Assessing Business Excellence

SITY OF ULSTER

To my wife, Norma, for her love and support.

(LJP)

To Andrew, Brigitte, Phil and Steve, who take credit for some of the ideas in this book. You were great people to work with.

(SJT)

Assessing Business Excellence

A guide to business excellence and self-assessment

Second edition

L. J. Porter

and

S. J. Tanner

Oakland Consulting plc

and

The European Centre for Business Excellence

AMSTERDAM BOSTON HEIDELBERG LONDON NEW YORK OXFORD
PARIS SAN DIEGO SAN FRANCISCO SINGAPORE SYDNEY TOKYO

Elsevier Butterworth-Heinemann
Linacre House, Jordan Hill, Oxford OX2 8DP
200 Wheeler Road, Burlington, MA 01803

First published 1996
Second edition 2004

British Library Cataloguing in Publication Data
A catalogue record for this book is available from the British Library

Library of Congress Cataloguing in Publication Data
A catalogue record for this book is available from the Library of Congress

ISBN 0 7506 5517 8

For information on all Butterworth-Heinemann publications
visit our website at http://books.elsevier.com

Typeset by Newgen Imaging Systems (P) Ltd., Chennai, India
Printed and bound in the Netherlands

Contents

Preface

When we decided to write the first edition of this book, we were heavily involved as assessors in the European Quality Award and UK Quality Award. This has continued and continues to be a great learning experience, which we would encourage the reader to get involved in if at all possible. Our experience as researchers and consultants in the field of business excellence has built on this experience and has encouraged us to share our experiences of the Award processes and organizational self-assessments. Having worked with many leading organizations on their journey to excellence, we are convinced that the Excellence frameworks used in the Award processes offer a unique opportunity to integrate the business excellence philosophy into standard business practice. In too many organizations excellence is a veneer rather than being integrated into the organization.

This book is written for those who need to assess business or organizational excellence with a view to improving the organization, and academics and students who are studying in this area. If an organization is to remain competitive, it requires that everyone must be committed to stakeholder satisfaction and understand how this can be improved. The book is based on our experiences of self-assessment in various organizations.

Part 1 of the book sets out the case for business excellence. Part 2 describes the main excellence frameworks. Part 3 describes the self-assessment process, and includes a 'Roadmap to Excellence'.

L. J. Porter
S. J. Tanner

Acknowledgements

So many people have helped us in the writing of this book that it is impossible to list them all. However, we have received support and encouragement from our colleagues in Oakland Consulting plc and from our colleagues in the European Centre for Business Excellence, the research and education division of Oakland Consulting plc. We are also indebted to the British Quality Foundation for their support. This book has drawn heavily on our experience and published materials from the various awarding bodies. We are very grateful to all these organizations, and openly acknowledge their contribution to this book. We must also thank all our friends in our excellence and self-assessment networks.

Finally, we must thank our families for supporting us in our efforts. Thanks to Norma for putting up with an overworked husband at weekends and holidays (LJP). Thanks to Pat for suffering the process of writing a book – even on holiday (SJT).

Part One

The Case for Business Excellence

Introducing business excellence

1.1 Introduction

In the last two decades, organizations have experienced a period of great change in their markets and operations. International competition has meant that many organizations have faced an increasingly turbulent and hostile environment. Customers have become more demanding, competition has become more intense and sophisticated, and the pace of technological change has quickened. Regulators and consumer groups have also added to these pressures. As a result, many organizations have adopted a range of improvement approaches in response to these forces. We have seen the growing adoption of quality management systems standards such as ISO9000, the emergence of total quality management (TQM), business process engineering (BPR), business excellence, performance excellence, lean thinking, Six Sigma etc. The battle weary could be excused from taking a rather jaundiced view of this ever lengthening list of 'quality' offers, but, by and large, they fit into an integrated approach to organizational improvement.

The involvement of people in the continuous improvement and transformation of business processes is a fundamental theme that runs through all of these quality improvement, process improvement and excellence approaches. By definition, this requires measurement and an understanding of how superior performance can be achieved. Assessing business excellence or organizational excellence is an essential part of a learning and measurement process, which involves people in self-assessment and allows organizations to identify strengths and improvement opportunities as well as enabling the progress of excellence programmes to be monitored in a systematic way. Self-assessment is a comprehensive, systematic and regular review of an organization's activities and results referenced against an appropriate business excellence model. These types of business or organizational assessments are one of the most powerful organizational learning tools available. In this book we describe the main excellence frameworks, and explain how they may be used to drive organizational improvement using the process of self-assessment.

As part of setting the scene for understanding where 'assessing business excellence' fits in, we need to understand the pedigree of the excellence models.

1.2 Business excellence – the pedigree

In the 1980s, many Western organizations woke up to the fact that quality was a strategic differentiator and not just the preserve of someone in quality control! The decade saw a shift in emphasis from quality control to quality assurance, and the emergence of ideas such as company-wide quality control, total quality (TQ), and total quality management (TQM). Quality systems standards such as BS5750:1979 and the international standard ISO9000:1987 were an important element of many quality programmes in the 1980s and 1990s; however, these standards had only a small impact on the early development of the award excellence frameworks, whereas TQ and TQM approaches had a profound influence.

Many of the ideas associated with TQM-type approaches have been used to develop the excellence frameworks that are the main subject of this book. Indeed all the excellence models are founded on TQM concepts, but they have also taken TQM thinking beyond its original remit to achieve better organizational integration. We need to be clear on what we mean by TQM, given the importance of TQM in the pedigree of all the excellence models.

Total quality management (TQM) is an approach that focuses on improving the organization's effectiveness, efficiency and responsiveness to customers' and other stakeholders' needs by actively harnessing people's skills and competencies in the pursuit of achieving sustained improvements to organizational performance. One of the critical success factors for TQM is strong leadership. Leaders need to be able to motivate and empower people to engage in TQM.

The achievement of business or organizational excellence is at the core of TQM. Results are the milestones of achievement and progress. If they are not captured on a regular basis, it becomes very difficult to maintain momentum, commitment and, more importantly, the motivation and desire to achieve higher performance standards. Furthermore the results captured must be consistent with the pursuit of improving the organization's overall performance. This requires a fundamental understanding of how sustained excellent organizational results are achieved. Customer perceived quality has been shown to be directly associated with profitability, and many studies have suggested a strong and identifiable link between a TQM approach and superior financial performance. These links will be explored in some detail in Chapter 2.

The 1990s saw the emergence of techniques such as business process re-engineering (BPR) and the balanced scorecard. Both these techniques had an influence on the development of the various excellence models; the influence of the scorecard being the greater. BPR brought a 'green field' approach to the radical redesign of key business processes by challenging basic assumptions and embracing change. The aim of BPR is to bring about a step-change in performance in cost, quality and customer satisfaction. The balanced scorecard is in essence a measurement system that enables the effective translation of strategy into action by developing an understanding of the cause and effect relationships that deliver the desired strategic outcomes. It attempts to link the 'people' dimensions of learning and growth to the process issues of quality and time, then to the customer dimensions of delivery and loyalty and, finally, to financial outcomes such as return on capital employed (ROCE). All the excellence frameworks include this fundamental conceptual thinking.

Whilst the interest in explicit TQM programmes has declined in some countries in recent years, its successor in all but name, Six Sigma, has seen a dramatic increase in application. Six Sigma is not new; its origins can be traced to Motorola in the early 1980s. Six Sigma is a disciplined methodology for improving organizations' processes, based on extremely rigorous data gathering and analysis. The approach focuses on helping organizations produce products and services better, faster and cheaper by improving the capability of processes to meet customer requirements. Six Sigma identifies and eliminates costs that add no value to customers. Unlike simple cost-cutting programmes, Six Sigma delivers cost cuts whilst retaining or improving value to the customer.

The term 'Six Sigma' is based on a statistical rationale. Six Sigma performance is the goal, and equates to 3.4 defects per million process, product or service opportunities. The focus is on reducing variability to achieve the goal. Many of the features of Six Sigma can be traced back to the earlier TQM thinking and, while Six Sigma has not really influenced the development of the excellence models, there is genuine interest about where Six Sigma fits into them. We address this in section 1.7.

Several common themes run through all the above 'quality' or 'excellence' approaches, and it is possible to identify several core concepts – the 'core themes of excellence'.

1.3 The core themes of excellence

Whilst most excellence approaches can trace their roots to TQM, the excellence concept as described in most excellence models is more holistic in nature than the earlier models of TQM. In particular, business excellence or organizational excellence provides for a complete integration of the improvement activity into the organization. Business excellence or organizational excellence is not a bolt-on to 'business as usual'. The core themes of excellence are:

- *Leadership.* The specific leadership behaviours of setting a clear direction and values for the organization, creating customer focus, and empowering the organization and its people in the pursuit of excellence are key to all excellence approaches.
- *Customer focus.* The customer is the final judge of product quality and service delivery. Customer loyalty and retention are best achieved by understanding the current and future needs of current and prospective customers. The voice of the customer is critical in designing the product or service 'offer', and in designing the processes that impact on the customer.
- *Strategic alignment.* All the excellence models stress the importance of strategic development, alignment and planning. In this respect, an excellence approach can be differentiated from many TQM-type programmes, where a lack of strategic integration frequently results in bolt-on quality programmes.
- *Organizational learning, innovation and improvement.* Stimulating individual and organizational learning, innovation and improvement through the effective sharing of knowledge and information is a critical element in an excellence approach.
- *People focus.* An organization's success is highly dependent upon the knowledge, skills, creativity and motivation of its people. This 'people potential' is best harnessed through shared values supported by a culture of trust and empowerment. Valuing people is a critical element in an excellence approach.
- *Partnership development.* Organizations need to develop longer-term strategic mutually beneficial partnerships with a range of external partners, including customers, suppliers and education organizations. Successful longer-term partnerships focus on delivering sustained value for the partners.

- *Fact-based processes management.* Processes are the 'engines' that deliver every organization's value proposition. The focus of all excellence approaches is on designing processes to meet customer requirements, systematically managing processes on the basis of facts and improving processes on the basis of customer feedback and feedback from the process itself. Process capability is based on the ability of the organization's processes to meet customer requirements.
- *Results focus.* Excellence is concerned with creating value for all the key stakeholders, including customers, employees, suppliers and partners, the public and the community at large. Balancing the needs of all these key stakeholders is a critical part of developing successful strategies.
- *Social responsibility.* Responsibility to the public, ethical behaviour and good citizenship are important in an excellence approach, and are critical to the longer-term interest of the organization.

1.4 Quality awards and excellence

Quality award frameworks have a long history. The Union of Japanese Scientists and Engineers (JUSE) established the Deming Prize in 1951 in honour of W. Edwards Deming's legendary impact on Japanese industry. The Prize was intended to recognize excellence in the implementation of company-wide quality control (CWQC). CWQC is, broadly speaking, the Japanese equivalent of TQM, although TQM takes a more holistic view.

Several decades passed before the Malcolm Baldrige National Quality Award was launched in 1988. The Malcolm Baldrige National Quality Award framework is probably the best-known excellence award model and the world's most widely used excellence framework for self-assessment. It is named in remembrance of Malcolm Baldrige, who served as the US Secretary of Commerce from 1981 until his untimely death in a rodeo accident in 1987. Baldrige was a champion of quality management as a key enabler of US prosperity and longer-term economic strength. The annual award was originally used to recognize US private sector companies for business excellence and quality achievement. In 1999, education and healthcare categories were introduced. The Baldrige Award criteria have played a major role in promoting excellence in the USA and around the world, and many of the other national and international quality awards can trace their parentage to the award. The criteria are designed to help organizations improve their competitiveness by focusing on two goals: continually delivering improved value to customers, and improving overall organizational performance. The Baldrige Model has evolved over the last decade and a half from a TQM model to a fully integrated performance excellence framework. The Baldrige criteria for performance excellence address:

- Leadership
- Strategic planning
- Customer and market focus
- Measurement, analysis and knowledge management
- Human resource focus
- Process management
- Business results (includes customer, product and service, financial and market, organizational effectiveness and governance, and social responsibility results).

The next significant development in quality awards occurred in 1991 with the launch by the European Foundation for Quality Management (EFQM) of the European Model for Total Quality Management. Although the European Model drew heavily on the experiences of the Deming and Baldrige Models, it offered a much greater business focus than these two 'quality frameworks'. The model, with its explicit reference to business results, led to the development of the business excellence concept. The European Model has seen similar developments over the last decade to the Baldrige Model, and is now known as the EFQM Excellence Model®. The criteria address:

- Leadership
- Policy and strategy
- People
- Partnerships and resources
- Processes
- Customer results
- People results
- Society results
- Key performance results.

The commonality between the two excellence frameworks is clear, as is their TQM parentage and the impact of concepts such as the balanced scorecard. The US and European award programmes led to an explosion of national quality and regional/state awards in America, Asia, Australia, Europe and New Zealand, using Baldrige- and/or European-based excellence frameworks.

Organizations pursuing an excellence strategy soon recognized that the award frameworks offered more than just a vehicle for recognition. The award frameworks were seen to be best-practice models for implementing excellence strategies, performing self-assessments, benchmarking, and ultimately delivering improved performance.

Over the last five years, the award frameworks and award processes across the world have continued to improve as the latest ideas on quality and excellence have been incorporated. In this process there has been increasing convergence of all the excellence models, and whilst we are still some way from a 'Unified Global Model', most of the models have a high degree of commonality.

1.5 The development of self-assessment

The quality award criteria, such as those for the Japanese Deming Prize, the American Malcolm Baldrige National Quality Award (MBNQA) and the European Foundation for Quality Management's Excellence Award, are increasingly being used by organizations in both the private and public sectors to carry out self-assessments in an attempt to measure their improvement progress and potential. Each of the award criteria provides a framework of standardized items against which an organization can measure its performance. This standardization allows comparisons to be made and best-in-class performance to be identified. Winning one of these annual awards is a prestigious event, but applicants frequently cite the most beneficial aspect as being the assessment process itself.

Thousands of organizations across the world now use self-assessment on a regular basis. Self-assessment is not only a means of measuring continuous improvement; it also provides an excellent opportunity for integrating business or organizational excellence into normal business activity.

In the following chapters we will consider the self-assessment process in some detail.

1.6 An overview of the self-assessment process

All self-assessment processes involve collecting data and information about the organization being assessed, and this is then subjected to the actual assessment process itself. There are many different ways in which an organization can position itself against a recognized excellence framework, and a flowchart of a typical process is shown in Figure 1.1. The key steps in this process are discussed briefly below, and the details of each step are discussed at greater length in subsequent chapters.

Define objectives and scope

A clear purpose for the assessment and well-defined objectives need establishing right at the start of the process. A small minority

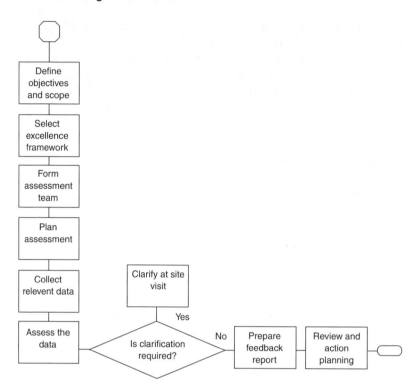

Figure 1.1 Overview of the self-assessment process

of organizations will be concerned with winning an award, but most organizations use self-assessment as an organizational improvement tool. This can be used at the very highest level in the organization, for example in business planning, or at relatively low levels as a means of identifying improvement opportunities.

The scope issue addresses the question of whether the assessment should cover the whole organization, a division, a business unit or a functional department.

Select excellence framework

The issues to be addressed include choosing between the various frameworks – for example, the Baldrige versus the EFQM Excellence Model® – and the development of the framework to suit the organization's needs. Many issues, including length of experience with self-assessment and geographical location, dictate the choice of the actual framework. At the detailed level within the frameworks, many organizations tailor the framework and terminology to improve its usability.

Form assessment team

Self-assessment is a team-based activity. No single person is likely to have the in-depth knowledge needed in all the areas of the chosen excellence framework to ensure an objective assessment. Also, the process of assessing business or organizational excellence relies on people being able to make an objective assessment of excellence. People's perception of excellence differs, and the team-based approach makes the whole process robust to those differing views and experiences.

Plan assessment

The planning stage addresses the issues of how the actual data and information about the organization will be collected and who will be involved in this process. The assessment of these data will also have to be planned. Will the team collecting the data assess it themselves; a true self-assessment? Alternatively, will the data collection and assessment phases be kept quite distinct and different teams be used for each step? It is important to develop a time-scaled action plan for the process. The self-assessment process can be a relatively lengthy and complex affair, and it is essential to control the process to deliver the end result in an efficient and timely manner.

Collect relevant data

Self-assessment is an organizational health check that is best based on fact and not opinion. However, there are a variety of ways of establishing the facts. The data collection phase is governed by two factors, namely the objectivity required and the resources available. Generally speaking, greater objectivity requires more resources.

In the major excellence award processes, the organization is required to produce a position statement of approximately 75 pages that explains what the organization has achieved and how it has achieved it. This is clearly a time-consuming process. However, there are a range of simpler data collection techniques, such as checklists and pro forma, that allow valuable assessments to be made without consuming too many resources.

Assess data

The assessment phase involves a combination of individual and team assessments of the data and information against the chosen excellence framework, and the process is facilitated by the involvement of experienced assessors. Assessors review the whole data and information to identify strengths, areas for improvement, and clarification or site-visit issues. This is initially done on an individual basis and then as a team to reach a consensus overview of the organization. The clarification or site-visit stage can be an integral part of the process for in-company assessments.

Individual assessment, consensus and site visits are key sub-processes of most award processes and the majority of self-assessment systems.

Prepare the feedback report

The feedback report is the major output from the assessment process. It is the final analysis of the organization, and contains the accumulated knowledge acquired by the assessor team. A good report is tactful and constructive, and is based on fact not opinion. It should encourage the organization to take improvement opportunities forward, and ensure that best practice is deployed across the organization.

Review and action planning

Any self-assessment cycle should be concluded with a post-completion review to identify what went well with the process, what could be improved, and what benefits have been or are likely to be achieved.

The culmination of the whole process is to take the feedback from the assessment and develop action plans that deliver increased levels of satisfaction for the stakeholders – namely customers, employees, society at large, and the shareholders or other financial stakeholders.

1.7 Achieving organizational excellence

Excellence approaches based on TQM are primarily concerned with improving the business or organization. However, excellence and TQM mean different things to different people, and we have already seen that there is a growing portfolio of tools and techniques at the disposal of the excellence champion. Organizations in the thick of excellence initiatives, such as business excellence, scorecards, benchmarking, Six Sigma etc., suffer the danger of paralysis by initiative! However, these activities are not in competition with each other; rather they should be seen as

Figure 1.2 The components of organizational excellence

complementary activities as part of a planned strategy to achieve organizational excellence.

Achieving organizational excellence requires the organization to practise a repeating cycle of the continuous improvement cycle plan: do, check and act (see Figure 1.2).

Strategy and business planning

In the strategy and planning phase, the results of self-assessment against an excellence framework provide the organization with insights into the strengths and weaknesses in its organizational capability. Scorecard development is instrumental in developing strategies and plans that focus on the balanced needs of all stakeholders. Scorecard deployment is the key goal deployment link that connects plans to the organization's key value-adding and support processes.

Processes

Excellent process management is critical to achieving organizational excellence. Three elements of process management can be identified:

1. *Process design*. This element may include elements of business process redesign (BPR).

2. *Process control.* This element will require the disciplines of statistical process control (SPC) and ISO9000:2000. This latest version of the ISO9000 standard has a heavy emphasis on process,
   customer and measurement, and provides a sound framework
   for process management. (Earlier versions of ISO9000 had a
   greater emphasis on procedures and were rightly subjected to
   some criticism on account of their contribution to quality
   bureaucracy rather than quality improvement).
3. *Process improvement.* This element relies on continuous techniques, such as Six Sigma and TQM. Business transformation
   techniques, such as BPR, are also needed if there are large gaps
   in process performance.

Self-assessment

Self-assessment against an excellence framework focuses on
performance excellence for the whole organization within the
context of an overall organizational framework. The assessment
process identifies and tracks all the important organizational
results, and provides feedback on organizational capability and
results to the strategy and planning process.

1.8 The Excellence Maturity Model

Having illustrated how the various techniques complement each
other, we need to understand when they should be used. Figure 1.3
illustrates the phasing of these complementary techniques.

Many organizations have tried self-assessment in the early
stages of their journey to excellence, only to be overwhelmed by
the number of areas for improvement. This can be quite a
discouraging start, and can result in a serious lack of focus. We
recommend that organizations should view the journey to excellence in three distinct phases:

1. *Gain control.* In this phase, it is essential to establish the basic
   business and operational controls that ensure a reasonably
   consistent mode of operation. Policies, procedures, and
   quality systems such as ISO9000:2000 are the appropriate
   approaches here. The performance improvement gap, whilst at
   its largest at this point on the journey, must be assessed against
   a reasonably stable baseline.
2. *Build on best practice.* Having established control, techniques to
   identify and adopt best practice now become appropriate.
   Benchmarking and internal self-assessment can be productively

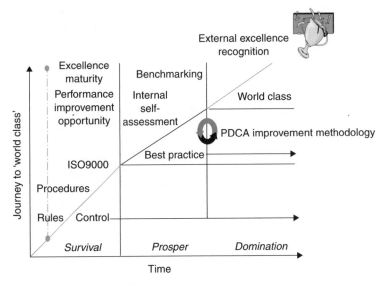

Figure 1.3 The Excellence Maturity Model

used at this stage of the journey. Self-assessment in this phase gives meaningful actionable results, whereas in the control phase it is difficult to separate real effects from the noise of out-of-control operations.

3. *Deliver world-class results.* Having built an excellence platform based on best practice, it is now time to harness this to deliver world-class results. The more powerful award-type self-assessment and process benchmarking is appropriate at this stage. External quality award applications and the attendant award assessment process can offer real opportunities for further organizational learning, and help move the organization up the performance curve to world-class performance. The ultimate attainment of world-class status manifests itself in sustained excellent performance.

1.9 Summary

In this chapter we have examined the pedigree and basic philosophy of excellence and explored how other activities, such as self-assessment, benchmarking, business process re-engineering, etc., are an integral part of excellence approaches.

The major excellence-based frameworks have been briefly introduced, and their use in self-assessment noted.

An overview of the self-assessment process has also been presented. The key steps in the process have been briefly discussed and some of the work issues raised. Self-assessment using one of the recognized excellence-based frameworks is at the core of assessing business excellence.

An excellence integration framework has illustrated how all the excellence tools and techniques fit together to deliver organizational excellence. Finally, a basic road map to excellence has illustrated how the different approaches are used in the different phases of the road to excellence. We will return to this road map towards the end of the book, once we have increased our understanding of the concepts and practices of excellence.

In the following chapters we will explore these frameworks in greater detail, and the self-assessment processes. We hope you benefit from this journey to business excellence.

The case for business excellence

2.1 Introduction

Back in 1995 when we wrote the first edition of *Assessing Business Excellence*, we included a chapter at the end entitled 'The experiences of some role model organizations'. This summarized the contents of a number of articles and some limited research that had been conducted on the benefits of business excellence. The purpose of including this chapter was to convince readers that it is good advice to implement business excellence and that it is logical to spend some time looking at the experience of companies that have achieved external recognition through one of the various award processes.

Time has led to many more articles and more rigorous research. Back in 1995 the EFQM Model was only a few years old, and most work had been centred on the Baldrige Model. At that time implementing business excellence had started to become a cult activity, and now it is more of a business imperative. It is therefore appropriate to tackle the issue of benefit head-on by reviewing the case for business excellence right at the start of the book.

In this chapter we have selected the important studies that have been published over the last 15 years. Some of the work has taken many years to complete, and the studies focus on a number of issues, from the benefits that may be achieved from implementing business excellence to the reasons why it has been implemented. The work includes key learning points and illustrations from successful organizations. Not all the messages are positive. Although there is compelling evidence that business excellence delivers benefit to the organization, it is clear that it does not work for everyone. Some of the research also questions the principles of some of the frameworks, and not all the studies are in agreement. The central message is that the framework chosen and the method of implementation should meet the needs of the organization. Part 2 of this book describes the most popular frameworks, and Part 3 the activity of self-assessment, which is the primary method of implementing business excellence.

This chapter presents the work in chronological order, and the studies included are listed in Table 2.1. This shows the primary objective of each piece of work, together with an outline of the methodology and the main findings. For the purpose of this review, the terms 'total quality management' and 'business excellence' have been considered to be interchangeable. The former is the term

Table 2.1: Studies covered in Chapter 2

Year	Subject	Reference
1983	Study on the benefits of the Deming Prize	JUSE (1983). Referenced in GAO (1991)
1991	US government-sponsored study on the performance improvement of Baldrige winners	GAO (1991)
1994	Case study on Philips Taiwan, one of the three organizations to win the Deming Prize and the only overseas company to be awarded the Japan Quality Medal	Williams and Boudewijn (1994)
1994	Review of Baldrige winners	Wisner and Eakins (1994)
1995	Share price performance of Baldrige winners	NIST (2002). Also see Helton (1995) for the original work
1995	Survey of firms to see what benefits are delivered through business excellence	Powell (1995)
1997	First major study on the uses of the EFQM Model across Europe	ECforBE (1997)
1999	Survey of 4000 firms to determine the benefits from business excellence	Terziovski and Samson (1999)

Table 2.1: Continued

Year	Subject	Reference
1999	First major study on the EFQM Award winners	ECforBE (1999); Oakland (1999)
2000	Publication of a collection of examples from various organizations that are conducting self-assessment using the EFQM Excellence Model©	ECforBE (2000); ECforBE (2002)
2000	Review into the effectiveness of business excellence within the automotive industry	Curkovic et al. (2000)
2000	UK government-sponsored review of the use of the EFQM Excellence Model® in UK public sector organizations	PriceWaterhouseCoopers (2000)
2000	Analysis of share price performance of award winners in the USA. The awards included company and independent awards such Baldrige	Hendricks and Singhal (2000, 2001a, 2001b)
2001	Investigation into the economic impact of quality awards in the USA	Fisher et al. (2001)
2001	Survey of hospitals to examine how business excellence implementation had an effect on organizational performance	Douglas and Judge (2001)
2001	Investigation into the impact of stakeholder management and social initiative participation on shareholder returns	Hillman and Keim (2001)
2001	Study to test the construction of the Baldrige Model	Pannirselvam and Ferguson (2001)
2002	Another stock performance study, but this one does not return such positive returns as other studies	Przasnyski and Tai (2002)
2002	Study of Danish organizations to examine the criterion weightings of the EFQM Excellence Model®	Eskildsen et al. (2002)

used in the American studies and the latter in European studies. At the end of the chapter we will pull together some key themes from the work.

2.2   JUSE Deming Prize winner study

A study published in 1983 by The Union of Japanese Scientists and Engineers looked at companies that had been awarded Deming Prizes between 1961 and 1980. The study considered the earnings rate, productivity, growth rate, liquidity and safety of the companies, and concluded that most companies had an upward trend in or maintained a favourable level of business perform-ance. A few companies showed a temporary upturn in perform-ance, and then maintained a performance level above the industry average.

JUSE concluded that results had been achieved across the following ten areas:

1. Quality stabilization and improvement
2. Productivity improvements/cost reductions
3. Expanded sales
4. Increased profits
5. Thorough implementation of management plans/business plans
6. Realization of top management's dreams
7. QC by total participation and improvement of the organiza-tional constitution
8. Heightened motivation to manage and improve as well as to promote standardization
9. Converged large power from the bottom of the organization and enhanced morale
10. Establishment of various management systems and the total management system.

2.3   General Accounting Office study of Baldrige winners

The first comprehensive study into the benefits of following a business excellence approach was conducted by the American General Accounting Office. This study, which was based on past Baldrige applicants, led to the publishing of government report number GAO/NSIAD-91-190 in May 1991.

The purpose of the study was to determine the impact of formal business excellence practices on the performance of selected US companies. The report discusses:

- What was achieved
- How it was achieved
- What lessons were applicable to US companies in general.

The study reviewed twenty companies that were among the highest-scoring applicants in the 1988 and 1989 Baldrige Award process. The overall summary concluded that:

1. Companies that adopted business excellence practices experienced an overall improvement in corporate performance. In most cases companies achieved better employee relations, higher productivity, greater customer satisfaction, increased market share and improved profitability.
2. Each of the companies studied developed its own unique environment that had its own opportunities and problems. There were, however, common features in their management approach that were major contributing factors to their improved performance.
3. Many different types of companies benefited from a business excellence approach, underpinning the fact that the practices were universally applicable.
4. None of the companies reaped the benefits of their approach immediately. It was concluded that allowing sufficient time for results to be achieved was as important as initiating a business excellence programme in the first instance.

To provide a general framework for examining the impact of business excellence practices in diverse organizations, a model for total quality management was developed. This is shown in Figure 2.1. This model is particularly interesting because it indicates the direction in which the various indicators are expected to move as

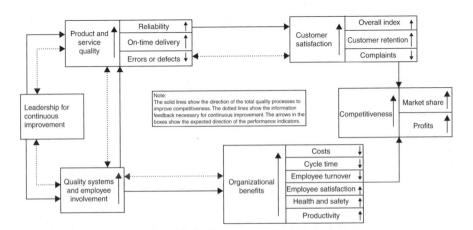

Figure 2.1 GAO Study TQM Model (Source: GAO (1991))

a result of applying business excellence practices. It is particularly powerful, as it is not based on theory but on the observation of the twenty companies in the study.

To determine the impact of business excellence on corporate performance, empirical data were analysed across four broad areas: employee relations, operating procedures, customer satisfaction and financial performance. The first three of these areas are major sections of the Baldrige framework. In each area a number of indicators were identified that could be used to measure performance. The results of the study in each of the four areas are given in Tables 2.2–2.5.

The companies studied represented a wide range of industries and competitive environments. Six interrelated features were identified that consistently appeared in the companies' total quality management approaches and that contributed to the improved performance. These six features were:

1. Corporate attention was focused on meeting quality requirements
2. Management led the way in disseminating TQM values throughout the organization
3. Employees were asked and empowered continuously to improve all key business processes

Table 2.2: GAO Study employee-related indicators

| Performance indicator | Number of responding companies | *Direction of indicator* | | |
		Positive (favourable)	Negative (unfavourable)	No change
Employee satisfaction	9	8	1	0
Attendance	11	8	0	3
Turnover	11	7	3	1
Safety/health	14	11	3	0
Suggestions received	7	5	2	0
Total	18*	39	9	4

*Indicates the total number of companies providing data, and not the total number of responses for all performance indicators.
Source: GAO (1991)

Table 2.3: GAO operating indicators

	Direction of indicator			
Performance indicator	*Number of responding companies*	*Positive (favourable)*	*Negative (unfavourable)*	*No change*
Reliability	12	12	0	0
Timeliness of delivery	9	8	1	0
Order-processing time	6	6	0	0
Errors or defects	8	7	0	1
Product lead time	7	6	0	1
Inventory turnover	9	6	1	2
Costs of quality	5	5	0	0
Cost savings	9	9	0	0
Total	20*	59	2	4

*Indicates the total number of companies providing data and not the total number of responses for all performance indicators.
Source: GAO (1991)

Table 2.4: GAO customer satisfaction indicators

	Direction of indicator			
Performance indicator	*Number of responding companies*	*Positive (favourable)*	*Negative (unfavourable)*	*No change*
Overall customer satisfaction	14	12	0	2
Customer complaints	6	5	1	0
Customer retention	10	4	2	4
Total	17*	21	3	6

*Indicates the total number of companies providing data and not the total number of responses for all performance indicators.
Source: GAO (1991)

Table 2.5: GAO financial performance indicators

		Direction of indicator		
Performance indicator	*Number of responding companies*	*Positive (favourable)*	*Negative (unfavourable)*	*No change*
Market share	11	9	2	0
Sales per employee	12	12	0	0
Return on assets	9	7	2	0
Return on sales	8	6	2	0
Total	15*	34	6	0

*Indicates the total number of companies providing data and not the total number of responses for all performance indicators.
Source: GAO (1991)

4. Management nurtured a flexible and responsive corporate culture
5. Management systems supported fact-based decision-making
6. Partnerships with suppliers improved product or service quality.

2.4 Philips Taiwan case study

With the growing interest in business excellence within Europe back in the early 1990s, the European Foundation for Quality Management published a case study on Philips Taiwan (Williams and Boudewijn, 1994). The purpose of publishing the case study was to give companies an insight into what world-class organizations were like at a time when there were no real benchmarks. It also illustrated the effort that was required to become world-class, which increased the value of the European Quality Award. The case study remains of interest, as it documents a journey that many organizations face today.

Philips Taiwan's journey towards becoming the second company outside Japan to be awarded a Deming Prize began in the most unlikely of places – Southampton, Hampshire. It was during a visit in 1982 to Philips' operation in Southampton that Mr Y. C. Lo, a General Division Manager from Taiwan, was given details of a complaint from a Japanese customer who used components from one of his plants. Apparently the customer was unhappy that when the product was looked at in a certain light, there were reflections on the surface that should not have been there. The component was not out of specification and the 'defect' would not have affected its performance. The Japanese customer said that if the surface looked that way, then he did not believe that the inside could be perfect either.

Following long debates, and after listening to presentations from other manufacturers, the management team in Taiwan concluded that as far as quality was concerned, it was all or nothing. If they wanted to compete in the market they had to improve their quality, so a decision was made to act.

The first step was to adopt a 'Crosby' approach, and this was launched in January 1983. This produced an early impact, as there was a reduction in component defect level from 9000 ppm at the start of 1982 to 3000 ppm at the end of 1983. Employee participation in Quality Circles grew, as did the number of suggestions – to a level of one suggestion per person per month in 1984. The adoption of suggestions also improved.

Although Philips Taiwan was proud of its achievements, it was beginning to realize that its approach to quality would have to go beyond employee suggestions and the use of simple quality tools. Important customers such as IBM and Ford were demanding that their suppliers use statistical process control.

At the same time, other challenges were starting to appear. For example, the expansion of the Taiwan economy meant that the demand for well-educated manpower outstripped supply. The retention of good personnel would be a factor of strategic and operational importance.

At the end of 1984, the management team laid down four principles of the approach to quality. These were:

1. Quality through discipline
2. Do it right the first time
3. Maximum process capability
4. Perfect customer service.

There was also a greater emphasis on the Deming 'plan–do–check–act' cycle and *Kaizen* improvement. Training in the seven 'new' management tools and statistical techniques was a priority.

In 1985, Mr Lo took responsibility for all of Philips Taiwan. In his first year he sold the concept of total quality control to his management team. The team committed to set a goal of five years to 'go to the top' and win a Deming Prize. This involved engaging Japanese consultants and visiting previous Deming Prize winners to study their approaches.

This new phase in Philips' development saw the introduction of many new Japanese techniques, such as quality function deployment, policy deployment, just in time, and internal QC-diagnosis 'President's audits'. These initiatives required considerable effort – for example, the preparation time for the first President's diagnosis was 40 man-days.

Employee involvement in quality circles and the number of suggestions per employee continued to grow, but it took two years for Philips to learn that everything had to be based on fact. If anybody put forward a proposal, the first thing that top management asked would be, 'where are the relevant facts and figures?'. The real tool for total quality control was statistics and the problem-solving methodology.

Just as the expansion of the Taiwan economy had given Philips a challenge in 1984, the strength of the New Taiwanese Dollar (NT$) had an impact in 1987. The exchange rate moved from NT$40 to US$1 in January to only NT$32 to US$1 in December 1987. The effect of this was the need for a 15 per cent reduction in cost at a time when the quality drive continued to sap resources. The policy chosen was to drive even harder with the quality programme, as the management believed that only by adoption of the programme could the major cost savings be achieved. This was not the end of the currency problems, and during 1988/1989 the value of the NT$ moved to NT$25 to US$1, prompting the need for another 10 per cent cost reduction.

In 1988, Philips had its first experience working with Deming consultants. As their English was relatively poor, translators were necessary, but it was not just the language that caused communication problems. The following extract is taken from the Philips Taiwan case study published by EFQM, and demonstrates the point.

> *They asked mostly questions and seldom told Philips Taiwan what to do. For example, they would always enquire what the actual targets are. 'Why do you have a sleeping target?' they would ask if they saw that the target line was flat. 'Where is your Plan–Do–Check–Action cycle?'. They would not suggest how to make one. This led to frustration until it finally became clear that they wanted Philips Taiwan not only to develop their own solutions, but also wanted to set in motion a process that would continuously develop and improve, what Mr Lo later would call, the intelligence of the organization. With these objectives in mind, it would have been totally unfit to tell what had to be done. Management and employees of Philips Taiwan had to find their own solutions to their problems and learn from them.*

Readers will recognize this as a QC-diagnosis in action.

Deming consultants were not the only consultants that Philips used. It also commissioned Japanese consultants who went for action-orientated short-term projects that would be finished within two to three days and achieve immediate results. After an initial investigation, these consultants astonished Philips by announcing that they could easily improve productivity by 50 per cent. In the end a target of 30 per cent was set, and that target was almost met by the end of 1989.

The drive to improve quality and increase productivity did not go unnoticed in the outside world. For example, Sony, a customer, recognized Philips Taiwan for its quality improvement. Whereas in the past it would not share its long-term development plans, now Sony began to share its three-year plans so that both parties could increase the value added to their relationship.

The next few years' effort was concentrated on preparing for the examination and the examination itself. It was 5 pm on 15 October 1991 that Mr Lo received a fax from the Deming Prize Committee to say that Philips Taiwan had been awarded a Prize. It was almost ten years since his visit to Southampton, yet he knew that much more work had to be done. As he explained:

Total Quality Control improves one's capability to identify strengths and weaknesses in the organization. The more you understand about TQC, the more weaknesses and therefore improvement opportunities you can identify. The point is that Philips Taiwan has a system in place that will help them to eradicate quality problems and to continually improve their business performance. Already, Philips Taiwan is moving its Quality Objectives relentlessly forward.

Since this case study was written, Philips has continued to face major challenges as an organization operating in a highly competitive industry. That the progress made was sustained is evidenced by the fact that in 1997 Philips Taiwan was awarded the Japan Quality Medal – the only overseas organization to achieve this high status.

2.5 Review of Baldrige winners

Research conducted by Wisner and Eakins studied the performance of Baldrige winners over the period 1986–1993. This research included four privately owned companies. Table 2.6 shows the results of key performance improvement indicators for five of the winners. These results are very impressive, and clearly demonstrate the value of a business excellence approach.

There are several common themes in Table 2.6. The decrease in costs and cycle times stands out, as does the increase in employee involvement and customer satisfaction. What is particularly interesting is that in one of the examples, AT&T Universal Card Services, there was a direct increase in sales volume. This point

Table 2.6: Key performance improvement indicators for five Baldrige winners

Motorola Inc.

- 150-fold improvement in in-process defects (1981–1989)

- 97% decrease in cycle time for cellular phones (1981–1989)
- 93% decrease in returned order costs (1981–1989)

- $2.2 billion in cost savings due to quality improvements (1986–1991)
- 90% increase in cellular phone reliability (1981–1989)
- 62% decrease in part count for cellular phones (1981–1989)

Zytech Corp.

- 50% increase in manufacturing yields (1988–1991)
- 26% decrease in manufacturing cycle times (1988–1991)
- 50% decrease in design cycle times (1988–1991)

- 13% increase in on-time deliveries (1988–1991)
- Tenfold increase in mean time between failures (1987–1991)
- 48% decrease in warranty costs (1988–1990)

AT&T Universal Card Services

- 500% increase in sales volume (1990–1992)
- Five decreases in the interest rate charged (1990–1992)

- Number two in sales among 6000 credit card users (1990–1992)

- Tenfold increase in employees (1990–1992)
- 40% increase in calling card revenues among Universal Card holders (1990–1992)
- Threefold increase in employee suggestions (1990–1992)

Granite Rock Co.

- 34% increase in on-time deliveries (1985–1991)

- 63% decrease in quarry-truck loading time (1985–1991)

- Revenue per employee 30% higher than industry average (1985–1991)
- Three times more training hours per employee than industry average (1985–1991)

The Ritz-Carlton Hotel Co.

- Threefold increase in TQM expenditure (1989–1991)

- 67% increase in supplier on-time deliveries (1989–1991)

- 47% decrease in employee turnover (1989–1991)

- 6% increase in employee satisfaction (1989–1991)

- 100% increase in predetermination of repeat customer needs (1989–1991)

- 8% decrease in hours worked per guest room (1989–1991)

Source: Wisner and Eakins (1994)

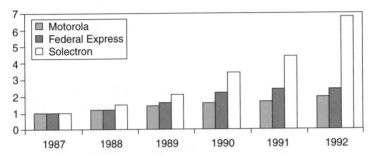

Figure 2.2 Indexed sales increases for three Baldrige winners (Source: Wisner and Eakins (1994))

is confirmed when comparing the increase in sales volumes for three other winners: Federal Express, Solectron and Motorola. Figure 2.2 gives the indexed increase in sales for these three publicly owned companies over the period 1987 to 1992.

A final area of interest from this study concerns the results from privately owned companies. It is difficult to get data on private companies, but Wisner and Eakins surveyed four such companies. The respondents cited financial improvements with respect to their industry, and attributed a significant portion of this improvement to their quality programmes. They also cited improvements in competitive characteristics, particularly in the areas of future competitiveness, overall product quality, product complaints and returns. Table 2.7 summarizes their findings.

The overall conclusions of the report are that, while winning the Baldrige Award has not guaranteed success, the award winners are generally recognized as profitable companies and exhibit strength in terms of market share, product quality and other performance benchmarks. Of particular importance is that the Baldrige Award winners provide examples that investment in quality programmes can result in cost savings, market share improvement, and impressive improvements in manufacturing and service performance.

Table 2.7: Results from the privately owned company Baldrige winners survey

Financial characteristics	Combined response	Competitive characteristics	Combined response
Overall financial performance		*Current overall competitiveness*	
Change with respect to industry	Positive	Change with respect to industry	Positive
Amount of change due to quality programme	58%	Amount of change due to quality programme	84%
Sales		*Projected future competitiveness*	
Change with respect to industry	Positive	Change with respect to industry	Positive
Amount of change due to quality programme	73%	Amount of change due to quality programme	91%
Previous five-year sales growth		*Overall product quality*	
Change with respect to industry	Positive	Change with respect to industry	Positive
Amount of change due to quality programme	70%	Amount of change due to quality programme	98%
Projected future sales growth		*Innovative product offerings*	
Change with respect to industry	Positive	Change with respect to industry	Positive
Amount of change due to quality programme	80%	Amount of change due to quality programme	65%
Return on sales		*Product complaints/returns*	
Change with respect to industry	Positive	Change with respect to industry	Positive
Amount of change due to quality programme	70%	Amount of change due to quality programme	93%

Table 2.7: Continued

Financial characteristics	Combined response	Competitive characteristics	Combined response
Return on assets		*Employees' job satisfaction*	
Change with respect to industry	Positive	Change with respect to industry	Positive
Amount of change due to quality programme	50%	Amount of change due to quality programme	57%

Source: Wisner and Eakins (1994)

2.6 NIST share price performance of Baldrige winners

There have been many studies on the share price performance of Baldrige winners. The original work was conducted by Helton (1995), and this was an important study because a couple of the early Baldrige winners actually ran into financial difficulty within a few years of winning the award, and this was not a good advertisement for the process. Such was the impact of Helton's work that each year the National Institute for Standards and Technology, which manages the Baldridge Awards, releases updated figures to reflect the latest data.

In order to perform the calculations, a hypothetical sum is invested in each of the 1991–2000 publicly-traded Baldrige Award recipient's common stock, in the year they applied for the award. The investment is tracked from the first business day of the month following the announcement of the award recipients (or the date when they began public trading, if it is later) through to the end of the year. A hypothetical $1000 is invested in each whole company, and for subsidiaries the sum invested is $1000 multiplied by the percentage of the whole company's employee base the subunit represented at the time of its application. The same total dollar amount is invested in the Standard & Poor's (S&P) 500 on the same day.

Taking the latest results in March 2002, adjusting for stock splits, the value on 3 December 2001 was calculated. Information is reported two ways: all publicly traded award recipients, and only whole-company award recipients (NIST, 2002). The results for both types of investment are given in Table 2.8.

Table 2.8: Award recipient share price performance

	$ Investment	$ Value (3 December 2001)	Change
1991–2000 publicly traded award recipients			
1991–2000 Award recipients	5291.21	22 370.00	322.78%
S&P 500	5291.21	11 094.39	109.68%
1991–2000 publicly traded whole-company award recipients			
1991–2000 whole-company Award recipients	3000	18 367.11	512.24%
S&P 500	3000	6455.19	115.17%

Source: NIST (2002)

The 21 publicly traded award recipients, as a group, outperformed the S&P 500 by approximately 2.94 to 1, achieving a 322.78 per cent return compared to a 109.68 per cent return for the S&P 500. The group of three publicly traded whole-company award recipients outperformed the S&P 500 by about 4.45 to 1, achieving a 512.24 per cent return compared to a 115.17 per cent return for the S&P 500.

Results have also been given for site-visited organizations. These are summarized in Table 2.9.

The 61 publicly traded site-visited applicants, as a group, outperformed the S&P 500 by approximately 1.15 to 1, achieving a 125.13 per cent return compared to a 108.52 per cent return for the S&P 500. The group of nine whole-company site-visited applicants outperformed the S&P 500 by approximately 1.48 to 1, achieving a 167.40 per cent return compared to a 113.28 per cent return for the S&P 500.

In releasing this information NIST also noted that while receiving a Baldrige Award or any other award is not a guarantee of success, to win the award organizations must show continuous and major improvements. For example, when Solectron Corp. won the Baldrige Award in 1991, revenue was $265 million with 1500 employees. When they won again in 1997, revenue was $4 billion with 18 215 employees. In 2001, Solectron's revenue was $18 billion with 60 000 employees. In another case, Federal Express Corp. won a Baldrige Award In 1990, and that year the company had revenues of $7 billion, 90 000 employees, and

Table 2.9: Award site-visited share price performance

	$ Investment	$ Value (3 December 2001)	Change
1991–2000 publicly traded site-visited award applicants			
1991–2000 site-visited applicants	18 986.15	42 743.05	125.13%
S&P 500	18 986.15	39 589.47	108.52%
1991–2000 publicly traded whole-company site-visited award applicants			
1991–2000 whole-company site-visited applicants	9000	24 065.59	167.40%
S&P 500	9000	19 195.10	113.28%

Source: NIST (2002)

1.5 million shipments a day. In 2001, Federal Express had revenues of $19.6 billion, 215 000 employees, and 5 million shipments a day.

Stock price performance is a popular way to research the benefits of the business excellence awards, and several other studies are described below. The approach for these studies is essentially the same but, as will become apparent, the selection of the comparison or benchmark group makes all the difference in how impressive the results appear.

To date no similar studies have been published on the EFQM Excellence Model®, but it is known that such work is currently taking place.

2.7 Powell's search for competitive advantage

In 1995 Powell conducted a survey of firms with the objective of identifying whether business excellence led to a competitive advantage (Powell, 1995). The survey was quite small, and of the 143 organizations approached only 36 returned their questionnaires. Such a low response rate is quite common in research.

The firms selected for the study included organizations that were considered to have implemented business excellence, and those that had not. Interviews were conducted with the Chief Executive Officers and Quality Executives in 30 of the 36 firms, to collect more information about their approaches and performance. A number of interesting conclusions were drawn from the work:

- The study concluded that business excellence could produce economic value to the firm, but not for all adopters
- Success depended on executive commitment, having an open organization, and employee empowerment
- Success depended less on benchmarking, training, flexible manufacturing, process improvement and improved measurement.

The overall conclusion from the study was that business excellence can produce a competitive advantage, but that it is not necessary for success in every instance. It was further suggested that business excellence's highest purpose and real contribution to US business is that it provides a framework that helps firms to understand and acquire resources as part of an integral change programme.

2.8 Study on self-assessment using the EFQM Excellence Model® across Europe

When this study was conducted back in 1997, there was little published information about the use of self-assessment based on the European Model for Total Quality Management (now the EFQM Excellence Model®). Indeed, at the time there was little published information on the use of total quality-based self-assessment in Europe *per se*. Hence there was a need for a research programme to evaluate the current use of self-assessment by European companies.

The research project sought to evaluate the operation of the European Quality Award (EQA) Model for self-assessment, and made use of the following research techniques:

- Telephone survey
- Postal questionnaire
- Structured interviews of senior management
- Semi-structured focus group discussions
- Site visits
- Literature searches
- Search of published information
- Computer database management
- Statistical data analysis.

There were approximately 50 respondents to the postal question-naire. This number allowed reasonable statistical analysis of the data. Twenty-five individual companies were selected for inter-views and site visits, stratified to reflect the European scope of this study, and provided 25 case studies of self-assessment using the EQA Model.

The project lasted for one calendar year, and was funded by the Chartered Institute of Management Accountants (CIMA), the European Foundation for Quality Management (EFQM), and the Norwegian Fellowship Programme in Leadership and Organization Development (STILO). It also had the backing of the British Quality Foundation (BQF).

The research led to a comprehensive report, and some of the results that are still relevant today are discussed here. First, Table 2.10 gives the reasons why organizations commenced self-assessment. This shows that the primary motive for commencing self-assessment was to drive improvement. Organizations were not starting self-assessment to enter for an award.

To supplement the results given in Table 2.10, the study also looked at the reasons for continuing to use self-assessment. These results, shown in Table 2.11, indicate that the main driver remained improvement and not external recognition through a quality award.

The results so far measured intentions. The study also looked at the benefits achieved through the activity of self-assessment. These perceptions of the benefits are given in Table 2.12, which shows that improvement activity, embedding a quality culture, and communication are all major benefits. This conclusion is fur-ther supported by the information in Figure 2.3, which charts the perceptions of the overall usefulness of self-assessment.

As mentioned above, 25 organizations were visited across Europe as part of the work. The main benefits of self-assessment identified by the case study organizations are described in Table 2.13. They are not ranked according to any order of importance, usage, or otherwise.

2.9 Survey of Australian and New Zealand organizations

Terziovski and Samson (1999) conducted a survey of 4000 Australian and New Zealand organizations in order to test the strength of the relationship between business excellence practice and organizational performance with and without the covariates of company size, industry type, and ISO9000 certification status.

Table 2.10: Ranked order of importance of reasons for starting self-assessment in current users

Reason	*Mean*	*Mode (0 = not important; 5 = very important)*
Provide driver for continuous improvement	4.48	5
Identify organization's areas for improvement	4.42	5
Increase TQ awareness throughout organization	4.11	5
Increase commitment of line management to TQM	3.84	5
Re-energize TQ effort	3.73	4
Take a 'base-line' measure of the organization	3.42	3
Identify organization's strengths	3.38	4
Use as an internal benchmarking tool	3.31	4
Next step in a planned implementation of TQM	3.30	4
Co-ordinate local/*ad hoc* improvement activities	3.18	4
Use as an external benchmarking tool	2.67	4
Compete for national/international quality award	1.68	0
Win a national/international award	1.42	0
Competitors using self-assessment	1.06	0

Source: ECforBE (1997)

Questionnaires were sent to 3000 Australian and 1000 New Zealand manufacturing sites. The selection of the sites was at random. A total of 962 Australian sites and 379 New Zealand sites responded to the questionnaire, which was filled out by the most senior manufacturing executive at the site. This represented

Table 2.11: Ranked order of importance of reasons for continuing to use self-assessment in current users

Reason	Mean	Mode (0 = not important; 5 = very important)
Drive continuous improvement	4.31	5
Identify further areas for improvement	4.27	4
Measure effectiveness of improvement plans from previous self-assessment	3.84	4
Increase commitment of line management to TQM	3.75	4
Involve employees in TQ efforts	3.74	4
Use as an internal benchmarking tool	3.56	4
Re-energize TQ effort	3.46	4
Successful first self-assessment	3.29	4
Identify further strengths	3.28	4
Use as an external benchmarking tool	2.80	4
Compete for a national/international quality award	1.90	0
Win a national/international quality award	1.65	0
Competitors still using TQ-based self-assessment	1.00	0

Source: ECforBE (1997)

response rates of 32 and 38 per cent respectively. In both countries, stratification of the sample was on the basis of twelve industry codes and three company size categories. These categories were: 'small' (20–49 employees), 'medium' (50–99 employees) and 'large' (100 or more employees).

The central finding of the study was that business excellence tends to have mixed results when analysed by company size and industry type. A typical manufacturing organization is more likely

Table 2.12: Benefits gained from using TQ-based self-assessment, and how important these have been

Benefit	Importance	
	Mean	*Mode (0 = not important; 5 = very important)*
Identified areas for improvement	4.44	5
Provided a focus for continuous improvement	4.29	5
Increased customer focus	3.90	5
Increased 'top-team' awareness of TQM	3.90	4
Increased organizational awareness of TQM	3.82	4
Increased visibility of TQ efforts/initiatives	3.82	4
Increased knowledge of business processes	3.75	4
Personal development of those involved in the self-assessment process	3.53	4
Identified key business processes	3.53	3
Identified key business performance indicators	3.52	3
Benefits to business planning	3.44	4
Established links between enablers (approach taken) and business results	3.39	4
Facilitated culture change	3.38	4
Improved business results	3.16	3
Increased profile of organization in industry/market	2.82	3
Obtained a 'score' for the business assessment	2.16	3
Won a national/international quality award/prize	1.67	0

Source: ECforBE (1997)

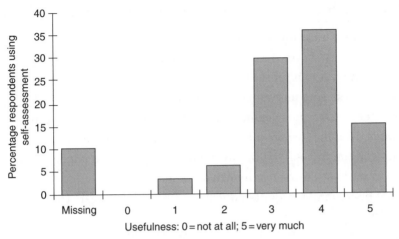

Figure 2.3 Overall usefulness of TQ-based self-assessment
(Source: ECforBE (1997))

to achieve better performance in employee relations, customer satisfaction, operational performance and business performance with business excellence than without it. In addition, business excellence was found to be significantly related to operational and business performance, employee relations, and customer satisfaction.

The effect of ISO9000 led to an interesting conclusion. The authors found that ISO9000 certification was not shown to have a significantly positive effect on organizational performance in the presence or absence of a business excellence environment. This supports the view that, on average, ISO9000 certification has little or no explanatory power regarding organizational performance. Based on the results of this study, the authors believe that ISO9000 certification can contribute to organizational performance if a climate of change is created. However, this is not yet happening on a widespread basis. ISO9000 certification may act as a foundation on which to build a quality organization where it is implemented as part of the business excellence philosophy and methods.

It was also found that there was a difference in relationship between business excellence and organizational performance across industry sector and size of organization. Like the Powell study described above, it was concluded that business excellence neither guarantees superior profitability nor that improved returns can only be obtained by those organizations with higher quality of products and services. It was found that there are certainly organizations that achieve good returns without TQM. On the other hand, there were TQM organizations that had not turned in a good profit record.

Table 2.13: Benefits of self-assessment for case study organizations

- Identified areas for improvement
- Provided a focus/driver for continuous improvement
- Coordinated *ad hoc* improvement activities
- Provided a base-line measure of the organization
- Encouraged senior management involvement in business excellence
- Encouraged line-management involvement in business excellence
- Encouraged employee/staff involvement in business excellence
- Provided motivation for results-driven managers
- External benchmarks provided a focus for senior managers (particularly awards)
- Effective means of implementing business excellence
- Added impetus to TQ implementation
- Key component in a 'phased' approach to business excellence
- Encouraged top-down and bottom-up communication
- Was an effective management development tool
- Increased employee/staff motivation
- Encouraged a team culture and integrated management
- Promoted a cross-functional (process) perspective
- Promoted sharing of skills/knowledge
- Encouraged key components of a learning organization
- Encouraged commitment to strategic directives
- Effective base for a collaborative management approach
- Gave a holistic view of the business
- Provided a business measurement framework
- Could be integrated into business planning

Source: ECforBE (1997)

2.10 *The x-Factor* report

The x-Factor report (ECforBE, 1999) presented the results of a research project on the linkages between business excellence activities, including self-assessment, and superior business performance and results. It also identified the best practices that led to these results.

The research uncovered a wealth of evidence, both anecdotal and empirical, which indicates that there are multiple benefits to be gained from adopting business excellence practices. In every case, the research showed that business excellence delivers positive and superior business results measured by a range of financial and non-financial indicators.

The research was carried out by the European Centre for Business Excellence (ECforBE) – the research and education division of Oakland Consulting plc. The work was funded by Transco and supported by the British Quality Foundation (BQF) and the European Foundation for Quality Management (EFQM). The main objectives of the research were to:

- Determine the links between business excellence practices, self-assessment and business performance
- Establish whether links between the 'enablers' of the business excellence model and 'results' could be demonstrated in role model organizations
- Determine best practice business excellence activities as measured by the business results criteria
- Examine whether there is evidence that the business excellence approach delivers sustained business benefits.

The research was structured around four phases: a review of literature from the USA, Europe and the UK; an analysis of European and UK Business Excellence Award winners' submission documents (over the last five years); in-depth interviews with selected award-winning organizations; and the production of 'The Route to Business Excellence'. As much of the literature has already been covered in this chapter, we will look at the findings from the case study research and the model that was produced as a result of the work.

The research provides an overwhelming amount of evidence and a compelling argument that organizations adopting business excellence principles and practices achieve excellent business performance across a set of balanced measures. The companies studied through the literature, award submissions documents, and interviews were found to be actively following and deploying best practice and, as a result of the benefits derived, were showing commitment to ongoing use of the business excellence model.

The submissions from fourteen European and UK Quality/ Business Excellence Award-winning companies were analysed regarding financial performance. The fourteen companies were assessed by a team of EQA/UK assessors who had awarded a high score for business results. Therefore, the sample represented a good cross-section of high-performing companies. The results

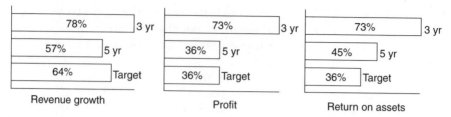

Figure 2.4 Percentage companies showing strong positive trends/sustained excellent performance (Source: ECforBE (1999))

were examined for:

- Three-year trends and sustained good performance
- Five-year trends and sustained excellent performance
- Favourable comparisons with set targets.

Benchmark comparisons were provided where sensible data were available, but it was found that the role model organizations had some difficulty in identifying suitable benchmarks and partners. Figure 2.4 shows the measures used and the percentage of companies showing strong positive trends and/or sustained excellent performance over three and five years (not a one-off snapshot), and favourable comparisons with their own targets.

Strong positive trends and/or sustained excellent performance over three years were demonstrated by over 70 per cent of the companies using three main financial measures:

1. Revenue growth
2. Operating profit
3. Return on assets.

Other financials against which these role model companies performed well, over three and five years and against targets/benchmarks, included:

- Cash flow
- Liquidity
- Debtor days
- Shareholder funds.

The x-Factor report covers all the results areas of the business excellence model as it was in 1998. As a summary the authors' report compiled a 'Business Excellence Scorecard', which gave the top five achievements in each of the four results areas (Figure 2.5). It should be noticed that at the time of research all the organizations were private sector organizations. Some indication as to the benefits obtained by public sector organizations is included in the

Customer satisfaction	People satisfaction
◆ Overall satisfaction	◆ Overall satisfaction
◆ Perception across a range of customer attributes	◆ Satisfaction across a range of people attributes
◆ Marker share	◆ Absenteeism
◆ Delivery performance	◆ Accident levels
◆ Defect, error etc. rate	◆ Labour/staff turnover
Impact on society	Business results
◆ Perception of corporate responsibility	◆ Revenue growth
◆ Support for charity	◆ Operating profit
◆ Support for educational institutions	◆ Return on equity/assets/capital
◆ Recycling	◆ Process performance measures such as cycle time
	◆ Supply chain indicators

Figure 2.5 The Business Excellence Scorecard top five achievements (Source: ECforBE (1999))

report of the evaluation of the public sector excellence programme discussed below.

In the final phase of the work, a framework or 'route map' to business excellence was developed from all the best practice activities identified. The affinity/interrelationship diagram (Figure 2.6) was created by grouping common themes and showing their relationships.

The route map maintains the integrity of the business excellence model whilst fleshing out some of the underlying themes. A clear path and linkages have been identified, from *Values and direction setting* through *Process management, Goal deployment, People management, Improvement and review* to targeted and measured achievements in the *Results* areas. In addition, the importance of *Planning, Self-assessment, Benchmarking, and Customer–Supplier Partnerships* is highlighted by this route map.

The report notes that the management of *People*, including *HR strategy, Competencies, Training, Conditions and benefits*, and *Recognition and reward*, is the fulcrum of achieving excellence in business and results.

2.11   *The Model in Practice*

Following *The x-Factor* report there was an additional piece of work by the ECforBE, which was commissioned by the British Quality Foundation. *The x-Factor* report had listed several 'best

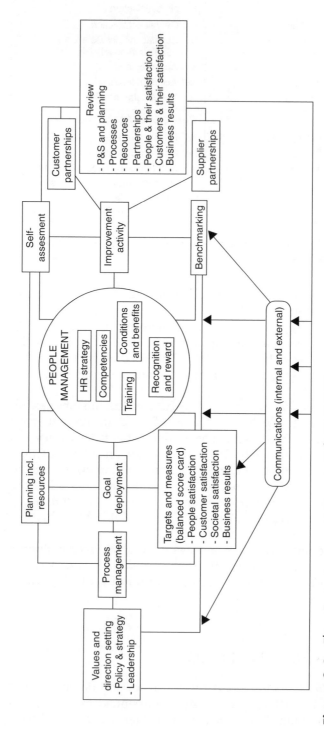

Figure 2.6 *The x-Factor 'route map'* (Source: ECforBE (1999))

practices' that had been found during the work, but limited details had been given on how the good practices actually operated. The report was also limited because all the case studies concerned large private-sector organizations. No public or small–medium enterprises had been included.

The Model in Practice (ECforBE, 2000)) sought to achieve three objectives:

1. To summarize the background to excellence to help organizations that were new to the subject
2. To provide a range of summary examples showing how aspects of the EFQM Excellence Model® had been implemented in all types of organization
3. To show that excellence was more than just about self-assessment, and how it could be used to drive change.

The result was a best-selling document that contains an introduction to the model and 99 short examples. The result was a best-selling document that contains an introduction to the model, together with a number of good practice examples for each of the 33 sub-criteria. The examples cover different types of organization including private sector, public sector and small organizations. Figure 2.7 provides an example of an entry from the 2002 version of *The Model in Practice*. The example, which is taken from a secondary school, is for sub-criterion 3E – *'People are rewarded, recognized and cared for'*. A description of the practice is given, followed by a classification showing how the practice supports the fundamental concepts of excellence. It should be noted that although this practice was found in a school, elements of it could be transferred to other organizations.

Not only does *The Model in Practice* provide a library of examples; it also includes a number of linkage diagrams for the purpose of identifying the linkages across the model. This was the first time such tables had been published in the public domain. These linkage tables will be discussed further in Chapter 12. The tables are designed to be used with an improvement approach that has four stages:

1. Establish and prioritize the improvement needs – the *Results* being aimed for
2. Select the improvement activity – the *Approaches* to be introduced or improved
3. Take action – deploy the new or revised Approaches
4. Confirm the improvement – *Assessment and Review*.

This approach is based on RADAR®, which is the evaluation approach behind the EFQM Excellence Model®. We will look at RADAR® in greater detail in Chapter 5, but it should be noted that this was the first time RADAR® had been used in this way.

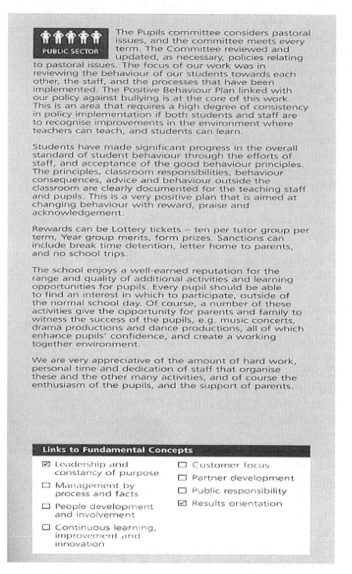

The Pupils committee considers pastoral issues, and the committee meets every term. The Committee reviewed and updated, as necessary, policies relating to pastoral issues. The focus of our work was in reviewing the behaviour of our students towards each other, the staff, and the processes that have been implemented. The Positive Behaviour Plan linked with our policy against bullying is at the core of this work. This is an area that requires a high degree of consistency in policy implementation if both students and staff are to recognise improvements in the environment where teachers can teach, and students can learn.

Students have made significant progress in the overall standard of student behaviour through the efforts of staff, and acceptance of the good behaviour principles. The principles, classroom responsibilities, behaviour consequences, advice and behaviour outside the classroom are clearly documented for the teaching staff and pupils. This is a very positive plan that is aimed at changing behaviour with reward, praise and acknowledgement.

Rewards can be Lottery tickets – ten per tutor group per term, Year group merits, form prizes. Sanctions can include break time detention, letter home to parents, and no school trips.

The school enjoys a well-earned reputation for the range and quality of additional activities and learning opportunities for pupils. Every pupil should be able to find an interest in which to participate, outside of the normal school day. Of course, a number of these activities give the opportunity for parents and family to witness the success of the pupils, e.g. music concerts, drama productions and dance productions, all of which enhance pupils' confidence, and create a working together environment.

We are very appreciative of the amount of hard work, personal time and dedication of staff that organise these and the other many activities, and of course the enthusiasm of the pupils, and the support of parents.

Links to Fundamental Concepts

☑ Leadership and constancy of purpose
☐ Management by process and facts
☐ People development and involvement
☐ Continuous learning, improvement and innovation
☐ Customer focus
☐ Partner development
☐ Public responsibility
☑ Results orientation

Figure 2.7 *The Model in Practice* example (Source: ECforBE (2002))

2.12 The effectiveness of business excellence in the automotive industry

Curkovic *et al.* (2000) conducted a survey of the top 150 (in revenue terms) independent automotive parts suppliers in the USA, with 57 responses (38 per cent response rate) being achieved.

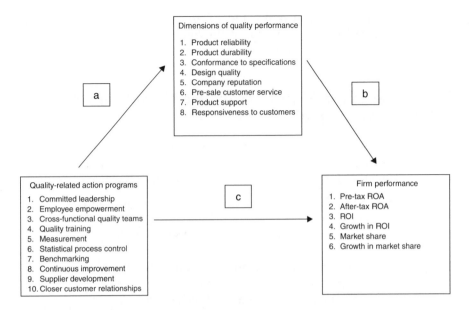

a = effects of quality-related action programs on dimensions of quality performance.
b = effects of dimensions of quality performance on firm performance.
c = direct effects of quality-related action programs in firm performance.
a,b = indirect effects of quality-related action programs on firm performance.

Figure 2.8 Study conceptual model (Source: Curkovic *et al.* (2000))

The research examined the relationship between 'Quality-related action programmes', 'Dimensions of quality performance' and 'Firm performance', using a model that had been derived from the literature. This model is shown in Figure 2.8.

The model shows that a number of 'quality-related action programmes' or common business excellence activities such as committed leadership, measurement and continuous improvement were examined to see what effects they had on several 'dimensions of quality performance' relating to product performance, which are covered by all the business excellence frameworks described in Part 2 of this book. It was of interest to the researchers to see whether the quality activities had had a direct or indirect effect on firm performance.

The research found that not all of the action programmes have pervasive direct effects on firm performance, but many have indirect effects. The main relationships found were the action programmes affecting product conformance, which in turn affected return on investment (ROI). It was also found that action programmes affect responsiveness to customers, which in turn affects ROI, ROI growth, market share and market share growth. This research is important because it is one of the few empirical studies that examines the relationships at the heart of the excellence models.

2.13   Use of the EFQM Excellence Model® in UK public sector organizations

In February 2000 the UK Cabinet Office commissioned a study to undertake an evaluation of the Public Sector Excellence Programme. The aim of the study was to answer four key questions:

1. What impact has the Excellence Model had on those organizations that have used it?
2. How effective a tool is the Excellence Model for the public sector?
3. How effective has the Public Sector Excellence Programme and its associated elements been?
4. What should the next steps be for the Cabinet Office?

The study was conducted by undertaking a survey of 3500 public sector organizations following the completion of a literature review. Eighty face-to-face and telephone interviews were then conducted, together with four facilitated workshops. The work led to the production of twelve case studies and a final report by PriceWaterhouseCoopers (2000).

The key findings arising from the evaluation are presented under the following headings:

- Baseline assessment of the take-up and use of the Excellence Model
- The effectiveness of the Excellence Model in the public sector
- The effectiveness of the Public Sector Excellence Programme.

Baseline assessment of the take-up and use of the EFQM Excellence Model®

The baseline assessment looked at the take-up and use of the Excellence Model by the public sector. It identified the drivers and barriers to improvement, how the Model is being used, the extent of deployment across organizations, implementation costs, and the level of integration within organizations. Some of the key findings were that:

- Ninety per cent of survey respondents had a strategy in place for improvement, and the majority of these stated it was incorporated within a corporate or business plan.

- Internal drivers, not government efforts, were cited as the more significant drivers for improvement with good leadership also being important.
- Uncommitted leadership at both executive and political levels was seen as the key barrier to driving forward excellence. Initiative overload, particularly from government-led initiatives, was also cited as a significant barrier to achieving excellence.
- Fifty-six per cent of survey respondents were current users of the EFQM Excellence Model®. The majority of non-users said they were using other approaches, or that the EFQM Excellence Model© was not part of their strategy
- For half of the organizations, implementation costs were believed to be below £20 000 – including staff time, training, consultancy and material costs.

The effectiveness of the EFQM Excellence Model® in the UK public sector

The effectiveness of the EFQM Excellence Model® was examined in terms of its 'fit' with other quality tools. The evaluation also examined whether improvement could be directly attributed to the implementation of the EFQM Excellence Model®. The key findings were that:

- The EFQM Excellence Model® was seen to be the overarching framework for organizations seeking continuous improvement. Other tools and schemes assist organizations in their performance improvement efforts, and greater benefit can be achieved when they are used in a 'joined-up' and complementary manner.
- Awareness and prior use of other quality tools and schemes was not found to be a prerequisite for the use of the EFQM Excellence Model®.
- Sixty-eight per cent of survey respondents considered the EFQM Excellence Model® to be either a strong or a very strong driver for improvement in the UK public sector.
- There was concern regarding the way that the inspectorate bodies are approaching the principles advocated by the EFQM Excellence Model® in promoting good practice and facilitating improvement.
- The EFQM Excellence Model® was seen as providing a common language and framework for carrying out organizational assessment and planning for improvement, and therefore has many practical advantages for the public sector.

The effectiveness of the UK Public Sector Excellence Programme

A key part of the evaluation was to assess the impact of the UK Public Sector Excellence Programme in driving forward excellence in the UK public sector. The key findings were that:

- It was felt that the Programme's original objectives had proved to be over-ambitious, and ultimately unachievable. Not enough had been done at the outset to enable monitoring to take place.
- The Programme lacked performance targets, and measures did not include any monitoring and review arrangements – for example, no formal evaluation was undertaken of the value and impact of the use of the training consultants.
- Most organizations saw benefits in using the EFQM Excellence Model®, and its main value was seen as an improvement diagnostic rather than as a scoring or performance measuring device.
- A great fear expressed by UK public sector organizations was that the government might in some way seek to enforce compulsory scoring of organizations and generate 'name and shame' league tables – a scenario that all commentators believed would be the death knell of the EFQM Excellence Model® in the UK public sector. Notwithstanding this, validated scoring creates a fairly robust method that indicates where organizations are on the 'improvement curve', and how they compare with others.

This work provides many learning points regarding both implementation and benefits of business excellence. It is clear that the introduction of the EFQM Excellence Model® has had major benefits for the UK public sector. The major benefits include driving continuous improvement, and these improvement activities are supported in most cases by integrating the improvement activities with the business plan. Leadership is a key enabler for success, and 'interference' from central government a potential barrier. A final key learning point is the need to install monitoring mechanisms.

2.14 Financial performance of US award winners

This piece of research by Kevin Hendricks, of the University of Western Ontario, and Vinod Singhal, of the Georgia Institute of Technology, has been loudly applauded across the world (Hendricks and Singhal, 1997, 2000, 2001a, 2001b). It was a study similar to the NIST study described above, but was more extensive because it included many types of excellence awards and not just the Baldrige Award. Although an American study, it has been accepted that the findings are applicable throughout the world, and work is currently being undertaken to replicate the work with European Award winners.

The work started as the researchers identified the need to investigate whether business excellence delivered benefit to organizations, given a number of articles that were appearing in the press questioning its value. The researchers also noted that some of the previous research had lacked rigour.

The research was conducted by using the receipt of a quality award as a 'proxy' for effective business excellence implementation. Winners from 140 different award bodies were selected, with a sample of about 600 publicly traded award winners being studied. These award bodies included independent national awards such as the Baldrige Award, regional/state awards, and customer awards given by third parties – such as manufacturers' awards for suppliers.

The organizations' performance during implementation, which was taken to be a five-year period before the award was given, was compared to the performance post-implementation, which was a five-year post-award period. The performance of the winners was compared with the performance of carefully chosen benchmark organizations. It should be noted that the share price performance was analysed alongside a number of other performance variables, such as growth in sales, return on assets and return on sales.

The first major conclusion from the research was that there was no difference in the performance of the award winners and the benchmark organizations in the period prior to winning the award. The performance post-awards was, however, significantly different. Figure 2.9 gives a comparison of the financial performance for the award winners against the benchmark organizations for the five-year period after winning the award.

Figure 2.9 demonstrates that in this study the post-implementation results indicate that award winners outperform benchmark organizations in a number of performance measures (e.g. operating income, sales, ROA, ROS). Figure 2.10 shows the results when segmented into independent awards and supplier awards, and these indicate that organizations receiving independent awards perform better than those receiving customer awards. This applies to performance data and stock performance. A further conclusion is that more benefit in percentage terms is achieved by small compared to larger organizations.

As mentioned above, the stock price performance was also evaluated. Figure 2.11 provides the summary results. It can be seen that with stock performance, award winners outperformed

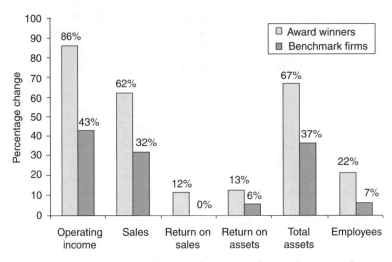

Figure 2.9 Comparison of the performance of award-winning firms and benchmark organizations during the post-implementation period (Source: Hendricks and Singhal (2001b))

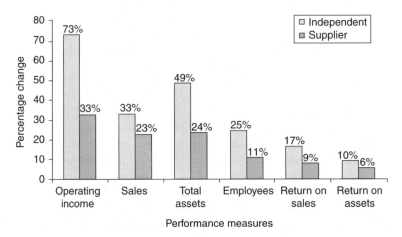

Figure 2.10 Comparison of the post-implementation period's benchmark-adjusted performance of independent award winners and customer award winners (Source: Hendricks and Singhal (2001b))

the S&P 500 and the control sample of benchmark organizations. This was the case even when adjusting the benchmark portfolio for industry and size.

The work by Hendricks and Singhal provides compelling evidence that business excellence is of benefit to organizations. The

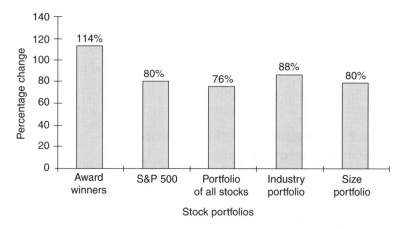

Figure 2.11 Comparison of the post-implementation period's stock price performance of award winners and various benchmark portfolios (Source: Hendricks and Singhal (2001b))

research papers include some other information that is also of interest, such as an analysis of self-assessment scores to see what factors drive the financial performance. The authors conclude that business excellence is not a tool or technique, a programme, or a replacement for corporate strategy, but it is a source of competitive advantage.

2.15 Study of the economic impact of quality awards in the USA

Unlike the previous study, this work does not provide strong evidence for the benefits of business excellence. It has been included because it does draw an important conclusion about the benefit of a business excellence approach that may explain some of the other research results.

Fisher *et al.* (2001) conducted a survey of the different USA State Awards, and compared some economic factors found in these States with those found in States that did not administer a State Award. The underlying principle of both the Baldrige and the EFQM European Quality Award® is that the promotion of such awards will lead to economic success. Logic thus dictates that if this is indeed the case, the economic performance within States with awards will be superior to that in those that do not.

The results indicated that there may be a relationship between States that demonstrate commitment to quality business practices, but it is accepted that many other factors have an influence on economic performance. This is an important conclusion, as several of the studies covered in this chapter conclude that business excellence is not a guarantee for success. The research supports these findings.

2.16 Effect of business excellence on organizational performance

This study is of interest, as it reaches a different conclusion to that of Hendricks and Singhal (see above) regarding when the benefits of business excellence are delivered to an organization. Douglas and Judge (2001) conducted a survey of general medical hospitals. The targets for the questionnaire were the CEO and Director of Quality, and 193 hospitals returned at least one questionnaire. An analysis of some secondary data was also conducted to assess financial performance.

The study concluded that there was strong empirical support for a positive relationship between the degree of business excellence implementation and organizational performance – the greater the degree of business excellence implementation, the greater the benefit achieved. Figure 2.12 best illustrates this relationship. It should be noted that this result is in contradiction to Hendricks and

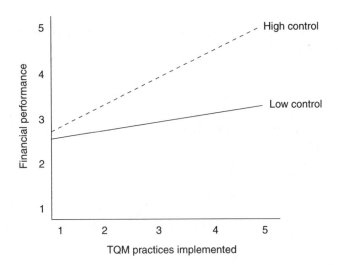

Figure 2.12 Relationship between quality practices implemented and financial performance (Source: Douglas and Judge (2001))

Singhal's conclusion, as they found no difference in performance between award-winning organizations and the benchmarks until the awards were given. This work by Douglas and Judge (2001) suggests that the delivery of the benefit increases in correlation with the implementation of the quality practices.

There was also some empirical evidence that the relationship between business excellence implementation and organizational performance was moderated by the organizational structure. This is shown by the two lines in Figure 2.12, which represent different levels of organizational control. The authors claimed that the study broke new ground in the business excellence literature by identifying a complex relationship between organizational structure and TQM implementation success.

2.17 Impact of stakeholder management social initiative participation on shareholder returns

This study, by Hillman and Keim (2001), tests another principle of business excellence. A business excellence approach requires that the needs of many stakeholders must be managed to deliver sustained success. The stakeholders include the shareholders, customers, suppliers, people, and society in general.

The study tested this principle by using data from the Stern Stewart Performance 1000 database and the KLD database. A sample of 308 firms was subjected to a quantitative analysis looking to test the relationship between stakeholder management and social issue participation on shareholder value creation. The results indicated a positive relationship between stakeholder management and shareholder value creation. This supports the principle that managing stakeholders will lead to financial success for the organizations. However, a negative relationship was found between social issue participation and shareholder value creation. This suggests that becoming involved with the community, which is a core principle of business excellence, could be detrimental to an organization.

The main conclusion was that investing in stakeholder management is of benefit to organizations, but social issue participation is not. This conclusion does not indicate support for the Corporate Social Responsibility Fundamental Concept, which is one of the eight building blocks of the EFQM Excellence Model®, or Public Responsibility and Citizenship, which is one of the Baldrige core values and concepts.

2.18 Share price performance considering market and industry effects

The most recent study on share price performance of private organizations in the USA, by Przasnyski and Tai (2002), does not confirm the huge benefits claimed by the other studies in this chapter. The study also drew some different conclusions regarding the timing of the delivery of the benefit from business excellence.

In their work the researchers conducted an assessment of stock performance of public traded Baldrige Award winners up to 1998, and included an adjustment for market and industry effects by taking matching companies. In effect, these researchers chose to use different benchmark organizations to those selected by Hendricks and Singhal.

The researchers concluded, unlike Hendricks and Singhal, that the benefit is delivered post-winning the award. Any increase in share price is built over a period as an organization builds its competence. In most cases there is no surprise element. Furthermore, Baldrige winners under-performed by 17 per cent when compared to stocks with a similar risk and type of industry. It was concluded that the 'spectacular' returns are due to market and industry factors.

The conclusion was not that there was no significant benefit. The Baldrige companies did outperform the S&P 500, but it was concluded that a higher return would have been achieved by investing in the matching companies. Only one company had a high return for low risk. Adjusting for risk and market movements, only about half of the companies outperformed the market.

Replicating the NIST work, a fictitious fund of all the Baldrige winners, when adjusted for risk, did outperform stocks with similar risk. The authors concluded that Baldrige winners can give a superior S&P 500 performance, but it is not as spectacular as that claimed by NIST.

This work should not be taken as undervaluing the studies described earlier in this chapter. However, it does give a sense of realism to the work that has been done to date. It is clear that business excellence delivers benefits, but the level of the benefit is dependent on the industry in which an organization competes. It is also suggested that the benefit comes over time, and not 'at the flick of a switch'. This would seem to be more realistic.

2.19 Study to test the structure of the Baldrige Model

Surprisingly little empirical work has been done to test the structures of the various business excellence models. These were generated based on expert opinion, and in the case of the EFQM Excellence Model® the model has been modified in the light of extensive feedback from member organizations. Pannirselvam and Ferguson (2001) attempted to assess the relationships within the Baldrige model, aiming their research specifically at answering the questions:

- Are the proposed relationships between the categories in the MBNQA framework valid?
- What is the strength of the relationships between the different quality management constructs prescribed by the MBNQA criteria?

These two questions were examined using data from a State quality award that mirrors the MBNQA award criteria and evaluation process. A state award was used because there was easier access to the data, the Baldrige data being kept confidential. The Arizona Governor's Quality Award (AGQA) was chosen, as this was the closest match to a set of predetermined criteria that included the purpose and structure of the award as well as the evaluation process.

The sample in this research consisted of the 69 organizations that applied to the AGQA in 1993. Of the 69 applicants, 26 were small businesses (less than 100 employees), 26 were medium-sized businesses (between 100 and 500 employees), and 17 were large businesses (greater than 500 employees). The number of employees ranged from seven to over 6000, and some of the applicants were divisions of national or multinational corporations. The sample included 19 manufacturing businesses, 36 service businesses, four healthcare organizations, four educational institutions, and six government agencies.

The Baldrige criteria represent leadership as the driving force that influences all other elements of quality management. The results from this research partially validated this, indicating that leadership significantly directly or indirectly affects all of the systems components except for strategic quality planning and information management, which was not tested in the model.

The Baldrige criteria also emphasize the need for good human resource practices and employee involvement in order for an organization to make substantial progress in its quest for quality. Human resources management is clearly an important part of an organization's quality management process, as it determines the effectiveness of the organization's product and process management and customer focus and relationship management efforts. Through these two components, human resources management has a significant indirect impact on the organization's performance. The results from this research provided ample evidence of the important role that human resources management plays in improving an organization's quality focus.

The Baldrige criteria emphasize that access to and use of company and industry information (through benchmarking) is essential to setting quality goals and allocating resources to achieve these goals. Information management is essential to effective planning and execution of the plans. This research provided strong support for this theory through the significant relationships between information management and the other infrastructure, core management practices, and performance constructs.

The greatest determinant of organization performance, in the market and internally, is customer focus and relationship management. This component examines the actions an organization takes to understand and anticipate its customers' needs and maintain a good relationship with its existing customer base. The results from this analysis underscore the value of customer focus and effective customer relationship management. This component had the most significant effect on both business results and customer satisfaction results. This focus on customers is also emphasized throughout the Baldrige criteria in its planning and execution of the other quality management constructs.

The researchers concluded that their analysis provided evidence to confirm the validity of the Baldrige criteria. They also noted that there had been changes to the Baldrige criteria since 1993, which was the year on which the analysis was based. They felt, however, that the conclusion was still valid.

2.20 Examination of the criterion weightings

The final piece of research reviewed in this chapter relates to work conducted in Denmark on the weightings placed on the criteria in both the Baldrige and EFQM Excellence Model®. Very little research has been carried out regarding the criterion weight structure, and this is a problem because it raises the question as to whether it makes sense to compare companies according to an arbitrary weighting score.

To test the score weightings, Eskildsen *et al.* (2002) used data from the Danish Excellence Index, which was established in 1998. The database contains data from over 9000 organizations in Denmark with over 20 employees, and an organization's position is evaluated using a questionnaire based on the EFQM Excellence Model®. In responding to the questionnaire the organization rates the importance of a number of statements, each being related to a criterion of the EFQM Excellence Model®.

To perform the analysis, a sample of responses was taken from the database and estimates made of the weightings given to the various criteria by the organizations. In doing this, the analysis

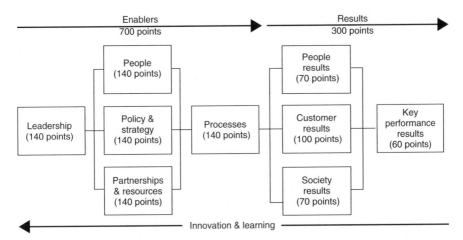

Figure 2.13 Empirical Excellence Model (Source: Eskildsen *et al.* (2002))

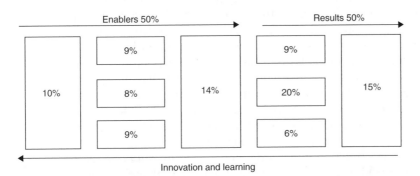

Figure 2.14 EFQM Excellence Model® criterion weightings (Source: EFQM (1999))

was addressing where the emphasis was being placed by the organizations. Weightings were calculated for each of the criteria, and the results are shown in Figure 2.13. The weightings of the EFQM Excellence Model® are shown in Figure 2.14 for purposes of comparison.

This analysis throws up a number of interesting points, the most obvious being the 70/30 split between enablers and results compared with the 50/50 arbitrary split in the EFQM Excellence Model®. It is also noted that all the enabler criteria have been given 140 points, and the weighting of the customer results and key performance results are much lower.

2.21 Summary

In this chapter we have examined the wealth of empirical research conducted to show the value that an organization may gain from adopting a business excellence philosophy. This work stretches back over a decade, and includes all the major business excellence frameworks that are covered in this book.

The first extensive survey was conducted on behalf of the American General Accounting Office, and focused on the first Baldrige Award winners. The research concluded that Baldrige-winning organizations were likely to experience higher customer and staff satisfaction, whilst at the same time reducing defects and costs. This research also reviewed earlier, less extensive research studies on the Deming Prize-winning organizations, concluding that all the research indicated consistent benefits.

A little later the first share-price studies were conducted, and these indicated that organizations winning the Baldrige award were likely to provide shareholders with a greater return over time than a non-award winning organization. There has been some debate regarding the actual level of share price advantage obtained, as the results are affected by other conditions such as market, industry and risk factors. Despite this complication it is clear that some level of share price advantage is obtained.

Research also indicates that business excellence delivers competitive advantage. Many researchers have shown a link between quality activities and organizational performance. It has been noted, however, that an excellence approach is not a guarantee of success. When the benefit is delivered is another talking point, with some research suggesting that it is not delivered until 'world-class' status is achieved. Other researchers, however, believe that the level of benefit increases as the maturity of the approaches increases.

A final point is that although a number of different methods have been used to conduct the research, most of the research has been focused on the US Baldrige framework. Perhaps it is time for more extensive studies in other parts of the world.

References

Curkovic, S., Vickery, S. *et al.* (2000). Quality-related action programmes: their impact on quality performance and firm performance. *Decision Sciences*, **31(4)**, 885–905.

Douglas, T. J. and Judge, W. Q. (2001). Total quality management implementation and competitive advantage: the role of structural control and exploration. *Academy of Management*, **44(1)**, 158–69.

ECforBE (1997). *Evaluating the Operation of the European Quality Model for Self-assessment.* Leeds: European Centre for Business Excellence, p. 106.

ECforBE (1999). *The x-Factor: Winning Performance through Business Excellence.* Leeds: European Centre for Business Excellence.

ECforBE (2000). *The Model in Practice.* London: British Quality Foundation.

ECforBE (2002). *The Model in Practice.* London: British Quality Foundation.

EFQM (1999). *The EFQM Excellence Model.* Brussels: European Foundation for Quality Management.

Eskildsen, J. K., Kristensen, K. *et al.* (2002). Trends in EFQM criterion weights. *Measuring Business Excellence*, 22–8.

Fisher, C., Dauterive, J. *et al.* (2001). Economic impact of quality awards: does offering an award bring returns to the state? *Total Quality Management*, **12(7 & 8)**, 981–7.

GAO (1991). *GAO Management Practices: US Companies Improve Performance through Quality Efforts.* Washington, DC: General Accounting Office.

Helton, R. (1995). The Baldie play. *Quality Progress.*

Hendricks, K. B. and Singhal, V. R. (1997). Does implementing an effective TQM program actually improve operating performance? Empirical evidence from firms that have won quality awards. *Management Science*, **44(9)**, 1258–74.

Hendricks, K. B. and Singhal, V. R. (2000). The long-run stock price performance of firms with effective TQM programs as proxied by quality award winners. *Management Science*, **47(3)**, 359–68.

Hendricks, K. B. and Singhal, V. R. (2001a). Firm characteristics, total quality management, and financial performance. *Journal of Operations Management*, **19**, 269–85.

Hendricks, K. B. and Singhal, V. R. (2001b). The impact of TQM on financial performance: evidence from quality award winners. In: *Stakeholder Value – The Path to Sustainable Growth.* Lucerne: EFQM.

Hillman, A. J. and Keim, G. D. (2001). Shareholder value, stakeholder management, and social issues: what's the bottom line? *Strategic Management Journal*, **22**, 125–39.

NIST (2002). *Baldrige Winners Beat the S&P 500 for the Eighth Year.* National Institute for Standards and Technology (www.quality.nist.gov).

Oakland, J. S. (1999). Winning performance through business excellence. *Credit Control*, **20(7)**, 25–31.

Pannirselvam, G. P. and Ferguson, L. A. (2001). A study of the relationships between Baldrige categories. *International Journal of Quality and Reliability Management*, **18(1)**, 14–34.

Powell, T. C. (1995). TQM as competitive advantage. A review and empirical study. *Strategic Management Journal*, **16**, 15–37.

PriceWaterhouseCoopers (2000). *Report on the Evaluation of the Public Sector Excellence Programme – Main Report*. London: PriceWaterhouseCoopers.

Przasnyski, Z. H. and Tai, L. S. (2002). Stock performance of Malcolm Baldrige National Award winning companies. *Total Quality Management*, **13(4)**, 475–88.

Terziovski, M. and Samson, D. (1999). The link between total quality management practice and organizational performance. *International Journal of Quality and Reliability Management*, **16(3)**, 226–37.

Williams, R. and Boudewijn, J. (1994). *Quality Leadership in Taiwan*. Brussels: European Foundation for Quality Management.

Wisner, J. D. and Eakins, S. G. (1994). A performance based assessment of the US Baldrige Quality Award winners. *International Journal of Quality and Reliability Management*, **11(2)**, 8–25.

Part Two

The Excellence Frameworks

Overview of the national and international quality awards

3.1 Introduction

The late 1980s and early 1990s saw a global realization of the strategic importance of quality, and many countries established programmes to recognize quality and excellence. These initiatives followed the earlier example of Japan, which started to recognize quality practices with the launch of the Deming Prize in 1951. The structure and criteria for these award programmes elevated quality to a strategic level, and resulted in some of the concepts of business excellence with which we are familiar today. The majority of these programmes have undergone continuous improvement in framework design and award administration.

Organizations pursuing an excellence strategy soon recognized that the award frameworks offered more than just a vehicle for recognition. The frameworks were seen to be best-practice models for implementing excellence strategies, performing self-assessments, benchmarking and, ultimately, delivering improved performance.

As such, quality award criteria such as the Japanese Deming Prize, the American Malcolm Baldrige National Quality Award (MBNQA), and the European Foundation for Quality Management's Excellence Award are continuously being used by organizations in both the private and public sectors to carry out self-assessments to measure their improvement progress and potential. Each of the award criteria provides a framework of standardized items against which an organization can measure its performance. This standardization allows comparisons to be made and best-in-class performance identified. Winning one of these annual awards is a prestigious event, but applicants frequently cite the most beneficial aspect as being the assessment process itself.

Over the last ten years, the award frameworks and award processes across the world have continued to improve as the latest ideas on quality and excellence have been incorporated. In this process there has been increasing convergence of all the excellence models and, whilst we are still some way from a 'Unified Global Model', most of the models have a high degree of commonality.

This chapter briefly introduces the main quality awards – the Deming Prize from Japan, the Malcolm Baldrige National Quality Award from the United States, the European Foundation for Quality Management's (EFQM) Excellence Model®, the Canada Awards for Excellence, the Australian Business Excellence Awards, and the Singapore Quality Award. The countries or continents covered by these awards represent over three-quarters of the world's gross domestic product. The ISO9000 quality system is also introduced, and the growing number of national and regional awards that are usually based on either the Baldrige or EFQM frameworks are listed.

3.2 A summary guide to the excellence models

A quick overview of each of the main quality awards follows. Each framework is subsequently discussed in greater depth in the following chapters.

The Deming Prize

The Union of Japanese Scientists and Engineers (JUSE) established the Deming Prize in 1951 in honour of W. Edwards Deming's legendary impact on Japanese industry. The Prize was intended to recognize excellence in the implementation of company-wide quality control (CWQC). CWQC is, broadly speaking, the Japanese equivalent of TQM, although TQM takes a more holistic view. There are three categories of The Deming Prize: the *Deming Prize for Individuals* and the *Quality Control Award for Factories* are restricted to Japanese applicants only; the *Deming Application Prize*, on the other hand, has been open to non-Japanese organizations since 1984, and is an annual award presented to:

> *companies or divisions of companies that have achieved distinctive performance improvement through the application of company-wide quality control using statistical methods. (JUSE, 1992)*

A total quality (TQ) based framework has been established for the award process that enables an organization's relative achievement of CWQC to be assessed against a series of ten equally weighted criteria. The criteria are not formally structured into a model framework, unlike other national quality awards.

The major significance of the Deming Application Prize is that it launched the practice of self-assessment and uses processes that are found in the more recent Malcolm Baldrige National Quality Award (MBNQA) and the European Quality Award (EQA).

The assessment process is both rigorous and exhaustive, and some applicants have sought guidance from JUSE counsellors, although this is by no means a prerequisite of winning the Prize. Florida Power and Light, which in 1989 became the first non-Japanese company to receive the Deming Prize, was counselled for four years before applying. Winning the Deming Prize does seem to have clear benefits. Previous recipients have demonstrated strong financial performances, with earning rates, productivity, growth rates, liquidity and net worth well above their industry sector averages. This has ensured a constant stream of applicants, and although non-Japanese companies have been eligible to apply for the Prize since 1984, preference is given to Japanese companies if the number of applicants in any one year is more than the Deming Prize Committee can examine. In 1992, Philips Taiwan became the second non-Japanese company to be awarded the Deming Prize, followed by ATandT in 1994.

Despite the high profile of the Deming Prize, there has been enormous ignorance in the West surrounding how judgements are made and what weightings have been given to the different categories. It is not generally known how assessors are trained. This has made it extremely difficult to transfer the framework and assessment processes to an internal self-assessment system.

The Malcolm Baldrige National Quality Award

The United States Government launched the Baldrige Award in 1987 to encourage US companies to adopt TQM to gain competitive advantage. The National Institute of Standards and Technology (NIST) administers the Award, and the American Society for Quality (ASQ) assists in the assessment process.

In an attempt to define quality performance, NIST developed a set of core principles for quality management: leadership, customer-driven quality, continuous improvement and learning, employee satisfaction, design quality and prevention, planning, corporate responsibility and citizenship, and results. The hundreds of companies that apply for this highly prestigious Award are assessed according to a comprehensive excellence framework, and Figure 3.1 is based on these core principles. The Award framework is probably the most widely used self-assessment framework in existence. To date, well over one million copies of the Award criteria have been distributed to organizations for self-assessment. The use of the Internet has led to even greater dissemination of the Baldrige criteria.

The assessment process developed as part of the award procedure has become the generic process of most self-assessment systems. The actual framework has also seen considerable development since its launch, and a significant change was made in 1995 with the introduction of a 'business results' category. This stronger emphasis on business results has resulted in an even more powerful framework for assessing business excellence, and has ensured the transformation of the Baldrige Model from a TQ framework to a performance excellence framework.

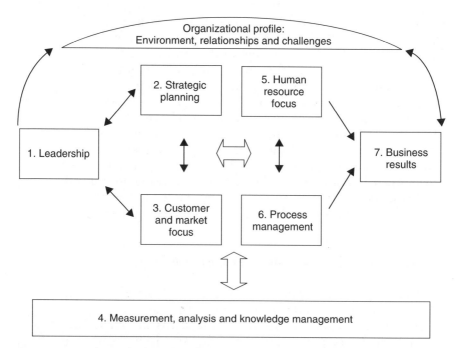

Figure 3.1 The Malcolm Baldrige Performance Excellence criteria

Winners include many role-model companies, such as 3M, Motorola, Milliken, AT&T, Texas Instruments, etc. More recently, the award process has been opened up to the public sector. A full listing of the winners is given in Chapter 4. The majority of winners and applicants can demonstrate significantly superior performance over a period of many years. The Baldrige Award has arguably made one of the greatest contributions to the practice of self-assessment in organizations in recent years through the development of a holistic performance excellence framework and a well-defined assessment process.

The EFQM Excellence Model®

In September 1988, the presidents of fourteen leading western European companies signed a letter of intent to establish the European Foundation for Quality Management (EFQM). The foundation was officially established in October 1989, with the goal of promoting business excellence and TQM in Europe and assisting its members in their TQM efforts. Recognition was seen as one of the main ways of promoting business excellence. In October 1991 the EFQM, with the support of the European Union and the European Organization for Quality (EOQ), launched the European Quality Award (EQA), based on the framework of the EFQM's European Model for Total Quality Management. The EQA Model was the first TQ-based self-assessment framework to place an emphasis on business results. Over the last decade the model has seen ongoing development, with a shift in emphasis from a TQM model to an excellence model

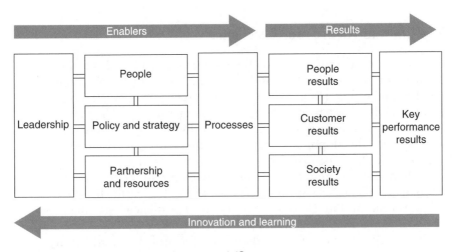

Figure 3.2 The EFQM Excellence Model®

(see Figure 3.2), although many of the TQ core values have been retained or enhanced. The EFQM Excellence Model® recognizes that there are many routes to achieving excellence, and that an excellent balanced scorecard of results is achieved by strong leadership driving policy and strategy through people, partnerships, and resources and processes.

The award process is very similar to the Baldrige process. Past 'large business' winners of the award include Rank Xerox (1992), Milliken European Division (1993) and Design to Distribution (1994), Texas Instruments Europe (1995), BRISA (1996), SGS-Thomson Microelectronics (1997), TNT United Kingdom Ltd (1998), Yellow Pages (1999), Nokia Mobile Phones, Africa and Europe (2000). A full listing of the award winners is given in Chapter 5.

The categories have changed over the years. In 1997 an SME category was introduced, and this was further split into independent and subsidiary SMEs in 1998. In 1998 a public sector category was introduced, and in 1999 a category for operational units. The year 2000 saw the first public sector award winner, the Inland Revenue Accounts Office Cumbernauld.

The launch of the award has generated a considerable interest in self-assessment in Europe. Many national awards (such as the UK Quality Award, administered by the British Quality Foundation) have subsequently been launched, and these have accelerated the use of self-assessment. In particular, the EFQM Excellence Model®, with its strong performance emphasis, has made a significant contribution to integrating excellence approaches and TQM into the mainstream business activities of many organizations.

The Canada Awards for Excellence

The Canada Awards for Excellence were introduced by the Ministry of Industry in 1984, and are administered by the National Quality Institute (NQI). The awards recognize outstanding achievement across major functions of an organization. The award framework was revised in 1989 to reflect the Baldrige Model, and subsequent developments have resulted in the Canadian Framework for Business Excellence, which is used by many Canadian-based organizations as a framework for promoting organizational excellence as well as being used by the NQI as the basis for adjudication of the Canada Awards for Excellence and many regional recognition programmes.

The NQI is an independent not-for-profit organization whose vision is 'to inspire organizational excellence' and whose

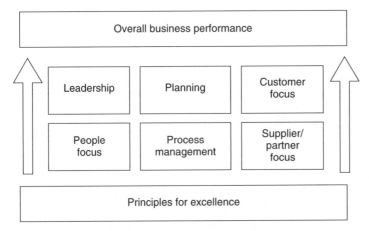

Figure 3.3 The Canadian Framework for Business Excellence

mission is:

> to assist organizations in Canada achieve excellence through a
> strategic approach and application of quality principles, practices
> and certification as embodied in the NQI criteria, and to
> recognize outstanding achievement through the Canada Awards
> for Excellence.

The Canadian Framework for Business Excellence (see Figure 3.3)
has many similarities to both the Baldrige and European Models.
The eight-section model includes Principles for excellence,
Leadership, Planning, Customer focus, People focus, Process
management, Supplier/partner focus, and Business performance.
The sections are further divided into subsections in a similar
structure to the Baldrige and European Models. The Canadian
Framework is supported by a ten-step 'Road Map to Excellence',
which outlines how the framework can be used to drive the quest
for excellence.

The Canada Awards for Excellence are Canada's premier
awards for recognizing outstanding achievement. The Canadian
Quality Award is presented to companies that meet or exceed the
intent of the Canadian Framework for Business Excellence.
Certificates of Merit are awarded to organizations that are clearly
on the road to excellence and are potential future award winners,
but need more time to achieve the desired outcomes.

The Australian Business Excellence Awards

The Australian Business Excellence Awards have been a vehicle
for recognizing outstanding Australian organizations since 1988.

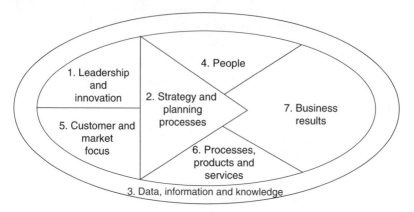

Figure 3.4 The Australian Business Excellence Framework

The Australian Quality Council (AQC) originally ran the awards, but in February 2002 Standards Australia International acquired a range of products and services previously owned by the AQC, including the rights to the Australian Business Excellence Awards. Business Excellence Australia, a division of Standards Australia International Limited, now runs the awards and also offers a range of excellence products.

Applicants go through a peer evaluation, and their performance is assessed against the categories and items in the Australian Business Excellence Framework (see Figure 3.4).

Seven organizational categories make up the Model:

1. Leadership and innovation
2. Strategy and planning processes
3. Data, information and knowledge
4. People
5. Customer and market focus
6. Processes, products and services
7. Business results.

Each category is made up of a number of sub-categories called 'Items', in a similar way to the Baldrige Model. Assessment is based on four dimensions:

1. Approach – this identifies the organization's vision of excellence and intent for the item
2. Deployment – this identifies the activities actually happening
3. Results – this demonstrates how measures are monitored
4. Improvement – this shows how the organization improves the approach and deployment.

The awards are open to all organizations operating in Australia, and there are two recognition categories:

1. Recognition at Award Level, where there are five levels of recognition
   - Excellence Medal
   - Gold Award
   - Silver Award
   - Bronze Award
   - Finalist Medal

2. Recognition at Category Level
   - Leadership Award
   - Strategy and Planning Award
   - Knowledge and Information Award
   - People Award
   - Customer and Market Focus Award
   - Innovation, Quality and Improvement Award
   - Success and Sustainability Award.

The Singapore Award

The Singapore Quality Award (SQA) was launched in 1994, and is awarded to organizations that demonstrate the highest standards of business excellence. The business excellence model underpinning the SQA, the Singapore Quality Award Framework, is based on the best practice embodied in the Baldrige Model, the EFQM Excellence Model®, and the Australian Business Excellence Framework. The aim of the award programme is to encourage organizations to strengthen their management systems, and enhance their capability and competitiveness.

The SQA is administered by the Standards, Productivity and Innovation Board (SPRING Singapore). SPRING is a member of the Guardians of Premier Excellence Model (GEMS). Other network members include the administrators of the Baldrige, European and Australian Awards. SPRING's membership of GEMS ensures that the SQA framework continues to reflect best practice.

SQA applicants are assessed using a framework of nine criteria, with Driver, System and Results elements (see Figure 3.5).

Previous winners of the SQA include a mix of private and public sector organizations: Texas Instruments Singapore Pte Ltd (1995), Asia Pacific Paging Subscriber Division (1996), Baxter Healthcare Pte Ltd (1997), Housing and Development Board (1997), Philips Electronics Singapore Pte Ltd, Turner Factory (1998), PSA Corporation Ltd (1999), STMicrolectronics (1999), Citibank N.A. Regional Cash Process Management Unit (2000),

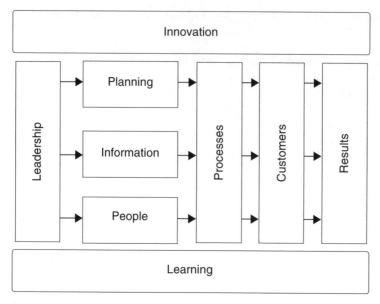

Figure 3.5 Singapore Quality Award Framework

Philips Electronics Singapore Pte Ltd, DAP Factory (2000), Sony Display Device (Singapore) (2001), The Ritz-Carlton Millenia Singapore (2001), Singapore Police Force (2002), and Singapore Technologies Engineering Ltd (2002).

SPRING has implemented the SQA Business Excellence Programme to assist organizations in their journey to world-class business excellence. Under this programme, organizations first undertake an assessment using a questionnaire based on the Singapore Quality Award Framework. Organizations scoring 400 points or more are site-visited to validate the score. Organizations with a validated score of 400 points or more are invited to join the Singapore Quality Class. Over time, with continuous and trans-formational improvement programmes, members of the Singapore Quality Class progress to become world-class organizations. They are then invited to apply for the SQA. The best of the best organ-izations are conferred with the Singapore Quality Award for their attainment of world-class standards of business excellence.

3.3 Comparison of the frameworks

The award frameworks share a similar purpose, similar core values and concepts, and similar criteria. A summary is presented in Table 3.1.

Table 3.1: Summary comparison of the major award programmes

Award	Purpose	Core values and concepts	Criteria
Deming Prize	To recognize those companies that have successfully applied company-wide quality control based on statistical control, and are likely to keep it up in the future	• Top management leadership; • Process control; • Kaizen improvement; • Future planning	1. Policies; 2. Organization; 3. Information; 4. Standardization; 5. Human resources; 6. Quality assurance; 7. Maintenance; 8. Improvement; 9. Effects; 10. Future plans
Malcolm Baldrige National Quality Award	1. To help improve organizational performance practices, capabilities and results; 2. To facilitate communication and sharing of best practices information among US organizations of all types; 3. To serve as a working tool for understanding and managing performance, and for guiding organizational planning and opportunities for learning	• Visionary leadership; • Customer-driven excellence; • Organizational and personal learning; • Valuing employees and partners; • Agility; • Focus on the future; • Managing for innovation; • Management by fact; • Social responsibility; • Focus on results and creating value; • Systems perspective	1. Leadership; 2. Strategic planning; 3. Customer and market focus; 4. Measurement, analysis and knowledge management; 5. Human resource focus; 6. Process management; 7. Business results
European Quality Award	1. To recognize European or global role models in their approaches and the results they achieve;	• Results orientation; • Customer focus; • Leadership and constancy of purpose; • Management by	1. Leadership; 2. Policy and strategy; 3. People; 4. Partnerships and resources; 5. Processes;

(continued)

Table 3.1: *Continued*

Award	Purpose	Core values and concepts	Criteria
	2. To provide independent feedback to organizations to help them on their continuing journey to excellence	processes and facts; • People development and involvement; • Continuous learning, innovation and improvement; • Partnership development; • Public responsibility	6. Customer results; 7. People results; 8. Society results; 9. Key performance results
Canada Awards for Excellence	1. To assist organizations in Canada in achieving excellence through a strategic approach and application of quality principles, practices and certification to the Canadian Excellence Framework; 2. To recognize outstanding achievement through the Canada Awards for Excellence	• Leadership through involvement; • Primary focus on stakeholders/ customers and the marketplace; • Cooperation and teamwork; • Prevention-based process management; • Factual approach to decision-making; • Continuous learning and people involvement; • Focus on continuous improvement and breakthrough thinking; • Fulfil obligations to all stakeholders and society	1. Leadership; 2. Planning; 3. Customer focus; 4. People focus; 5. Process management; 6. Partnership; 7. Business performance
Australian Business	To promote, nurture, recognize	• Customers define quality;	1. Leadership and innovation;

Table 3.1: *Continued*

Award	Purpose	Core values and concepts	Criteria
Excellence Awards	and celebrate organizational excellence in all its forms	• Understand process variability; • Process improvement; • Fact-based decision making; • Improvement should be planned; • System thinking – people work in a system; • People are the most important resource; • Leadership, direction and support are essential; • Continuous improvement requires continual learning	2. Strategy and planning processes; 3. Data, information and knowledge; 4. People; 5. Customer and market focus; 6. Processes, products and services; 7. Organizational results
Singapore Quality Award	To: 1. Promote understanding of the requirements for business and organizational excellence; 2. Enhance organizational performance practices and capabilities; 3. Promote sharing of best practice information amongst organizations	• Visionary leadership; • Customer-driven quality; • Innovation focus; • Organizational and personal learning; • Valuing people and partners; • Agility; • Knowledge-driven system; • Societal responsibility; • Results orientation; • Systems perspective	1. Leadership; 2. Planning; 3. Information; 4. People; 5. Process; 6. Customers; 7. Results

All the award programmes emphasize fact-driven continuous improvement and learning through a focus on customer-driven quality, leadership, strategic alignment, people and partners, effective and efficient processes, and a balanced scorecard of results.

The programmes share a similar assessment process in which assessors, who are trained in the assessment process and the excellence award models and criteria, subject applicants' submissions to an objective evaluation. The assessment process shares some basic common features:

- Assessors or examiners carry out an initial individual assessment
- The assessors or examiners meet or are in dialogue to form a consensus view and score
- High-scoring applicants are site-visited to verify and clarify their applications
- Awards are given to organizations that demonstrate excellence in both their approaches and their results when referenced against the respective excellence frameworks.

All the award criteria are periodically updated so that they continue to reflect best practice.

Further analysis of the award criteria highlight seven common themes of excellence that run through each award framework. Table 3.2 presents a summary of how each award criterion addresses the common themes of leadership, strategy and planning, customer focus, people focus, suppliers and partnerships, process management, and a balanced scorecard of results. All the awards encourage continuous improvement and learning.

3.4 The ISO9000:2000

An introductory discussion of the main quality frameworks would be incomplete without considering the ISO9000:2000 Quality Management System. The ISO9000 quality system is one of the most widely used quality frameworks. We are not claiming that ISO9000 is TQM, or that the ISO system is a fully comprehensive business excellence framework; however, ISO9000 is a useful first step on the journey to excellence.

The ISO9000 standard was introduced in 1987, was subsequently revised in 1994, and underwent a major revision in 2000. This latter review resulted in a much greater emphasis on processes, customers and continuous improvement, with two frameworks being presented within the ISO9000 series, the second of which (ISO9004) could be considered a TQM framework. The auditing and management review processes described in the

Table 3.2: The common excellence themes

	Deming Prize	Baldrige Award	European Quality Award	Canadian Awards for Excellence	Australian Business Excellence Awards	Singapore Quality Award
Leadership	Policy and organization for leadership; supporting supervision	Guiding the organization, governance and organizational performance	Setting direction and values and creating an environment for excellence	Establishing unity of purpose and direction. Enabling change for improvement	Executive, company and community leadership	Senior executive leadership, organizational culture, community and environment responsibility
Strategy and planning	Future plans, quality control focus and initiatives	Action plans – strategy into action plans, key performance measures and projecting future performance	Implementing the vision and mission via a clear stakeholder-focused strategy	Linking planning to strategic direction. Implementing and measuring performance to assess progress	Policy, value integration and the strategic process	Strategy development and deployment

(continued)

Table 3.2: *Continued*

	Deming Prize	*Baldrige Award*	*European Quality Award*	*Canadian Awards for Excellence*	*Australian Business Excellence Awards*	*Singapore Quality Award*
Customer focus	Service activities and customer relationships	Market requirements, customer relationships and satisfaction	Leaders' involvement with customers, customer relationship management, customer satisfaction measurement and feedback	Focus on the customer and marketplace and on the achievement of customer satisfaction and loyalty	Customer needs awareness, customer relationship management and satisfaction measurement	Establishing customer requirements, managing the relationship and measuring satisfaction
People focus	Training and motivation of skilled labour	Human resource focus and emphasis on approaches to promote high performance	Releasing the full potential of people through trust and empowerment	Encouraging and enabling people to contribute to the organization's goals whilst realizing their full potential	Developing potential through effective people management, involvement, training and communication	People approach emphasizes planning and enabling people performance through development, involvement, care and recognition

Suppliers and partnerships	Vendor training and associations of related companies	Improvement of partnering process and evaluation of supplier performance	Beneficial partnerships built on trust, sharing of knowledge and integration	Building key external relationships that are critical to the organization's strategic objectives	Building 'quality' relationships	Effective supplier and partnering process
Process management	Standardization, quality assurance, maintenance and improvement	Value creation and support processes – design, control and improvement	Process design, management and improvement. Generating value for customers and other stakeholders	Process management to support the organization's strategic direction with an emphasis on prevention and continuous improvement	Quality of product design and services, supplier relationships and improvement	Focus on the innovation process and process management and improvement

(continued)

Table 3.2: Continued

	Deming Prize	Baldrige Award	European Quality Award	Canadian Awards for Excellence	Australian Business Excellence Awards	Singapore Quality Award
Balanced scorecard of results	Quality, delivery, cost, profit, safety and environmental effects of quality control	Customer, product and service, financial and market, human resource and organizational effectiveness results	Perception and performance indicators for customers, people and society. Key performance outcomes and indicators	Customer, people, process, partnership, societal and owner/ shareholder measures	Organizational performance – customers, shareholders, employees and community	Customer, financial and market, people and operational results

Note: This table is based on an analysis originally presented by Vokurka et al. (2000), in *Quality Progress*

standard contain elements of self-assessment, and many organizations are developing integrated auditing and self-assessment processes. When used correctly, ISO9000 can make a contribution to business improvement; used incorrectly, it can result in a bureaucratic system that constrains the organization.

3.5 Award listings and contact points

The main international and national excellence awards are listed in Table 3.3. This table does not include the industry specific awards – e.g. automotive awards, government awards, awards given by companies, or awards to individuals. The American Society for Quality lists these in its annual Quality Awards Listing in the journal *Quality Progress*.

Table 3.3: International and national awards

Award	Recognition criteria	e-Information	Notes
International			
Deming Application Prize	Awarded to applicant organizations that effectively practise TQM suitable to their management principles, type of industry and business scope	www.deming.org	Open to all types of industries and any organization – public or private, large or small, domestic or overseas. Autonomous divisions may also apply
European Quality Award	Presented to European organizations that can demonstrate organizational excellence when assessed against the EFQM Excellence Model	www.efqm.org	Open to large businesses and business units, operational units of companies, public sector organizations, and SMEs

(continued)

Table 3.3: *Continued*

Award	Recognition criteria	e-Information	Notes
Malcolm Baldrige National Quality Award	Awarded to applicant organizations that can demonstrate performance excellence against the Baldrige criteria. Business, education and healthcare criteria exist	www.quality.nist. gov; www.asq.org	Open to businesses – manufacturing, service and small businesses, plus education and healthcare organizations. US subunits of foreign companies may apply
National			
Australian Business Excellence Awards	Recognized as Australia's premier business awards, the Australian Business Excellence Awards are the showcase for organizations that have achieved business excellence across all the categories in the framework	www.businessex cellenceaustralia. com.au	Three entry levels: General entry level; Award Gold Level (only open to former general entry level winners); Australian Business Excellence Prize (only open to former Award winners)
Austrian Quality Award	Recognizes achievement in excellence	www.afqm.at; www.oevq.at	Based on the EFQM Excellence Model®
Belgium Quality Award	Recognizes achievement in excellence	www.btqm.be; www.vck.be	Based on the EFQM Excellence Model®. Co-sponsored by the Belgium Association for Total Quality Management and Vlaams Centrum voor Kwaliteitszorg

Table 3.3: *Continued*

Award	Recognition criteria	e-Information	Notes
Brazil National Quality Award	Recognizes organizational excellence	www.fpnq.org.br	Seven-category model, very similar to Baldrige
Canada Awards for Excellence	Recognizes Canadian organizations through two awards; Quality Award, and Healthy Workplace Award	www.nqi.ca	Seven-category model (similar to Baldrige but excludes Information and Analysis) includes partnerships as a criterion
Danish Quality Prize	Recognizes achievement in excellence	www.kvalitespris.dk	Based on the EFQM Excellence Model®
Dubai Quality Award	Two Awards; Dubai Quality Award for Private Enterprise, and Appreciation Programme for Small and Medium-sized Organizations	www.dqg.org	Based on the old version of the EFQM Quality Award Model. Open to private enterprises and small and medium-sized organizations
Finnish Quality Award	Recognizes achievement in excellence	www.laatukeskus.fi	Based on the EFQM Excellence Model®
French Quality Award	Recognizes achievements in quality	www.mfq.asso.fr	Not based on EFQM model®
German National Quality Award	Recognizes achievement in business excellence	www.dgq.de; www.deutsche-efqm.de	Based on the EFQM Excellence Model®

(continued)

Table 3.3: *Continued*

Award	Recognition criteria	e-Information	Notes
Hellenic National Quality Award	Award being developed	www.eede.gr	Based on the EFQM Excellence Model®
Hungarian Quality Development Centre Award	Recognizes achievement in business excellence	www.eoq.org; details from the European Organization for Quality	Based on the EFQM Excellence Model®
Irish Business Excellence Award	Recognizes achievement in business excellence	www.excellence-ireland.ie	Based on a nine-element model similar to Baldrige
Italian Quality Award	Recognizes achievement in business excellence	www.aicq.it	Based on the EFQM Excellence Model®
Korea National Quality Management Award	Awarded to the company scoring highest against a five-criterion framework	www.ksa.or.kr	Baldrige based framework. Award administered by the Korea Standards Association
Mexican Quality Award	Awarded to applicant organizations demonstrating commitment to continuous improvement and quality achievements	e-mail: fundamec@data.net.mx	Main criteria – continuous improvement and customer satisfaction. Co-sponsored by the Mexican Quality Foundation and the Ministry of Industry and Trade

Table 3.3: *Continued*

Award	Recognition criteria	e-Information	Notes
Netherlands National Quality Award	Recognizes achievement in business excellence	www.nederland se-kwaliteit.nl	Based on the EFQM Excellence Model® with some small modifications
Norwegian Excellence Award	Recognizes achievement in business excellence	www.exno.no	Based on the EFQM Excellence Model®
New Zealand Business Excellence Award	Recognizes business excellence achievement according to a 'ladder' – recommendation of progress, commendation (bronze), achievement (silver) and world-class (gold)	www.nzquality. org.nz	Assessment framework distillation of Baldrige and EFQM Excellence Model®
Northern Ireland Quality Awards	Recognizes achievement in organizational excellence	www.cforc.org	Fully aligned with the EFQM Excellence Model®
Scottish Awards for Business Excellence	Recognizes achievement in organizational excellence	www.qualityscot land.co.uk	Fully aligned with the EFQM Excellence Model®. Open to four categories – company, service, public sector, SMEs
Singapore Quality Awards for Business Excellence	Recognizes achievement in organizational excellence	www.spring. gov.sg	Based on best practice from Baldrige, EFQM and Australian Models

(*continued*)

Table 3.3: *Continued*

Award	Recognition criteria	e-Information	Notes
South African Performance Excellence Award	Recognizes organizations with sound leadership, continuous improvement in the delivery of products and services, and provision for satisfying and responding to customers	www.saef.co.za	Open to companies, small and medium-sized enterprises and public organizations in South Africa
Spain – Prince Felipe Industrial Quality Award	Recognizes quality achievement in industrial companies	www.aec.es	Based on the EFQM Excellence Model®
Swiss Quality Award	Recognizes achievement in excellence	www.saq.ch	Based on the EFQM Excellence Model®
UK Business Excellence Award	Recognizes exceptional organizations that demonstrate a high level of commitment to the fundamental concepts of business excellence	www.quality-foundation.co.uk	Fully aligned with the EFQM Excellence Model®. Open to six categories – large businesses and business units, medium-sized businesses, operational units of companies, large public sector organizations, small and medium-sized public sector organizations, small businesses

Table 3.3: *Continued*

Award	Recognition criteria	e-Information	Notes
Vietnam Quality Award	Awarded to Vietnamese manufacturing and service organizations that produce high quality products and services	www.moste. gov.vn	Criteria very close to Baldrige core values
Wales Quality Award	Recognizes achievement in organizational excellence	www.walesquali tycentre.org.uk	Fully aligned with the EFQM Excellence Model®. Open to manufacturing and the service sector, SMEs, education and healthcare providers

3.6 Summary

In this chapter we have introduced the major award programmes and excellence frameworks, and the ISO9000 Quality Management System. The various models of excellence are built on broadly similar core values, and differ mainly in the lower-level detail rather than in the higher-level construct. The award processes also share many common features, and the award self-assessment processes have stimulated the practice of self-assessment in both private and public sectors. Frameworks such as the Baldrige Model and the EFQM Excellence Model® have had a profound effect on the development of the ISO9000 standard and quality management in general. In the following chapters, we will explore these awards and excellence frameworks in greater detail.

The Malcolm Baldrige National Quality Award

4.1 Introduction

The Malcolm Baldrige National Quality Award framework is probably the best-known excellence award model, and the world's most widely used excellence framework for self-assessment. It is named in remembrance of Malcolm Baldrige, who served as the US Secretary of Commerce from 1981 until his untimely death in a rodeo accident in 1987. Baldrige was a champion of quality management as a key enabler of US prosperity and longer-term economic strength. The annual award was originally used to recognize US private sector companies for business excellence and quality achievement. In 1999, education and healthcare categories were introduced.

The Baldrige Award criteria have played a major role in promoting excellence in the USA and around the world. Many of the other national and international quality awards can trace their parentage to the Baldrige Award. The criteria are designed to help organizations improve their competitiveness by focusing on two goals: continually delivering improved value to customers, and improving overall organizational performance. In this chapter we will examine the Baldrige framework, the award process, and its role in self-assessment.

4.2 Background to the Baldrige Award

The Malcolm Baldrige National Quality Award was created by Public Law, and was signed by President Reagan on 20 August

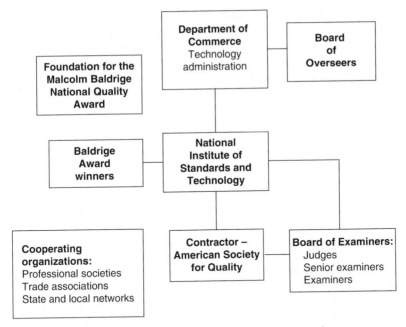

Figure 4.1 The Malcolm Baldrige Award organization chart

1987. The Baldrige National Quality Program led to the creation of a new partnership between the government and the private sector, aimed at promoting quality and performance excellence. Private sector support for the Program comes in the form of funds, volunteer efforts, and knowledge transfer.

The Malcom Baldrige Award organization is shown in Figure 4.1. The Foundation for the Malcolm Baldrige National Quality Award was created to foster the success of the Award Program. The Foundation's prime objective is to raise funds to endow the Award Program permanently. Prominent leaders from US organizations serve as the Foundation's trustees.

The National Institute of Standards and Technology (NIST), an agency of the US Department of Commerce – Technology Administration, is responsible for developing and administrating the award, with the cooperation and support of the private sector. Actual administration of the award process is subcontracted to the American Society for Quality (ASQ). The Board of Overseers advises the Department of Commerce on the Baldrige National Quality Program. The Board is appointed by the Secretary of Commerce, and consists of distinguished leaders from all sectors of the US economy.

The Board of Examiners evaluates the award applications and prepares feedback reports. The Panel of Judges, part of the Board of Examiners, makes award recommendations to the Director of

NIST. The Board consists of leading business, education and healthcare experts. NIST selects members through a competitive application process. The Board has approximately 400 members, including nine judges (who are appointed by the Secretary of Commerce) and 70 senior examiners.

The purpose of the award is twofold:

1. To promote the awareness of performance excellence as an increasingly important element in competitiveness
2. To promote information sharing of successful performance strategies and the benefits derived from using these strategies.

The award is given to manufacturing businesses, service businesses, small businesses, education organizations and healthcare organizations. Any for-profit organization with headquarters in the USA or its territories may apply for the award, including US subsidiaries of foreign companies. To participate in the award process, an organization must submit an application that addresses all the elements of the Baldrige criteria. The awards are traditionally handed out by the President of the United States of America at a gala presentation in Washington, DC. award recipients may publicize and advertise their awards, and are expected to share information about their successful approaches and results with other organizations.

Up to three awards may be given in each category each year; if the standards of the applications are not high enough, no awards are given. The list of companies that have received awards contains many household names – or companies that have become household names since they won the award. These include AT&T, Boeing, Motorola, IBM, Eastman Chemical Company, and Xerox. A full list of award winners is given in Appendix 4.1 to this chapter.

The trend in applications since the award was launched in 1987 is shown in Figure 4.2. The number of applications grew from 66 in 1988 to a peak of 106 in 1991. The period 1991 to 1997 saw a steady reduction in applications, perhaps reflecting the fact that only the top percentile of American companies can compete in the process as only a small percentage have been on the excellence journey long enough ago to reap the benefits today. The downward trend may also be due to the increasing number of state awards, and the fact that many companies are investing their time and effort in other quality initiatives such as becoming ISO 9000:2000 certified. The downward trend has been reversed in recent years, and the smaller number of applications does not reflect the interest in the award framework expressed by US business and public sector organizations. Interest in the Baldrige Award continues to grow both nationally and internationally. For example, participation in local and state Baldrige-based awards

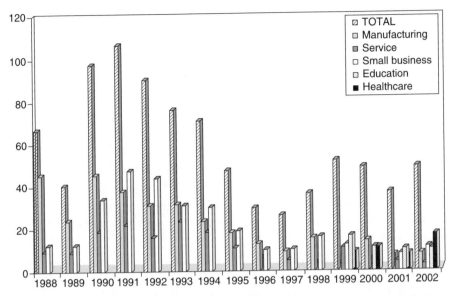

Figure 4.2 Baldrige Award applications 1988–2002 (Source: American Society for Quality)

has increased significantly over the last decade, and the number of states with Baldrige-based awards has increased from 10 to 43 over the period. Internationally, approximately 60 quality awards have been established; most of these can trace their parentage to the Baldrige Award.

Although the number of applications remains relatively low for such a large potential market, the number of sets of guidelines issued since the launch of the Baldrige Program in 1988 is in excess of two million, demonstrating how popular the adoption of the framework is. Further heavy reproduction and electronic access multiply this number many times, giving an indication of the number of companies that are now using the Baldrige framework for self-assessment purposes.

4.3 The Baldrige Award criteria purpose and goals

The Malcolm Baldrige National Quality Award criteria are the basis for making the awards and for giving feedback to applicants. The criteria have been modified over the years since their inception, and section 4.7 below includes a discussion of how they have changed over the years. The comments contained in this chapter are based on the award criteria booklets for business, education and healthcare, which are available from the American Society for Quality. Electronic copies of the award criteria are freely available via the NIST website at http://www.quality.nist.gov

Three important roles aimed at strengthening US competitiveness are stressed in the business criteria. These are:

1. To help improve organizational performance practices, capabilities and results
2. To facilitate communication and sharing of best-practices information among and within US organizations of all types
3. To serve as a working tool for understanding and managing performance, and for planning and opportunities for learning.

The award criteria are designed to help organizations utilize an integrated approach to organizational performance management that results in:

- Delivery of ever-improving value to customers, contributing to marketplace success
- Improvement of overall organizational operational effectiveness and capabilities
- Organizational and personal learning.

4.4 The criteria's core values and concepts

The Baldrige criteria are published in three variants:

1. Criteria for performance excellence – applicable to manufacturing, service and small businesses
2. Education criteria for performance excellence – applicable to education organizations
3. Healthcare criteria for performance excellence – applicable to healthcare organizations.

The award criteria are built upon a set of eleven core values and concepts that are the foundation for integrating the overall customer and organizational operational performance requirements. These core values and concepts are broadly the same across the three variants, and are outlined below. The main differences for the Education and Healthcare criteria are discussed in full in Appendices 4.2 and 4.3.

Visionary leadership

This has four dimensions:

1. *Setting direction.* An organization's senior leaders should set direction, create a customer focus, and establish clear and

visible values and high expectations. All this should be done in a way that balances the needs of all stakeholders.

2. *Providing a framework for achieving excellence.* Leaders should ensure the development and deployment of strategies and a system for achieving excellence, stimulating innovation, and building knowledge and capability.

3. *Inspiring and motivating.* Senior leaders should inspire and motivate the entire workforce and should encourage all employees to contribute, to develop and learn, to be innovative, and to be creative.

4. *Serving as role models.* Senior leaders should serve as role models and reinforce the values through their ethical behaviour. They should be personally involved in developing the organization's future leadership capability, reviewing organizational performance, and employee recognition.

Customer-driven excellence

Five dimensions can be identified for the business criteria:

1. *Understanding customer requirements.* The customer ultimately judges the qualities of an organization's products and services. The organization must take into account all product and service features and all customer access channels that add value for customers and result in customer acquisition, improved satisfaction, positive referral, and retention and business expansion.

2. *Customer relationship management.* Value and satisfaction may be influenced by many factors throughout the customer experience cycle – purchase, ownership and service experience. These factors include the organization's relationship with customers, which helps to build trust, confidence and loyalty.

3. *Striving to eliminate customer dissatisfaction.* Reducing defects and errors and eliminating the causes of dissatisfaction and their impact on customer satisfaction are important in achieving customer-driven excellence. Success in how an organization recovers from defects and mistakes is also crucial in retaining customers and building customer relationships.

4. *Differentiation.* Customer-driven organizations address the features and characteristics that differentiate their products and services from competing offerings, as well as addressing their own fundamental product and service characteristics.

5. *Sensitivity to changing customer and market trends.* Customer-driven excellence demands that organizations be sensitive to and anticipate changing and emerging customer and market requirements, and the factors that drive customer satisfaction and retention. Awareness of developments in technology and

competitors' offerings, as well as rapid and flexible response to customer and market requirements, is essential.

Organizational and personal learning

Four themes can be identified:

1. *An integrated approach to learning.* Achieving the highest levels of business performance requires a well-executed approach to organizational and personal learning. Organizational learning includes both continuous improvement of existing approaches and adaptation to change, leading to new goals and/or approaches. Learning needs to be embedded in the way the organization operates. This means that learning is a regular part of daily work; is practised at personal, work unit, and organizational levels; results in solving problems at their source ('root cause'); is focused on sharing knowledge throughout the organization; and is driven by opportunities to effect significant change and to do better. Sources for learning include employees' ideas, research and development (R&D), customers' input, best-practice sharing, and benchmarking. Organizational learning can result in: enhancing value to customers through new and improved products and services; developing new business opportunities; reducing errors, defects, waste, and related costs; improving responsiveness and cycle time performance; increasing productivity and effectiveness in the use of all resources throughout your organization; and enhancing the organization's performance in fulfilling its public responsibilities and service as a good citizen.

2. *Providing increasing learning opportunities.* Employees' success depends increasingly on having opportunities for personal learning and practising new skills. Organizations invest in employees' personal learning through education, training, and other opportunities for continuing growth. Such opportunities might include job rotation and increased pay for demonstrated knowledge and skills. On-the-job training offers a cost-effective way to train and to link training to your organizational needs and priorities.

3. *Technology-enhanced learning.* Education and training programmes may benefit from advanced technologies, such as computer- and internet-based learning and satellite broadcasts.

4. *Organizational performance.* Personal learning can result in: more satisfied and versatile employees who stay with the organization; organizational cross-functional learning; and an improved environment for innovation. Thus learning is directed not only toward better products and services, but also toward

being more responsive, adaptive, and efficient – giving the organization marketplace sustainability and performance advantages.

Valuing employees and partners

Three themes can be identified:

1. *Commitment to employees.* An organization's success depends increasingly on the knowledge, skills, creativity and motivation of its employees and partners. Valuing employees means committing to their satisfaction, development, and wellbeing. Increasingly, this involves more flexible, high-performance work practices tailored to employees with diverse workplace and home life needs.
2. *Motivating employees.* Major challenges in the area of valuing employees include: demonstrating leaders' commitment to employees' success; recognition that goes beyond the regular compensation system; development and progression within the organization; sharing the organization's knowledge so employees can better serve customers and contribute to achieving strategic objectives; and creating an environment that encourages risk-taking and creativity.
3. *Partnership development.* Organizations need to build internal and external partnerships in order better to accomplish overall goals. Internal partnerships might include labour-management cooperation, such as agreements with unions. Partnerships with employees might entail employee development, cross-training, or new work organizations, such as high-performance work teams. Internal partnerships also might involve creating network relationships among work units to improve flexibility, responsiveness and knowledge sharing. External partnerships might be with customers, suppliers and education organizations. Strategic partnerships or alliances are increasingly important kinds of external partnerships. Such partnerships might offer entry into new markets, or a basis for new products or services. Also, partnerships might permit the blending of an organization's core competencies or leadership capabilities with the complementary strengths and capabilities of partners. Successful internal and external partnerships develop longer-term objectives, thereby creating a basis for mutual investments and respect. Partners should address the key requirements for success, means for regular communication, approaches to evaluating progress, and means for adapting to changing conditions. In some cases, joint education and training could offer a cost-effective method for employee development.

Agility

Two themes are considered here:

1. *Responsiveness.* Success in competitive markets demands agility – a capacity for rapid change and flexibility. Businesses face ever-shorter cycles for the introduction of new/improved products and services.
2. *Cycle time.* All aspects of time performance are important, and cycle time is a critical process measure in meeting increasing competitive challenges. Cycle time improvements drive organizational improvements, and improvements in quality, cost and productivity.

Focus on the future

Three themes are evident:

1. *Understanding business drivers.* It is important to understand the short- and long-term factors that influence the business and its market.
2. *Commitment.* Pursuit of market leadership requires a strong future orientation and a willingness to make long-term commitments to all stakeholders.
3. *Planning.* Planning needs to anticipate the many types of changes that will affect customers' future expectations of products and services.

Managing for innovation

The main theme here is innovation, as a driver of improvement to an organization's products, services, and processes, and to create new value for the organization's stakeholders. Innovation should lead the organization to new levels of performance. Innovation is not just restricted to the research and development departments; it is important for all aspects of business and all processes. Organizations should be led and managed so that innovation becomes part of the culture and is integrated into daily work.

Management by fact

Three themes can be identified here:

1. *Strategy.* The measurement system should be derived from the company's strategy, and include all key processes and outputs as a result of the processes.

2. *Data types.* The data required for performance improvement will be of many types and cover many aspects. For example, the data is likely to include measures of customer satisfaction, product and service performance; comparisons of operational, market, and competitive performance; and supplier, employee, cost and financial performance.
3. *Analysis.* The analysis of the data may be performed in many ways – for instance, trends, projections, comparisons etc. Whatever the analysis method, it is important that the analysis leads to information that drives performance improvement.

Social responsibility

Five themes can be identified:

1. *Corporate responsibility.* An organization's leaders should stress its responsibilities to the public and practise good citizenship. Corporate responsibility covers many things, from business ethics to the protection of public health, safety and the environment. The scope of responsibility covers the organization's operations and the life cycle of its products and services.
2. *Conserving resources.* Organizations should emphasize resource conservation and waste reduction at source.
3. *Design impact.* Design has a major impact on production processes and the use and disposal of products. Design strategies should anticipate growing environmental concerns and responsibilities.
4. *More than compliance.* Organizations should treat all statutory and regulatory requirements as opportunities for improvement beyond mere compliance.
5. *Leadership and support.* Good citizenship requires leadership and support, within the limits of an organization's resources, for publicly important causes. Examples might include improving education and healthcare in the community, environmental excellence, resource conservation, community service, improving industry and business practices, and sharing non-proprietary information. Influencing other organizations to work in partnership on these causes is also important.

Focus on results and creating value

The key themes of results focus and balance are stressed:

1. *Results focus.* An organization's performance measurement system needs to focus on results.

2. *Balance.* Results should be balanced in the interests of all the stakeholders: customers, employees, stockholders, suppliers and partners, the public and the community. The business strategy should address all stakeholder requirements to avoid the impact of conflicts between differing stakeholder needs. The use of a balanced composite of leading and lagging indicators is also essential.

Systems perspective

Two themes can be identified:

1. *Systems thinking.* The Baldrige criteria provide a systems perspective for managing the organization to achieve performance excellence. The core values and the seven Baldrige categories form the building blocks and the integrating mechanism for the system. However, successful management of overall performance requires organization-specific synthesis and alignment. Synthesis means looking at the organization as a whole and building upon key business requirements, including strategic objectives and action plans. Alignment means using the key linkages among the requirements given in the Baldrige categories, including the key measures/indicators.
2. *Strategic alignment.* Alignment is depicted in the Baldrige framework in Figure 4.3. Alignment includes the senior leaders' focus on strategic directions and on customers. It means that senior leaders monitor, respond to and manage performance based on business results. Alignment includes using measures/ indicators to link key strategies with key processes and align resources to improve overall performance and satisfy customers. Thus, a systems perspective means managing the whole organization, as well as its components, to achieve success.

4.5 Baldrige Award criteria framework

The business, education and healthcare criteria are all built on the above core values and concepts, and share the same seven-category performance excellence framework:

1. Leadership
2. Strategic planning
3. Customer and market focus (*student, stakeholder and market focus in the education criteria; focus on patients, other customers and markets in the healthcare criteria*)
4. Measurement, analysis and knowledge management

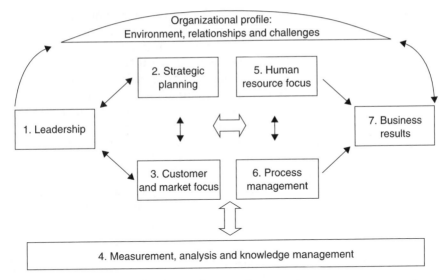

Figure 4.3 2003 Baldrige Award criteria framework – a systems perspective (Source: 2003 Award Criteria Booklet (NIST, 2003))

5. Human resource focus (*faculty and staff focus in the education criteria; staff focus in the healthcare criteria*)
6. Process management
7. Business results (*organizational performance results in the education and healthcare criteria*).

The rationale for using the same framework across business, education and healthcare is that it is adaptable to the requirements of all types of organization. The dynamic relationships of the above criteria are shown in Figure 4.3.

The basic framework elements

The framework has three basic elements:

1. *Organizational profile*. This describes the organization's operating environment, key working relationships, and strategic challenges. These factors should shape the organizational performance management system.
2. *System operation*. The system comprises of the six Baldrige categories at the centre of Figure 4.3, defining the organization, its operations and results. Two triads can be identified:
   - The leadership triad – Leadership, Strategic planning, and Customer and market focus – stresses the importance of a leadership focus on strategy and customers

- The results triad – Human resources focus, Process management and Business results. The organization's employees and key processes accomplish the work of the organization that delivers business results. Business results take a balanced view of customer, financial and operational performance results, including human resource results and public responsibility. The role of leadership in driving business results and the importance of feedback in effective performance management is emphasized by the two-headed horizontal arrow in the centre of Figure 4.3.

3. *Systems foundation*. Measurement, analysis and knowledge management are critical to the successful management of an organization, and serve as the foundation for the performance management system.

Key characteristics of the criteria

There are several important key concepts implicit in the framework. These include:

1. *Focus on organizational results*. Key areas of organizational performance for business, education and healthcare are outlined in Table 4.1. The use of this mix of indicators is intended to ensure that strategies are balanced – that they ensure appropriate treatment of all key stakeholder objectives, and that short-, medium- and longer-term goals are taken into account.
2. *Being non-prescriptive and adaptable*. Although the criteria detail results-orientated requirements, they do not prescribe:
   - How the organization should be structured
   - That different units in the organization should be managed in the same way
   - That the organization should or should not have departments for quality, planning, or other functions.
3. *Systems perspective*. A systems perspective to goal alignment is inherent in the Baldrige framework. Alignment is built around the connecting and reinforcing measures that translate the organization's strategy into the areas of people and process. The measures serve as a communication tool, and provide a basis for deploying consistent overall performance requirements. The systems perspective includes dynamic linkages between the criteria items, and ensures an effective response to changes in strategy and goals. Action-orientated cycles of learning take place via feedback between processes and results. The learning cycles have four stages:
   - Planning, including design of processes, selection of measures, and deployment of requirements

Table 4.1: Baldrige results focus

Business	*Education*	*Healthcare*
Customer-focused results	Student learning results	Patient- and other customer-focused results
Product and service results	Student- and stakeholder-focused results	Healthcare results
Financial and market results	Budgetary, financial and market results	Financial and market results
Human resource results	Faculty and staff results	Staff and work systems results
Organizational effectiveness results, including operational and supplier performance	Organizational effectiveness results, including key operational performance measures	Organizational effectiveness results, including key internal operational results
Governance and social responsibility results	Governance and social responsibility results	Governance and social responsibility results

- Execution of plans
- Assessment of progress – internal and external results
- Revision of plans based upon assessment findings, learning, new inputs, and new requirements.

4. *Goal-based diagnosis.* The criteria and the scoring guidelines provide a two-part assessment or diagnostic system. The criteria describe nineteen performance-orientated requirements. The scoring system evaluates the organization against these performance requirements on a basis of the excellence of the approach, deployment of the approach, and the results achieved – i.e. approach, deployment, results. The assessment provides a profile of strengths and opportunities for improvement relative to the nineteen performance-orientated requirements.

Category structure

Each category within the framework is itself split down into several criteria items or sub-categories (Figure 4.4), and against each

Category

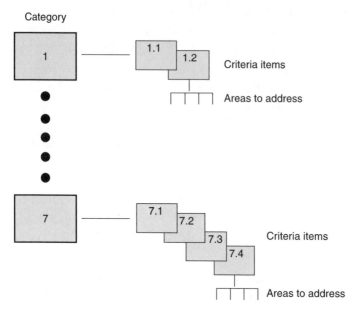

Figure 4.4 Baldrige system for evaluation – criteria item structure

examination item there is a list of areas to address. There are 19 criteria items and 32 areas to address in total. All the criteria language is in question format. Appendix 4.4 shows a complete breakdown for the first element, Leadership, as an example of how the framework is structured.

The main Leadership category 1.0 gives a general description of what is being looked for under the Leadership category.

1.0 The Leadership Category examines how your organization's senior leaders address values, directions and performance expectations, as well as a focus on customers and other stakeholders, empowerment, innovation and learning. Also examined are your organization's governance and how your organization addresses its public and community responsibilities.

Below this headline level there are two items that address specific areas of Leadership. The items ask the organization to describe how they tackle each specific area:

1.1 Organizational Leadership
Describe how senior leaders guide your organization. Describe your organization's governance system. Describe how senior leaders review organizational performance.

1.2 Social Responsibility
Describe how your organization addresses its responsibilities to the public, ensures ethical behaviour and practices good citizenship.

'Areas to Address' list the specific information required in each item – for example, 1.1b Organizational Governance:

How does your organization address the following key factors in your governance system:

- *management accountability for the organization's actions*
- *fiscal accountability*
- *independence in internal and external audits*
- *protection of stockholder and stakeholder interests, as appropriate.*

'Notes' provide supplementary points of clarification.

Table 4.2 lists all the main categories and items for the business, education and healthcare criteria.

The Baldrige Award Guidelines give a full description of all the framework categories. A summary description, emphasizing the main points, is given below.

P Organizational profile

The organizational profile is a brief resumé of the organization, the key influences on its operations, and the key challenges it faces. It plays a key part in providing the context for the category and item descriptions, which follow. The category is split into two parts: organizational description, and organizational challenges.

P.1 Organizational description
The organization must describe its operating environment and key relationships with customers, suppliers and other partners. *Customers equate to students and stakeholders in the education criteria, and patients and other customers in the healthcare criteria.* The organization description includes details of the organizational environment, including a description of:

- The organization's main products/services and how these are delivered to customers. *Educational programmes and services equates to products/services in the education criteria; a description of the main healthcare services and delivery to patients is required in the healthcare criteria.*
- The organizational culture. This may include the vision, mission and values.
- The employee profile, including educational levels, diversity, bargaining units, use of contract employees, and any special

Table 4.2: 2003 Baldrige categories and items

Main categories	Business items	Education item variants	Healthcare item variants
P. Preface: Organizational Profile	P.1 Organizational Description P.2 Organizational Challenges		
1.0 Leadership	1.1 Organizational Leadership 1.2 Social Responsibility		
2.0 Strategic Planning	2.1 Strategy Development 2.2 Strategy Deployment		
3.0 Customer and Market Focus (Education – Student, Stakeholder and Market Focus; Healthcare – Focus on Patients, Other Customers, and Markets)	3.1 Customer and Market Knowledge 3.2 Customer Relationship and Satisfaction	3.1 Student, Stakeholder, and Market Knowledge 3.2 Student and Stakeholder Relationships and Satisfaction	3.1 Patient, Other Customer and Health Care Market Knowledge 3.2 Patient and Other Customer Relationships and Satisfaction
4.0 Measurement, Analysis and Knowledge Management	4.1 Measurement and Analysis of Organizational Performance 4.2 Information and Knowledge Management		

Business/Organizational	Education Focus	Healthcare Focus
5.0 Human Resource Focus (Education – Faculty and Staff Focus; Healthcare – Staff Focus)		
5.1 Work Systems		
5.2 Employee Learning and Motivation	5.2 Faculty and Staff Learning and Motivation	5.2 Staff Learning and Motivation
5.3 Employee Well-being and Satisfaction	5.3 Faculty and Staff Well-being and Satisfaction	5.3 Staff Well-being and Satisfaction
6.0 Process Management		
6.1 Value Creation Processes	6.1 Learning-Centred Processes	6.1 Health Care Processes
6.2 Support Processes	6.2 Support Processes	6.2 Support Processes
7.0 Business Results (Education and Healthcare – Organizational Performance Results)		
7.1 Customer-Focused Results	7.1 Student Learning Results	7.1 Healthcare Results
7.2 Product and Service Results	7.2 Student and Stakeholder-Focused Results	7.2 Patient- and Other Customer-Focused Results
7.3 Financial and Market Results	7.3 Budgetary, Financial, and Market Results	7.3 Financial and Market Results
7.4 Human Resource Results	7.4 Faculty and Staff Results	7.4 Staff and Work System Results
7.5 Organizational Effectiveness Results		
7.6 Governance and Social Responsibility Results		

Source: 2003 Award Criteria Booklet (NIST, 2003)

safety requirements. *Employees are termed faculty and staff in the education criteria, and staff in the healthcare criteria.*

- Major technologies, equipment and facilities.
- The regulatory environment under which the organization operates – occupational health and safety regulations; accreditation requirements; environmental, financial and product regulations.

The other key part of this section is a description of the organizational relationships. This includes a description of:

- Organizational structure and governance systems, reporting relationships between the board of directors, senior leaders and parent organization.
- The key customer groups and/or market segments and the key requirements in these groups and segments. *Key customers equate to key student and stakeholders in the education criteria, and key patient/customer groups in the healthcare criteria.*
- The supply chain requirements – suppliers, dealers, etc. – including the key supplier and customer partnering mechanisms.
- Key customer and supplier partnering arrangements.

P.2 Organizational challenges

The key requirement here is a description of the organization's competitive environment, its key strategic challenges, and the system for performance improvement. Specific details are required of:

- The competitive environment, including competitive position and principal factors that determine the success of the organization relative to competitors.
- Strategic challenges, including operational, human resource, business and global as appropriate. *Education, learning and community challenges are included in the education criteria.*
- The performance improvement system, including how the organization maintains a focus on performance improvement.

1.0 Leadership

The leadership category, assessed on the basis of approach and deployment, examines how the organization's senior leaders address values, direction and performance expectations, as well as focus on customers' and other stakeholders' empowerment, innovation and learning. Also examined is the organization's governance and how the organization addresses its public and community responsibilities. The criteria item details are the same across the business, education and healthcare criteria.

This category is split into two items: organizational leadership, and public responsibility and citizenship.

1.1 Organizational leadership

The organization must describe how senior leaders guide the organization, establish governance systems and review organizational performance. This will include:

- How they set and deploy organizational values, short- and longer-term direction and performance expectations including how they balance value for customers and other stakeholder needs.
- How they communicate values, direction and expectations throughout the organization's leadership system, and to all employees, key suppliers and partners.
- How they ensure two-way communication on these topics.
- How they create an environment for empowerment, innovation, organizational agility, and organizational and employee learning.
- How they create an environment that fosters and requires legal and ethical behaviour.
- How the organization addresses key factors in its governance system, including: management accountability for the organization's actions; fiscal accountability; independence in internal and external audits; protection of stockholder and stakeholder interests.
- How they review overall organizational performance and capability.
- How they translate the findings from these reviews into continuous and breakthrough improvement.
- What key performance measures are regularly reviewed.
- How they evaluate the performance of senior leaders, including the chief executive and the board of directors.

It should be noted that almost every item has a requirement to review and improve the approach taken, as has just been described for item 1.1 in the paragraph above. In the interests of brevity, this requirement will not be repeated in the remaining item descriptions.

1.2 Public responsibility and citizenship

The organization has responsibilities to the public, and should ensure ethical behaviour and practise good citizenship. Responsibilities to the public include the need to:

- Ensure a positive impact on society of the organization's products, services and operations.
- Anticipate the current and future public concerns about the organization's products, services and/or operations.
- Accomplish ethical business practices in all stakeholder transactions and interactions.

- Support key communities – how does the organization, senior leaders and employees actively support and strengthen the organization's key communities?

2.0 Strategic planning

The strategic planning category examines how the organization sets strategic direction, and how it determines key planning requirements. The deployment of planning requirements to all organizational units through the performance management system is also considered. There are two items in this section: strategy development, and strategy deployment.

2.1 Strategy development

Ideally an organization will have short-term (one to three years) and longer-term (three or more years) planning processes for enhancing its competitive position and for overall performance improvement. The ways in which these processes (or what may be one process covering the two timeframes) are deployed throughout the organization is also important. The key areas covered within this item include:

- A description of the main steps in the strategic planning process.
- The key inputs used to develop the strategy and plans. These will typically include: customer and market requirements and the expected evolution of these requirements; projections of the competitive environment; technology and other changes impacting upon the organization's products and services; an assessment of internal capability including human and other resources; an assessment of supplier/partner strengths and weaknesses; risks, such as financial, market, technological and societal risks.
- A statement of the key strategic objectives (goals/targets), and a timetable for accomplishing them.
- How the strategic objectives address the key organizational challenges and achieve balance between all key stakeholder needs.

2.2 Strategy deployment

Item 2.2 focuses on how the strategies are converted into plans. Taking the key business drivers outlined under sub-criteria 2.1, the organization should describe how these drivers are translated into action plans. Key areas within this item include:

- How the organization develops and deploys action plans to achieve strategic objectives. These plans will address resource implications.

- A statement of the short- and longer-term action plans. These will include overall plans, human resource plans, etc.
- Key performance measures/indicators used to track performance against plan. In particular, the performance measurement system must achieve organizational alignment and cover all key deployment areas and stakeholders.
- Performance projection – the organization should show how its performance projects into the future relative to competitors and key benchmarks. This includes actual measures and targets that the organization needs to achieve in order to be successful.

Minor differences are apparent in the education criteria relating to customers, which are defined as students and stakeholders.

3.0 Customer and market focus

The customer and market focus category examines the organization's systems for learning about customer and market requirements, expectations and preferences, and for building and maintaining customer relationships. The key factors that drive marketplace competitiveness need to be clearly understood. Also examined are the organization's methods to determine the factors that lead to customer acquisition, satisfaction, loyalty and retention, and business expansion.

There are two criteria items in this category: customer and market knowledge, and customer relationship and satisfaction.

3.1 Customer and market knowledge

The organization should have a clear understanding as to how it determines the requirements, expectations and preferences of its customers and markets to ensure the continuing relevance of its products and services and to develop new opportunities.

The organization should demonstrate how:

- Customer groups and/or market segments are determined or selected.
- The organization listens and learns to determine key customer requirements.
- Specific product and service features and the relative importance of these features to customer groups or segments are determined.
- Other key information and data, such as complaints, gains and losses of customers and product/service performance, are used to support the determination of customer intentions.

In the education criteria, a broadly similar structure is followed but with the emphasis on determining student and market needs and expectations. In the healthcare criteria, the emphasis is on patient/customer and healthcare market knowledge.

For the long term, the organization should define how it addresses future requirements and expectations of customers or students or patients, outlining how it keeps its listening and learning methods current with the organization's needs and direction.

3.2 Customer relationship and satisfaction

This item is concerned with how the organization builds relationships to acquire, satisfy and retain customers, to increase customer loyalty, and to develop new opportunities and determine customer satisfaction. Key areas include:

- How the organization builds relationships to acquire customers and meet and exceed their expectations, which leads to increased loyalty and repeat business and positive referrals.
- How the organization establishes key access mechanisms for customers to seek information, conduct business and make complaints.
- How the organization deals with complaints. This includes how complaints are resolved effectively and promptly, and how the learning from this activity drives improvement.
- How the organization determines customer satisfaction. Customer satisfaction is a central pillar of performance excellence and total quality management. The organization must therefore understand how it determines customer satisfaction and dissatisfaction, customer repurchase intentions, and customer satisfaction relative to its competitors, and how it uses this information to drive improvement.
- How the organization follows up with customers on products/services and transactions to receive prompt and actionable feedback.
- How the organization obtains and uses information on customer satisfaction relative to customer satisfaction with competitors and/or industry benchmarks.
- How approaches to building customer relationships, providing customer access and determining customer satisfaction are kept current with the organization's needs.

A similar structure is adopted in both the education and health-care criteria.

Customer satisfaction measurement might include both a numerical rating scale and descriptors. An effective (actionable) customer satisfaction measurement system is one that provides the organization with reliable information about customer ratings of specific product and service features, and the relationship between these ratings and the customers' likely future market behaviour. Customer dissatisfaction indicators may also be included here. These include complaints, claims, refunds, recalls, returns, repeat services, litigation, replacements, downgrades, repairs, warranty work, warranty costs, mis-shipments, and incomplete orders.

4.0 Measurement, analysis and knowledge management

The measurement, analysis and knowledge management category examines how the organization selects, gathers, analyses, manages and improves its performance data, information and knowledge assets. The category has two criteria items: measurement and analysis of organizational performance, and information management.

4.1 Measurement and analysis of organizational performance

This item is concerned with how the organization provides effective performance management systems for measuring, analysing, aligning and improving performance at all levels and in all parts of the organization. Areas to address include aspects of performance measurement and analysis. For performance measurement, key areas include how the organization:

- Selects and aligns measures/indicators for tracking daily operations and overall organizational performance.
- Gathers and integrates data and information from all sources to support operations and organizational decision-making.
- Selects and ensures the effective use of key comparative data and information.
- Keeps the performance measurement system current with the business need and direction.

For performance analysis, the key areas to address include:

- Analysis to support the senior leaders' organizational performance review and the strategic planning process.
- How the organization communicates the results of organizational-level analysis throughout the organization to enable effective support for decision-making.

4.2 Information management

This item addresses how the organization ensures the quality and availability of needed data and information for employees, suppliers/partners and customers, and how it builds and maintains its knowledge assets. The areas addressed include data and information availability, and organizational knowledge requirements.

For data and information availability, the areas to address include how the organization:

- Makes needed and appropriate data and information available to employees, suppliers/partners and customers.

- Ensures that hardware and software are reliable, secure and user friendly.
- Keeps data and information availability mechanisms, including hardware and software, current with business needs and direction.

For organizational knowledge, the areas addressed include how the organization:

- Manages organizational knowledge.
- Ensures the integrity, timeliness, reliability, security, accuracy and confidentiality of data, information and organizational knowledge.

There are no major variations on the key themes addressed above in either the education or the healthcare criteria.

5.0 Human resource focus

The human resource focus category examines how the organization's work systems, employee learning and motivation enable employees to develop their full potential in support of the organization's overall objectives and action plans. The organization's efforts to build and maintain an environment for performance excellence conducive to full participation and personal and organizational growth are also examined.

There are a total of three criteria items in this section: Work systems, employee learning and motivation, and employee wellbeing and satisfaction.

5.1 Work systems

This item considers how the organization's work and jobs, compensation, career progression and related workforce practices motivate and enable employees and the organization to achieve high performance. Areas addressed include how the organization:

- Organizes and manages the work and jobs to promote cooperation, initiative and innovation, promotes the organizational culture, and ensures agility in line with current business needs.
- Ensures work systems capitalize on the diverse ideas, cultures and thinking of employees and the communities with which the organization interacts.
- Achieves effective communication and knowledge transfer across work units, jobs and locations.
- Employee performance management system, including feedback to employees, supports high performance and customer and business focus.
- Motivates employees to develop and utilize their full potential – formal and informal mechanisms are included here.

- Ensures that compensation, recognition and related reward and incentive practices reinforce high performance work and customer and business focus.
- Accomplishes effective succession planning for the senior leadership and throughout the organization.
- Identifies the skills and competencies needed by potential and existing employees.
- Recruits, hires and retains new employees and addresses diversity issues.
- Work systems capitalize on the diverse ideas, cultures and thinking of the communities with which it interacts.

5.2 Employee learning and motivation

An important part of human resource management is the way in which all employees are educated, trained and developed. The way that individual development needs are established and how these are aligned with organizational performance goals has to be understood. This item considers how the organization's education and training support the achievement of overall objectives, including building employees' knowledge, skills and capabilities.

The key areas addressed include how the organization:

- Designs and deploys education and training in support of its short- and longer-term organizational objectives and employees' needs.
- Seeks and uses feedback from employees and their supervisors/managers in the development and delivery of education and training.
- Addresses specific organizational needs via its education and training programmes. Examples include changes in technology, management/leadership development, new employee induction, safety and health, diversity etc.
- Delivers education and training programmes – this will include formal and informal mechanisms.
- Evaluates the effectiveness of education and training.
- Reinforces the use of skills and new knowledge on the job.

5.3 Employee wellbeing and satisfaction

An organization should maintain a work environment that is conducive to the wellbeing and growth of all employees. Under these conditions, where levels of employee satisfaction and the opportunities for growth are high, it is more likely that employees will contribute to the success of the business and will be customer focused. This item specifically considers how the organization maintains a work environment and an employee support climate that contributes to the wellbeing, satisfaction and motivation of all employees. The key areas addressed include how the organization:

- Improves workplace health, safety and ergonomics. This includes how employees contribute to improvement.
- Determines the key factors that affect employee wellbeing, satisfaction and motivation.
- Supports employees via services, benefits and policies.
- Assesses employee wellbeing, satisfaction and motivation, both formally and informally.
- Uses other indicators such as employee retention, absenteeism, grievances, safety, and productivity to assess and improve employee wellbeing, satisfaction and motivation.
- Uses the results from assessments to identify priorities for improving the work environment and employee support climate.

The category and item details for the education and healthcare criteria are almost identical to the business criteria, with the proviso that reference is made to faculty and staff in the education criteria, and staff in the healthcare criteria.

6.0 Process management

The process management category examines the key elements of process management, including key product, service and business processes for creating customer and organizational value, and key support processes. The category examines how all work units, including research and development units and suppliers, contribute to the overall quality and operational performance requirements. There are two criteria items in this section: value creation processes, and support processes.

6.1 Value creation processes

This criteria item requires the organization to describe how the organization identifies and manages its key processes for creating customer value and achieving business success and growth. The areas addressed include:

- How the organization determines its key value creation processes, and how they create value and contribute to profitability and business success.
- How the requirements for the key value creation process are determined, incorporating input from customers, suppliers and partners.
- How these processes are designed to meet all the key requirements.
- How new technology and organizational knowledge are incorporated into the design of these processes.

- How effectiveness and efficiency measures are incorporated into the design of these processes.
- Identification of the key performance measures or indicators used for the control or improvement of these processes.
- How overall costs associated with inspection, tests and audits are minimized.
- How defects and rework are prevented and warranty costs minimized.
- How value creation processes are improved to achieve better performance and reduce variability.
- How improvements are shared with other organizational units and processes.

The education and healthcare criteria for process management broadly follow the same pattern, but the wording of each is sufficiently different to merit a full exposition.

6.1 Learning centred processes (education criteria)

This criteria item describes how the organization identifies and manages its key processes for creating student and stakeholder value and maximizing student learning and success. Areas addressed include:

- How the organization determines its key learning centred processes, how these create value, and how they contribute to learning and success.
- How the organization determines key learning centred process requirements, incorporating input from students, faculty staff, stakeholders, suppliers and partners.
- How these processes are designed to meet all the key requirements.
- How new technology and organizational knowledge are incorporated into the design of these processes.
- How effectiveness and efficiency measures are incorporated into the design of these processes.
- Identification of the key performance measures or indicators used for the control or improvement of these processes.
- How the organization incorporates a measurement plan that makes effective use of formative and summative assessment.
- How student learning processes are improved to achieve better performance and reduce variability.
- How improvements are shared with other organizational units.
- How the organization ensures that faculty and staff are properly prepared to implement educational programmes and offerings.

6.1 Healthcare processes (healthcare criteria)

This item addresses how the organization designs and manages its key processes for delivering patient healthcare services. Areas addressed include:

- How the organization determines its key healthcare and service delivery processes, how these create value, and how they contribute to improved healthcare for patients.
- How the organization determines key healthcare process requirements, incorporating input from patients and other customers, suppliers and partners.
- How these processes are designed to meet all the key requirements, including patient requirements, regulatory accreditation, and payor requirements.
- How new technology and organizational knowledge are incorporated into the design of these processes.
- How patients' expectations are managed, addressed, considered and taken into account in shaping the delivery of healthcare processes.
- How day-to-day operation of healthcare processes ensures that process, patient safety, regulatory, accreditation and payor requirements are met.
- How overall costs associated with inspection, tests and audits are minimized.
- How defects and rework are prevented.
- How healthcare processes are improved to achieve better performance and reduce variability.
- How improvements are shared with other organizational units and processes.

6.2 Support processes

This criteria item addresses how the organization manages its key processes that support the value creation processes. Areas addressed include:

- How the organization determines its key support processes.
- How the organization determines key support process requirements, incorporating input from internal and external customers, suppliers and partners.
- How these processes are designed to meet all the key requirements.
- How new technology and organizational knowledge are incorporated into the design of these processes.
- How effectiveness and efficiency measures are incorporated into the design of these processes.
- How processes are implemented to ensure they meet design requirements.

- Identification of the key performance measures or indicators used for the control or improvement of these processes.
- How overall costs associated with inspection, tests and audits are minimized.
- How defects and rework are prevented and warranty costs minimized.
- How support processes are improved to achieve better performance and reduce variability.
- How improvements are shared with other organizational units and processes, as appropriate.

The education criteria for item 6.2 broadly follow the same pattern, but there is an emphasis on incorporating input from faculty, staff, students, stakeholders, suppliers and partners in determining key process requirements.

The healthcare criteria for item 6.2 are very similar to those of the business version of 6.2.

7.0 Business results

Category 7 deals with results. All results items are concerned with trends and current performance of key organizational measures, together with the performance of competitors and relevant benchmarks. The business results category examines the organization's performance and improvement trends in six key business areas: customer-focused results, product and service results, financial and market results, human resource results, organizational effectiveness results, and governance and social responsibility results.

7.1 Customer-focused results

Item 7.1 is concerned with the organization's key customer-focused results, including customer satisfaction and customer perceived value, segmented by customer group or market as appropriate. Areas addressed include current levels and trends in key measures/indicators of:

- Customer satisfaction and dissatisfaction, including comparisons with competitors' levels of customer satisfaction.
- Customer-perceived value, customer retention, positive referral, and/or other aspects of building relationships with customers, as appropriate.

7.2 Product and service results

Item 7.2 is concerned with the organization's key product and service performance results. Areas addressed include current levels and trends in key measures/indicators of product and service performance.

7.3 Financial and market results

Item 7.3 looks at the organization's key financial and marketplace performance results by market segments, as appropriate. Areas addressed include current levels and trends in key measures/indicators of:

- Financial performance, including aggregate measures of financial return and/or economic value, as appropriate.
- Marketplace performance, including market share/position, business growth, and new markets entered, as appropriate.

7.4 Human resource results

This item is concerned with the organization's key human resource results, including employee wellbeing, satisfaction and development, and work system performance. Results are segmented as appropriate to address the diversity of the workforce and the different types and categories of employees, as appropriate. Areas addressed include current levels and trends in key measures/indicators of:

- Work system performance and effectiveness.
- Employee learning and development.
- Employee wellbeing, satisfaction and dissatisfaction, and development.

7.5 Organizational effectiveness results

Item 7.5 is concerned with the organization's key performance results that contribute to the achievement of organizational effectiveness. Areas addressed include current levels and trends in key measures/indicators of:

- The operational performance of key value creation processes, including productivity, cycle time, supplier/partner performance, and other appropriate measures of effectiveness and efficiency.
- The operational performance of key support processes, including productivity, cycle time, supplier/partner performance, and other appropriate measures of effectiveness and efficiency.
- The accomplishment of organizational strategy.

7.6 Governance and social responsibility results

Item 7.6 is concerned with the organization's key governance and social responsibility results, including evidence of fiscal accountability, ethical behaviour, legal compliance and organizational citizenship. Areas addressed include current levels and trends in key measures/indicators of:

- Fiscal accountability – internal and external.
- Ethical behaviour and stakeholder trust in the organization's governance.
- Regulatory and legal compliance.
- Organizational citizenship in support of the organization's key communities.

The results categories in the education and healthcare criteria are significantly different, and merit separate explanations.

Regarding the education criteria, the organizational performance results category examines student learning results; student- and stakeholder-focused results; budgetary, financial, and marketplace performance; faculty and staff results; organizational effectiveness results; and governance and social responsibility results.

7.1 Student learning results (education criteria)
This item is concerned with the organization's key student learning results, segmented by student groups and market segments, as appropriate. Results required include current levels and trends in key measures/indicators of student learning and improvement in student learning, segmented by student groups and market segments, as appropriate, and comparisons to competitors and other appropriate student populations.

7.2 Student- and stakeholder-focused results (education criteria)
This item is concerned with the organization's key student- and stakeholder-focused results, including student and stakeholder satisfaction. Results required include current levels and trends in key measures/indicators of:

- Current and past student and key stakeholder satisfaction and dissatisfaction, including comparisons with competitors' and/or comparable organizations' levels of student and stakeholder satisfaction.
- Student and stakeholder perceived value, persistence, positive referral, and/or other aspects of building relationships with students and stakeholders, as appropriate.

7.3 Budgetary, financial and market results (education criteria)
This item is concerned with the organization's key budgetary, financial, and market performance results by segments, as appropriate. Results required include current levels and trends in key

measures/indicators of:

- Budgetary and financial performance, including measures of cost containment, as appropriate.
- Market performance, including market share and new markets entered, as appropriate.

7.4 Faculty and staff results (education criteria)

This item is concerned with the organization's key faculty- and staff-related results, including faculty and staff wellbeing, satisfaction, and development and work system performance. Results should be segmented to address the diversity of the workforce and the different types and categories of faculty and staff, as appropriate. Results required include current levels and trends in key measures/indicators of:

- Faculty and staff work system performance and effectiveness.
- Faculty and staff learning and development.
- Faculty and staff wellbeing, satisfaction and dissatisfaction.

7.5 Organizational effectiveness results (education criteria)

This item addresses the organization's key performance results that contribute to opportunities for enhanced learning and/or the achievement of organizational effectiveness. Results required include current levels and trends in key measures/indicators of:

- The performance of key learning centred processes, including school capacity to improve student performance, student development, the education climate, indicators of responsiveness to student or stakeholder needs, supplier/partner performance, and other appropriate measures of effectiveness and efficiency.
- The performance of key support processes – productivity, cycle time, supplier and partner performance.
- Accomplishment of organizational strategy.

7.6 Governance and social responsibility results (education criteria)

This follows the same structure as the business guidelines.

Regarding the healthcare results, the organizational performance results category examines the organization's performance and improvement in key areas – healthcare results, patient-/ customer-focused results, financial and marketplace results, staff and work system results, organizational effectiveness results, and governance and social responsibility results. Performance levels relative to those of competitors and other organizations providing similar healthcare services are also examined.

7.1 Healthcare results (healthcare criteria)

This item looks at key healthcare performance results segmented by customer group and market segment as appropriate. An indication should be given of those measures that are mandated by regulatory, accreditor or payor requirements. Results required include current levels and trends in key measures/indicators of:

- Healthcare outcomes.
- Healthcare service delivery results.
- Patient safety.
- Patients' functional status that are important to patients and other customers.

7.2 Patient- and other customer-focused results (healthcare criteria)

This item addresses the organization's key patient- and other customer-focused results, including patient/customer satisfaction and patient/customer perceived value. Results are segmented by customer groups and market segments, as appropriate. Results required include current levels and trends in key measures/indicators of:

- *Patient and other customer satisfaction and dissatisfaction, and satisfaction relative to competitors and other organizations providing similar healthcare services.*
- *Patient/customer perceived value, patient/customer retention, positive referral, and/or other aspects of building relationships with patients/customers, as appropriate.*

7.3 Financial and market results (healthcare criteria)

This is almost identical with the business criteria.

7.4 Staff and work systems results (healthcare criteria)

This is almost identical to human resource results in the business criteria.

7.5 Organizational effectiveness results (healthcare criteria)

This item addresses the organization's key performance results that contribute to the achievement of organizational effectiveness. Results required include current levels and trends in key measures/indicators of:

- The key healthcare processes – productivity, cycle time, supplier and partner performance and other effectiveness and efficiency measures.
- Key support and business processes – productivity, cycle time, supplier and partner performance, and other effectiveness and efficiency measures.
- Accomplishment of organizational strategy and action plans.

7.6 **Governance and social responsibility results (healthcare criteria)**
This follows the same structure as the business guidelines.

4.6 The award process

Organizations that decide to submit an application for the Baldrige Award must check their eligibility before informing the award administrators of their intention to apply for the award by April of the year they wish to submit the application. They then have until May to submit the application together with the application fee.

Although an organization has just over a month from the date it registers its interest in applying for the award to submitting the award, normally it would have been working on the application when the award guidelines were issued in the autumn of the year before the application is submitted. The application itself takes the form of a written report in which the company describes how it addresses the specific areas of the framework. Such a report would normally take over six months to complete and would typically consist of around 70 pages, depending on whether the application was from a large or small organization. The report has two main sections:

- An organizational profile, which should not exceed five single-sided pages
- The response to all the criteria, which should not exceed 50 single-sided pages.

For large or complex organizations, a third main section is included to ensure an effective examination:

- Supplemental information addressing all the criteria areas, which should not exceed 35 pages.

The award process itself starts long before the closing date for the submissions. Experienced quality professionals and senior managers are invited to apply to become examiners for the award process annually. Over 1500 people apply to be examiners, and of these only around 400 are selected to serve. All the examiners have to attend a two-day training course during which they go through a simulation of the award process evaluating a fictitious case study. Even if examiners have served in a previous year, they still have to take part in the training, as the award criteria are changed from year to year. Of the examiners that are trained, between 40 and 50 are appointed as senior examiners to lead the assessment teams. There are also around nine judges, who are appointed to ratify the recommendations of the examination teams and oversee the process.

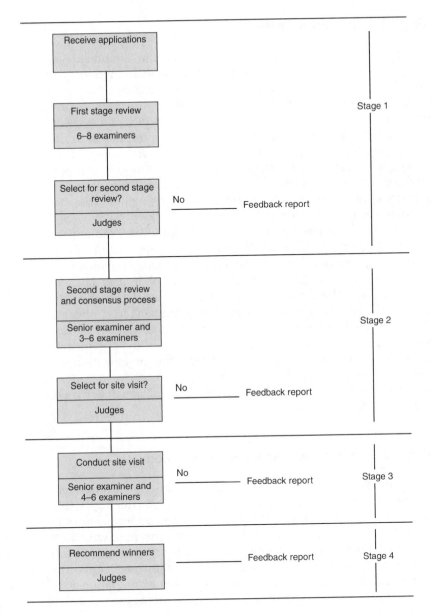

Figure 4.5 The Baldrige Award process

The examination process itself takes around eight months to complete, from receipt of the applications in April to the award ceremony in Washington, DC in December. Figure 4.5 shows the full evaluation process, which is broken down into four stages. Each stage is described below.

Stage 1 – first stage review

On receipt of the applications, the submission documents are assigned to examination teams. Provided the examiners confirm that there is no conflict of interest, the applications are issued to the examiners, who individually score the application. Scoring the application is central to the evaluation process, and is treated in a separate section below. At this point it is important to note that during the scoring process each examiner will create a list of 'Strengths', 'Areas for improvement' and 'Site-visit issues', together with their 'Score' for a particular item. This analysis is performed at the examination item level. For example, there is a separate section for 1.1, 1.2, 2.1 etc.

When all the examiners have individually scored the application, the judges, who select the highest scoring applications for the second stage, review the scores. Applications not going forward to the second stage receive a feedback report that lists both the 'Strengths' and the 'Areas for improvement', together with a summary of the scores. Specific scores are not fed back to applicants.

The feedback report is arguably the most important output from the award process, as it recognizes the efforts of the organization as well as offering advice as to where the organization can improve. Everyone applying for the award receives a feedback report – even the award winners. An example of a feedback report is given in Appendix 4.5.

Stage 2 – consensus and site-visit selection

Applications reaching the second stage first undergo the consensus process. When the examiners individually score the application during the first stage, they are not aware of the scoring of the other members of their team. During the consensus meeting, which can take place by physically meeting each other or by making a conference telephone call, the examiners compare their individual scores and agree on a common score for each examination item. The actual consensus process is considered in greater detail in later chapters. Another output from the consensus meeting is agreement on the 'Strengths', 'Areas for improvement' and 'Site-visit issues'. This information is used when compiling the feedback reports, and the 'Site-visit issues' will be used to plan the site visit.

When all the consensus meetings have taken place, the judges meet to decide which companies will go on to the third stage, a site visit. Analysis of the results from previous years shows that approximately 25 per cent of applicants receive a site visit.

Table 4.3: Purpose of a site visit

Clarification	The consensus meeting will have raised several 'Site-visit issues' that will need clarification during the site visit
Verification	It is important to ensure that the application is a true reflection of the company's system
Resolution	During the site visit, conflicts in the company's system may become apparent that require resolution
Investigation	Some information is difficult to establish from a written submission – areas that spring to mind are deployment, integration into business as usual, and ownership

Stage 3 – site visit

A team of six to eight members of the Board of Examiners, led by a Senior Examiner, conduct the site visit. The purpose of a site visit is not to collect additional information or data that were missing in the original application, and neither is it an ISO9000 quality audit. The purposes are essentially clarification, verification, resolution and investigation. These are described in Table 4.3.

Organizations are additionally expected to provide updates for their results provided in the application. The output from a site visit is a site-visit report. On the basis of this report, the examiners either recommend the company for an award or decline an award. They also prepare a feedback report for the company. There is no set score that must be achieved to receive a recommendation for an award, as this is based solely on the site-visit experience. The scoring of a Baldrige application is used exclusively for determining which companies will receive a site visit.

Stage 4 – confirmation of awards

Using all the information available, for example the consensus and site visit reports, the judges consider the examination team's recommendation and make recommendations to the Director of NIST on whether to confer an award or not. The Director of NIST conveys the recommendations to the Secretary of Commerce, who makes the final determination of award receipts. Although there is no set score to win an award, it is unlikely that an award would be given for an application scoring less than 600 points after consensus. A more likely score is in the region of 700.

The number of awards given varies from year to year. There are a total of fifteen on offer (three per category), but the highest number of awards given in any one year is five – in 1992 and again in 2001. The average number of awards given per year is four.

Scoring an application

Scoring is key to the evaluation process. The scoring system has three design elements:

1. It provides for assigning a numerical score to measure the degree of attainment for each item on the Baldrige criteria
2. It provides a system that generates essentially the same numeric scores when applied by independent examiners
3. It is based on a three-dimensional scoring system.

The three dimensions are approach, deployment and results. These dimensions are expanded in Table 4.4. Not all the dimensions are applicable to each examination item – for example, only 'Approach' and 'Deployment' are applicable to examination item 1.1, 'Senior executive leadership', whereas only 'Results' is considered when scoring examination item 7.2, 'Financial and market results'.

To score an examination item, the examiners list all the 'Strengths' and 'Areas for improvement' against the item, using the examination item details as a reference point. The examiner then turns to the scoring guidelines (Table 4.5) and, taking 50 per cent as the starting point, decides where on the scoring guidelines the application sits.

The examiner also knows from the application guidelines which dimensions of the scoring system should be addressed for the examination item (see Appendix 4.6).

The examiner will score each item based on a 100 per cent score. Each examination item does not attract the same score, and the percentile scores are therefore adjusted at the end so that the final score is based on a maximum total of 1000 points. The weighting of the examination items is shown in Table 4.6. The scoring process is one of the critical processes in self-assessment, and is covered in greater detail in Chapter 9.

4.7 How the Baldrige Award framework has evolved

As with any major initiative, the Baldrige Award has received a substantial amount of both praise and criticism. One benefit of this debate has been the continued refinement of the award's criteria and guidelines by the organizers.

Table 4.4: Baldrige three-dimensional scoring system

Dimension	Definition	Evaluation points
Approach	Refers to the methods the organization uses to achieve the purposes addressed in the examination items	• Appropriateness of the methods to the requirements • Effectiveness of the use of the methods • Degree to which the approach is repeatable, integrated and consistently applied • Degree to which the approach embodies effective evaluation/improvement/learning cycles • Degree to which the approach is based on information that is objective and reliable • Alignment with organizational needs • Evidence of beneficial innovation and change
Deployment	Extent to which approaches are applied to all relevant areas and activities addressed and implied in examination item	• Use of the approach in addressing relevant and important item requirements • Use of the approach by all appropriate work units
Results	Outcomes in achieving the requirements addressed and implied in examination item	• Current performance • Comparison with appropriate comparisons and/or benchmarks • Rate and breadth of performance improvement • Linkage of results to enabling activities – action plans, processes etc.

Table 4.5: Scoring guidelines

Score	Approach/deployment
0%	No systematic approach evident; anecdotal information
10% to 20%	Beginning of a systematic approach to the basic requirements of the item Major gaps exist in deployment that would inhibit progress in achieving the basic requirements of the item Early stages of a transition from reacting to problems to a general improvement orientation
30% to 40%	Effective systematic approach evident, responsive to the basic requirements of the item Approach deployed although some areas are in the early stage of deployment Beginnings of a systematic approach to evaluation and improvement of the basic item processes is evident
50% to 60%	Effective systematic approach, responsive to the overall requirements of the item and key business processes is evident Approach well deployed although extent of deployment may vary A fact-based systematic evaluation and improvement process is in place for improving the efficiency and effectiveness of key processes The approach is aligned with basic organizational needs identified in other criteria
70% to 80%	Effective, systematic approach responsive to the multiple item requirements and changing business needs evident Approach is well deployed, with no significant gaps Fact-based systematic evaluation and improvement process and organizational learning/sharing are key management tools; clear evidence of refinement and improved integration as a result of improvement cycles, learning and analysis The approach is well integrated with organizational needs identified in other criteria
90% to 100%	Effective, systematic approach, fully responsive to all the item requirements and current and changing business needs evident Approach is fully deployed without any significant weaknesses or gaps in any areas or work units

Table 4.5: *Continued*

Score	Approach/deployment
	A very strong, fact-based, systematic evaluation and improvement process and extensive organizational learning/sharing are key management tools; strong refinement and integration, backed by excellent organizational-level analysis, is evident The approach is fully integrated with organizational needs identified in other criteria

Score	Results
0%	No results or poor results in areas reported
10% to 30%	Some improvements and/or early good performance levels in a few areas Results not reported for many to most areas of importance to the applicant's key organizational requirements
30% to 40%	Improvement trends and/or good performance levels reported in many areas of importance to the organization's key business requirements Early stages of developing trends and obtaining comparative information are evident Results are reported for many to most areas of importance to the organization's key business requirements
50% to 60%	Improvement trends and/or good performance levels reported in most areas of importance to the organization's key business requirements No pattern of adverse trends and no poor performance levels are evident in areas of importance to the organization's key business requirements Some trends and/or current performance levels – evaluated against relevant comparisons and/or benchmarks – show areas of strength and/or very good relative performance levels Business results address most key customer, market, and process requirements
70% to 80%	Current performance is good to excellent in areas of importance to the organization's key business requirements

(*continued*)

Table 4.5: *Continued*

Score	Approach/deployment
	Most improvement trends and/or current performance levels are sustained Many to most trends and/or current performance levels – evaluated against relevant comparisons and/or benchmarks – show areas of leadership and very good relative performance levels Business results address most key customer, market, process requirements and action plan requirements
100%	Current performance is excellent in most areas of importance to the organization's key business requirements Excellent improvement trends and/or sustained excellent performance levels in most areas Evidence of industry and benchmark leadership demonstrated in many areas Business results fully address key customer, market, process requirements and action plan requirements

Source: 2003 Award Criteria Booklet (NIST, 2003)

Table 4.6: **Examination items and scores**

		Score	Points
1.0	**Leadership**	–	**120**
	1.1 Organizational leadership	–	70
	1.2 Social responsibility	–	50
2.0	**Strategic planning**	–	**85**
	2.1 Strategy development	–	40
	2.2 Strategy deployment	–	45
3.0	**Customer and market focus**	–	**85**
	3.1 Customer and market knowledge	–	40
	3.2 Customer relationship and satisfaction	–	45
4.0	**Measurement, analysis and knowledge management**	–	**90**
	4.1 Measurement and analysis of organizational performance	–	45
	4.2 Information and knowledge management	–	45

Table 4.6: *Continued*

		Score	Points
5.0	**Human resource focus**	–	**85**
	5.1 Work systems	–	35
	5.2 Employee education, training, and development	–	25
	5.3 Employee wellbeing and satisfaction	–	25
6.0	**Process management**	–	**85**
	6.1 Value creation processes	–	50
	6.2 Support processes	–	35
7.0	**Business results**	–	**450**
	7.1 Customer-focused results	–	75
	7.2 Product and service results	–	75
	7.3 Financial and market results	–	75
	7.4 Human resource results	–	75
	7.5 Organizational effectiveness results	–	75
	7.6 Governance and social responsibility results	–	75
	Total points		**1000**

Source: 2003 Award Criteria Booklet (NIST, 2003)

A look at the original framework as launched in 1988 shows at a glance how it has changed (see Figure 4.6). Not only has the framework changed, but also the base concepts, scoring system, categories, examination items and areas to address. It could easily be concluded that the only elements that remain after eight years are the name, the public law that brought about the award, and the number of categories.

Two distinct development phases can be identified:

1. Development from a quality framework to a business framework
2. Development of a performance excellence framework.

Development from a quality framework to a business framework (1988–1996)

The evolution of the award from 1988 to 1996 is shown schematically in Figure 4.7. This illustration captures the increasing conceptual richness that has been added over the years. Some of the

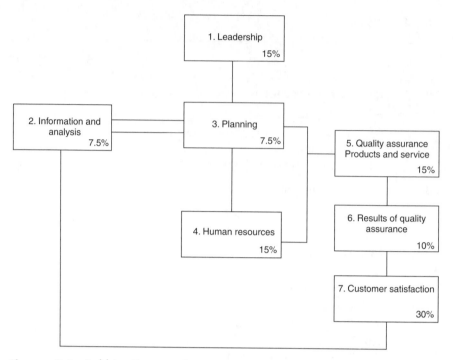

Figure 4.6 Baldrige Framework in 1988

reasons for the change in emphasis come from a reinterpretation of the original public law. Point 8 (C) of the law calls for the establishment of the guidelines and criteria that will allow businesses to evaluate their quality improvement efforts. To fill this mandated goal, the Baldrige Award organization has continually reflected on the purpose of the award criteria. In 1988, the Baldrige Award organization stated that the purpose of the criteria was to 'test all elements of a total quality system'. In 1989, the purpose was changed to 'permit the evaluation of the strengths and areas for improvement in the applicant's quality systems and quality results'.

In 1991, however, two distinct objectives were identified: to be a standard for organizations seeking the highest levels of overall quality performance and competitiveness, and to be a framework that can be used by organizations to tailor their systems and processes towards ever-improving quality performance. In 1992 these objectives were further expanded: to help evaluate quality standards and expectations, and to facilitate communication and sharing among and within organizations of all types based on common understanding of key quality requirements. In addition, they served as a working tool for planning, training, assessment, and other uses. As stated in the 1994 guidelines, the criteria are now

Framework	1988	1989	1990	1991	1992	1993	1994	1995	1996
	Simple	Developed						Migration towards EFQM Model	Further migration towards EFQM Model
Business performance measures								Introduced	Human resource results item introduced
Examination guidelines						Introduced	Expanded	Simplified	'Preparing the overview' added and 'Response guidelines' revised
Performance issues					Introduced	Developed	Developed	Developed	Developed
Key concepts				6 concepts	10 core values	10 core values	10 core values	11 core values	11 core values
Examination characteristics				Incipient	12 areas	Simplified	Simplified	Simplified	–
Business factors			Introduce	Detailed explanation	Brief presentation	Simplified	Dropped		–
Scoring method		Criteria	Dimensions	Dimensions and guidelines	Dimensions and guidelines	Dimensions and guidelines	Dimensions and guidelines	Dimension and guidelines	Dimensions and guidelines
Areas to address	278	182	133	99	89	92	91	54	52
Items	62	44	33	32	28	28	28	24	24
Sub-categories	42	27	–	–	–	–	–	–	–
Categories	7	7	7	7	7	7	7	7	7

Figure 4.7 Evolution of the Baldrige Award criteria framework, 1988–1996 (Source: Adapted from Neves and Nakhai (1994))

designed to help any organization to achieve ever-improving value for customers and to improve overall company performance.

Further major change to the examination criteria came in the 1995 guidelines, as there was a sharper focus on the area of business results. In 1995 the criteria continued to evolve in four major ways:

1. Toward comprehensive coverage of overall performance, including customer-driven quality performance
2. Toward better integration of overall performance, including employee performance, with business strategy
3. Toward further strengthening of the financial and business rationale for improvement priorities
4. Toward increasing emphasis on results.

The improvements resulted in a decrease in the number of areas to be addressed by 40 per cent, which represented a major reduction in complexity. Clarification was also provided regarding which examination elements are 'enablers' and which are 'results' and should be evaluated as such. A small but psychological change was the removal of the word 'quality' wherever possible from the criteria. This was replaced by 'business performance'.

Development of a performance excellence framework (1997–)

1997 saw further major change; the title 'award criteria' was replaced with 'criteria for performance excellence', the categories were re-ordered, and the framework was redesigned to emphasize the systems perspective currently used. The criteria were re-ordered and consolidated to make them easier to understand; criteria items were reduced by 17 per cent (to 20) and the number of areas to be addressed was cut by 42 per cent (to 30). The new framework, with all seven criteria under an umbrella of 'Customer and market-focused strategy and action plans', was redesigned to highlight the importance of a customer- and market-driven strategy, the role of information and strategy, and the goal of improved business results.

The criteria continued to evolve in 1998, with a further strengthening of the systems view of performance management, a greater emphasis on the alignment of company strategy, customer and market knowledge, a high performance workforce, key company processes and business results. Increased focus was placed on all aspects of organizational and employee learning. The number of areas to address was reduced from 30 to 29.

In 1999, education and healthcare criteria were introduced in addition to the business criteria. A new, easier to use format was introduced, with a series of key questions covering the seven category areas.

For 2000, there were no changes to the item requirements, but important changes were made to:

- The core values – these remained constant at eleven, but changes were made to achieve better alignment with the foundation for the current criteria
- The 'Glossary of key terms' – this was revised and expanded
- The category and item descriptions – these were rewritten and reformatted
- Scoring guidelines – these were revised for approach/deployment items
- The 'Guidelines for responding to approach/deployment items' – these were modified to explain the desired responses for 'how'-type and 'what'-type questions.

Further change took place in 2001, including the following:

- The number of items was reduced from 19 to 18
- The number of areas to be addressed was increased from 27 to 29
- A new organizational context section, the 'Organizational profile', was introduced to replace the 'Business overview' section
- The 'Glossary of key terms' was revised and expanded
- Category 4, Information and analysis, was rewritten to recognize the importance of e-commerce and the Internet
- Category 6, Process management, was redesigned to address all key product, service and other business processes.

No major revisions were made to the 2002 criteria, although the glossary of key terms was almost doubled in size and a new diagram was added to describe a mature process approach.

In the 2003 criteria, much greater attention has been put on governance and ethics, the need to capitalize on knowledge assets, the need to create value for customers and the business, and the alignment of all aspects of the organization's performance management system with results measurements. Criteria questions have been better aligned to improve the Baldrige framework as an assessment tool, and to identify gaps in approach, deployment and results.

Two underlying concepts guided the changes in 2003: the first was the need to have a set of criteria for evidence-based management, and the second was to focus on the dual challenge of 'running the business as usual' and 'changing the business'. The most significant changes are that:

- The number of criteria items has been increased from 18 to 19
- The number of areas to be addressed has been increased from 29 to 32
- All criteria language has been converted to question format

- The leadership criterion now includes an increased focus on governance and leadership responsibility for the organization's legal and ethical behaviour
- The measurement, analysis and knowledge management criterion has a greater emphasis on knowledge management
- The process criterion now addresses process management in the two key areas of value creation processes and support processes
- The business results criterion now includes a separate results item on governance and social responsibility.

As the administration of the award has evolved, the purposes of the award criteria have been interpreted more broadly and explained more thoroughly. The Baldrige Award organizers are now closer to fulfilling its original mandated goal of establishing criteria and guidelines for organizations to follow in their efforts to achieve excellence in performance.

4.8 Summary

In this chapter we have looked at the Malcolm Baldrige National Award, which is the world's most studied and developed award process. It is particularly significant because it is also the world's most widely adopted excellence framework against which self-assessment is carried out by organizations.

The award process is more transparent than that used by the Deming Prize, which has also helped its adoption as a self-assessment framework. The way in which organizations can assess their approach, deployment and results achieved using the three-dimensional scoring system is significantly more advanced than that used as part of normal quality assurance/ISO9000 methodology. With the latter, approach is not really questioned, and interpretation and deployment are the pivotal points.

Owing to the number of years the Baldrige Award has been running, it has been possible to conduct a review into the effectiveness of the framework, or more particularly the effectiveness of adopting a performance excellence approach within an organization. It will be recalled that the Baldrige Award process was established to promote prosperity within American businesses. A report by the private Council for Competitiveness entitled 'Building on Baldrige: American Quality for the 21st Century' states: '...more than any other programme, the Baldrige Quality Award is responsible for making quality a national priority and disseminating best practices across the United States'.

A further report, published by NIST, entitled *An Economic Evaluation of the Baldrige National Quality Program* (NIST, 2001), estimated social benefits to the US economy of $26.45 billion and a conservative benefit to cost ratio of 207 to 1.

References

American Society for Quality (2002). *Baldrige Award Applications 1988–2002*. Gaithesburg: ASQ.

Neves, J. and Nakhai, B. (1994). The evolution of the Baldrige Award. *Quality Progress*, **27(6)**, 65–70.

NIST (2001). *An Economic Evaluation of the Baldrige National Quality Program*. Gaithesburg: National Institute of Standards and Technology.

NIST (2003). Baldrige Award criteria framework – a systems perspective. *2003 Award Criteria Booklet*. Gaithesburg: National Institute of Standards and Technology.

Appendix 4.1 Baldrige Award winners

2002	*Manufacturing* Motorola Commercial, Government & Industrial Solutions Sector *Small Business* Branch-Smith Printing Division	*Healthcare* SSM Health Care
2001	*Manufacturing* Clarke American Checks, Inc. *Small Business* Pal's Sudden Service	*Education* Chugach School District Pearl River School District University of Wisconsin-Stout
2000	*Manufacturing* Dana Corporation – Spicer Driveshaft Division Karlee Company Inc *Small Business* Los Alamos National Bank	*Service* Operations Management International Inc.
1999	*Manufacturing* STMicrolectronics Inc – Region Americas *Small Business* Sunny Fresh Foods	*Service* BI The Ritz-Carlton Hotel Company, LLC

Appendix 4.1 *(Continued)*

1998	*Manufacturing* Boeing Airlift & Tanker Programs Solar Turbines Inc. *Small Business* Texas Nameplate Company Inc.	
1997	*Manufacturing* 3M Dental Products Division Solectron Corporation	*Service* Merrill Lynch Credit Corporation Xerox Business Services
1996	*Manufacturing* ADAC Laboratories *Small Business* Custom Research Inc. Trident Precision Manufacturing Inc.	*Service* Dana Commercial Credit Corporation
1995	*Manufacturing* Armstrong World Industries Inc Corning Incorporated, Telecommunications Products Division	
1994	*Small Business* Wainwright Industries Inc.	*Service* AT&T Consumer Communications Services Verizon Information Services
1993	*Manufacturing* Eastman Chemical Company *Small Business* Ames Rubber Corporation	
1992	*Manufacturing* AT&T Network Systems Group – Transmission Systems Business Unit Texas Instruments Incorporated Defence Systems & Electronics Group *Small Business* Granite Rock Company	*Service* AT&T Universal Card Services The Ritz-Carlton Hotel Company

Appendix 4.1 (*Continued*)

1991   *Manufacturing*
        Solectron Corporation
        Zytec Corporation
        Small Business
        Marlow Industries Inc

1990   *Manufacturing*   *Service*
        Cadillac Motor Car Company   Federal Express
        IBM Rochester   Corporation
        Small Business
        Wallace Co Inc.

1989   *Manufacturing*
        Milliken & Company
        Xerox Corporation, Business
        Products & Systems

1988   *Manufacturing*
        Motorola Inc.
        Westinghouse Electric
        Corporation Commercial
        Nuclear Fuel Division
        Small Business
        Globe Metallurgical Inc.

Appendix 4.2 Education criteria core values and concepts

The core values and concepts are:

- Visionary leadership
- Learning-centred education
- Organizational and personal learning
- Valuing faculty, staff and partners
- Agility
- Focus on the future
- Managing for innovation
- Management by fact
- Social responsibility
- Focus on results and creating value
- Systems perspective.

Several of these themes are sufficiently different from the business criteria to merit further discussion.

Learning-centred education

Three dimensions can be identified:

1. *Understanding student needs.* If students are to realize their potential, education organizations need to offer them opportunities to pursue a variety of avenues to success. Learning-centred education supports this goal by placing the focus of education on learning and the real needs of students, which are in turn derived from market and citizenship requirements.

2. *Creating an effective learning environment.* Learning-centred organizations need to understand student requirements and translate them into appropriate curricula and development experiences. The requirements of the modern world require education organizations to focus more on students' active learning and on the development of problem-solving skills. Educational offerings also need to be built around effective learning, and effective teaching needs to stress promotion of learning and achievement.

3. *Sensitivity to changes in the education environment.* Learning-centred education demands that education organizations be sensitive to and anticipate changing and emerging student, stakeholder and market requirements, and the factors that drive student learning, satisfaction and persistence. It demands anticipating changes in the education environment, as well as rapid and flexible responses to student, stakeholder, and market requirements.

The education criteria also detail key characteristics of learning-centred education. These are summarized below:

- Standards – high developmental expectations and standards are set for all students.
- Learning styles – students learn in different ways and at different rates. Learning-centred organizations must understand the factors that contribute to effective learning, and constantly search for alternative ways to enhance learning.
- Active learning – a primary emphasis on active learning must be provided. This may require a wide range of techniques, materials and experiences to engage student interest.
- Assessment – assessment systems addressing formative, summative and self-assessment are required to measure learning and track progress.
- Focus on key transitions – a focus on key transitions is required, i.e. school to school and school to work.

Organizational and personal learning

In the education criteria, similar themes to the business criteria can be identified:

- *Integrated approach.* Achieving the highest levels of performance requires a well-executed approach to organizational and personal learning. Organizational learning includes continuous improvement of existing approaches, and adaptation to change, leading to new goals and/or approaches. Learning needs to be embedded in the way the organization operates. This means that learning (1) is a regular part of the daily work of all students, faculty, and staff; (2) is practised at personal, work unit/department, and organizational levels; (3) results in solving problems at their source ('root cause'); (4) is focused on sharing knowledge throughout the organization; and (5) is driven by opportunities to effect significant change and to do better. Sources for learning include faculty and staff ideas, education and learning research findings, student and stakeholder input, best-practice sharing, and benchmarking.
- *Design for learning.* Improvement in education requires a strong emphasis on the effective design of educational programmes, curricula, and learning environments. The overall design should include clear learning objectives, taking into account the individual needs of students. Design must also include effective means for gauging student progress. A central requirement of effective design is the inclusion of an assessment strategy. This strategy needs to emphasize the acquisition of formative information – information that provides an early indication of whether or not learning is taking place – to minimize problems that might arise if learning barriers are not promptly identified and addressed.
- *Providing personal learning opportunities.* Faculty and staff success depends increasingly on having opportunities for personal learning and practising new skills. Organizations invest in personal learning of faculty and staff through education, training, and other opportunities for continuing growth. Such opportunities might include job rotation, and increased pay for demonstrated knowledge and skills.
- *Enhancing learning through technology.* Educational and training programmes may benefit from advanced technologies, such as computer and internet-based learning and satellite broadcasts.
- *Organizational improvement.* Personal learning can result in: (1) more satisfied and versatile faculty and staff who stay with the organization; (2) organizational cross-functional learning;

and (3) an improved environment for innovation. Thus, learning is directed not only toward better educational programmes and services, but also toward being more responsive, adaptive, and flexible to the needs of students, stakeholders, and the market.

Valuing faculty, staff and partners

In the education criteria, broadly similar themes to the business criteria can be identified but the term 'employees' is replaced with 'faculty and staff'.

Additional items in education include the need to develop faculty not only by building discipline knowledge but also knowledge of student learning styles and of assessment methods.

For staff, development might include classroom and on-the-job training, job rotation, and pay for demonstrated skills. Increasingly, training, education, development, and organizational structure need to be tailored to a more diverse workforce and to more flexible, high-performance work practices.

Agility

In the education criteria, the need for responsiveness is based on agility as an important measure of organizational effectiveness.

Appendix 4.3   Healthcare criteria core values and concepts

The core values and concepts are:

- Visionary leadership
- Patient-focused excellence
- Organizational and personal learning
- Valuing staff and partners
- Agility
- Focus on the future
- Managing for innovation
- Management by fact
- Social responsibility and community health
- Focus on results and creating value
- Systems perspective.

Several of these themes are sufficiently different from the business criteria to merit further discussion.

Patient-focused excellence

Three dimensions can be identified:

1. *Understanding patient desires.* The delivery of healthcare services must be patient-focused. All attributes of patient care delivery factor into the judgement of satisfaction and value. Satisfaction and value to patients are key considerations for other customers. Understanding current patient desires and anticipating future patient desires and healthcare marketplace offerings is vital.
2. *Patient-focused delivery.* Value and satisfaction may be influenced by many factors during a patient's experience of healthcare provision. These may include a clear understanding of likely health outcomes, relationship with the healthcare provider and ancillary staff, cost, responsiveness, and continuing care and attention. For many patients, the ability to participate in making decisions on their own healthcare is considered an important factor. This requires patient education for an informed decision. Characteristics that differentiate one provider from another also contribute to the sense of being patient-focused.
3. *Sensitivity to emerging patient desires.* Patient-focused excellence demands rapid and flexible responses to emerging patient desires and healthcare market requirements, and to the measurement of the factors that drive patient satisfaction. It also demands awareness of new technology and new modalities for delivery of healthcare services.

Organizational and personal learning

Similar themes to the business criteria are evident:

- *Integrated approach.* Achieving the highest levels of performance requires a well-executed approach to organizational and personal learning. Organizational learning includes both continuous improvement of existing approaches and adaptation to change, leading to new goals and/or approaches. Learning needs to be embedded in the way the organization operates. This means that learning: (1) is a regular part of daily work; (2) is practised at personal, department/work unit, and organizational levels; (3) results in solving problems at their source ('root cause'); (4) is focused on sharing knowledge throughout the organization; and (5) is driven by opportunities to effect significant change and to do better. Sources for learning include staff ideas, healthcare research findings, patients' and other customers' input, best-practice sharing, and benchmarking. Organizational learning can result in: (1) enhanced value to patients through new and improved patient care services; (2) development of new healthcare opportunities; (3) reduction in errors, defects, waste, and related costs; (4) an improvement in responsiveness and cycle time performance; (5) increased productivity and effectiveness in the use of all resources throughout the organization; and (6) enhanced performance of the organization in building community health and fulfilling its public responsibilities.

- *Providing personal learning opportunities.* Staff success depends increasingly on having opportunities for personal learning and practising new skills. Organizations invest in personal learning through education, training, and other opportunities for continuing growth. Such opportunities might include job rotation and increased pay for demonstrated knowledge and skills. On-the-job training offers a cost-effective way to train and to link training better to organizational needs and priorities. For healthcare providers, personal learning includes building discipline knowledge, discipline retraining to adjust to a changing healthcare environment, and enhancing knowledge of measurement systems influencing outcome assessments and clinical guidelines, decision trees, or critical paths.
- *Enhancing learning through technology.* Education and training programmes may benefit from advanced technologies, such as computer- and internet-based learning and satellite broadcasts.
- *Organizational improvement.* Personal learning can result in: (1) more satisfied and versatile staff who stay with the organization; (2) organizational cross-functional learning; and (3) an improved environment for innovation. Thus, learning is directed not only toward better healthcare services but also toward being more responsive, adaptive, and efficient – giving the organization healthcare marketplace sustainability and performance advantages.

Appendix 4.4 Example of breakdown of categories

Leadership (120 points)

The *Leadership* category examines how your organization's senior leaders address values, directions, and performance expectations, as well as having a focus on customers and other stakeholders, empowerment, innovation, and learning. Also examined are your organization's governance and how your organization addresses its public and community responsibilities.

Organizational leadership (70 points)

Describe how senior leaders guide your organization.
Describe your organization's governance system
Describe how senior leaders review organizational performance.

Within your response, include answers to the following questions:

a. Senior leadership direction

How do senior leaders:

- Set and deploy organizational values, short- and longer-term directions, and performance expectations?
- Include a focus on creating and balancing value for customers and other stakeholders in their performance expectations?
- Communicate organizational values, directions, and expectations through your leadership system and to all employees and key suppliers and partners?

How do senior leaders create:

- An environment for empowerment, innovation and organizational agility?
- An environment for organizational and employee learning?
- An environment that fosters and requires legal and ethical behaviour?

b. Organizational governance

How does your organization address the following key factors in your governance system?

- Management accountability for the organization's actions
- Fiscal accountability
- Independence in internal and external audits
- Protection of stockholder and stakeholder interests, as appropriate.

c. Organizational performance review

1. How do senior leaders:
   - Review organizational performance and capabilities?
   - Use these reviews to assess organizational success, competitive performance, and progress relative to short- and longer-term goals?

- Use these reviews to assess your organizational ability to address changing organizational needs?

2. What are the key performance measures regularly reviewed by your senior leaders? What are your key recent performance review findings?
   - How do senior leaders translate organizational performance review findings into priorities for continuous and break-through improvement of key business results, and into opportunities for innovation? How are these priorities and opportunities deployed throughout your organization? When appropriate, how are they deployed to your suppliers and partners to ensure organizational alignment?
   - How do you evaluate the performance of your senior leaders, including the chief executive? How do you evaluate the performance of members of the board of directors, as appropriate? How do senior leaders use organizational performance review findings to improve both their own leadership effectiveness and that of your board and leadership system, as appropriate?

Source: NIST (2003) Baldrige National Quality Program 2003, Criteria for Performance Excellence. *National Institute for Standards and Technology.*

Appendix 4.5 Sample feedback report comments

The comments given below are based on a feedback report used in the 2001 Baldrige Award Examiner Preparation Course. The comments are about a fictitious service sector organization, TriView National Bank, and are representative of the specific, actionable feedback companies will receive. The relevant Baldrige Award criteria item is given in parentheses.

Strengths

The Executive Management Committee addresses the impacts on society during the annual Strategic Planning Process through an environmental scan. This includes a review of regulations and laws that may impact bank services and products. A specific EMC member is responsible for ensuring compliance with regulatory and legal requirements. (1.2 Public responsibility and citizenship)

TriView National Bank has defined criteria for categorizing customers into Consumer, Small Business, or Commercial Accounts. Defined asset-based and liability-based products are associated with each customer segment. (3.1 Customer and market knowledge)

As part of the design and delivery of key business processes, TriView National Bank uses critical performance measures to monitor process quality, timeliness, cost and cycle time of selected key processes. These measures align with key customer requirements. Each functional area is responsible for managing and improving business processes. (6.2 Business processes)

Areas for improvement

Although one of TriView National Bank's key strategic challenges is the high level of competition, it is not clear what information is covered in the competitive scan and whether TriView National Bank addresses its capabilities relative to its competitors, including the levels of performance required for competitive leadership. (2.1 Strategy development)

TriView National Bank does not appear to align branch-level measurement and analysis with organizational measurement and analysis. This may make it difficult for the Bank to ensure operational focus and improvements are supportive of strategic objectives. (4.1 Measurement and analysis of organizational performance)

It is not clear how TriView National Bank addresses diversity in recruiting in order to capitalize on the diversity of the communities in which it serves. While the Bank states that diversity goals exist, they were not explicitly identified, and current workforce diversity is not described in the organizational profile. (5.1 Work systems)

Source: ASQ Award Literature.

Appendix 4.6   Examination items scoring dimensions

Category/item	Approach	Deployment	Results
1.0 Leadership			
1.1 Organizational leadership	✓	✓	
1.2 Social responsibility	✓	✓	
2.0 Strategic planning			
2.1 Strategy development	✓	✓	
2.2 Strategy deployment	✓	✓	

3.0	**Customer and market focus**		
	3.1 Customer and market knowledge	✓	✓
	3.2 Customer relationships and satisfaction	✓	✓
4.0	**Measurement, analysis and knowledge management**		
	4.1 Measurement and analysis of organizational performance	✓	✓
	4.2 Information and knowledge management	✓	✓
5.0	**Human resource focus**		
	5.1 Work systems	✓	✓
	5.2 Employee learning and motivation	✓	✓
	5.3 Employee wellbeing and satisfaction	✓	✓
6.0	**Process management**		
	6.1 Value creation processes	✓	✓
	6.2 Support processes	✓	✓
7.0	**Business results**		
	7.1 Customer-focused results			✓
	7.2 Product and service results			✓
	7.3 Financial and market results			✓
	7.4 Human resource results			✓
	7.5 Organizational effectiveness results			✓
	7.6 Governance and social responsibility results			✓

Source: NIST (2003) 2003 Performance Excellence Criteria. National Institute for Standards and Technology.

The European Quality Award

5.1 Introduction

The European Quality Award is the European equivalent of the Baldrige Award. The European Award took the Baldrige Award as a starting point, and refined it so that it had a similar but unique focus on the adoption of total quality as a business improvement vehicle. This development led to an approach that at the time was more business orientated than that of the Baldrige Award. However, in recent years both models have evolved, and both now have a high degree of business orientation.

The award framework discussed in this chapter was developed by the European Foundation for Quality Management (EFQM), and as such they remain the custodians of the framework. Most European countries have adopted the European model and award process for their national awards. The EFQM notes that the number of organizations using its framework across Europe is rapidly growing, with over 20 000 organizations currently using the model to drive their improvement activities.

5.2 Background to EFQM and the awards

On 15 September 1988, fourteen chief executives of leading European companies formed the European Foundation for Quality Management (EFQM) with the aim of enhancing the competitive position of European companies in the world market. In doing this an organization was formed that is the strongest executive management-led organization addressing strategic quality issues in Europe.

The fourteen founding members came from both service and manufacturing industry sectors. The membership of EFQM has grown to over 750 members, from most European countries and most business sectors.

The EFQM sees itself as having a key role to play in enhancing the effectiveness and efficiency of European organizations through the promotion of the use of its model. The EFQM's mission is to be the driving force for sustainable excellence in Europe, with a vision of a world in which organizations in Europe excel. The EFQM forms the centre of an excellence network, and as such is supported by many National Partner Organizations across Europe. Each partner organization runs its own national quality awards using the EFQM Excellence Model®, and provides a distribution channel for EFQM's products and services.

To achieve the mission and vision, the EFQM has a structure of a governing committee, an advisory committee, and a number of steering groups. A key thrust for the EFQM is around the area of recognition, and it was the Recognition Steering Group activity that led to the creation of the European Quality Awards. The objective of the awards is to recognize top quality performance of people and performance in Europe. Originally a number of awards were established, but today all the awards fall within the framework of the 'Levels of Excellence' scheme. Since late 2001 there have been three Levels of Excellence:

1. The European Quality Award
2. Recognized for Excellence
3. Committed to Excellence.

The scheme was originally designed so that the levels operated independently. In practice, however, organizations that do not achieve the standard required in order to be considered for the European Award may be considered for the 'Recognized for Excellence' scheme if they achieve a score of above 350 at the end of the consensus meeting and of above 400 at the end of the site visit. They also have to indicate that they want to be considered for an award under this scheme on the application form. For the purpose of this chapter, we will consider only the European Quality Award (EQA). More details on the other levels may be obtained from EFQM.

Within the European Quality Award there are three levels, as summarized in Table 5.1.

The EFQM lists many benefits for organizations that apply and win awards. The benefits of winning relate to the promotion the organization receives, which is particularly valuable for private

Table 5.1: European Quality Award levels

European Award level	Explanation

Award Winner	This award is given to the organization that is judged to be the best in each of the award categories, providing they meet certain requirements set by the jurors. The award categories are:
	
	• Large and business units
	• Operational units
	• Public sector
	• Small and medium-sized enterprises (SMEs), of which there are two sub-categories:
	  • Independent SMEs, and
	  • Subsidiary (Business Unit) SMEs

Special Prizes	Introduced in 2003, these are given to organizations that excel in some of the fundamental concepts that underpin the EFQM Award framework. Special Prizes will be given for: • Leadership and consistency of purpose • Customer focus • Corporate social responsibility • People development and involvement • Results orientation In making this change, which has the objective of promoting role model practices in the areas, the EFQM notes that organizations will have the opportunity of winning more than one prize
Finalist	Finalists are organizations that are short-listed for the award and prizes but do not achieve the required level of achievement to be confirmed as one of the winners in any of the levels above. Finalists receive a framed certificate, and may publicize that they were short-listed

Table 5.2: EFQM Award and prize winners 1992–2003

Year	Large and business units		Small and medium-sized enterprises (SMEs)		Public sector organizations		Operational units	
	Award Winner	Prize Winners	Award Winner	Prize Winners	Prize Winners	Prize Winners	Award Winner	Prize Winners
1992	Rank Xerox Limited	BOC Limited, Special Gases Industrias del Ubierma SA – UBISA Milliken European Division	No such award	No such award	No such award	No such award	No such award	No such award
1993	Milliken European Division	ICL Manufacturing Division	No such award	No such award	No such award	No such award	No such award	No such award
1994	D2D (Design to Distribution) Ltd	Ericsson SA IBM (SEMEA)	No such award	No such award	No such award	No such award	No such award	No such award
1995	Texas Instruments Europe	TNT Express United Kingdom Limited	No such award	No such award	No such award	No such award	No such award	No such award
1996	BRISA	British Telecom NETAS – Northern Electric	No such award	No such award	No such award	No such award	No such award	No such award

Year							
		Telekomunikasyon AS, TNT United Kingdom Limited					No such award
1997	SGS-THOMSON Microelectronics	British Telecom, NETAS – Northern Electric Telekomunikasyon AS, TNT United Kingdom Limited	Beksa	Gasnalsa		No such award	No such award
1998	TNT United Kingdom Ltd	BT Communications Northern Ireland, NETAS – Northern Electric Telekomijnikasyon AS, Sollac Yellow Pages	Landhotel Schindierhof (Independent), BekoTicaret (Subsidiary)	DIEU (Independent)	No award winner declared	AVE (a division of RENFE) Inland Revenue Cumbernauld	No such award
1999	Yellow Pages	BT Communications Northern Ireland, Elais, Sollac	DIEU (Independent), Servitique Network Services (Subsidiary)	Banca Internacional d'Andorra i Banca Mora (Subsidiary), Burton-Apta Refractory Manufacturing Ltd (Subsidiary)	No award winner declared	No prize winner declared	Volvo Cars Gent, No prize winner declared

(continued)

Table 5.2: *Continued*

Year	Large and business units		Small and medium-sized enterprises (SMEs)		Public sector organizations		Operational units	
	Award Winner	*Prize Winners*	*Award Winner*	*Prize Winners*	*Prize Winners*	*Prize Winners*	*Award Winner*	*Prize Winners*
2000	Nokia Mobile Phones, Europe and Africa	Arçelik A.S. Eczacibasi Vitra Irizar	Burton-Apta Refractory Manufacturing Ltd. (Subsidary)	Water Team (Independent) Zahnarztpraxis (Independent) Avaya Ireland (Subsidiary)	Inland Revenue, Accounts Office Cumbernauld	Arbejdsformidlingen – Ringkoebing AMT Foxdenton School and Integrated Nursery	No award winner declared	No prize winner declared
2001	No award winner declared	DHL Portugal Westel Mobile Telecommunications Co. Ltd	Zahnarztpraxis Switzerland (Independent)	Siemans Tele Industry SA Greece (Subsidiary) Maxi Coco-Mat SA Greece (Independent) QMS AG Quality Management Services AG Germany (Independent)	St Mary's College Northern Ireland	No prize winner declared	No award winner declared	No prize winner declared

2002	2003
No prize winner declared	No winners
DEXIA – SOFAXIS	Siemens Nederland NV, the Netherlands (*Results Orientation, Leadership and Constancy of Purpose*)
Springfarm Architectural Mouldings Ltd (Independent)	Maxi COCOMAT, Greece Edinburgh International Conference Centre, United Kingdom
Banca Internacional d'Andorra i Banca Mora (Subsidiary) ASLE, "Workers incorporated companies association" (Independent) Maxi Coco-Mat SA (Independent)	Maxi COCOMAT, Greece (*Results Orientation*) Edinburgh International Conference Centre, United Kingdom (*People Development and Involvement*) Hunziker and Co, Switzerland (*Customer Focus*) Microdeco, Spain (*Corporate Social Responsibility*) Robur S.p.A., Italy (*Leadership and Constancy of Purpose*) Schindlerhoff Hotel, Germany (*Customer Focus*)
No prize winner declared	Runshaw College, United Kingdom
Customs and Tax Region Aarhus	Runshaw College, United Kingdom (*Leadership and Consistency of Purpose*) Kocaeli Chamber of Industry, Turkey (*Results Orientation*)
No prize winner declared	Bosch Sanayi ve Ticaret AS, Turkey
Bosch Sanayi ve Ticaret AS	Bosch Sanayi ve Ticaret AS, Turkey (*Leadership and Consistency of Purpose*) Grundfos A/S, Denmark (*Leadership and Constancy of Purpose*) Solvay Martorell Site, Spain (*Corporate Social Responsibility*) TNT Post Group Information Systems, United Kingdom (*People Development and Involvement*)

Note: The European Prize was replaced by Special Prizes in 2003.

organizations. Table 5.2 lists all the award and prize winners to date, and it can be seen that there is a range of organizations, many of whom may not have been readily recognizable before winning the award.

All organizations that apply for an award, be it at a European, national or regional level, gain substantial benefits. These include:

- Enabling comparison of the organizations' profile against other organizations
- Receipt of a detailed feedback report listing both strengths and areas for improvement (this feedback is provided by practising managers who are completely independent)
- The opportunity to learn from others though good-practice sharing
- If a winner or finalist, public recognition.

The profile and feedback relate to the application of the EFQM Excellence Model®. The background to the model, its composition, and how it is used during the award process are discussed in the following sections.

5.3 The development of the EFQM Excellence Model®

Introduction

The European Model for Total Quality Management began life in 1990 through a series of workshops that were run in Brussels. Drawing on the experience of both the American Baldrige Award and the Japanese Deming Prize for companies, a basic model was developed, a simple form of which is shown in Figure 5.1. The philosophy of this model was that superior performance is achieved by involving people in improving their processes. This basic model was developed further by drawing on the experiences and thoughts of Tito Conti, and by consulting with many EFQM representatives and other leading bodies. Over 1000

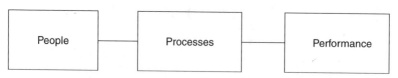

Figure 5.1 Basic Excellence Model

people were consulted as part of the formulation of the final model and award process.

The eight fundamental concepts

Although the EFQM Excellence Model® is used as the basis of the European Quality Award, it is important not to lose sight of the fact that the model itself is only a schematic representation of the fundamental concepts of excellence. These concepts were introduced to complement the original model. They were reviewed and endorsed in 1999, when the model underwent a major change. More recently, in 2002, they were reviewed for a second time, with one fundamental, 'Public responsibility', being given the more modern title of 'Corporate social responsibility'. At this time a more detailed explanation was given for each fundamental concept. The current fundamental concepts are given in Table 5.3.

Excellent organizations strive to satisfy their stakeholders' needs, and take pride in the way that they achieve their success. They do this by embracing the fundamental concepts. The premise is that:

Excellent results with respect to Performance, Customers, People and Society are achieved through Partnerships and Resources, and Processes.

The EFQM Excellence Model®, which is a schematic representation of the fundamental concepts, is shown in Figure 5.2. Details of both the enablers and results are given below.

The way in which an organization evaluates itself against the model will be discussed in section 5.5. At this point, it is worth noting that not all the criteria or sub-criteria carry equal weighting. There is a 50/50 split between the enablers and results criteria, but the enablers and results criteria have different weights within this split to reflect their perceived importance. For example, 'Leadership' carries a weighting of 10 per cent, whereas 'Processes' accounts for 14 per cent. Similarly with the results criteria, 'People results' is worth 9 per cent, compared with 20 per cent for 'Customer results'.

Although the model is presented as a two-dimensional framework, there are links across the criteria that are not obviously apparent. For example, there is a close correlation between 'People' and 'People results', and between 'Policy and strategy' and 'Key performance results'. There have been arguments to present the model in three dimensions or perhaps in a cyclical format, but these schematics should not distract from the power of the relationships between the enablers and results. The BQF

Table 5.3: EFQM: the eight fundamental concepts

Fundamental concept	Definition	Explanation
Results orientation	Excellence is achieving results that delight all the organization's stakeholders	Excellent organizations are seen as those who measure and anticipate stakeholder needs. The information is used to plan the operation of the organization. Stakeholders include customers, people, society and shareholders/funding bodies
Customer focus	Excellence is creating sustainable customer value	This concept relates to understanding customers, appreciating the impact they have on the business, and creating an environment that supports meeting their needs
Leadership and constancy of purpose	Excellence is visionary and inspirational leadership, coupled with alignment of purpose	Leaders need to communicate a clear direction, and unite and motivate their people. They also have to be role models, leading by example. Leadership is not confined to the top, but must be prevalent at all levels throughout the organization
Management by process and fact	Excellence is managing the organization through a set of	An effective management system will deliver the needs and expectations of

interdependent and interrelated systems, processes and facts		stakeholders. The processes should be deployed consistently throughout the organization, and managed for improvement on a continuous basis. Decisions are made on hard data and not just on perceptions
People development and involvement	Excellence is maximizing the contribution of employees through their development and involvement	Excellence requires the identification of the competencies needed now and in the future to implement the organization's policies, strategies, objectives and plans. Personal development is promoted and supported, allowing people to realize their full potential. The intellectual capital of the people is also important, as is the way that employees are rewarded and recognized
Continuous learning, innovation and improvement	Excellence is challenging the *status quo* and effecting change by utilizing learning to create innovation and improvement opportunities	Learning from their own and others' activities is a key component of continuous improvement. This goes further than the activity of benchmarking, and includes consideration as to the way that knowledge is shared and barriers to implementation are reduced

(continued)

Table 5.3: *Continued*

Fundamental concept	Definition	Explanation
Partnership development	Excellence is developing and maintaining value-adding partnerships	Developing partnerships is becoming an important way of delivering enhanced value to stakeholders. Partnership may be with a number of stakeholders, including suppliers, society, customers and even competitors. These partnerships should be identified based on mutual benefit with partners working together with shared values and goals
Corporate social responsibility	Excellence is exceeding the minimum regulatory framework in which the organization operates, and striving to understand and respond to the expectations of its stakeholders in society	Based on the organization's values, it will seek to adopt a highly ethical approach, being transparent and accountable to stakeholders. Promoting opportunities to work on mutually beneficial projects is important, alongside the organization having an awareness of its current and future impact on the community

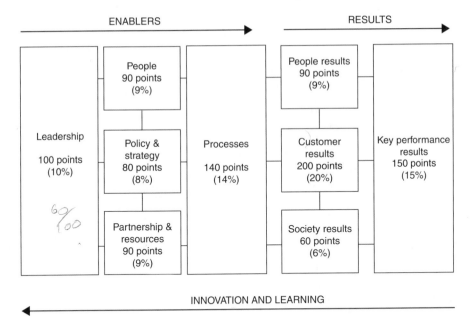

Figure 5.2 EFQM Excellence Model®

book *The Model in Practice* includes a number of diagrams show-ing the linkages between the criteria, and their use in aiding the preparation of an award submission is explained in Chapter 12.

To complete our review of the EFQM Excellence Model®, the sub-criteria and their purposes are briefly described below. A detailed description is available in one of the many EFQM or National Partner Organization publications, such as the British Quality Foundation's *The Model in Practice*, mentioned earlier. Unlike the Deming Prize and the American Baldrige award, the EFQM raises funds by invoking copyright protection on the full details of the model.

The enabler criteria

The enabler criteria are concerned with the organization's approach to running its business. They represent the 'hows' rather than the 'whats'. Information is required regarding the excellence of the approach and the degree of deployment of the approach throughout the organization, both vertically and horizontally. Although the model is not designed to be prescrip-tive, the criteria are split down into several sub-criteria (Figure 5.3). Under each sub-criterion there are several 'guidance points'. All of the sub-criteria have an equal weighting within

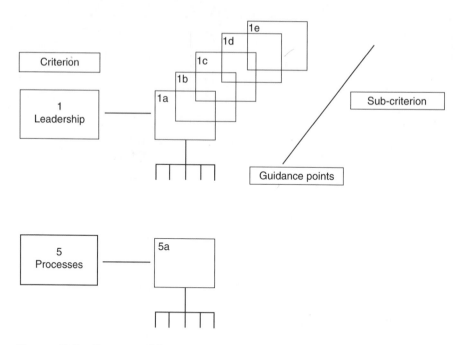

Figure 5.3 Structure of the criterion

their criterion, except for 'Customer results', 'People results' and 'Societal results'. Table 5.4 describes the various weightings.

The criteria are reviewed below.

Criterion 1: Leadership

Excellent leaders develop and facilitate the achievement of the mission and vision. They develop organizational values and systems required for sustainable success and implement these via their actions and behaviours. During periods of change they retain a constancy of purpose. Where required, such leaders are able to change the direction of the organization and inspire others to follow.

The Leadership criterion is split down into five sub-criteria:

1a   Leaders develop the mission, vision, values and ethics and are role models of a culture of Excellence
It is important for leaders to be fully involved developing the organization's mission and vision, and supporting the evolution of the culture to a culture that is consistent with an Excellence philosophy. Acting as role models and stimulation and encouragement of improvement, creativity and innovation are all important features.

Table 5.4: Criteria and sub-criteria weightings

Criterion	Weighting (%)	Number of sub-criteria	Sub-criteria weighting
Enabler criteria Comprising:	*50*		
1. Leadership	10	5	Equal
2. Policy and strategy	8	4	Equal
3. People	9	5	Equal
4. Partnerships and resources	9	5	Equal
5. Processes	14	5	Equal
Results criteria Comprising:	*50*		
6. Customer results	20	2	6a 75% 6b 25%
7. People results	9	2	7a 75% 7b 25%
8. Society results	6	2	8a 25% 8b 75%
9. Key performance results	15	2	Equal

1b   Leaders are involved in ensuring the organization's management system is developed, implemented and continuously improved
An Excellence approach demands that the organization's strategy and objectives are delivered through a process structure and leaders have a key role in establishing this structure. Within this management system there is clear ownership of processes, and the processes cover all aspects of the business including both operational and support processes.

1c   Leaders interact with customers, partners and representatives of society
Working with partners is becoming more important to the success of organizations, and this sub-criterion reinforces the need for

leaders to be actively involved with partners. Establishing partnerships, understanding and responding to their needs, and participating in joint improvement activity are some of the behaviours that are encouraged.

1d Leaders reinforce a culture of Excellence with the organization's people

Communication, accessibility and responding to people's needs are key requirements of this sub-criterion. Leaders also need to provide appropriate resources and assistance, including helping to set priorities for improvement activities and releasing people to participate in improvement activities. Recognizing both team and individual efforts in a timely and appropriate manner is also of paramount importance.

1e Leaders identify and champion organizational change

A sub-criterion introduced with the 2003 model, the need for leaders to understand the drivers of change and to take a key role in leading change has been recognized. Activities include securing investment and resources, managing stakeholders, communicating change agendas, and reviewing the effectiveness of change.

Criterion 2: Policy and strategy

Excellent organizations implement their mission and vision by developing a stakeholder-focused strategy that takes into account the market and sector in which it operates. Policies, plans, objectives, and processes are developed and deployed to deliver the strategy.

It is important to understand exactly what is meant by terms like 'mission' and 'vision'. Table 5.5 gives the EFQM's definitions.

The Policy and strategy criterion is split into four sub-criteria.

2a Policy and strategy are based on the present and future needs and expectations of stakeholders

Given the keen focus on the stakeholder throughout the model, this sub-criterion looks at the approaches used by the organization to identify and anticipate stakeholder needs in preparation for the formulation of the policy strategy. Understanding the marketplace and the potential changes is also part of this sub-criterion. From a traditional strategy standpoint, this sub-criterion covers parts of both the external and internal scans in relation to strategic positioning.

2b Policy and strategy are based on information from performance measurement, research, learning and external related activities

This sub-criterion focuses more on hard data than does sub-criterion 2a. Current performance levels, best in class performance and partners' core competencies are all areas to consider.

Table 5.5: Criterion 2: Policy and strategy definitions

Term	Definition
Policy and strategy	The top-level statements of the organization that set out its underlying mission, values, vision, objectives and strategies
Mission	The purpose of the organization – a statement of why the business exists
Vision	Statements that describe the kind of organization it wishes to become
Values	The understandings and expectations that describe how the organization's people behave and upon which all business relationships are based, for example trust, support, truth etc.

The sub-criterion also calls for some external data, such as demographic and economic data. From a traditional strategy standpoint, again we have components of the external and internal scans under this area.

2c Policy and strategy are developed, reviewed and updated
Once information has been collected through the approaches meeting the 2a and 2b requirements, this sub-criterion considers how the policy and strategy are actually developed. Balancing stakeholders' needs, identifying core competencies and determining competitive advantage are key activities. Alignment with partners is also considered important, as is the management of risk.

2d Policy and strategy are communicated and deployed through a framework of key processes
This is a natural follow-on from the previous sub-criterion as the policy and strategy are deployed. Here we have a direct link with sub-criterion 1b, where leaders have the task of establishing a process-based management system. Often performance measurement frameworks/balanced scorecards and business plans are used to facilitate this and to track progress. Communication should be to all stakeholders, and there is a need to ensure that awareness of the policy and strategy is evaluated.

Criterion 3: People management

Excellent organizations manage, develop and release the full potential of their people at an individual, team-based and organizational level.

They promote fairness and equality and involve and empower their people. They care for, communicate, reward and recognize, in a way that motivates staff and builds commitment to using their skills and knowledge for the benefit of the organization.

This criterion is broken down into five sub-criteria.

3a People resources are planned, managed and improved

It is important that the human resource policy, strategy and plans are completely aligned with the high-level strategy, and that there is a clear process for human resource planning. There is also a need to ensure that there is alignment between the human resource plans, the organization's structure, and the framework of key processes. Recruitment, career development and succession planning within an equal opportunities framework are also considered.

3b People's knowledge and competencies are identified, developed and sustained

In a changing environment, it is possible that the skills and capabilities of the organization's people are at variance with the organization's requirements. The first stage in bridging the gap is to have clear processes for establishing the requirements and evaluating the skills and capabilities of the people. The establishment and execution of training plans will be a key enabler. It is also usual for people to be developed through teamwork or work experience. Personal objective setting, appraisal and mentoring are also covered by this sub-criterion.

3c People are involved and empowered

The ways in which individuals and teams contribute to improvement activities are covered by this sub-criterion. The organization may make use of devices such as in-house conferences, ceremonies and team-working. It is also important to understand how people are empowered to take action, and how the effectiveness of the approach is reviewed. One change in the 2003 Model criteria was to introduce the concept of the development of guidelines to steer empowerment.

3d People and the organization have dialogue

The area of communication is covered as an integral part of most other sub-criteria. This sub-criterion is really an overview of the communication processes, and seeks to evaluate how the needs of the organization are evaluated, how top-down and bottom-up communication is achieved; and how the effectiveness of the communication is reviewed and improved. Communication under this sub-criterion includes providing opportunities to share best practice and knowledge.

3e   People are rewarded, recognized and cared for

In the context of this sub-criterion, reward relates to aspects such as remuneration, redundancy and other terms of employment, which should be aligned with the policy and strategy. Recognition is also important, with the objective of promoting and sustaining involvement and empowerment.

Promotion of personal welfare, including health and safety and a concern for the environment, are features of an Excellence organization. Diversity and appreciation of different cultural backgrounds are also important.

Criterion 4:   Partnerships and resources

Excellent organizations plan and manage external partnerships, suppliers and internal resources in order to support policy and strategy and the effective operation of processes. During planning and whilst managing partnerships and resources they balance the current and future needs of the organization, the community and the environment.

This criterion is broken down into five sub-criteria. Each sub-criterion deals with a different type of resource.

4a   External partnerships are managed

Although sub-criterion 1c examined leaders' involvement with partners, this sub-criterion looks at the approaches that are used on a day-to-day basis. These include the identification of the partnership opportunities in line with the policy and strategy. The focus is on getting partnerships and supplier relationships to deliver maximum value to the organization. Such relationships may be either up- or downstream in the supply chain.

4b   Finances are managed

Financial resources are defined as the short-term funds required for the day-to-day operation of the business, and the capital funding from various sources (shareholder equity, loan capital retained earnings, government grants etc.) required for the longer-term financing of the business. The financial strategy should underpin the top-level policy and strategy.

This sub-criterion also examines financial planning and reporting to ensure that there are sound financial procedures in place. The requirements also extend to areas such as managing risks and governance processes at all levels of the organization.

4c   Buildings, equipment and materials are managed

The focus in this sub-criterion is on maximizing the value of all assets and minimizing their effect on the environment. To maximize the value of fixed assets, increasing the total life cycle by careful management and maintenance is advocated, and security of all assets is a key consideration. Preventative action should be taken to minimize the effect of assets on the environment and community, so recycling waste is important. Optimizing the consumption of utilities is another key activity. There is a close link between the way that the assets are managed and the results presented in Criterion 8, Society results.

4d Technology is managed

The application of technology covers how the organization develops and protects technologies, including information technologies, that are the basis of its products, processes and systems, and how it explores related and new technologies that may be of benefit to the business. This includes the use of technology to support improvement. Alternative and emerging technologies should be identified and evaluated according to their impact on the business.

4e Information and knowledge are managed

Information resources are defined as business and technical data and other information in all its forms. The means of making the business information available and accessible to both internal and external users are considered. It should be noted that this sub-criterion not only concerns itself with computer systems. Control of paper-based information systems also needs to be considered.

The way an organization manages its information and knowledge is of paramount importance. The information strategy must support the top-level policy and strategy, and the way in which this is formulated needs to be considered. The validity, integrity, security and scope of the information need to be assured and improved, and appropriate and relevant information needs to be accessible. Management of intellectual property is also considered under this criterion.

Criterion 5: Processes

Excellent organizations design, manage and improve processes in order to fully satisfy, and generate increasing value for, customers and other stakeholders.

For the purposes of this criterion, a process is defined as a sequence of activities that adds value by producing required outputs from a variety of inputs. In any organization a network of processes will exist, all of which need to be managed and improved. Amongst the processes there will be those that are critical to the success of the business. The 1999 revision of the model led to a restructuring of this criterion so that the first two sub-criteria consider how processes are designed and managed, and how they are improved. The next three sub-criteria consider three core activities of any organization: developing products and services, delivering products and services, and managing customer relationships.

5a Processes are systematically designed and managed

The way that all processes are designed, including the key processes that support policy and strategy, is considered within this sub-criterion. This includes identifying the process stake-holders, and managing interface issues inside and external to the organization. These processes go to form the process management system that was covered in sub-criteria 1b and 2d. How system standards such as the ISO standards are applied is also of inter-est, as is the way that process indicators are used and perform-ance targets are set.

5b Processes are improved, as needed, using innovation in order to fully satisfy and generate increasing value for customers and other stakeholders

This sub-criterion is all about improvement, and includes the identification of opportunities for both breakthrough and incre-mental improvement. Such opportunities come about through a variety of sources, including the review of current performance against targets or benchmarks, the discovery of new process designs, and ideas generated from people. The management of process change is also included, providing a close link with sub-criterion 1e, where leaders consider how they lead change.

5c Products and services are designed and developed based on customer needs and expectations

The analysis of market research, customer surveys and other feed-back mechanisms may be used to determine customer needs and expectations, both at the current time and in the future. Based on this information, new products and services may be designed, sometimes with the participation of customers and partners, tak-ing into account the impact of existing or new technology. Use of creativity, innovation and key competencies from both internal people and external partners can lead to competitive products opening up new markets.

5d Products and services are produced, delivered and serviced

Once designed, products and services have to be delivered. This may be though procurement or through the use of the organiza-tion's own resources, such as production activities. Delivery and servicing of products and services is also considered, as is the disposal of products through recycling, if appropriate.

5e   Customer relationships are managed and enhanced

Managing customer relationships is becoming more important. The activities under this sub-criterion include the management of day-to-day contact, as well as the handling of enquiries and complaints. Measurement of customer satisfaction with regard to the delivery of the products and services is also covered here.

The results criteria

The results criteria are concerned with what the organization has achieved and is achieving, and they are split down into two sub-criteria. The results criteria are best summarized by way of a table that shows the main focus areas. This summary is given in Table 5.6.

On reviewing Table 5.6 some observations may be made, and we will return to these when discussing how an organization evaluates itself against the EFQM Excellence Model®. First, the results that are used are highly specific to the organization. The full EFQM criteria listing does give a number of suggestions as to what could be presented as evidence, but it should always be remembered that the criteria should be used in a structural and not a prescriptive manner.

Secondly, there is an important relationship between the 'A' and 'B' sub-criteria. This relationship is explained in Figure 5.4.

The 'A' sub-criteria contain the outcome or lagging measures – outcome measures because they are measures of what the organization wants to achieve as its outcomes, and lagging measures because it takes time before the activities of the organization have an impact on the actual result. Excellent customer satisfaction and people satisfaction are built up over many years, and are normally not changed 'by the flick of a switch'. These measures are normally recorded at low frequency intervals, such as annually or bi-annually.

The 'B' sub-criteria measures are timelier, in that they can be measured on a more regular basis, and they may be used to 'indicate' levels of future outcome performance. They are referred to as 'leading' measures.

The examples in Figure 5.4 reinforce these points. If customer complaints are high, it is likely that future customer satisfaction will be poor. If involvement in the community is high, it is likely that the community's perception of the organization will be good. Note that the approach is used for both the perception-based measures and the key performance outcome measures. If operating costs are kept low, then at the end of the year profitability will be higher.

This completes a brief description of the EFQM Excellence Model®. In the next section we will look at the way in which an

Table 5.6: EFQM Excellence Model® results criteria

Results criterion	Definition	Focus of 'A' sub-criterion	Focus of 'B' sub-criterion
6. Customer results	Excellent organizations measure the perceptions of their external customers and the organization's performance with respect to them	Customer perceptions, such as their perception of the products and services, sale and after sales support, and their intention to remain loyal	Internal measures that predict future levels of satisfaction, such as defect rates, complaints, and duration of relationship
7. People results	Excellent organizations measure the perceptions of their people and the organization's performance with respect to them	Employee perceptions, such as their perception of the level of motivation, quality of communication and general satisfaction	Internal measures that predict future levels of satisfaction, such as sickness levels, grievances and levels of training and development
8. Society results	Excellent organizations measure the perceptions of their society and the organization's performance with respect to them	Society perceptions, such as their perception of the performance of the organization as a responsible citizen, level of involvement in community activities, and its approach towards the environment	Internal measures that predict future levels of satisfaction, such as actual involvement in community activities, levels of waste and cycling, and number of complaints

(continued)

Table 5.6: Continued

Results criterion	Definition	Focus of 'A' sub-criterion	Focus of 'B' sub-criterion
9. Key performance indicators	Excellent organizations measure their performance with respect to the key elements of their policy and strategy	This area looks at the achievements against the objectives outlined in the strategic plan. The actual results will be specific to the organization, but the results are likely to include financial outcomes such as turnover and profitability, and non-financial outcomes such as market share and success rates	This area examines the operational measures that are used to monitor the processes and act as an indicator of the achievement of the outcomes cited in 9A. Again the actual results will be specific to the organization, but are likely to include financial outcomes such as costs and cash flow, and non-financial outcomes such as process performance, partnership performance, asset use, technology use, and information and knowledge use

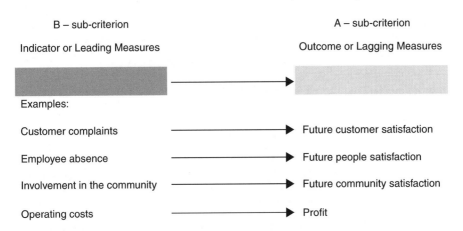

Figure 5.4 Relationship between 'A' and 'B' sub-criteria

organization is evaluated as part of the European Quality Award process.

5.4 The European Quality Award process

Figure 5.5 gives an overview of the award process as it appears to the applicant.

The guidelines for the European Quality Award process and the Application Brochure are published in the October prior to the year in which an application for an award will be made. The application guideline document, which covers all aspects of the Levels of Excellence scheme, is available from the EFQM website.

The application form is also available from the website, and it is important to check the entry criteria at this point as not everyone can apply. For example, the award process is not open to organizations that only have a minority interest in Europe, and nor can voluntary organizations apply at this time. A non-returnable fee of Euro1000 is also payable on completion of the application form.

The EFQM provides the opportunity for potential award applicants to attend a Submission Writing workshop. On reviewing the list of previous winners, it can be seen that several organizations did not win an award at the first attempt. The Submission Writing workshop is designed to ensure that organizations are not disadvantaged due to inexperience with the requirements of the award process.

Each year there is a call for Assessors, who are selected from senior managers, quality professionals and academics from the

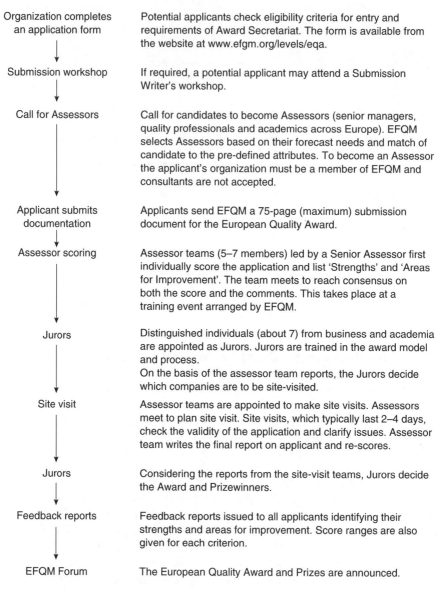

Organization completes an application form	Potential applicants check eligibility criteria for entry and requirements of Award Secretariat. The form is available from the website at www.efgm.org/levels/eqa.
Submission workshop	If required, a potential applicant may attend a Submission Writer's workshop.
Call for Assessors	Call for candidates to become Assessors (senior managers, quality professionals and academics across Europe). EFQM selects Assessors based on their forecast needs and match of candidate to the pre-defined attributes. To become an Assessor the applicant's organization must be a member of EFQM and consultants are not accepted.
Applicant submits documentation	Applicants send EFQM a 75-page (maximum) submission document for the European Quality Award.
Assessor scoring	Assessor teams (5–7 members) led by a Senior Assessor first individually score the application and list 'Strengths' and 'Areas for Improvement'. The team meets to reach consensus on both the score and the comments. This takes place at a training event arranged by EFQM.
Jurors	Distinguished individuals (about 7) from business and academia are appointed as Jurors. Jurors are trained in the award model and process. On the basis of the assessor team reports, the Jurors decide which companies are to be site-visited.
Site visit	Assessor teams are appointed to make site visits. Assessors meet to plan site visit. Site visits, which typically last 2–4 days, check the validity of the application and clarify issues. Assessor team writes the final report on applicant and re-scores.
Jurors	Considering the reports from the site-visit teams, Jurors decide the Award and Prizewinners.
Feedback reports	Feedback reports issued to all applicants identifying their strengths and areas for improvement. Score ranges are also given for each criterion.
EFQM Forum	The European Quality Award and Prizes are announced.

Figure 5.5 European Award process

EFQM member organizations. The award organizers try to ensure that there is a balanced representation from countries across Europe and from different industry sectors, and that Assessors with various levels of experience are included. Assessors must work for organizations that are EFQM members and, to maintain independence, external consultants are not selected to act as assessors.

In the past, all Assessors attended a three-day training programme that required them to complete a pre-course 12–16-hour case study before attending training. The programme itself was aimed at training individuals so that they could serve in any assessment team and be 'calibrated' against each other. In more recent times, as the level of experience has increased, the need to put busy Assessors through a case study every year has become of less value. As a consequence, the Assessor training process has been split into two stages, with Stage 1 covering the basic Assessor training and Stage 2 concentrating on the assessment process itself. Only first-time Assessors attend the Stage 1 training, unless an Assessor feels that he or she would benefit from attending Stage 1 again, or the Senior Assessor recommends re-attendance. The EFQM publishes an overview of the desirable requirements for Assessors, which include skills, availability, and the ability to meet their own costs in the early part of the process.

Before meeting for the first time at a Stage 2 training event, Assessors are allocated to teams and asked to work on an actual application. The focus of the training has become one of support, and the team is developed during the training week as it meets for the first time, reaches consensus and plans for its site visit.

Application for the award requires a submission of up to 75 pages addressing the criteria of the EFQM Excellence Model®. The EFQM has made available case studies that help applicants with the preparation of their self-assessment, and the preparation of the submission is similar to that of the Baldrige Award described in Chapter 4. It is not unusual to take about six months to prepare the submission, which has some specific requirements. Chapter 12 gives some advice on how to complete this task effectively and efficiently.

When the submission is sent to the EFQM for assessment, the second stage of the application fee must be paid. This varies from Euro3000 for an independent SME or small public sector organization to Euro11 000 for a large organization or operation unit with over 1000 employees.

On receipt of the applications, the submission documents are subject to confirmation that there are no conflicts of interest and are assigned to an assessor team for individual scoring. Each team consists of between five and seven members, with an appointed Senior Assessor to lead the team. Unlike the Baldrige award described in Chapter 4, all applications for the European Quality Award go through a consensus process where the team meets to agree on common 'strengths', 'area for improvement' and 'site-visit issues'. This now takes place as part of the assessor training workshop. The way the team evaluates the self-submission against the European Model will be described in greater detail in Chapter 9.

The Jurors, who are a team of around seven distinguished individuals, review all of the applications to decide the ones that will be site-visited for the purpose of deciding upon an award or prize. The site visits take typically two to four days, during which the application is validated and the points identified as 'site-visit issues' during the initial stages of the evaluation are clarified. Sometimes, owing to other commitments, the site-visit team members are different to the ones that evaluated the original application. This does not present any problems, and can actually add value to the process.

If the applicant is selected as a finalist, it can still receive a site visit under the 'Levels of Excellence' scheme. Provided the organization has requested the visit during the application and has scored over 350 points, a site visit will be conducted. If the final score after the site visit is above a fixed threshold score, the jury has the power to award a 'Recognized for Excellence' certificate.

After the site visit, the assessment team reviews their feedback and re-scores the application. The Jurors decide the Award and Prize winners after considering the site-visit report and amended scores. The winners are announced at the annual EFQM forum.

The last stage in the process is when all applicants, including the winners, receive a feedback report written by the assessment team. These feedback reports are a re-write of the original

Table 5.7: Timetable for the European Quality Award process

Event	Timescale
Application form and Levels of Excellence available from the EFQM website	October
Submission Writers' workshop	November
Call for Assessors	November
Closing date for receipt of application form	December
Closing date for receipt of submission	March
Initial assessment of applications during assessor training	April and May
Site visits take place	June
Last feedback reports to applicants	July
Award presentation	October

consensus report, updated to take into account feedback from the site visit (if conducted). They contain the assessment team's view of the applicant's 'strengths' and 'areas for improvement'. Score ranges are also given for each criterion.

Table 5.7 gives approximate timescales for the award process.

5.5 Evaluation against the EFQM Excellence Model®

Figure 5.6 outlines the European Quality Award assessment process. The key steps in this process – individual assessment,

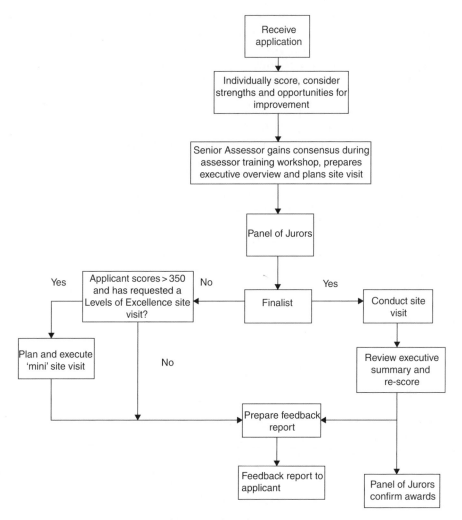

Figure 5.6 European Quality Award evaluation process

consensus, site visit and feedback – are all considered in detail in Chapter 9.

Individual Assessors go through the submission noting any 'strengths' or 'areas for improvement' in their 'Scorebook' against particular sub-criteria. Where some points need clarification, they will be listed as 'site-visit issues'.

The individual assessments based on strengths and areas for improvement are subsequently refined during the consensus process involving an assessor team. The team or consensus view is the basis of the feedback report, which will be further refined if the application goes to a site visit. It is widely acknowledged that a site visit may not make a huge difference to the score, but it will make a significant difference to the quality and accuracy of the feedback.

The scoring system for the European Quality Award is somewhat different to that of the Baldrige Award. The original 'Blue Card' scoring system that was based on Baldrige was radically changed as part of the model review in 1999. This led to the RADAR® scoring system, which is a developed form of 'Plan–Do–Check–Act'.

In assessing an application, the enablers and results are assessed using a matrix on a 0–100 per cent scale, but the elements examined vary, with Approach, Deployment, and Assessment and review being used for the enablers, and Results for the results. Like the detail of the EFQM Excellence Model®, the details of the RADAR® scoring system are protected by copyright. RADAR® consists of four elements, the explanation of which are given in Table 5.8.

Several authors have noted that the RADAR® logic may be applied to more than just the purpose of self-assessment. For example, the EFQM suggests that it can be used to develop a management system, and in BQF's *The Model in Practice*, RADAR® is used to drive change in an organization.

5.6 How the EFQM Excellence Model® has evolved

In its short life since 1992 the EFQM Excellence Model® has undergone some major revisions. The first major revision took place in 1995, when the 'Results' criteria were each split down into two sub-criteria and each part given appropriate weighting.

The next major change took place in 1999, when the model was completely overhauled and the RADAR® logic was introduced.

Table 5.8: EFQM RADAR® logic

Element	Explanation	Applied to	Components of the RADAR® scoring system
The logic states that an organization needs to:			
Results	Determine the Results it is aiming for as part of its policy- and strategy-making process. These Results cover the performance of the organization, both financially and operationally, and the perceptions of its stakeholder	Results	The Excellence of the Results is considered alongside the scope of the Results. To evaluate the Excellence, the trend performance, performance against own targets and performance against any external data are evaluated. Whether the Results are caused by the Approaches is also considered. For scope, the Results must address relevant areas of performance and be available where expected, for example, for all products and/or customers
Approach	Plan and develop an integrated set of sound Approaches to deliver the required Results both now and in the future	Enablers	The Approach must have a clear rationale and process, which focuses on stakeholder needs. It should also support policy and strategy and be aligned to other Approaches

(continued)

Table 5.8: *Continued*

Element	Explanation	Applied to	Components of the RADAR® scoring system
Deployment	Deploy the Approaches in a systematic way to ensure full implementation	Enablers	The Approach should be implemented where relevant across and to all levels of the organization. It should also be deployed in a structured way
Assessment and review	Assess and review the Approaches followed, based on monitoring and analysis of the results achieved and ongoing learning activities	Enablers	There are three components to Assessment and review: first, the effectiveness and efficiency of the deployed Approaches should be evaluated; secondly, account should be taken of what others are doing through learning; finally, the measurement and learning should lead to improvement

This version saw changes at the criteria level, where Partnerships were added to Resources, and three Results areas were changed from 'Satisfaction' to 'Results'. The emphasis on the leading and lagging measures was also strengthened.

The most recent change was in 2003, when there was some revision at the sub-criterion level. The most significant change at this time was the review of the eight fundamental concepts, which, although they remain essentially the same, were given some additional explanation.

As the team at EFQM are committed to continuous improvement, the model is likely to see further change. At the time of writing, a fundamental change is planned for 2004.

5.7 Summary

In this chapter we have examined the EFQM Excellence Model®. Although the award process was only launched in 1991, with the first winners being announced in 1992, it has already started to gain a substantial following among European companies. Its main asset is its focus on key performance outcomes as a key deliverable from an Excellence approach.

The framework behind the model has both strengths and weaknesses. On one hand it has the advantage of having been established on the basis of two existing total quality frameworks – the Malcolm Baldrige Award and the Deming Prize. As such, it has learned from the operation of both these processes. On the other hand, it is disadvantaged in that there is insufficient history at this time to show that it is a rigorous model for business effectiveness. To date, there is only limited empirical evidence to support the benefit from its use.

The next chapter considers the Deming Prize. This has significant historical importance, as it was the first award of its kind.

Reference

ECforBE (2000, 2002) *The Model in Practice.* London: British Quality Foundation.

The Deming Prize

6.1 Introduction

The Japanese Deming Prize is significant for several reasons. Its introduction launched the practice of self-assessment, and the concepts of scoring and site visits in an award process were developed. This has ultimately led to the process by which both the more recent Malcolm Baldrige and European Quality Awards are operated.

It is generally difficult to get information about the Deming Prize in the Western world. As most of the documentation surrounding the award is written in Japanese, and little has been translated into English, there is a general lack of information in the normal quality literature. Even part of the award application for English-speaking nations must be in Japanese! The most useful source of information comes from the publication *The Deming Prize Guide For Overseas Companies*, which is the primary source for this chapter. The Union of Japanese Scientists and Engineers publish the guide. Use has also been made of material found on the worldwide web.

This situation is not helped by the attitude of Dr Deming himself. Whilst Dr Deming was very honoured by the dedication of the Deming Prize, he did not play an active role in either its creation or its administration. The late Mr Kenichi Koyanagi, who in 1951 was the managing director of the Union of Japanese Scientists and Engineers (JUSE), established it following a proposal. Dr Deming's main connection (apart from the name) comes from his early sponsorship, as he donated the royalties from one of his books, *Some Theory of Sampling*, and from other works published in Japan, such as *Elementary Principles of the Statistical Control of Quality*, to form the Deming Prize fund. The Prize is now completely funded by JUSE.

Dr Deming did not generally support quality awards. He felt that quality awards create winners and losers, and that the achievement of an award can be seen as some sort of end-point. Dr Deming clearly saw continuous improvement as being an endless process. These views have led the societies who follow his work, such as the now sadly defunct British Deming Association, to dissociate themselves from the prizes and not promote them in any way, even for self-assessment purposes. This is an interesting reaction, given the emphasis the Japanese place on *shindin*, or QC-diagnosis.

The philosophy of Deming is the key feature to the prize. The approach promotes self-discovery in a company so that continuous improvement processes are embedded and will survive even if there is a change of leadership. Senior executive leadership is important for any quality initiative to succeed. Imagine the breakthrough point beyond which even poor leadership cannot stop progress! This is the point that the Deming framework aims for.

6.2 Background to the Deming Prize

The quality movement started in Japan in 1946 through the birth of the Union of Japanese Scientists and Engineers (JUSE). In 1949, the Quality Control Research Group in JUSE was formed to give lectures and education on the principles of quality control both in the JUSE and the Japanese Standards Association (JSA). In 1950, Dr W. Edwards Deming was invited by JUSE to give seminars on statistical process control. Deming is now seen as the father of the worldwide quality movement, and was the pre-eminent quality guru until his death in 1993. His impact on Japanese industry is legendary and all too evident, and his philosophies continue to have a major impact in most developed economies.

In 1951 the Deming Prize was instituted in honour of W. Edwards Deming, and the Deming Prize Committee was formed. The first prizes were given in 1951 to four Japanese companies. Over the last four decades the award process has undergone significant evolution, details of which are shown in Table 6.1.

The prize now has three award categories:

- The Deming Prize for Individuals
- The Deming Application Prize
- The Quality Control Award for Factories.

Table 6.1: Evolution of the Deming Prize

Date	Event
1951	On 22 September, the first Prizes were awarded at a ceremony at the Osaka Chamber of Commerce and Industry
1957	The Deming Application Prize for small companies was created
1965	The Deming Application Prize for Divisions was created
1970	The Japanese Quality Control Medal was introduced for companies who had won the Deming Prize five years previously
1972	A system of honouring a single establishment or place of business via the Deming Factory Prize was adopted
1974	The Deming Prize for Individuals was introduced
1984	The Deming Application Prize became an international award, and overseas companies could apply for it
1994	The Deming Prize criteria were refined
1995	The Application Prize categories were abolished

The *Deming Prize for Individuals* is awarded to individuals who have conducted excellent research in the theory or application of statistical techniques, or who have made remarkable contributions to the dissemination of statistical control methods. Past winners include Ishikawa, who is famed for the development of the 'Fishbone' diagram cause-and-effect problem-solving technique.

The *Deming Application Prize* is awarded to organizations that have achieved distinctive performance improvement through the application of company-wide quality control. It is the only Deming Prize that is available outside of Japan. Prior to 1995 the Deming Application Prize had four categories, each introduced at different times:

- The Deming Application Prize for Organizations
- The Deming Application Prize for Divisions
- The Deming Application Prize for Small Companies
- The Deming Application Prize for Overseas Companies.

Since 1995 these categories have been discontinued, but the award is still applicable to small companies, overseas companies, and divisions, as well as Japanese organizations.

The *Deming Factory Prize* is awarded to factories or plants that have achieved distinctive performance improvement through the application of quality control/management in the pursuit of company-wide quality control. The Deming Factory Prize introduced a system of honouring a single establishment or place of business.

Table 6.2 shows the numbers of prizes given between 1951 and 1999. Since the introduction of the applicability of overseas companies for the Deming Application Prize, only three overseas companies have won. These were Florida Power and Light (USA) in 1989, Philips Taiwan Ltd in 1991, and AT&T Power Systems in 1994. As an example of the effort required, AT&T Power Systems worked for four years and spent $250 000 to win the Deming Prize. In addition, Florida Power and Light's application has been reported as being approximately 1000 pages long.

Winners of the Deming Prize are given the chance to apply for the Japan Quality Medal every five years. This award was created to commemorate the world's first International Conference on Quality Control, which was held in 1969 in Tokyo. Its purpose is to upgrade the level of company-wide quality control of the Deming Prize recipients.

Applications for the medal are accepted only when the applicant company has been awarded the Deming Prize more than five years previously. The examination is carried out on the implementation of company-wide quality control subsequent to winning the original prize, reinforcing the fact that the quest for quality improvement does not stop and the journey for continuous learning

Table 6.2: Numbers of Deming Prize winners 1951–1999

Deming Prize type	*Number of recipients 1951–1999*
Individual Prizes	62 prizes awarded since the prizes' introduction in 1974
Application Prizes	*Company (1951–1994):* 88 prizes awarded
	Small Company (1957–1994): 36 prizes awarded
	Division of a Company (1965–1994): 5 prizes awarded
	Overseas (1984–1994): 3 prizes awarded
	All categories (1995–1999): 20 prizes awarded
Factory Prizes	17 prizes awarded

continues. The method of judging the award is the same as for the Deming Application Prize, and during the period 1969 to 1999 only fifteen organizations were honoured in this way. The last recipient of the Japan Quality Medal was Philips Taiwan in 1997, which is the only overseas organization ever to win the award.

The Deming Prize Committee was established as a requirement of the Deming Prize Regulations. This committee, which is chaired by the Chairperson of JUSE or by another person recommended by the JUSE board, consists of members from the field of quality control who are academicians or officials of organizations. The Deming Prize Committee oversees the examination process and awards the Deming Prizes. Five sub-committees have been established to carry out the examinations and related activities.

6.3 The Deming Prize framework

The remainder of this chapter focuses on the 1994 version of the Deming Application Prize, which is the prize that is applicable outside Japan and is the one that has greatest relevance to a discussion of business improvement. From here on, the 'Deming Application Prize' will be referred to as the 'Deming Prize'.

The Deming Prize was originally established to ensure that improved performance is achieved through the successful implementation of company-wide quality control activities. It is interesting to consider JUSE's definition of company-wide quality control:

> *CWQC is a system of activities to assure that quality products and services required by customers are economically designed, produced and supplied while respecting the principle of customer-orientation and the overall public well-being. These quality assurance activities involve market research, research and development, design, purchasing, production, inspection and sales, as well as other related activities inside and outside the company. Through everyone in the company understanding both the statistical concepts and methods, through their application to all the aspects of quality assurance and through the repeating cycle of rational planning, implementation, evaluation and action, CWQC aims to accomplish business objectives.*

This definition will come as a surprise to people who consider that the Deming Prize is just based on the application of statistical techniques to manufacturing processes. Whereas the Baldrige Award and European Quality Award take a much deeper look at customer satisfaction and service quality as excellence criteria, there is no doubt that some of these principles are embedded in the Deming framework. The most recent (1994) version of the framework has a significant change of language away from 'quality control' to 'total quality management'. It also introduces some of the features of the Baldrige and EFQM frameworks, such as corporate social responsibility.

It is true, however, that the main strengths of the Deming Prize criteria are the focus they have on top management leadership, process control, *Kaizen* improvement activities and on future planning to ensure that the gains will be sustained. *Kaizen* is a philosophy of continuous improvement of all the organization's employees, so that they can make an incremental contribution to continuous improvement each day.

The framework looks specifically at the role and effectiveness of the senior management team. The term 'control' in Japanese implies management, and hence 'Japanese' quality control really means quality management. In the Western world we have a different perception of the term 'quality control'.

The purpose of the award, as first defined by JUSE, is:

> *To award prizes to those companies that are recognized as having successfully applied Company-wide Quality Control based on statistical control and are likely to keep it up in the future.*

Consequently, criteria such as company policy and planning, results and future plans are primarily concerned with quality assurance activities and quality results, especially the elimination of defects.

The Deming Prize's framework actually consists of two frameworks or 'viewpoints'. The first is centred on the implementation of a set of principles and techniques, many of which may be found in the other frameworks in this book. It seeks to evaluate the organization against ten criteria, and a full list of these criteria is shown in Table 6.3.

The second framework seeks to evaluate the role of senior executives within an organization. It does this by looking for evidence across five criteria. A full list of the criteria, together with a list of points to check and relevant remarks, is included in Table 6.4.

The viewpoints can be simplified into the framework illustrated in Figure 6.1. The framework, which covers the role of both the senior executives and the organization, has been broken down into ten areas for simplicity. First, the corporate policy process that sets the direction is examined. This is followed by the support activities, such as the organization, information management and people management. Implementation consists of the quality assurance activities, maintenance/control activities and improvement activities. The results obtained follow implementation, and finally planning for the future is examined.

Table 6.3: Deming examination viewpoints

Viewpoint	Sub-components
1 Top management leadership, vision, strategies	*1.1 Top management leadership.* Recognizing its roles (sense of mission, responsibilities, authorities, ethics, etc.), top management leads the organization for effective utilization of management resources and achievement of business plans
	1.2 Organizational vision and strategies. Management principles, vision, and strategies, which are based on the organizational mission, are clearly defined. A management structure is in place to respond quickly to the changes in business environment and to involve employees in working together for achieving business objectives. (Top management is involved in establishing management principles, vision, and strategies; and exercises its leadership in developing the management structure for materializing these principles, vision, and strategies)
2 TQM frameworks	*2.1 Organizational structure and its operations.* The consistency between business management systems and the organizational structure is well thought out. The interdepartmental activities are well coordinated. Meetings and committees are operating efficiently and effectively
	2.2 Daily management. Operational accountabilities are clearly established, and management resources are properly allocated for carrying out the operations. Standardization is recognized for its importance and is carried out efficiently and effectively. Through maintaining and improving standards, favourable results are achieved
	2.3 Policy management. There is a well-developed management system that covers from establishing, deploying, and implementing policies to evaluating

the achievement of business objectives. Together with top management diagnosis and other activities, the management system is contributing to the company's business performance. In the case where its objectives are not achieved, the cause analysis on these objectives is properly carried out. The system is well coordinated, with cross-functional management systems

2.4 Relationship to ISO9000 and ISO14000. When ISO9000 and ISO14000 are implemented, the consistency between TQM and these systems is assured and executed

2.5 Relationship to the other management improvement programmes. When TPM, JIT, and the other management improvement programmes are implemented, the consistency between TQM and these systems is assured and executed

2.6 TQM promotion and operation. The objectives of TQM introduction and promotion are clearly communicated to and understood by employees. According to the structure and the master plan in place for TQM promotion, improvement efforts are made to remove obstacles and to achieve the objectives. (The company understands that TQM is a long-lasting activity, not a temporary programme. It has a clear direction for how TQM should be promoted)

3 Quality assurance system

3.1 Quality assurance system. Understanding the complexity and diversity of quality assurance, an integrated quality assurance system is established and properly managed. The status of quality assurance is grasped with indicators such as customer satisfaction. (The key is that necessary activities to improve customer satisfaction are well coordinated and implemented under an integrated system)

3.2 New product and new technology development. Effectively using tools such as quality analysis, quality function deployment, and design review, the company is active in developing new product and new technologies. Through these activities, the company improves customer satisfaction and business

(*continued*)

Table 6.3: Continued

Viewpoint	Sub-components
	performance. (It is important that the company's efforts to develop new products and new technologies are constant and active, its use of the concepts and tools is appropriate, and the development activities are producing favourable results)
	3.3 Process control. Process analysis and improvement is actively carried out. Understanding their importance, processes are controlled properly. (Not only manufacturing, but also administration and service functions implement active process analysis, improvement, and control)
	3.4 Test, quality evaluation, and quality audits. Quality evaluation and quality audits are conducted properly. Quality assurance, which is based on tests, is carried out effectively and efficiently. Reliability, safety, and product liability are taken into consideration
	3.5 Activities covering the whole life cycle. At each stage of the life cycle of products and services, necessary activities are carried out properly. (The company carries out necessary quality assurance activities covering the whole life cycle from market survey, planning, development, designing, engineering, production, purchasing, procurement, sales, and to after-sales services)
	3.6 Purchasing, subcontracting, and distribution management. From a global perspective, the management system for purchasing, subcontracting, and distribution provides technological support and cooperation to necessary parties. (The company carries out its purchasing, subcontracting, and distributing activities in an organized global manner, including doing these activities overseas from a viewpoint of internationalization)

4 Management systems for business elements

4.1 Cross-functional management and its operations. Cross-functional elements for management are properly selected. For the selected cross-functional management systems, their meeting structures, committees, and executives in charge are clearly defined. The cross-management systems are well coordinated with the other management systems and operating smoothly. (The elements selected for cross-functional management systems are appropriate. To effectively operate the systems, their implementation structures are established. These cross-functional management systems are carried out consistently with policy management, business plans, and other management systems)

4.2 Quantity/delivery management. A system to manage the quantity/delivery of products and services is established. Using appropriate indicators, the company manages effectively its production progress, inventories, lead-time, etc. (Through an appropriately established management system for quantity/delivery of products and services, the company shortens the time required from planning to delivery and, as a result, improves customer satisfaction)

4.3 Cost management. A cost management system, which begins with cost planning, is established. The system provides a structure to produce products while balancing costs with quality. Using appropriate tools, the company carries out cost reduction activities effectively. (The established cost management system, which takes procurement from overseas into consideration, is used effectively and promotes active cost reduction activities)

4.4 Environmental management. An environmental management system is established. Considering the effects of the company's operations on its communities and environment, it actively addresses the issues such as ISO14000, LCA (life cycle assessment), and eco-marks. (Recognizing the

(continued)

Table 6.3: Continued

Viewpoint	Sub-components
	importance of the global environment, the company addresses the environmental issues and problems enthusiastically)
	4.5 *Safety, hygiene, and work environment management.* Employees' safety and hygiene are managed properly in the workplace. Safety education is conducted in a planned manner. (From a viewpoint of employee satisfaction, the company addresses actively the issues of employee safety, hygiene, and work environment)
5 *Human resources development*	5.1 *Positioning of 'people' in management.* Recognizing 'people' as the most important management resources, the company promotes each individual employee's self-actualization through putting the right person in the right post
	5.2 *Education and training.* To improve each individual employee's abilities, a system for education and training is established. The company's technological expertise is passed down efficiently from one generation to the next. The company gives consideration to providing assistance and support to its affiliated companies' needs for education and training
	5.3 *Respect for people's dignity.* Employees exhibit their autonomy and creativity fully, demonstrate their high morale and enthusiasm, participate in group activities such as QC circles, and produce good results
6 *Effective utilization of information*	6.1 *Positioning of 'information' in management.* A system for collecting, analysing, and utilizing information regarding the company's business and business environment is established. By sharing information, the company manages its operations efficiently and effectively. (Recognizing information as

an important management resource, the company utilizes information effectively, including digging out potential information, for its business management)

6.2 Information systems. Effectively utilizing information technologies, the company has an established information system, which effectively manages important databases on quality technologies, customers, and others. (The company has a systematic approach to its efforts to bringing the state of art technologies into its management, and establishing and operating necessary databases)

6.3 Support for analysis and decision-making. Techniques and tools for information analysis are utilized effectively. Computer systems are also utilized effectively for management functions and operations. Thus, a system for logical decision-making is established. (The effective use of techniques and tools includes both quantitative and qualitative information analysis. The structure in place allows the company to make decisions speedily and to produce favourable business results)

6.4 Standardization and configuration management. A coding system for parts and other items as well as an overall database are established. For changes and renovations, configuration management is carried out properly. (Documentation needs to be computerized as much as possible so as to improve learning efficiency through information sharing and to manage changes and renovations properly)

7.1 Quality. Understanding the importance of quality in management, the company shares its understandings throughout its organization as well as to the outside. The company carries out activities to improve customer satisfaction

7 *TQM concepts and values*

(continued)

Table 6.3: Continued

Viewpoint	Sub-components
	7.2 Maintenance and improvement. The company respects the facts, regards its processes as important, and understands the significance of rotating the PDCA cycle. Based on the concepts of prevention and prediction, upstream management is practised to achieve good results. Understanding the importance of improvement, standardization and breakthrough activities are carried out effectively
	7.3 Respect for humanity. Understanding the significance of TQM that requires every employee's participation, the well-organized workplace environment promotes employees' self-actualization through self-development and mutual development by learning from each other
8 Scientific methods	*8.1 Understanding and utilization of methods.* To achieve objectives, appropriate methods are used effectively. The use of these methods contributes to technological improvement and the development of new methods. (The use of methods includes not only statistical methods but also other methods suitable for specific problems. It is important that the use of these methods contributes to the improvement and the accumulation of technologies, skills, and know-how related to the problems. If necessary, the company should develop new methods and new applications of the existing methods)
	8.2 Understanding and utilization of problem-solving methods. Recognizing the importance of solving problems scientifically, the company uses analytical problem-solving methods (QC story) and design-orientated problem-solving methods (quality function deployment, QC story for achieving tasks, etc.). The use of these methods contributes to achieving the results. (To solve problems,

the company should effectively use not only QC story but also other methods such as system analysis and design technique

9 Organizational powers
(core technology, speed, vitality)

9.1 Core technology. Recognizing its core competencies (core competitive advantages) including core technology, the company has clearly defined strategies for technologies. It also has an established system for managing patents and intellectual ownership. (Based on the understanding of what makes up the core competencies for the company, its strategies are established and materialized)

9.2 Speed. The company's decision-making process is clear and speedy. A network system for business management is established, and it allows the organization to respond to changes as they come. (Amidst the highly competitive era, the company understands the importance of speedy decision-making, and has an established system for coping with this requirement of speed)

9.3 Vitality. Executives and managers are full of entrepreneur and venture spirit. Employees show high morale and enthusiasm for challenging any initiatives. (All members of the organization work toward self-actualization through carrying out their jobs with enthusiasm)

10 Contribution to realization of corporate objectives

10.1 Customer relations. Measures are taken to establish, maintain, and enhance favourable customer relations. These measures result in improving customer satisfaction

10.2 Employee relations. Work environment and conditions for employees are well established, and safety and hygiene consideration is evident. Both the retention rate and the morale of employees are high. Employee satisfaction has an improving trend

(continued)

Table 6.3: Continued

Viewpoint	Sub-components
	10.3 Social relations. As a good corporate citizen, the company maintains its management transparency and fairness. Its concerns for coexistence with local communities, contribution to society, and environmental issues are well thought out and carried out to achieve favourable results
	10.4 Supplier relations. Having a friendly rivalry with its suppliers, the company strives for coexistence and co-prosperity through fair trade with them
	10.5 Shareholder relations. From a long-term perspective, the company secures profits consistently, pays a fair dividend to shareholders, and maintains a reasonable stock price
	10.6 Realization of corporate mission. Understanding the organizational mission correctly, the company has an established structure to achieve the mission in a planned manner. It properly evaluates the achievement level of the mission and makes itself an organization of high quality and with respectable presence
	10.7 Continuously securing profits. From a long-term perspective, the company secures reasonable profits. Through promoting TQM, the company improves its total organizational power, and thus possesses the capabilities to continuously produce profits

Source: Deming Prize Criteria (2000)© JUSE. Used with kind permission

Table 6.4: Deming examination viewpoints for senior executives

Viewpoint	Details
1 *TQM understanding and enthusiasm*	1. Demonstrate enthusiasm for TQM promotion, and take a strong leadership
	2. Understand both the effectiveness and the limitations of TQM, and provide appropriate promotion and support for TQM
	3. Clearly define and realize the objectives of TQM introduction and promotion
	4. Clearly understand the relationship between TQM and the other management activities and methods
	5. Fully understand the status and the features of their company's quality and TQM
2 *Top management leadership, vision, strategies, and policies*	6. Accurately understand and exercise the top management roles in TQM
	7. In anticipating changes in business environment and progress in science and technology, strive to cope with these predictions
	8. Grasp the changes of customer requirements, and aim to respond to these changes
	9. Establish sound quality and TQM policies, and position them appropriately in the total framework of business management
	10. Aim to utilize TQM effectively for future plans
	11. Assure the continuity of TQM practices into the future
3 *Organizational powers (core technology, speed, vitality)*	12. Clearly understand what core technologies are the source of competitive advantages and what roles TQM should play to uplift the level of these core technologies

(*continued*)

Table 6.4: *Continued*

Viewpoint	Details
	13. Take proper actions to improve the speed of development and decision-making, and clearly understand the roles of TQM for these actions
	14. Precisely understand what senior executives must do to strengthen the organizational powers and how it relates to TQM
	15. Have a well-thought-out evaluation system for measuring the improvement of the organizational powers
	16. Consider and incorporate the relations with the affiliated companies into the improvement of the organizational powers
4 Human resources development	17. Have a clear philosophy for hiring, developing, and utilizing human resources
	18. Provide employees with education and training in a planned manner, and secure the necessary funds and time for education and training
	19. Adequately communicate the policies for TQM education and training to the organization, and grasp its implementation status
	20. Adequately communicate the policies for specialized education and training, which correspond to their future plans, to the organization, and grasp its implementation status
	21. Understand and develop QC circles and other activities
5 Corporate social responsibilities	22. Strive to build a structure that secures reasonable profits long-term
	23. Think out employees' wellbeing (wage levels and working hours), and encourage them for their self-actualization

Table 6.4: *Continued*

Viewpoint	Details
	24. Accurately grasp the relations with the affiliated companies, and strive to improve the relations
	25. Clearly understand the company's contribution to society and to the environment as well as its social relations, and aim to build sound relations
	26. Accurately grasp the company's stockholder relations, and strive to build sound relations

Source: *Deming Prize Criteria (2000)*© JUSE. Used with kind permission

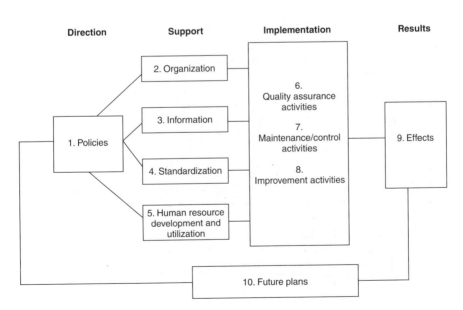

Figure 6.1 A simplified Deming Prize framework

The following simplified checklist is indicative of the range of activities addressed in Japan under the TQ banner.

Deming Prize checklist:

1. Policies
   - Quality and quality control policies and their place in overall business management
   - Clarity of policies (targets and priority measures)
   - Methods and processes for establishing policies
   - Relationship of policies to long- and short-term plans
   - Communication (deployment) of policies, and grasp and management of achieving policies
   - Executives' and managers' leadership.
2. Organization
   - Appropriateness of the organizational structure for quality control and status of employee involvement
   - Clarity of authority and responsibility
   - Status of interdepartmental coordination
   - Status of committee and project team activities
   - Status of staff activities
   - Relationships with associated companies (group companies, vendors, contractors, sales companies, etc.).
3. Information
   - Appropriateness of collecting and communicating external information
   - Appropriateness of collecting and communicating internal information
   - Status of applying statistical techniques to data analysis
   - Appropriateness of information retention
   - Status of utilizing information
   - Status of utilizing computers for data processing.
4. Standardization
   - Appropriateness of the system of standards
   - Procedures for establishing, revising and abolishing standards
   - Actual performance in establishing, revising and abolishing standards
   - Content of standards
   - Status of utilizing and adhering to standards
   - Status of systematically developing, accumulating, handling down and utilizing technologies.
5. Human resources development and utilization
   - Education and training plans and their results
   - Status of quality consciousness, consciousness of managing jobs, and understanding of quality control

- Status of supporting and motivating self-development and self-realization
- Status of understanding and utilizing statistical concepts and methods
- Status of QC circle development and improvement suggestions
- Status of supporting the development of human resources in associated companies.

6. Quality assurance activities
   - Status of managing the quality assurance system
   - Status of quality control diagnosis
   - Status of new product and technology development (including quality analysis, quality deployment and design review activities)
   - Status of process control
   - Status of process analysis and process improvement (including process capability studies)
   - Status of inspection, quality evaluation and quality audit
   - Status of managing production equipment, measuring instruments and vendors
   - Status of packing, storage, transportation, sales and service activities
   - Grasping and responding to product usage, disposal, recovery and recycling
   - Status of quality assurance
   - Grasping of the status of customer satisfaction
   - Status of assuring reliability, safety, product liability and environmental protection.

7. Maintenance/control activities
   - Rotation of management (PDCA) cycle
   - Methods for determining control items and their levels
   - In-control situations (status of utilizing control charts and other tools)
   - Status of taking temporary and permanent measures
   - Status of operating management systems for cost, quantity, delivery, etc.
   - Relationship of quality assurance system to other operating management systems.

8. Improvement activities
   - Methods of selecting themes (important problems and priority issues)
   - Linkage of analytical methods and intrinsic technology
   - Status of utilizing statistical methods for analysis
   - Utilization of analysis results
   - Status of confirming improvement results and transferring them to maintenance/control activities
   - Contribution of QC circle activities.

9. Effects
   - Tangible effects (such as quality, delivery, cost, profit, safety and environment)
   - Intangible effects
   - Methods for measuring and grasping effects
   - Customer satisfaction and employee satisfaction
   - Influence on associated companies
   - Influence on local and international communities.
10. Future plans
   - Status of grasping current situations
   - Future plans for improving problems
   - Projection of changes in social environment and customer requirements, and future plans based on these projected changes
   - Relationships among management philosophy, vision and long-term plans
   - Continuity of quality control activities
   - Concreteness of future plans.

6.4 Evaluation against the framework – the role of the QC-diagnosis

For any framework to be of value in business improvement, an organization must be able to evaluate itself against the criteria so that it can obtain feedback on which to base improvement actions. Using the Deming criteria outside the award process suffers from the drawback that not much is known about the evaluation process outside of JUSE.

On examining the actual Deming framework (see Table 6.3), it can be seen that evaluation of some of the criteria parts is subjective. For example, it is difficult to imagine how 'consistency between business management systems and the organizational structure are *well thought out*' could be objectively and consistently evaluated. The 1994 version of the framework is better in this area than the previous version, as this had items such as '*invisible effects*'. It is likely, however, that something had been lost in the translation.

Applying different weightings to the different criteria, which is the situation in both the Baldrige and the European Quality Award frameworks, does not complicate evaluation against the framework. However, the application and interpretation of the Deming Prize criteria by JUSE examiners have been described as 'highly qualified and sophisticated'. For instance, the guidelines for judges include consideration of aspects such as cost, productivity, delivery, safety and environment. The examiners are typically university professors with areas of expertise in quality management, and they have often spent their entire careers studying and improving quality and the management systems of companies with whom they have worked.

JUSE offers some advice to companies wishing to apply for the Deming Prize, noting that:

- The emphasis of the examination is on finding out how effectively the applicant company or division is implementing TQM by focusing on the quality of its products and services within the scope of its own business.
- TQM practices that only concentrate on format, or that establish unnecessary regulations and standards, are not favourably considered.
- A successful applicant is not necessarily one that uses advanced statistical methods. Even if a company is small or performs small-lot/large-variety production, it is still a qualified candidate for the Prize if it practises TQM and achieves good results with an organization-wide understanding of the statistical way of thinking.
- The examination in the non-production areas and at a non-manufacturing company will follow a pattern similar to that of the production department. For example, an examination will be performed to see if the respective department's role is clearly identified in assuring the quality of products and services.

Work published outside Japan indicates that the West has misunderstood the approach taken by the Japanese to evaluate their progress towards total quality control. The Japanese use a technique referred to as QC-diagnosis, or *shindan*. *Shindan* is sometimes translated into English as 'QC-audit'. Although some of the principles and objectives are similar to an audit approach, QC-diagnosis is a different concept. The Deming Committee examination is a form of QC-diagnosis.

QC-diagnosis was developed based on an idea from Juran in 1954. It differs from an audit in that the focus is not on compliance but on problems and what is being done to overcome these problems, or 'countermeasures'. In this way the diagnosis process focuses on the capability of an organization to learn from its current performance and to implement improvement action.

Another powerful form of QC-diagnosis is an internal 'President's' diagnosis. For example, past Deming Prize winners have implemented presidents' diagnosis up to four times a year to track their company's progress towards total quality control.

A typical diagnosis involves the most senior executive and the management team examining areas such as:

- The corporate culture or constitution – is it robust enough for its vision of the middle- and long-range plan to be realized?
- Problems in merchandise planning
- Problems in quality assurance
- Problems in research and development
- Problems in the reporting by the executives in the president's diagnosis.

To help companies who wish to implement company-wide quality control using the Deming Prize criteria, JUSE offers a 'QC-diagnosis' conducted by members of the Deming Application Prize sub-committee. The purpose of the QC-diagnosis is to advance the promotion of effective quality control/management in companies. The QC-diagnosis and resulting guidance is provided from an objective viewpoint. The process for the QC-diagnosis is a mirror of the Deming Application Prize process described below, with the exception that it can be carried out any time of year. It is not a prerequisite that a company undergoes a QC-diagnosis before applying for a Deming Prize. Any company requesting a QC-diagnosis is not allowed to apply for the Prize until the following year.

6.5 Deming Prize award process

Figure 6.2 shows the application and examination process for the Deming Prize, and Table 6.5 shows a timetable for the award process. As can be seen in the preceding chapters, the process is very similar to the processes for both the Baldrige and the European Quality Awards.

It is not a requirement that a company must seek pre-application counselling from Union of Japanese Scientists and Engineers (JUSE) consultants to improve its application of total quality control techniques. Past overseas prize winners have, however, engaged JUSE consultants for about four years before applying for the award.

As can be seen in Figure 6.2, the application and examination process is essentially a six-stage process.

Stage 1: Application process

Before applying for the prize, the applicant contacts the JUSE secretariat to confirm the application procedures and eligibility. Although in theory any company can apply for a prize, it is recognized that the process is an exclusive 'by invitation only' process.

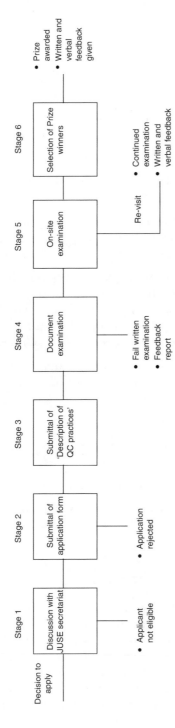

Figure 6.2 Deming Prize application and examination process

Table 6.5: Deming Prize application and examination timetable

Timing	Event
September	*The Deming Prize Guide (for Overseas Companies)* is distributed to the relevant parties
October	The applicant needs to consult with the JUSE secretariat for the application procedures
January	The application deadline
Early February	JUSE notifies applicants whether their application has been accepted or rejected
March	The deadline for an applicant to submit its Description of QC Practices, Terminology Glossary, and Description of Business Activities to JUSE
April–May	Examiners examine documents, decide if the applicant is eligible to stand for the on-site examination, notify the applicant of their decision, and, if accepted, provide the on-site examination schedule and the names of the examiners
June	The applicant's business orientation meeting and preparation meeting with the examiners for the on-site examination
July–September	The on-site examination
Mid-October	Selection, notification and public announcement of successful applicants
November	Deming Prize award ceremony and celebration party
November	Report and lecture by prize winners

Stage 2: Submittal of the application form

The application form is a simple form on which a company indicates the year in which the prize is sought, the name of the company, a principal contact name, and whether the application is for an entire company, a division of a company, or a small company. The reason why the company is applying must also be stated. In years where there are a high number of applications that may stretch JUSE resources, JUSE reserve the right to delay an application until the following year.

Stage 3: Submittal of the description of QC practices

During this stage of the process, the applicant submits a description of its company-wide quality control activities and its business activities. The timetable allows about six weeks from notification by JUSE that an application has been accepted until the description of QC practices must be submitted. However, in practice companies take about a year to complete the report.

The written report describes the applicant's promotion and implementation of quality control/management activities from the time of introduction up to the time of examination, including effects and results. The reports must be written in the Plan–Do–Check–Act format and be 'word-poor and data rich', because the Deming examiners want applicants to talk about facts. Numerous graphs and tables make up the heart of the report.

The Deming report and the reports expected for the European and Baldrige award processes (see Chapters 9–12) reinforce an important difference in the emphasis of the processes. Whereas the European and Baldrige processes require comparison of performance with own targets and benchmarks in the written submission for each set of data submitted, the Deming process is more interested in continuous improvement trends. This is not to say that comparisons with benchmarks are not important, and a statement of the standing of the company against other companies is a requirement of the report.

A 'Description of QC Practices' should be prepared for each business unit, as well as a corporate report. These submission documents will be used as a source document for the on-site examination, if this later stage is reached.

The Corporate Description of QC Practices should encompass all of the business units' activities. It is advised that the contents be organized along the lines of the following, with the senior executive's thoughts on QC practices at the end:

1. Outline of the company
2. Reason for QC introduction
3. Policies
4. Organization and operation
5. Employee development
6. Standardization
7. Quality assurance
8. Cost management
9. Effects of QC practices
10. Future plans.

Each business unit's Description of QC Practices should describe the details of the unit's QC activities. The format of the description is open, but it should include the following points:

1. An outline and features of the business unit, and an overview of its products and services
2. The relationship between the business unit head's policies and the corporate management and quality policies (short, mid and long term)
3. The organization of the business unit and its relationship to the quality management organization
4. The history of the business unit's QC practices (how the methods of QC management have evolved), the historical QC policy changes, and the current QC policies
5. The unique features of the business unit's QC management (areas of emphasis)
6. Self-evaluation of product and service quality and the use of data obtained to determine where the company stands in comparison to other companies
7. Both tangible and intangible effects of the QC practices at the business unit
8. The remaining problems and the future plans for the business unit's QC practices.

Whereas it is allowable to submit the business units' Description of QC Practices in English, the Corporate Description must be in Japanese. There is also a limitation on the size of the description, based on the number of employees – for example, this ranges from less than 50 pages for an organization with less than 100 employees to 75 pages for one with 2000 employees.

The last document that has to be submitted is the Description of Business Activities. This document provides an explanation of such things as the products and services offered by the company, business performance, and glossary of terms.

Stage 4: Document examination

The document examination is conducted on the documents submitted to determine if quality control/management is practised systematically and effectively throughout the company. During the document examination, the examiners may request additional documents for the purposes of clarification. No information is published regarding how this examination is conducted.

When an applicant passes the document examination, it is recommended for an on-site examination. If the company fails the document examination, it will be given a written report detailing the examiner's findings and the reasons for failure.

Stage 5: On-site examination

Depending on the company's size and organizational structure, the scope of its business and its geographical location(s), the on-site examination is carried out according to the following plans:

- Plan A: the examination is scheduled and conducted separately for the head office and the business units (e.g. divisions, plants, factories etc.). The on-site examination is not necessarily conducted in every business unit.
- Plan B: the examination is scheduled and conducted together for all business units. In this case, the entire company constitutes an examination unit.

A business unit selected for the on-site examination is referred to as an 'Examination Unit'. The Deming Application Prize subcommittee chooses which business units will be examined, and these will be at least ten employees in size. Sampling may be used if deemed necessary, based on a statistical approach.

The number of examiners per unit is typically between two and six, with one examiner acting as the lead examiner. The length of an on-site visit is between one and three days per Examination Unit. For the site-visit examination of Philips Taiwan, sixteen Deming examiners were used over a period of six days.

The process also allows additional material to be presented, which is in contrast to the process followed by both the Baldrige and the European Quality Awards (see Chapters 4 and 5), where new data must not be introduced during the assessment process.

The on-site examinations take place following a specific schedule that has the four elements shown in Figure 6.3. Each element is discussed briefly below.

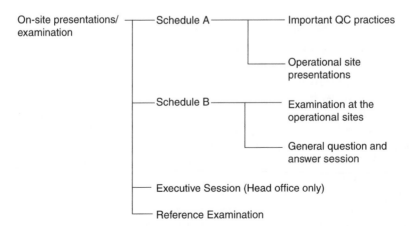

Figure 6.3 On-site examination schedules

Schedule A

Schedule A is the time allocated for the company to present its important QC practices to the examiners. The company determines the schedule for schedule A in consultation with each examination unit's lead examiner. The schedule will include a presentation covering the business unit's important QC practices, and one or more operational site presentations.

The presentation on QC practices should highlight points contained in the 'Description of QC Practices' that was submitted for documentation examination. It should also include any changes since the description was submitted, and allow time for questions from the examiners.

The operational site presentation should focus on explaining to the examiners the key processes, management methods and products and services offered. It should also allow time for questions.

Schedule B

Schedule B is the examiner-initiated part of the examination, and so it will be presented to the business unit after the completion of Schedule A. The format of the Schedule B examination depends on the unit under examination, and is at the discretion of the examiners. It will always include time for general questions and answers.

Executive Session

The Executive Session is carried out after the Schedule B on-site examination that covers the head office. The members of the company that should attend the Executive Session are agreed during the preparation meetings with the lead examiner.

Reference Examination

The Reference Examination is unique to the Deming Prize, as it is carried out on companies associated with the applicant's product and service quality assurance system – particularly group companies, subcontractors, vendors and distributors. The objective is not to evaluate these associated companies, but to consider the information from them in evaluating the applicant company. This examination is usually carried out at the associated companies' sites.

Not every examination unit will have a Reference Examination. In cases where a division of a company is applying for a prize, other parts of the organization that have functions that support the applicant may be considered as reference sites. For example, a Reference Examination may be conducted at a division's corporate headquarters.

Stage 6: Selection of prize winners

The results of the documentation examination and on-site examination are reported to the chairperson of the Deming Prize Committee. The Deming Prize Committee discusses the application and decides either to 'pass' the applicant or categorize the applicant as 'continued examination'.

If an applicant is given 'continued examination' status, this means that in effect it failed the on-site examination. Subsequent examinations are limited to twice during the next three years, and these examinations focus on what was highlighted at the previous examination and what has changed since then. The applicant is recognized as having passed the examination when it has significantly improved upon the previously noted issues and has achieved the necessary level to pass.

The *Overseas Deming Prize Guidelines* state that the examination process is not open to the public. However, the Deming Prize Committee defines the pass level even if it does not publish an objective measure that can be correlated to the way that the score was determined.

On the basis of a score of 100 possible points, all the following conditions must be met:

The Executive Session	70 points or more
Whole company average, excluding Executive Session	70 points or more
Any Examination Unit	50 points or more

There are also some guidelines given on the scoring method:

1. Each examiner evaluates each examination unit on the basis of 100 possible points
2. The score for each examination unit is the median value of the points awarded by each examiner
3. The score for the whole company is the weighted average of the scores achieved by each examination unit, excluding the Executive Session
4. The on-site examination of the head office and the Executive Session are scored separately.

The applicants receive a written report on the examination findings approximately six weeks after the examination. Successful companies are required to deliver a report on their QC practices and experiences at the Report and Lecture meeting.

In the event that a company receives 'continued examination' status, two or more examiners will visit the company with a written report to explain the examination findings.

6.6 How the Deming Prize has evolved

The Deming Prize has not undergone as many revisions as the other frameworks in this book, but the changes have been significant. In particular, there has been a move away from the 'quality control' focus to one of total quality management. The latest version also pays more attention to the results achieved, with Viewpoint 10 (Contribution to realization of corporate objectives) being similar to Baldrige's 'Business results' category. The Deming Viewpoint covers customer satisfaction, employees' satisfaction, social results, supplier results, shareholder return, and profit generation.

A number of other factors have been introduced that move the Deming framework towards the Western frameworks. For example, information and use of technology now feature, as does the need for a management framework. On the latter point, the Deming approach is less prescriptive than the EFQM approach, which dictates that a process infrastructure be installed to deliver the organization's objectives.

6.7 Summary

In this chapter we have considered the Deming Prize. Its original focus was mainly on the application of statistical quality control techniques with a view to improving process performance, thereby leading to an increase in company prosperity. In recent years, however, the main Deming Application Prize framework has integrated some of the factors within the other frameworks, which significantly widens its scope. The process improvement that is sought remains primarily that of the *Kaizen* incremental type as opposed to the 'step changes', or *Kaikaku*, which the newer frameworks like Baldrige encourage.

We have also seen the emphasis that the Deming approach puts on an organization's ability continually to learn and to take 'countermeasure' action as a result of identifying problems. The QC-diagnosis method supports a company in its implementation of continuous improvement processes.

A study of the Deming Application Prize award process reveals the rigour that companies who apply for the award go through. The time it takes to achieve a Deming Application Prize is around two to five years from initial contact with the Union of Japanese Scientists and Engineers. This time is somewhat longer than that normally associated with the Baldrige and European Quality Award processes, but as this includes all the preparatory work, the timescales are very similar.

One key difference between the Deming Prize and the other frameworks discussed in this book is that the prize process is more of an experience than a process. The prize is not given when a particular standard is reached, but when the examiners are convinced that the philosophy taken on by the applicant is fully embedded. This is achieved when the approach has been organically grown over a period of years.

The frameworks that support the Deming Application Prize at first glance appear to be internally focused, with limited emphasis on customer and people satisfaction as a specific goal. The award process does include, however, the provision to talk directly with suppliers and distributors on the subject of product quality, which makes it unique. The ability of an organization to produce products or services that meet customers' requirements is also central to the evaluation process.

The frameworks are also less dependent on external techniques such as benchmarking, or on the requirement that the company must be financially successful. It would appear that success is defined in terms of the application of an idealistic approach.

These points should be borne in mind as our discussion moves in the next chapter to review some of the other frameworks that are used around the world.

7

National and regional quality awards

7.1 Introduction

The preceding chapters have reviewed in some detail the US, Japanese and European Awards. Whilst these have been important in shaping our thinking on organizational excellence, they have also been instrumental in creating renewed interest in excellence at the national and regional levels.

In this chapter we review the Canadian, Australian, Singapore and UK national and regional awards. All of these award frameworks can trace their parentage to either the Baldrige or the European Award.

7.2 The Canada Awards for Excellence

The Canada Awards for Excellence were introduced by the Ministry of Industry in 1984, and are administered by the National Quality Institute (NQI). They recognize outstanding achievement across major functions of an organization. The award framework was revised in 1989 to reflect the Baldrige Model, and subsequent developments have resulted in the Canadian Framework for Business Excellence. This is used by many Canada-based private organizations as a framework for promoting organizational excellence, as well as being used by the NQI as the basis for adjudication of the Canada Awards for Excellence and many regional recognition programmes.

The NQI is an independent not-for-profit organization whose vision is 'to inspire organizational excellence' and whose mission is 'to assist organizations in Canada achieve excellence through a strategic approach and application of quality principles, practices and certification as embodied in the NQI criteria, and to recognize outstanding achievement through the Canada Awards for Excellence'.

The Canadian Framework for Business Excellence (Figure 7.1) has many similarities to both the Baldrige and European Models. The eight-section model includes Principles for Excellence, Leadership, Planning, Customer focus, People focus, Process management, Partnership, and Business performance. The sections are divided into subsections in a similar structure to the Baldrige and European Models.

The Canada Awards for Excellence are Canada's premier awards for recognizing outstanding achievement. The Canadian Quality Award is presented to companies that meet or exceed the intent of the Canadian Framework for Business Excellence. Certificates of Merit are awarded to organizations that are clearly on the road to excellence and are potential future award winners, but need more time to achieve the desired outcomes. Key features of the award framework and assessment process are outlined below. This information is based on materials in the public domain, and further details can be obtained from the National Quality Institute at www.nqi.ca.

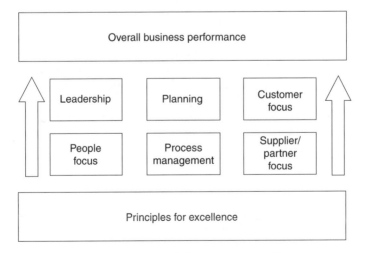

Figure 7.1 The Canadian Framework for Business Excellence

The road map to excellence

The Canadian Framework for Business Excellence is supported by a ten-step 'road map to excellence', which outlines how the framework can be used to drive the quest for excellence. The road map has several key steps:

1. *Support the principles.* The first step in the road map is to review the principles and discuss with everyone within the organization how they apply them and how they should be implemented in the workplace.
2. *Understand and review the Canadian Framework.* Step 2 starts with the organization looking at the Canadian Framework itself. Using a small team, the organization familiarizes itself with the contents and the scope of the Framework.
3. *Take the NQI assessment.* The next stage in the road map is to reach consensus on how the practices within the organization are currently working, by conducting a check-up using the NQI assessment. After completing the check-up, the team can identify any 'gaps' highlighted by the self-assessment.
4. *Develop the improvement plan.* Building on the results of the NQI assessment, the next step is to talk to customers and partners about their needs and relationship with the organization. There is also an internal need to discuss and gain consensus on the priority areas for improvement. From this data the organization needs to plan the actions that are required to facilitate the improvement. Also key here is the identification of the measurable targets to put the organization on the road to excellence.
5. *Spread the message.* Everyone in the organization should hear about the principles, the Canadian Framework, and the commitment of the organization to continuous improvement. Communicating the message will assist everyone in becoming involved, and sets the scene for the next step in the road map.
6. *Put the improvement plan into action.* This is the time to put the plan created at Step 4 into action. Clarity regarding the organization's improvement goals is paramount, as is training staff in the use of improvement tools to assist in the delivery of the plan.
7. *Monitor the improvement plan.* Now is the time to monitor and evaluate the progress made towards meeting the goals of the improvement plan by keeping close watch on the targets set in Step 4. The organization should ensure that support is available for improvement teams who need help to achieve their goals. Celebration of the positive steps taken is encouraged.

8. *Take the NQI assessment.* Step 8 suggests the organization conducts another NQI assessment to capture the gains and measure progress. This self-assessment also serves as the basis of the next improvement plan, looping back to Step 4 of the road map. However, no indication is given as to the approximate timing of this second assessment.

9. *Maintain the gains.* Here the organization embeds the commitment to continuous improvement by applying quality assurance approaches to every aspect of the business. This ensures that approaches are standardized and the gains made are consolidated. Quality assurance methods, such as the ISO9000 series of standards, are mentioned as useful for keeping the organization on track.

10. *Focus on continuous improvement.* At this step the NQI highlights that nothing stays the same. The world and your competitors are always moving, and as an excellent organization you also need to move forward. This step emphasizes the importance of maintaining the commitment to continuous improvement and making the Canadian Framework part of the organization's culture – in other words, the way the business is managed.

The principles for excellence

The eight excellence principles form the foundation for long-term improvement and excellence, underpinning the Canadian Framework for Business Excellence.

1. *Leadership through involvement.* Developing an approach to excellence involves a transformation in management thinking and behaviour, at all levels. This can only be achieved by the active involvement of senior management in establishing unity of purpose and direction, and facilitating, reinforcing, communicating and supporting the changes necessary for improvement.

2. *Primary focus on stakeholders/customer and the marketplace.* In order to achieve its goal, the primary aim of everyone in the organization must be fully to understand, meet and strive to exceed the needs of customers.

3. *Cooperation and teamwork.* Teamwork is nurtured and recognized within and between organizations as a cornerstone for the development of win–win relationships.

4. *Prevention-based process management.* An organization is a network of interdependent value-adding processes, and improvement is achieved through understanding and changing these processes to improve the total system. To facilitate long-term

improvements, a mindset of prevention as against correction must be applied to eliminate the root causes of errors and waste.

5. *Factual approach to decision-making.* Decisions are made based on measured data, internal and external comparisons, and understanding of the cause and effect mechanisms at work; not simply on the basis of instinct, authority or anecdotal data.

6. *Continuous learning and people involvement.* At all levels of the organization, everyone must be given the opportunity to develop their full potential and to use their creativity and make a positive contribution to the organization's pursuit of excellence.

7. *Focus on continuous improvement and breakthrough thinking.* A focus on continuous improvement is the cornerstone for breakthrough thinking and innovation. No matter how much improvement has been accomplished, there are always practical and innovative ways of doing even better, and of providing improved service or products to the customer.

8. *Fulfil obligations to all stakeholders and society.* An organization is seen as part of society, with important responsibilities to satisfy the expectations of its people, customers, partners, owners and other stakeholders, including exemplary concern for responsibility to society.

The Canadian Framework for Excellence criteria

The Framework contains seven main criteria, each divided into subsections with a number of key points or areas to address within each. Six of the seven criteria deal with how the organization conducts and manages activities within the relevant headings. The final subsection in each of these main criteria addresses continuous improvement and relates to the ongoing improvement cycle – namely, how the organization evaluates the effectiveness of its approaches and uses the information to make further improvements.

Section 1: Leadership

This section focuses on creating the culture, values and overall direction from lasting success, and has three subsections.

1.1 Strategic direction

a. A mission and vision statement is in place, reinforcing the organization's core values, and has been communicated to all levels in the organization.

b. Strategic objectives, key success factors and priorities have been determined and link to strategic direction.

c. Responsibility to society and the environment is considered in decision-making.

1.2 Leadership involvement

a. Senior management demonstrates a commitment to continuous improvement.

b. Functions across the organization work together to identify and reduce barriers in order actively to pursue the vision, mission and goals.

c. Responsibility, accountability and leadership are shared throughout the organization.

d. The organization learns from ideas and good practices, and shares them internally and with other organizations.

1.3 Continuous improvement

a. The organization evaluates the effectiveness of its approach to leadership, and uses this information to make further improvements.

Section 2: Planning

This section examines business planning, incorporating improvement plans, the linkage of planning to strategic direction/intent, and the implementation and the measurement of performance to assess progress.

2.1 Plan development

a. The organization gathers, analyses and uses factual information to provide input for the business planning process, including a formal internal organizational assessment.

b. The business plan identifies, prioritizes and incorporates a balanced set of objectives, and measures the initiatives necessary to support the strategic direction. Balanced objectives are not solely financial, but include customer service targets, people-focus issues, team targets etc.

c. The organization involves its people in the planning process, including strategic planning, and effectively communicates plans and progress to all levels of the organization.

d. The organization integrates the components of the business plan internally, as well as with key customers and partners. Examples of components of the plan may be regional, departmental or functional.

2.2 Plan implementation and review

a. The organization allocates resources to ensure effective implementation of the plan. The term 'resources' includes financial, assets, materials, information systems, and people.
b. Implementation of the components of the business plan are monitored and reviewed, with appropriate action taken.
c. The organization monitors and reviews the effectiveness of the business plan, using a performance measurement system that is linked to appropriate action.

2.3 Continuous improvement

a. The organization evaluates the effectiveness of its approach to business planning and uses this information to make further improvement.

Section 3: Customer focus

This section examines the organization's focus on the customer and the marketplace, and on the achievement of customer satisfaction and loyalty.

3.1 Customer, market and product knowledge

a. The organization defines its markets and/or customer groups.
b. Information is gathered, analysed, and evaluated to determine current and future customer needs and expectations. This includes factual information on customer perception, customer loyalty, product/service value, and competitive comparison.
c. The organization measures customer satisfaction to gain information for improvement.
d. The organization uses its market, partner and customer knowledge in defining or enhancing products and/or services provided.
e. The organization communicates the value of its products and/or services to employees and current and potential customers.

3.2 Management of customer relationships

a. The organization ensures that everyone is aligned on the importance of customer satisfaction, and trains and empowers employees to be advocates for the customer.
b. The organization makes it easy for customers to conduct business and to provide feedback – for example, in seeking assistance or registering complaints.
c. The organization responds successfully to customer feedback – for example, linking input to process improvement.
d. The organization ensures positive customer experiences by identifying and managing customer contact points – for example, communication, advertising, product, distribution, service.

3.3 Continuous improvement

a. The organization evaluates the effectiveness of its approaches to customer focus and uses this information to make further improvements.

Section 4: People focus

This section examines how people are encouraged and enabled to contribute and involved in contributing to the achievement of the organization's goals, while reaching their full potential.

4.1 Human resource planning

a. Human resource planning supports the organization's goals and objectives.
b. The organization recruits and selects people for mutual success.
c. The organization links reward and recognition to its strategic direction, based on individual, team and organizational performance.

4.2 Participatory environment

a. The organization ensures that people at all levels understand the strategic direction and the business plan, and that individuals and teams are committed to achieving the organization's goals and objectives.
b. People's suggestions and ideas are encouraged and implemented.
c. The organization encourages its people to innovate and take risks in order to achieve goals.

4.3 Continuous learning

a. Education and development needs are determined and addressed to support both organizational and individual goals, helping people to reach their full potential.
b. The organization evaluates the effectiveness of education and development processes.
c. Knowledge and experience are captured, managed, shared and utilized throughout the organization.

4.4 Employee satisfaction and wellbeing

a. The organization ensures a healthy workplace environment and involves its people in addressing issues related to employee wellness and wellbeing – for example, in physical and social environments, and support of personal health/wellness practices.
b. The organization measures employee satisfaction and wellbeing, and links feedback to achieving strategic objectives.

4.5   Continuous improvement

a. The organization evaluates the effectiveness of its approach to people focus, and uses this information to make further improvements.

Section 5: Process management

This section examines how processes are managed to support the organization's strategic direction, with a specific focus on prevention, as against correction, as well as continuous improvement. Process management applies to all activities within the organization, in particular those that are critical/key for success. Process improvement priorities are derived from goals established within other sections, notably Sections 2 (Planning) and 3 (Customer focus).

5.1   Process development

a. Key processes capable of developing and delivering products and/or services that meet customer needs are identified, designed, documented and implemented.
b. Inputs from employees, customers and partners are incorporated into process development.
c. The organization identifies process performance indicators that are linked to customer requirements and strategic objectives.

5.2   Process control

a. Process ownership has been determined and is maintained.
b. Key processes are monitored to ensure consistency in products and/or services provided.
c. Process problems are analysed, root causes identified, and actions taken and communicated to prevent recurrence.

5.3   Process improvement

a. The organization involves employees, customers and partners in continuous improvement activities.
b. Key processes are analysed to determine opportunities for continuous improvement, through incremental refinement and/or fundamental redesign. For example, the analysis may include internal or external benchmarking.
c. Opportunities for improvement are evaluated and prioritized.
d. Process improvements are implemented and monitored for effectiveness.

5.4   Continuous improvement

a. The organization evaluates the effectiveness of its approach to process management, and uses this information to make further improvements.

Section 6: Partnership

This section examines the organization's external relationships with other organizations, institutions and/or alliances that are critical to meeting its strategic objectives. Such working relationships may include suppliers, partnerships, distributors/dealers, joint ventures, insourcing/outsourcing, regulatory bodies and franchises. Suppliers can be external or internal (i.e. units of the parent organization that provides goods/services).

6.1 Partnering
a. The organization selects capable suppliers and develops appropriate partnerships that link to its strategic objectives.
b. Key suppliers/partners are involved in the development of the organization's business plans and strategic objectives.
c. The organization identifies product and service opportunities within partnerships that link to its strategic objectives.
d. Impacts on customers and employees are considered when making key supplier and/or partnership arrangements.

6.2 Supplier/partner management
a. Communications and business relationships with suppliers/partners are managed for the benefit of all parties.
b. Effectiveness of working relationships with key suppliers/partners is measured, and issues and concerns are addressed.

6.3 Continuous improvement
a. The organization evaluates the effectiveness of its approach to supplier/partner focus, and uses this information to make further improvements.

Section 7: Business performance

This section examines the following outcomes from overall organizational achievements.

7.1 Customer focus
a. Levels and trends in customer satisfaction, loyalty and retention.
b. Levels and trends of the performance of products and/or services provided – for example, warranty claims, refunds, repairs, replacements.
c. Levels and trends in sales growth, market share and/or 'customer share' – for example, share of customers' business.

7.2 People focus
a. Levels and trends of the effectiveness of education and development.

b. Levels and trends of involvement and effectiveness in improvement activities that link to the objectives and goals of the organization.
c. Levels and trends in employee wellness/wellbeing and satisfaction – for example, healthy workplace, environment issues and job satisfaction.
d. Levels and trends in measures of dissatisfaction – for example, employee turnover, absenteeism and complaints.

7.3 Process management
a. Indicators of the effectiveness of the design process for new products and/or services, such as cycle times, for example time to market, and frequency of design changes.
b. Levels and trends in overall efficiency and effectiveness of key production processes and/or service delivery, including support administrative processes – for example, productivity, cycle time, responsiveness, error and waste reduction, cost reductions, inventory turnover etc.

7.4 Partnerships
a. Indicators of positive working relationships with qualified suppliers/partners. Examples include efficiency and effectiveness.

7.5 Responsibility to society
a. Indicators of the extent to which responsibility to society and the environment is considered and measured.

7.6 Owner/shareholder focus
a. Levels and trends in measures of overall financial performance – for example, revenues, costs, profits, return on investment, return on assets.
b. Levels and trends of formal assessment findings. Examples include organizational excellence assessment ratings and/or scores.

Canadian Public Sector Award

The National Quality Institute has also developed the Canadian Quality Criteria for the Public Sector. The public sector criteria are based on the NQI's original Canadian Quality Criteria, and serve as the basis for adjudication of the public sector quality awards, part of the Canadian Awards for Excellence programme.

Although the public sector quality criteria are founded on nine quality principles, as against the eight in the Canadian Framework for Excellence, the underlying messages behind the principles are the same. In addition the road map to excellence is relabelled as the NQI Quality Compass for the Public Sector.

As with the Framework for Excellence, the Canadian Quality Criteria for the Public Sector are divided into sections and subsections. The main section headings are the same in both, but the subsections contain more detail and address additional points.

Award winners

The Quality Award Trophy has been awarded since 1991. Prior to this, Gold Winners were awarded in a number of areas such as Entrepreneurship, and Quality and Innovation. Table 7.1 shows the Quality Award Trophy winners since 1991.

Table 7.1: Canadian Business Excellence Award winners

Year	Organization
2002	Dana Canada Inc. – Spicer Driveshaft Group
	Canada Post Corporation – Saskatoon Operations
	Homewood Health Centre
	Mullen Trucking
2001	The Cardiac Care Network of Ontario
	Dana Canada Inc. – Spicer Driveshaft Group
	Diversicare Canada Management Services Inc. – Ontario Region
	IBM Solution Delivery Services
2000	Aeronautical and Technical Services
	Natural Resources Canada
	British Columbia Transplant Society
	Delta Hotels
	Honeywell Water Controls Business Unit
1999	Telus – Operator Services
1998	Amex Canada Inc.
	Flemington Public School
	John Deere Ltd
	Telus Mobility Inc.

(continued)

Table 7.1: *Continued*

Year	Organization
1997	BC Tel Education
	Brock Telecom
	Dominion Directory Information Systems
	Orillia Soldiers' Memorial Hospital
1996	Baxter Corporation – Alliston Plant
	Harris Farinon Canada
	IBM Canada – Customer Service
	KI Pembroke
1995	Alcan Cable – Usine Lapointe
	Joyce Public School
	Markham Stouffville Hospital
1994	None awarded
1993	Ford Electronics Manufacturing Corporation – Markham Plant
	IBM Canada Ltd – Toronto Manufacturing Plant
1992	General Motors of Canada Ltd – Windsor Trim Plant
	Texas Instruments Canada Ltd – Materials and Controls Group
1991	Chrysler Canada Ltd – Windsor Minivan Assembly Plant
	Linamar Machine Ltd

7.3 The Australian Business Excellence Awards

The Australian Business Excellence Awards have been the vehicle for recognizing outstanding Australian organizations since 1988. The Australian Quality Council (AQC) originally ran the awards, but in February 2002 Standards Australia International acquired a range of products and services previously owned by the AQC, including the rights to the Australian Business Excellence Awards. Business Excellence Australia, a division of Standards Australia International Limited, now runs the Awards and also offers a range of excellence products. Further details can be found on www.businessexcellenceaustralia.com.au.

The Framework

Applicants go through a peer evaluation, and their performance is assessed against the categories and items in the Australian Business Excellence Framework (see Figure 7.2).

Seven organizational categories make up the model:

1. Leadership and innovation
2. Strategy and planning processes
3. Data, information and knowledge
4. People
5. Customer and market focus
6. Processes, products and services
7. Business results.

Each category is made up of a number of sub-categories called items, in a similar way to the Baldrige Model. Assessment is based on four dimensions:

1. Approach – identifies the organization's vision of excellence and intent for the item
2. Deployment – identifies the activities actually happening
3. Results – demonstrates how measures are monitored
4. Improvement – shows how the organization improves the approach and deployment.

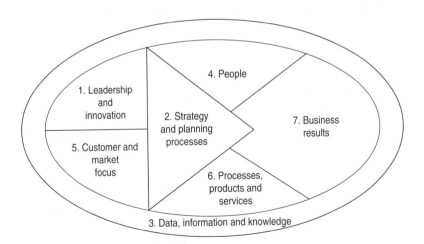

Figure 7.2 The Australian Business Excellence Framework

The awards are open to all organizations operating in Australia, and there are two recognition categories:

1. Recognition at Award Level – five levels of recognition
   - Excellence Medal
   - Gold Award
   - Silver Award
   - Bronze Award
   - Finalist Medal.

2. Recognition at Category Level
   - Leadership Award
   - Strategy and Planning Award
   - Knowledge and Information Award
   - People Award
   - Customer and Market Focus Award
   - Innovation, Quality and Improvement Award
   - Success and Sustainability Award.

Award winners

The programme seems to have stalled in 2002, when Business Excellence Australia took over the running of the awards from the AQC. There were no awards in 2002. However, the programme is now active again. Award winners for 2001 and 2003 are listed in Table 7.2.

Table 7.2: Australian Business Excellence Award winners

Year	Award	Organization
2003	Excellence Medal	Boeing Australia Limited
	Silver Award	Boeing Australia Limited CORE – the Public Correctional Enterprise
	Bronze Award	Freemantle Ports Tasmanian Alkaloids
	Finalists	Corporate Capability Development, QLD Department of Employment and Training Counter Disaster and Rescue Services, QLD Department of

Table 7.2: **Continued**

Year	Award	Organization
		Emergency Services
		Open Learning Institute of TAFE, QLD
		Safety and Health Division, Department of Natural Resources and Mines
	Strategy and Planning Award	Australia Post Shared Services Division
	Information and Knowledge Award	City of Perth
	People Award	Riteway Express
2001	Gold Award	Schefenacker Vision Systems Australia
	Finalist	City of Wodonga
		Kangan Batman TAFE
	Progress towards Business Excellence	Child Support Agency
		Knox City Council
		TAFE NSW – South Western Sydney Institute
		Queensland Ambulance Service
		SA Ambulance Service
		Port of Brisbane Corporation
	Foundation in Business Excellence	City of Melville
		ACT Community Care
		Navy Headquarters Tasmania
		Defence National Storage and Distribution Centre
		Queensland Health Human Resource Management Information Systems Project
		Tenix Defence Pty Ltd, Marine Division, WA & Naval Systems
		South Gippsland Shire Council

7.4 The Singapore Quality Award

The Singapore Quality Award (SQA) was launched in 1994, and is awarded to organizations that demonstrate the highest standards of business excellence. The business excellence model underpinning the SQA, the Singapore Quality Award Framework, is based on the best practice embodied in the Baldrige Model, the EFQM Excellence Model® and the Australian Business Excellence Framework. The aim of the award programme is to encourage organizations to strengthen their management systems, and enhance their capability and competitiveness.

The SQA is administered by the Standards, Productivity and Innovation Board (SPRING Singapore). SPRING is a member of the Guardians of Premier Excellence Model (GEMS) organizations. Other network members include the administrators of the Baldrige, European and Australian Awards. SPRING's membership of GEMS ensures that the SQA Framework continues to reflect best practice.

SQA applicants are assessed using a nine-criterion framework with Driver, System and Results elements (see Figure 7.3). The SQA adopts a three-tier administrative structure in its annual assessment and award process. The Singapore Quality Award (SQA) is managed by the Governing Council, which draws up policies and guidelines for the award programme and approves the award recipients. A management committee, comprising experienced assessors and business practitioners from the award members and award recipients, supports the Governing Council. The committee reviews the award criteria, develops the system for training and certifying the assessors, and shortlists award applicants. The Board of Assessors is made up of business excellence assessors nominated from organizations in both the public and private sectors, including the past Singapore Quality Award (SQA) winners. The business excellence assessors evaluate the applications against set criteria using a weighted scoring system, conduct site visits, and prepare feedback reports. They volunteer their time in the assessment process, without being paid for their services. To ensure integrity and objectivity in the assessment process, assessors abide by a code of confidentiality and conduct. Assessors are also required to attend compulsory preparatory training before they can evaluate applications.

SPRING has implemented the SQA Business Excellence Programme to assist organizations in their journey to world-class business excellence. Under this programme, organizations first undertake an assessment using a questionnaire based on the Singapore Quality Award Framework. Organizations scoring 400 points or more are site-visited to validate the score, and organizations with a validated score of 400 points or more are invited

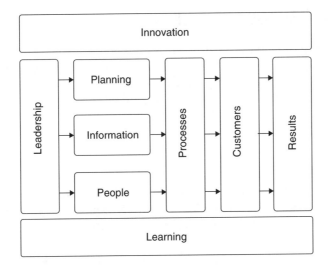

Figure 7.3 Singapore Quality Award Framework

to join the Singapore Quality Class. Over time, with continuous and transformational improvement programmes, members of the Singapore Quality Class progress to become world-class organizations. They are then invited to apply for the SQA. The best of the best organizations are conferred with the Singapore Quality Award for their attainment of world-class standards of business excellence. The core values and award criteria are outlined below, and further details can be obtained from www.spring.gov.uk.

Core values

The Singapore Quality Award criteria are built on a set of core values and concepts. These values and concepts are the foundation for the integration of the key performance requirements that exist within the criteria framework. They are:

- Visionary leadership
- Customer-driven quality
- Innovation focus
- Organizational and personal learning
- Valuing people and partners
- Agility
- Knowledge-driven system
- Societal responsibility
- Results orientation
- Systems perspective.

SQA criteria for business excellence

Each of the nine criteria within the excellence framework has a number of categories, which in turn have a series of excellence indicators. These excellence indicators are a set of statements reflecting approaches that excellent organizations will have in place.

1 Leadership

This criterion demonstrates what excellent organizations have in place in the categories of Senior executive leadership, Organizational culture, and Responsibility to community and the environment.

1.1 *Senior executive leadership* covers the requirement to have developed a clear and understandable vision and mission that drives the organization towards excellence. It also looks at how the vision, mission and goals of the organization are regularly reinforced throughout the organization both through special programmes and in day-to-day activities, and how the organization's goals are systematically cascaded to all levels of the organization. Throughout the category evidence is required to demonstrate the extent to which the senior managers are personally and visibly involved in performance improvement activities and in communicating the organization goals and quality corporate values to all levels of employees.

1.2 *Organizational culture* reflects the 'feel' of the organization and how senior managers within an excellent organization ensure a culture of providing opportunities for staff to try new ideas, experiment, innovate and take responsible risks. Employees at all levels should confirm that the senior management strongly supports and drives corporate culture through a variety of feedback sources, such as 360-degree appraisal to evaluate and take actions to improve leadership. This will result in employees showing a strong sense of identity and commitment towards the organization's vision, and practising the corporate values in their day-to-day work.

1.3 *Responsibility to community and the environment* asks the organization to demonstrate that it has a well-defined policy and goals in relation to its contribution to the community and the environment in which it operates, and how it involves employees in programmes to achieve its public responsibility objectives. These programmes may include community service, donations to charity, environmental conservation activities, hosting educational visits etc.

2 Planning

All of the excellence indicators within this criterion are evaluated under the category of Strategy development and deployment.

2.1 *Strategy development and deployment* looks for evidence that planning is a systematic and closed-loop process using inputs from a variety of people at all levels throughout the organization, and involves regular review and modifications when necessary. The planning process should be based on analysis of both internal data (for example, operational performance, quality indicators etc.) and external data (such as customer feedback, market intelligence, industry trends etc.). The planning process should produce a balanced business plan, with the long-term and short-term goals well defined in measurable terms, that is systematically cascaded down to all levels, and corporate goals should be translated into departmental and individual objectives with challenging and achievable targets set. It is also expected that appropriate indicators and data be regularly monitored to track the achievement of its plans and targets. Around all of this is the overall evaluation of the planning process itself, and the ability of the organization to make improvements to planning cycle time, planning accuracy and plan deployment.

3 Information

This criterion has two categories against which organizations are evaluated; Management of information, and Comparison and benchmarking.

3.1 *Management of information* asks organizations to demonstrate that they use carefully selected data and information. Information from a broad spectrum of areas, including financial, sales and marketing, production, product and service quality, supplier quality and customer satisfaction, should be used in management decision-making and to track the organization's performance against its corporate objectives. Excellent organizations would also be expected to have integrated data on various aspects of performance into a few key indicators – for example, through a balanced scorecard – to track overall performance. There should be an effective and integrated system to collect and manage data and information that are used in day-to-day management, and to drive performance improvements with assigned owners who review and ensure the accuracy, reliability, and accessibility of the data/information used for performance measurement. Closing the loop requires the organization regularly to evaluate and improve its management of data and information.

3.2 *Comparison and benchmarking* looks at how the organization regularly obtains the new knowledge it needs to create value for stakeholders, and checks that systems exist to capture and disseminate knowledge – such as ensuring that overseas benchmarking visits result in a report that contributes to organizational learning. It also requires the organization to have a systematic process to collect and analyse comparative data and information, and to use this information to set 'stretching' or challenging goals and drive performance improvements whilst systematically benchmarking its processes against best-in-class organizations and feeding best practices into the organization to improve organizational performance.

4 People

This criterion is divided into five categories, emphasizing the importance the Award process puts on to the people element – which is also reflected in the scoring mechanism. The categories are: Human resource planning; Employee involvement and commitment; Employee education, training and development; Employee health and satisfaction; and Employee performance and recognition. There is a general item that closes the feedback loop on all of the categories by examining how the organization regularly evaluates and improves on its HR planning process, employee participation, training and development process, employee satisfaction approach, and recognition and reward systems.

4.1 *Human resource planning* looks at how HR is proactively involved in the strategic planning process, providing its inputs as well as developing appropriate plans to support the organization's short- and long-term goals. HR's own plans will cover all key issues, including recruitment, retention, training and development, leadership succession, employee participation, recognition and reward, management-labour relations and employee satisfaction.

4.2 *Employee involvement and commitment* examines the need for organizations to have a wide variety of mechanisms to encourage employee participation at all levels, promote teamwork, and tap on the innovative potential of its employees.

4.3 *Employee education, training and development* ensures the organization systematically identifies training and development needs for all levels of employees, taking into account skills requirements and current skills inventory. It emphasizes the importance of assessing the effectiveness of training and development undertaken.

4.4 *Employee health and satisfaction* looks for evidence that the organization measures employee satisfaction, and has other mechanisms in place to obtain feedback from employees. Action taken on issues arising from such feedback should be in evidence.

4.5 *Employee performance and recognition* examines that the organization has a fair and effective system to measure employee performance and has a wide variety of reward and recognition schemes, linked to the corporate objectives and values, that support high performance, innovative and creative behaviour.

5 Processes

Innovation process, Process management and improvement, and Supplier and partnering are the categories covered in this criterion.

5.1 *Innovation process* examines what systematic processes exist to acquire, evaluate and implement creative ideas from a wide range of sources and to translate customer requirements and expectations into product or service design, production and delivery. It looks at how external parties, including customer, suppliers, and business partners, are involved in key aspects of the design process. There is also a need to ensure that the innovation and design processes are evaluated for improvements such as the shortening of cycle time, improvements in design quality and a reduction in costs.

5.2 *Process management and improvement* looks for key processes to have clear objectives and targets linked to business and quality goals. It examines how the organization manages all key and support processes through systematic measurement, using analysis of root causes to drive prompt corrective action and prevent future recurrence when a process fails to meet specified standards or the targets set. Organizations can use a variety of methods (such as internal assessment, third-party audit and customer audit) to assess regularly the quality and performance of the organization's key business processes and supporting processes, but should have a systematic approach to act on the results of the various assessments.

5.3 *Supplier and partnering* covers the management of suppliers and partners, including how the organization identifies and selects its suppliers and partners, communicates and proactively ensures that suppliers have the capability and capacity to meet its requirements through the use of supplier audits, supplier rating and certification systems, and has plans and actions to help key suppliers improve their abilities to meet key quality and response-time requirements.

6 Customers

Focusing on Customer requirements, Customer relationships and Customer satisfaction, this criterion encompasses all aspects of how an organization interfaces with its customers. Again, the review loop is closed with how the organization regularly evaluates and improves on its processes and methods.

6.1 *Customer requirements* looks for the organization to demonstrate that a wide variety of 'listening posts' (such as focus groups, frontline employees, surveys, feedback forms etc.) exist to determine both current and future customer requirements, which are then used as inputs in the planning process and incorporated into the strategic business and improvement plans. Excellent organizations ensure that this customer feedback is turned into actionable information. This category also looks for the organization to anticipate potential opportunities to exploit competitive advantage.

6.2 *Customer relationships* covers how the organization ensures the ease of customer contact through such methods as toll-free lines etc. and the setting of service standards for the various interfaces with the customer. Customer-contact employees should be adequately trained and empowered, within limits, to manage customer relationships and delight customers. It also examines how the organization records, resolves and tracks customer complaints, and uses the information to initiate prompt corrective action to prevent future recurrence.

6.3 *Customer satisfaction* examines the methods and indicators used to measure customer satisfaction, such as customer surveys, complaints/compliments etc., and that these are regularly and systematically monitored to ensure progression beyond customer satisfaction to customer loyalty and retention. It also examines whether the organization's ability to satisfy customers has been recognized in the form of customer awards or other forms of recognition schemes.

7 Results

The Results criterion is divided into four categories: Customer results, Financial and market results, People results, and Operational results. The excellence indicators are applied to all of the categories, and factors include evidence of:

- A clear link between the strategy of the organization and what it measures with key indicators in all categories
- Clear linkage of results to approach and deployment
- Targets and trends that consistently meet or exceed targets for three years or more, with adverse trends explained and corrective action demonstrated
- Absolute results being high relative to competitors or industry standard

- Comparisons being made with benchmarks within the industry and across industries
- Best-in-class results in some or most of its key indicators.

The award criteria weightings are shown in Table 7.3.

Award winners

Previous winners of the SQA include a mix of private and public sector organizations. Details are given in Table 7.4.

Table 7.3: Singapore Award criteria weightings

	Categories/items	*Points value*
1	*Leadership*	*120*
1.1	Senior executive leadership	50
1.2	Organizational culture	50
1.3	Responsibility to community and the environment	20
2	*Planning*	*80*
2.1	Strategy development and deployment	80
3	*Information*	*80*
3.1	Management of information	55
3.2	Comparison and benchmarking	25
4	*People*	*110*
4.1	Human resource planning	20
4.2	Employee involvement and commitment	20
4.3	Employee education, training and development	30
4.4	Employee health and satisfaction	20
4.5	Employee performance and recognition	20
5	*Process*	*100*
5.1	Innovation process	40
5.2	Process management and improvement	40
5.3	Supplier and partnering process	20

(*continued*)

Table 7.3: *Continued*

	Categories/items	Points value
6	Customers	110
6.1	Customer requirements	40
6.2	Customer relationships	40
6.3	Customer satisfaction	30
7	Results	400
7.1	Customer results	140
7.2	Financial and market results	90
7.3	People results	80
7.4	Operational results	90
Total points		1000

Table 7.4: Previous winners of the Singapore Quality Award

Year	Organization
2002	Singapore Police Force
	Singapore Technologies Engineering Ltd
2001	Sony Display Device (Singapore)
	The Ritz-Carlton Millenia Singapore
2000	Citibank N.A. Regional Cash Process Management Unit
	Philips Electronics Singapore Pte Ltd, DAP Factory
1999	PSA Corporation Ltd
	STMicrolectronics
1998	Philips Electronics Singapore Pte Ltd, Turner Factory
1997	Baxter Healthcare Pte Ltd
	Housing & Development Board
1996	Asia Pacific Paging Subscriber Division – Motorola Electronics Pte Ltd
1995	Texas Instruments Singapore Pte Ltd (now Micron Semiconductor Asis Pte Ltd)

7.5 The UK Excellence Award

The UK Excellence Award is organized and administered by the British Quality Foundation, a not-for-profit membership organization that promotes business excellence to private, public and voluntary sector organizations in the UK. There are currently close to 1800 member organizations of all sizes that have joined since the Foundation began in late 1993. The mission of the BQF is 'The British Quality Foundation exists to help organizations of all kinds to improve their performance', and it works under the following set of values:

- We are committed to delighting our customers
- We aim for excellence in all we do
- We are a learning organization
- We work as a team and involve others in key partnerships.

Award details

Founder/sponsor and key members of the Foundation help sponsor the UK Business Excellence Award, an annual award which, over the past six years, has quickly established itself as the UK's premier business prize.

The Foundation promotes business excellence through numerous activities, but at the core of all the programmes is the EFQM's Excellence Model®. Thousands of organizations in the UK now use this model to plan their improvements and monitor progress through regular self-assessment. The EFQM Excellence Model® was fully outlined in Chapter 5.

The UK Business Excellence Award was launched in 1994 to recognize organizations that have excelled when measured against the EFQM Excellence Model®. The UK Business Excellence Award is recognized as the UK's top business award, identifying and celebrating organizations that show the highest level of commitment to improving their business performance and increasing their competitiveness. Winning the UK Business Excellence Award is one of the highest accolades any organization in the UK can achieve. To date there have been more than 200 applicants, with 50 organizations achieving finalist status and 20 winning Awards. The high profile promotion of an Award winner, together with the opportunity to use the Award logo, confirms the organization's position as one of the most successful in the United Kingdom.

Entry to the UK Business Excellence Award is open to all organizations within the UK, and there are six entry categories:

1. Large Business and Business Units – whole companies or parts of companies, run as independent business units, with more than 250 employees
2. Medium-sized Businesses – whole companies and independent business units with fewer than 250 employees
3. Small Businesses – independent legal entities with fewer than 50 employees
4. Operational Units of Companies – parts of companies run as a cost centre
5. Large Public Sector Organizations – units operating within the public or voluntary sector, with more than 250 employees
6. Small and Medium-sized Public Sector Organizations – units operating within the public or voluntary sector, with less than 250 employees.

There are some minor restrictions on eligibility, although the award is intended to be as open as possible. The general rules that are applied include:

- Demonstration of three years of continuous operating history in the UK
- 50 per cent or more of the employees or asset base must reside in the UK
- There may be a maximum of four applications in any one year from a parent organization
- The organization may not have won the UK Business Excellence Award in the last three years.

To apply for the UK Business Excellence Award, applicants prepare a submission document with a maximum of 75 pages. Certain standards and styles of formatting are required, as is the number of copies that must be submitted. The submission document must present the organization's achievements across a range of specific areas relating to each of the criteria in the EFQM Excellence Model®. As the model is non-prescriptive, each applicant organization is able to present the information that is relevant to its own specific situation. The submission document should detail the approaches taken by the organization, with examples to show how each approach is used. The results sections should show clear trends and relevant comparisons, and provide a commentary. The Award assessors look for clear factual information, and what is deemed to be anecdotal will be scored poorly.

Teams of between three and eight assessors, depending on the size of the applicant organization, assess the applicant for 'strengths' and 'areas for improvement', and score these on a scale of 0–1000 points using the EFQM Excellence Model®. The assessors initially assess as individuals, then meet as a team to reach a consensus view on the organization. From this initial assessment, organizations with a score of more than 350 points are eligible for a site visit. The purpose of the site visit is to check the validity of the submission document and to clarify issues of understanding, and scores can be adjusted either up or down as a result. After the site visit, the Award Jury reviews the revised scores and makes a final decision on the winners and finalists.

The assessor team prepares a final feedback report, and awards are given to organizations demonstrating the highest standard of excellence. The Award Jury can determine that no award will be presented if no organization has achieved an appropriate level of excellence.

Assessors, who are mainly experienced, practising managers from UK organizations, are trained to use the RADAR® scoring process to allocate points and arrive at a total score out of 1000. A score in excess of 600 points is considered to be approaching world-class. The British Quality Foundation enjoys the voluntary services of about 200 assessors every year to help with its annual award programme. The time commitment from these volunteers can be anything from 10 to 15 working days per year.

Other recognition within the UK Business Excellence Awards

As well as the UK Business Excellence Award, the BQF also runs a Recognized for Excellence programme. This is run in conjunction with the main award, and is for organizations not selected as winners or finalists. Qualification for the Recognition for Excellence requires an application for the UK Business Excellence Award, and a score of more than 400 points. Organizations achieving this level are considered to be well managed, and can use a 'Recognition' logo in their commercial and promotional material. In 2003 the BQF is also introducing four British Quality Foundation Achievement Awards for Excellence in Leadership, Employee Satisfaction, Customer Satisfaction, and Corporate Social Responsibility. As it is impossible to assess and judge for one of the specific awards without examining its impact on other aspects of the organization, these new awards will only be open to entrants for the UK Business Excellence Awards, and each entrant will undergo a full assessment. There will be one winner or joint winner for each award, which will only be selected from those organizations that do not win a UK Business Excellence Award. Awards will only be made to those applicants deemed to have reached the standard as defined by the jury, and it is possible for no award to be made.

Table 7.5: UK Excellence Award winners

Year	Award winners and finalists
2002	*Winners*
	Siemens Communications
	Runshaw College
	Finalists
	AMS Operations Hillend
	AMS Operations Division Broad Oak
	Coors Brewers Limited (Alton)
	TPG Information Systems
	Vertex Customer Management
2001	*Winners*
	Northern Ireland Electricity
	NSK Bearings, Peterlee
	Rolls-Royce Airlines Operations
	Finalists
	Alenia Marconi Systems, Broad Oak
	Inland Revenue Accounts Office, Shipley
	Scottish Courage Brands
	Siemens Communications Systems
2000	*Winners*
	Inland Revenue Accounts Office, Cumbernauld
	St Mary's College
	Springfarm Architectural Mouldings
	Vista Optics
	Finalists
	City Technology College, Kingshurst
	Marriott Hotels
	Northern Ireland Electricity
	NSK Bearings

Table 7.5: Continued

Year	Award winners and finalists
2000 (*cont.*)	*Finalists (cont.)*
	Turners Optometrists
	Unipart DCM
1999	*Winners*
	British Aerospace, Military Aircraft & Aerostructures
	Foxdenton School
	NatWest Insurance Services
	Finalists
	Barclays Direct Loan Services
	NatWest Mortgage Services
	Springfarm Architectural Mouldings
	Vista Optics
1998	*Winners*
	Nortel Networks
	BT Payphones
	Seaview Hotel, Isle of Wight
	Finalists
	DHL Worldwide Express
	NatWest Insurance Services
	Post Office Counters Ltd
	Inland Revenue Accounts Office, Cumbernauld
	Vista Optics
1997	*Winners*
	The Dell Primary School
	BT Northern Ireland
	Hewlett-Packard (UK)
	BT National Business Communication

(*continued*)

Table 7.5: *Continued*

Year	Award winners and finalists
1997 (*cont.*)	*Finalists*
	Nortel Northern Ireland
	NatWest Life Assurance
1996	*Winners*
	Mortgage Express
	Ulster Carpet Mills
	Finalists
	BT Northern Ireland
	Griffin Factors
	Lawson Mardon Plastics
	NatWest Life Assurance
	Nortel
1995	*Winners*
	ICL High Performance Technology
	Finalists
	Avis Europe
	BT Northern Ireland
	ICL Customer Services
1994	*Winners*
	Rover Group
	TNT Express
	Finalists
	Avis Europe
	BT Northern Ireland
	ICL Customer Services

UK Business Excellence Award winners

Table 7.5 shows the winners of the UK Business Excellence Award since its inception in 1994.

7.6 UK Regional Quality Awards

Within the UK a number of regional quality organizations have been created to make excellence more accessible to companies and organizations within their regions – especially those companies that fall into the small to medium category. Many of these regional quality organizations organize and administer a Quality Award based on the EFQM Excellence Model®. The Regional Awards, whilst prestigious within their own region, are viewed as a stepping-stone to the UK Excellence Award and the EFQM Excellence Award. A few regional quality organizations do not organize a separate award programme. Table 7.6 lists the main regional award organizations, and an outline of the main awards is given below.

Table 7.6: UK Regional Award organizations

Organization	*e-mail contact details*
Quality Scotland Foundation	mail@qualityscotland.co.uk
Centre for Competitiveness, Northern Ireland	compete@cforc.org
Wales Quality Centre	wqc@newi.ac.uk
London Excellence	excellence@london-excellence.org.uk
Midlands Excellence	midex@midlandsexcellence.org.uk
Excellence South East	info@excel-se.com
East of England Excellence	excellence@eee.org.uk
Excellence North West	mail@excellencenorthwest.co.uk
Excellence South West	mail@esw.org.uk
Excellence North East	mcnaught@onenortheast.co.uk
Excellence Yorkshire	enquiries@excellence-yorkshire.org.uk

Quality Scotland Foundation

This was established in 1991 to develop a quality culture in Scotland that would allow organizations to respond to the competitive threat coming, in particular, from abroad. From its original base of fourteen members, Quality Scotland now has a membership in excess of 200 organizations, the majority of which feature among the top companies in Scotland. The Quality Scotland Foundation is an independent, non-profit-making and non-political organization.

Since 1994, the QSF has presented annual awards in four categories:

1. Company
2. Service
3. Public Sector
4. Small and Medium-sized (less than 250 employees).

The applicants submit a 75-page document, which is assessed by an independent team of assessors who are trained by Quality Scotland. Finalists in each category are selected and presented to a judging panel, which recommends those that should be visited by the assessment team. A second judges' meeting decides the winners and highly commended in each category. All applicants receive a feedback report listing their strengths and areas for improvement.

Wales Quality Centre

This is a membership organization funded by sponsors. Founded in 1988, it has had an award process based on the EFQM Excellence Model®. Its mission is 'To make Wales second to none for business improvement within Europe'. Its award process is conducted on the same basis as the BQF Excellence Awards, with 95 per cent of the 300 assessors coming from Wales. They receive approximately 50 applications for the award each year, and this number is rising. There is an overall award, and the Wales Quality Centre sponsors give additional awards for achievement within sector – for example, Public Sector, Manufacturing etc.

Centre for Competitiveness, Northern Ireland

This excellence award programme was until recently administered by the Northern Ireland Quality Centre. This body has now completed a merger with the Northern Ireland Growth Challenge to form the Centre for Competitiveness (CforC). The CforC is a private sector, not-for-profit membership organization actively supporting the development of an internationally competitive economy in

Northern Ireland through innovation, productivity improvement and quality excellence in the private, voluntary and public sectors. The primary role of the Centre is to assist local organizations, particularly SMEs, to achieve sustainable competitive advantage. In pursuing this commitment to helping organizations on their journey to excellence, the CforC has developed a series of recognition stages to assess and reward organizations for progress. These schemes use the EFQM Excellence Model®, and include the:

- EFQM Committed to Excellence
- Steps to Excellence and Competitiveness Index
- Mark of Excellence & EFQM Recognized for Excellence
- Northern Ireland Quality Award.

London Excellence

This is a membership organization that provides services to London-based organizations of all sizes and from all sectors. London Excellence's primary goals are to:

- Grow awareness of excellence within London
- Provide innovative membership services
- Support personal development with respect to excellence
- Recognize achievements.

London Excellence does not sponsor an award as such, but it does have a 'Commitment to Excellence Recognition' scheme. This is a non-competitive system of recognition of achievement for organizations in London that can demonstrate their commitment to continuous improvement through the use of excellence disciplines.

Midlands Excellence

This is a registered charity dedicated to improving the performance and competitiveness of all organizations in the region. Established in 1996, Midlands Excellence runs a number of activities, including Investors in Excellence and an annual awards process based on performance against the EFQM Excellence Model®. The Midlands Excellence Awards are open to all organizations or operational units in the private, public and voluntary sectors. There are award categories for large, medium and small companies, public bodies and not-for-profit organizations of any size, plus operational units. All applications are considered automatically for three additional awards:

- The Society Award
- The Midlands Equal Opportunities Employer
- The Most Improved Organization (since last submitting an application).

Applications are assessed and scored against the EFQM Excellence Model®. All entrants prepare a submission document, which is then assessed by a team of trained Midlands Excellence assessors who produce a comprehensive feedback report identifying strengths and areas for improvement. Entrants also receive a site visit from their assessment team, which is made up of volunteers from a range of organizations across the Midlands.

East of England Excellence

This is a not-for-profit organization, and the award programme is subsidized by sponsorship. The annual award programme is open to organizations, both large and small, operating in the public, voluntary and private sectors. The programme is provided to help organizations on their journey to excellence using the EFQM Excellence Model®, and to provide role models for others to use as benchmarks. Although run on similar lines to the UK Excellence Award, the submission document can consist of as few as 35 pages – i.e. one page per 32-criteria part, plus a brief overview – up to a maximum total of 75 pages.

Excellence Yorkshire

This is a not-for-profit organization that is committed to championing business excellence in the Yorkshire and Humberside regions. It encourages the widespread use of the EFQM Excellence Model® throughout the region, and recognizes and rewards best practice through an annual Excellence Yorkshire Award. The award process aim is to encourage organizations to progress and improve, and there is a progression ladder, similar to the BQF's 'Recognition for Excellence' scheme, to help organizations to achieve excellence. This recognizes an organization's achievement, and provides a target for the continuing journey of improvement.

The first rung of the ladder is 'Committed to Excellence'. To qualify for the Excellence Yorkshire Committed to Excellence award, an organization must have:

- Undertaken a review using the principles of the EFQM Excellence Model®
- Identified areas for improvement
- Developed a plan to act on those areas for improvement
- Taken action towards improving those areas for improvement.

Organizations can apply for Committed to Excellence at any time of the year, as the process is separate to that of the annual award process. A qualified assessor visits the organization. The visit is a meeting, which lasts for two hours or so, during which the organization will be asked to explain and provide evidence to demonstrate the above criteria. Recognition is in the form of a certificate.

To get onto the second or subsequent rungs, organizations apply for the full award. In addition to the three formal awards, it also makes awards to organizations at individual model criteria level.

The Excellence Yorkshire Awards are:

- *Bronze*, which is awarded to organizations that have progressed beyond the first steps of improvement and are actively seeking continuous improvement in the future.
- *Silver*, which is awarded to those organizations that have made significant progress in terms of improvement, but still have areas where effort is required to achieve a higher level.
- *Gold*, which is awarded to organizations that have reached a level of performance regarded as regionally excellent. Such organizations will be very well placed to progress to the UK Quality Awards run by the British Quality Foundation.

Excellence North West

Established in 1994, Excellence North West is a not-for-profit membership organization that spans the public, private and voluntary sectors. Its mission is to stimulate the performance of organizations in the northwest by encouraging the pursuit of quality and organizational excellence. The award process is based on a simple workbook that asks specific questions in each of the criterion parts of the EFQM Excellence Model®. Awards are determined by an independent jury, in five categories:

1. Private sector organizations with more than 250 employees
2. Private sector organizations with less than 250 employees
3. Public sector organizations with more than 250 employees
4. Public sector organizations with less than 250 employees
5. Charities and not-for-profit sector organizations.

There are also special awards for organizations demonstrating outstanding achievement in the fields of:

- Leadership
- People and people results
- Customer results
- Environmental and social sustainability. This is the Brian Redhead Award, and is sponsored by the BBC.

A team of assessors assesses the workbook in the same manner as for other awards.

7.7 The Common Assessment Framework

The Common Assessment Framework (CAF) is a free system for organizational self-assessment in the public sector, and the Framework is based on the EFQM Excellence Model®. Jointly managed by the Member States of the European Union, it has been developed to strengthen and support quality development in public administration. The CAF was pilot tested in 2000 before it was officially presented at the First Quality Conference for Public Administration in the EU, in Lisbon in May 2000. A new CAF version (CAF 2002) was finalized in October 2002, which will serve as a basis for providing average scores once a sufficient number of assessment forms have been received by the European Institute of Public Administration (EIPA). The EIPA is a unique establishment, poised between the training needs of the European institutions, the Member States of the European Union, and the countries that have applied for accession. The new version of the CAF is now starting to be used by public administrations across Europe. However, it will continue to be reviewed and improved over the next few years. Improvements will be of a practical nature, rather than changing its basic character as an easy-to-handle introductory tool for quality management in the public sector.

The Common Assessment Framework consists of a CAF assessment form and guidelines on how to conduct organizational self-assessment. The CAF form, which is produced in several European languages, is completed online by the organization and sent back to EIPA. Organizations completing an assessment will receive a feedback report, and will be listed in the CAF database kept at EIPA. Only part of the content of this database is accessible to external organizations, and the results of self-assessments conducted by individual organizations with the CAF remain confidential. The database does not therefore contain information on the overall results obtained by any organization, or on its performance with respect to the different criteria handled by the CAF. However, the database does contain basic information that should allow other organizations interested in sharing experiences and international benchmarking to identify possible partner organizations.

The database also includes basic information on the strengths of individual organizations using the CAF. This information may not, however, be fully reliable. Self-assessment with the CAF introduces the fundamental concepts of quality, and is relatively easy to use. However, the results obtained are less rigorous than those obtained using more demanding and complex quality management models, and do not involve any element of external evaluation. The result of the self-assessment relies entirely on the process of conducting the self-assessment within the group. The results may therefore not be entirely representative, or may be influenced by other factors, and are thus not necessarily fully reliable. This should be borne in mind when using the areas of strength to find partner organizations for sharing experiences or benchmarking.

The database also links to the overall scoring average of all organizations that have used the CAF and reported back to EIPA, enabling organizations to check their own performance against the average of other organizations. Future plans will enable organizations to check their own performance against that of other organizations in the same sector.

One of the objectives of the Common Assessment Framework is to enable public sector organizations to learn from the experiences of other organizations and to encourage benchmarking activities between public sector organizations throughout Europe. During 2003, 'good practice' profiles of individual public sector organizations that have used the CAF and have won an award in a national or other quality award will be available online. This criterion for selection as a 'good practice' profile ensures that the results of the assessment include an element of external verification. There will also be a link to the European Benchmarking Network, a network for sharing benchmarking practices in the public sector across EU countries. Further details on this framework can be found via the EFQM's website (www.efqm.org).

7.8 Summary

We have reviewed some of the national award programmes in this chapter. The countries or continents covered by the awards described in Chapters 4–6, together with those covered in this chapter, represent over three-quarters of the world's gross domestic product.

All the national and regional award programmes described in this chapter can trace their parentage to either the Baldrige or the European Award. They generally share a common framework, or a hybrid framework based on several models, and they share similar assessment processes. This is not to lessen the contribution these national programmes have had on the larger US and European programmes. Much of the thought leadership that has been harnessed in developing the excellence frameworks has come from national groups.

The national and regional awards are the key drivers in promoting organizational excellence within their own countries.

Acknowledgement

The authors gladly acknowledge the contribution of Kay Aitkin in writing this chapter.

8

The ISO9000 Quality Management System

8.1 Introduction

In this chapter we discuss how the ISO9000 framework can be used as a vehicle for business improvement. We are not primarily concerned with the process of achieving ISO9000 registration, or with the debate about its application or benefits to different industries. These areas are covered by many other books and articles. The process of assessing an organization for conformance to a Quality Management System, such as ISO9000, and the review process are important elements in the process of continuous improvement.

Traditionally authors have referred to 'audits' when discussing ISO and to 'assessment' when discussing the excellence models. However, in organizations that are more advanced on their excellence journey, there is generally not a lot of difference between the two approaches. These organizations have moved on from conformance auditing to organizational assessments. We have therefore used the terms 'assessment' and 'assessing' throughout this chapter.

8.2 Background to the standard

The ISO9000 series of standards were first introduced in 1987, and soon became the established global Quality Assurance Standards. National standards around the world were word for word the same as the ISO standards.

A revision took place in 1994 that shifted the balance of the standards more towards a business excellence approach. Changes included more emphasis on the need for an implemented quality policy, and the addition of preventative action to complement corrective action. More recently the year 2000 versions of the standards have been introduced, and this takes the standards even further towards a business excellence approach. The way that third-party assessments are conducted has also been totally revised by the more credible certification bodies, such as the British Standards Institution.

In the UK, these standards are known as BS EN ISO9000:2000. Table 8.1 lists the range of standards. In this chapter we will be looking at both the 9001 and 9004 standards.

Table 8.1: Main components of the BS EN ISO9000:2000 series

Standard	*Description*
BS EN ISO9000:2000	*Fundamentals and vocabulary* This describes fundamentals of quality management systems, and specifies the terminology for quality management systems
BS EN ISO9001:2000	*Requirements* This specifies requirements for a quality management system where an organization needs to demonstrate its ability to provide products that fulfil customer and applicable regulatory requirements, and aims to enhance customer satisfaction
BS EN ISO9004:2000	*Guidelines for performance improvements* This provides guidelines that consider both the effectiveness and efficiency of the quality management system. The aim of this standard is improvement of the performance of the organization and satisfaction of customers and other interested parties
BS EN ISO19011:2000	*Guidelines for auditing* This provides guidance on auditing quality and environmental management systems

Source: ISO9000 (2000)

Organizations choose to adopt ISO9001 for many reasons. These include:

- The need to comply with customers who require ISO9001 as a requirement of placing an order. This is particularly the case when selling to the European Union markets or tendering for public sector work
- To improve the quality system
- To minimize being subjected to repeated assessments by similar customers
- To improve suppliers' performance.

A number of benefits from applying ISO9000 have also been noted. These include:

- Achieving a better understanding and consistency of all quality practices throughout the organization
- Ensuring continued use of the required quality system year after year
- Improving documentation
- Improving quality awareness
- Strengthening the organization and improving customer confidence and relationships
- Yielding cost savings and improving profitability
- Forming a foundation and discipline for improvement activities within the quality management system.

Research commissioned by the British Standards Institution in 2000 and conducted by the European Centre for Business Excellence looked at both the benefits of the previous 1994 version of ISO9000 and the reasons why organizations have decided to adopt the standard. Based on a total of seventeen case studies that were taken from a mixture of organizations, the research reached several conclusions, which are summarized in Figure 8.1. The case studies themselves are available on the BSI website at www.BSI-global.com/iso9000casestudies.

A survey conducted in the USA in 1999 by Quality Systems identified the reasons why organizations maintain their registration, the main ones being operational benefits, customer demands and the fear of falling behind the competition. The results are shown in Figure 8.2. All three reasons were cited by around 50 per cent of those surveyed, and the benefit to the organization was in line with customer demands. This is an important finding, as it suggests that there are real benefits associated with ISO9000 registration as well as complying with customer demands.

- Almost 62 per cent of organizations stated requirement by customers as a reason that led to the implementation of ISO9000. As a result, many organizations were able to gain additional sales and secure existing business. One organization stated that $6 million of sales by a key customer had been secured. Another company was able to tender for government contracts accounting for additional 8 per cent of total turnover. £15 million per year of additional contracts was won by an organization. These examples show the decision to implement an ISO quality management system resulted in immediate benefits. Many companies were also certain that the system was useful for long-term business success.
- Using the ISO9000 quality management system provided remarkable operational benefits, which was most frequently mentioned by almost 81 per cent of organizations. In particular, the interviewees mentioned, for example, continuity, improvement, efficiency, effectiveness, 100 per cent consistency, uniformity, accuracy, focus, less duplication and less accidents as operational benefits gained by the systems.
- Support and continuous improvement were the most frequently perceived benefit gained through the help of BSI, both were mentioned by almost 81 per cent. The organizations interviewed believed that BSI provided an excellent support not only throughout the registration process but also afterwards. The guidance and feedback was seen as very valuable to the development and maintenance of the system. In addition, BSI played an important role by convincing people at all levels of the usefulness of ISO9000. One company said that BSI handled change well and diplomatically. Continuous improvement was achieved by pointing out opportunities on a regular basis. These opportunities covered both issues concerning the management system and an organization's business.

Figure 8.1 Conclusions from European Centre for Business Excellence Case Studies (Source: ECforBE (2000))

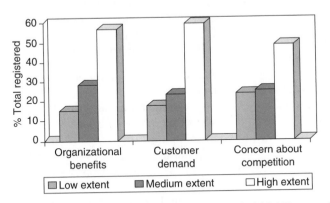

Figure 8.2 Reasons for maintaining registration (1999 US survey) (Source: Naveh *et al.* (1999))

The US survey also examined reasons for the implementation of ISO9000, and identified four implementation strategies: customization, routinization, learning, and going beyond. The features of each of these strategies are defined in Table 8.2.

Table 8.2: Four ISO9000 implementation strategies

Implementation strategy	Features
Customization is defined as the extent to which the standard is tailored to specific company circumstances	Coordination with suppliers Coordination with customers Based on learning from other companies already registered Integrated with practices already in place Based on an analysis of internal processes and performance A springboard to introduce new practices Customized to company needs
Routinization is defined as the extent to which ISO9000 is used in daily practice	Changes have been made since registration Documents are used in daily practice Documents are regularly updated The system is applied to operations such as marketing, etc. Managers value internal audits ISO9000 has led to the discovery of improvement opportunities Preparations for the external audit are not made at the last minute The system is not regularly ignored The system is not an unnecessary burden It has changed daily practice It has become part of a regular routine
Learning is defined as the extent to which the standard is used to make improvements	Audit findings are incorporated into training Top management uses the data to find solutions to the company's business problems Top management uses the data to find solutions to the company's technical problems ISO9000 has helped prevent problems
Going beyond corresponds to the extent to which implementation moves beyond the minimum requirements	ISO9000 is a starting point for introducing other more advanced practices ISO9000 is a catalyst for rethinking the way you do business ISO9000 is understood as an opportunity to innovate

Source: Naveh *et al.* (1999)

What is also of interest is how much benefit from ISO9000 is derived from each of the various strategies. The researchers measured the level of benefit for each strategy under different cultural conditions, the cultures being defined as 'low performance', 'medium performance' and 'high performance'. The results are shown in Figure 8.3, and two main conclusions may be drawn from them. The first is that some benefit is achieved in all cultures and with all implementation strategies but, not surprisingly, the high-performance culture delivers the highest benefit. Secondly, routinization would appear to be the most effective implementation strategy under all cultural conditions.

The increasing global interest over the past decade in a range of activities connected with quality assurance and quality management is definitely linked with the development and adoption of the ISO9000 standards. The success of the ISO9000 family of standards is still growing, and the number of countries where ISO9000 is being implemented has increased. Every year the International Standards Organization conducts a survey, and in the tenth survey (ISO 2002) it was found that up to the end of December 2000, over 400 000 ISO9000 certificates had been awarded in 158 countries worldwide. This was an increase of 64 988 ISO9000 certificates over the end of December 1999, when the total stood at 343 643 for 150 countries.

Looking at the different regions of the world, Europe, with 220 127 certificates awarded, was found to be still increasing its number of certificates rapidly, with 29 879 more than in 1999, while the Far East, with 81 919 certificates awarded, showed a 25 271 increase, confirming the growing interest of the region's industries in the ISO9000 certification process. Figure 8.4 gives

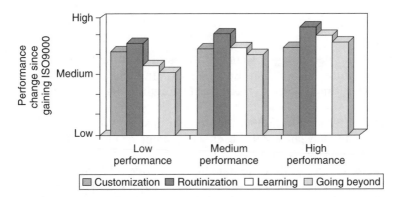

Figure 8.3 Organizational culture and implementation success (1999 US survey) (Source: Naveh *et al.* (1999))

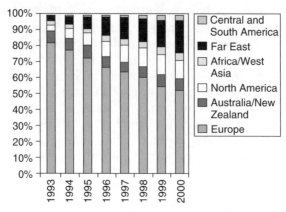

Figure 8.4 ISO9000:1994 certifications over an eight-year period (Source: ISO (2002d))

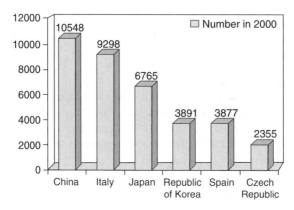

Figure 8.5 New certificate numbers 2000 (Source: ISO (2002d))

the trends for the percentage of certifications over an eight-year period. This figure shows that Europe's dominance has been decreasing over time, with the Far East showing the greatest growth.

The growth in interest in ISO9000 in the Far East is particularly interesting. Figure 8.5 shows the highest number of certificates awarded in 2000, for the top six countries.

It must be remembered that the data shown above relate to the 1994 version of the ISO9000 standard. This chapter will focus on the new standards, which, despite being entitled the 2000 version, did not come into force in full until late 2003. It has been possible to achieve certification against the 2000 standard since 2001, but organizations that have certification to the 1994 version have to migrate to the new standard by 15 December 2003. This long transition period reflects the change of the standard away from conformance to creating value within an organization by managing at a process level. Getting process management under control is a longer-term objective.

8.3 Applying the ISO9000 standard

Ask for a word to describe ISO9000, and the answers may well include 'bureaucratic', 'procedures', 'inflexible' and 'nit-picking'. However, there is more to the application of the standard than these perspectives, and these terms are becoming very out of date. It is true that there is a sharp focus on the control of processes through the use of procedures, but there are as many management processes that need to be under control.

The ISO framework also gives improvement opportunities through reviewing past performance. For example, it can be correlated against Deming's Plan–Do–Check–Act cycle. As shown in Figure 8.6, the main steps in applying the standard are:

- Define customer needs and expectations
- Establish objectives to reflect these needs and expectations
- Identify the processes to achieve the objectives
- Review the operation of the processes
- Improve the processes
- Review customer needs and expectations.

Viewing the standard in this way puts it into a completely new perspective, and we will build on this as we discuss its content in more detail. First we will review the ISO9001:2000 standard, which is the requirements standard, and then we will move on to ISO9004: 2000, which is the standard for performance improvement.

The 2000 version of the ISO9000 series of standards is based on eight management principles that are designed to lead an organization towards improved performance. It will be noted that these eight principles have a close similarity to the Baldrige core values and concepts described in Chapter 4, and the EFQM's eight fundamental concepts described in Chapter 5. The ISO9000 management principles are detailed in Table 8.3.

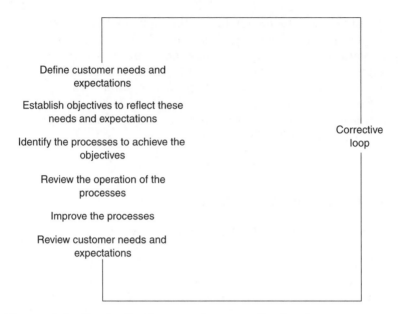

Figure 8.6 The Quality System and never-ending improvement

As can be seen from Table 8.3, there is a correlation between the ISO management principles and the Baldrige and EFQM equivalents. Where Baldrige and EFQM go beyond the ISO principles are in the areas of results orientation, a focus on the future, and corporate and social responsibility. These former two points do have an emphasis in the ISO9004:2000 performance improvement standard, and elements of corporate and social responsibility are covered by the ISO14001 environmental standard.

8.4 ISO9001:2000 – the requirements standard

It is not the purpose of this chapter to discuss the contents of the standard in great detail; we will only focus on the key points that relate specifically to business excellence. Figure 8.7 shows the relationship of the paragraphs of ISO9001 schematically.

The model is based on a Plan–Do–Check–Act Deming cycle. The elements of this are:

Plan: establish the objectives and processes necessary to deliver results in accordance with customer requirements and the organization's policies.

Table 8.3: ISO9000 eight management principles

Management principle	Explanation	Baldrige equivalent	EFQM equivalent
Customer focus	Organizations depend on their customers and therefore should understand current and future customer needs, should meet customer requirements and strive to exceed customer expectations	Customer-driven excellence	Customer focus
Leadership	Leaders establish unity of purpose and direction of the organization. They should create and maintain the internal environment in which people can become fully involved in achieving the organization's objectives	Visionary leadership	Leadership and constancy of purpose
Involvement of people	People at all levels are the essence of an organization, and their full involvement enables their abilities to be used for the organization's benefit	Valuing employees and partners	People development and involvement

(continued)

Table 8.3: *Continued*

Management principle	Explanation	Baldrige equivalent	EFQM equivalent
Process approach	A desired result is achieved more efficiently when activities and related resources are managed as a process	Systems perspective	Management by process and facts
Systems approach to management	Identifying, understanding and managing interrelated processes as a system contributes to the organization's effectiveness and efficiency in achieving its objectives	Systems perspective	Management by process and facts
Continual improvement	Continual improvement of the organization's overall performance should be a permanent objective of the organization	Organizational and personal learning	Continuous learning, improvement and innovation
Factual decision-making	Effective decisions are based on the analysis of data and information	Management by fact	Management by process and facts
Mutually beneficial supplier relationships	An organization and its suppliers are interdependent, and a mutually beneficial relationship enhances the ability of both to create value	Valuing employees and partners	Partnership development

Source: ISO (2000a)

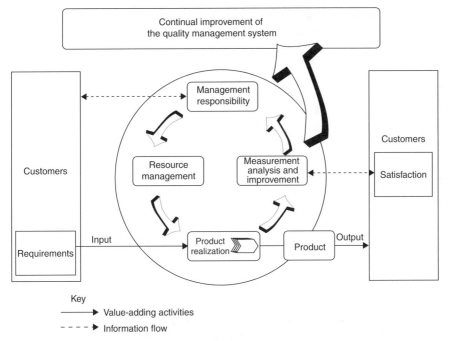

Figure 8.7 The ISO9001:2000 process-based quality management system (Source: ISO (2000b))

Do: implement the processes.
Check: monitor and measure processes and product against policies, objectives and requirements for the product and report the results.
Act: take actions to continually improve process performance.

This should not be confused with the cycle shown in Figure 8.6, which relates to the implementation of the quality management system – including the need to document the procedures. The points above relate to the choice of the activities that must be implemented to meet the customer needs. This reflects how far the ISO9000 series of standards has developed, as they are now totally process based. ISO9001:2000 notes that when used within a quality management system, a process approach emphasizes the importance of:

- Understanding and meeting requirements
- The need to consider processes in terms of added value
- Obtaining results of process performance and effectiveness
- Continual improvement of processes based on objective measurement.

As an illustration of the change in emphasis between the 1994 and 2000 standards, Table 8.4 shows a count of the number of times various terms are used in the two standards.

Table 8.4: Change in ISO9001 vocabulary

Term	Count, 1994 version	Count, 2000 version
Improvement	0	16
Processes	21	33
Procedures	36	9
Customer	15	30
Competency	0	3
Capability	5	1
Analyse(is)	0	5

Source: J. Hele of BSI. Used with kind permission

The core structure of the standard reflects the central wheel in Figure 8.7. Figure 8.8 lists the particular sections that make up the core requirements, and a summary of the contents of each of these sections follows.

Section 4: Quality management system

There is a need to ensure that the quality management system provides products and services that meet customer requirements. The quality management system should also be capable of improving the organization's ability to continuously improve.

The quality management system normally contains a variety of documents, which may all be electronic, as non-virtual written procedures are more widely accepted today. Figure 8.9 shows the structure of a typical quality management system.

The primary role of the quality management system is to enable the translation of policies into ways of working. The 'policies and direction' are normally defined in strategy documents. The 'systems architecture' relates to the way that the quality management system is defined, and this is normally captured in a top-level quality manual. Below this a number of processes are defined, and these lead to effective and efficient ways of working. The ways that processes are operated are normally defined in procedures or work instructions, and a number of other documents such as inspection records provide evidence that the processes have been operated consistently.

4	5	6	7	8
Quality management system	Management responsibility	Resource management	Product realization	Measurement, analysis and improvement
4.1 General requirements	5.1 Management commitment	6.1 Provision of resources	7.1 Planning of product realization	8.1 General
4.2 Documentation requirements	5.2 Customer focus	6.2 Human resources	7.2 Customer-related processes	8.2 Monitoring and measurement
	5.3 Quality policy	6.3 Infrastructure	7.3 Design and development	8.3 Control of non-conforming product
	5.4 Planning	6.4 Work environment	7.4 Purchasing	8.4 Analysis of data
	5.5 Responsibility, authority and communication		7.5 Production and service provision	8.5 Improvement
	5.6 Management review		7.6 Control of monitoring and measuring devices	

Figure 8.8 ISO9001:2000 section breakdown (Source: ISO (2000b))

Hence within a quality management system there is a need to identify the core processes of the organization, and the ways in which they will be measured, monitored and analysed so that they may be continually improved. There is a need to ensure that all the documentation of the quality management system is kept in line with the management of the processes.

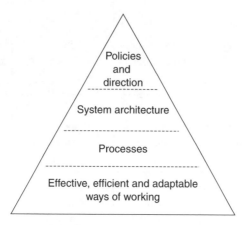

Figure 8.9 A typical quality management system

Section 5: Management responsibility

The top management team should take a leading and visible role in defining, implementing, administering and improving the quality management system. It is also important that the team ensures that the quality management system meets the needs of the customers.

Under the 'management commitment' subsection, the top management team has to demonstrate its commitment to the development and the improvement of the quality management system. It also has to communicate the importance of meeting customer, regulatory and legal requirements, and ensure the availability of necessary resources. Management review calls for a variety of inputs, such as internal assessments, customer feedback and process performance, to be considered when reviewing the effectiveness and efficiency of the quality management system. The review will lead to a number of improvement actions for both the processes and the quality management system.

Customer focus calls for top management to ensure that customer needs and expectations are determined, and converted into requirements. It is the fulfilment of these requirements that leads to the achievement of customer satisfaction. This commitment to meeting customers' and other requirements will normally be defined in a quality policy. The quality policy will also provide a framework for establishing and reviewing the quality objectives of the organization. These quality objectives should be deployed to all relevant functions and levels throughout the organization. It is also necessary to ensure that the relevant resources are identified to ensure that customer requirements are met, and that the quality management system and processes are continuously reviewed.

Section 6: Resource management

Resource management is the process of identifying, providing and managing all required resources. This includes both physical and human resources, so that they are available to meet the requirements of the quality management system.

For physical resources, there is a need to identify the facilities required and to ensure that they are maintained to achieve conformity of products and services such that customer satisfaction is maintained. There is also a need to ensure that the facilities are improved.

For people, the competencies required to perform the various functions should be identified. A training plan is often a supporting mechanism, and the effectiveness of any training that is required to ensure that the levels of competency are achieved should be evaluated.

Section 7: Product realization

The ISO9001:2000 has a focus on the processes that deliver the product or service, but the principles in this section could equally be applied to all processes. The objective is to have plans in place to ensure that all the delivery processes are operated and thus that the quality objectives are met.

There is a need for evidence of planning for the core delivery processes, including ensuring that:

- Objectives are set
- The process tasks are identified and planned
- Equipment is suitable and a suitable environment is ensured
- Any need for documented instructions and necessary records is identified
- Processes are monitored and approved
- Workmanship and acceptance criteria are established
- Plans for verification and validation of activities are prepared.

The core delivery processes are broken down into four categories, and each of these is defined in Table 8.5.

The final subsection relates to the control of monitoring and measuring devices. Often referred to as calibration, these activities ensure that any inspection, measuring and test devices are

Table 8.5: ISO9001:2000 product realization process categories

Process category	Definition
Customer-related processes	These are the processes that make certain that the organization can meet the customer needs before accepting the order. These also include the processes that determine the regulatory and legal requirements, and the processes that communicate product and service information to customers
Design and development processes	These processes ensure that the products and services meet all specified design requirements set by the customer, regulatory agencies and the law. Review, verification and validation activities as appropriate at each stage of the design are also included. There is also a need to evaluate the ability of the organization to fulfil the design requirements and to identify any problems so that action may be taken
Purchasing	These processes ensure that the products and services received from suppliers meet the organization's requirements. There is a need to demonstrate the effective operation of the processes covering areas such as: • Supplier evaluation • Purchasing data • Verification of purchased product/service at supplier's site • Verification of purchased product/service at organization's site
Production and service processes	These are the processes that deliver the products and services within the organization. There is a need to ensure that the processes are operated under controlled conditions

capable of consistently providing the specified measurement requirements so that proper decisions can be made for the control and acceptance of the products and services.

Section 8: Measurement, analysis and improvement

Monitoring and measurement activities are needed to ensure conformity and to accomplish improvement by defining, planning and implementing such activities. These improvement activities are based on the input from a number of sources, including customer satisfaction/dissatisfaction, process performance, and internal assessment.

There are essentially two aspects to this section. First there are the activities that relate to the collection and the analysis of the data. The second aspect relates to the way that corrective and preventative action is taken in a controlled manner. In conducting both these activities, there is a close link with the requirements of subsection 5.6, which relates to management review.

This completes our brief run-through of the ISO9001:2000 standard. From our discussions it can be concluded that there are many disciplines in the standard that support business improvement, and that the standard is totally process-based. Before reviewing the ISO9004:2000 performance improvement standard, we will move on to a brief discussion regarding the way in which the standard is normally applied through the achievement of certification – which is usually the root cause of criticism of the standard. Certification is the ISO9000 series' answer to the award processes discussed in the previous chapters.

8.5 The certification process

To evaluate whether an organization meets ISO9001:2000, an assessment of its quality system is performed. The concept of assessment will be discussed from two viewpoints: first, briefly, from a certification point of view; secondly, in section 8.6 of this chapter, from an internal/business improvement point of view.

A key factor with assessments is striking a balance between conformance to the standard and the opportunity for improvement. There can be a tendency to be excessively concerned with detail. A modern quality assessor would note but not dwell on the discovery of a piece of paper with a missing reference or page number. An old-style auditor could compete with Judge Jeffries! Consequently auditing has received bad press – unfortunately in some cases quite deservedly. With the introduction of ISO9001:2000, the more reputable certification bodies have retrained their assessors to move them away from conformance assessment against the standard to conformance assessment against the customer requirements. It has been stated that many old-style assessors have not made the grade.

The certification process conducted by a third party 'certification' body assesses an applicant to see if the organization meets the standard. A mistake that is often made is that companies think they are 'accredited' to ISO9001. In fact companies are actually 'certified', which in turn leads them to become 'registered' in the certification body's register of certified companies, should it keep such a register.

There are many approaches to ISO9001 registration that have been described in many publications. The description of the certification process is here broken down into three phases: pre-assessment, assessment and maintenance.

Phase 1 – Pre-assessment

The pre-assessment activities are where the initial benefits from adopting a quality system are gained. This is also the phase where most effort is required.

The starting point is to examine the organization's current and planned activities in order to establish the needs and the scope of the quality system, based on the requirements of the customers. Deciding the scope of the quality management system is very important, as this has a direct impact on the processes that will need documenting under Section 7 of the standard. By scope, we mean the areas that will seek registration. It is a common misunderstanding that an entire organization has to apply for certification at the same time. In some large organizations it is not practical for the organization or the certification body to certify the entire organization in one exercise. In fact there are distinct advantages in not doing this, the main one being that a specialized support function – such as training and development, information technology, or maintenance – would receive an assessment focused on its operation by assessors more familiar with current practices. There is a risk that an assessment of such a unit could be lost in the scope of an assessment of an entire organization.

The next step is to interpret the standard for the organization. Some paragraphs of the standard are universally acceptable, whereas some are extremely specific. Fortunately with many industries the interpretation of the standard is eased, as guidance is available through 'quality assessment schedules' and 'guidelines' that are published by certification bodies.

From experience, the majority of organizations find that the area requiring most attention and effort is documenting the quality system. The organization must be able to demonstrate to a third-party assessor that it is in control. This means having a quality manual, procedures and instructions, and detailed records of quality-related measurements. There is no requirement for these documents to be paper-based.

Usually the procedures are constructed from observation of current practice. It is also important to remember that there are several control processes that have to be implemented at an early stage of the proceedings. Examples of these control procedures are internal assessments, monitoring of supplier performance, and management review.

Phase 2 – Assessment

The assessment processes used by the various certification bodies may vary slightly, but in principle they are all the same. The assessment process described here is based on the one followed by the British Standards Institution Management Systems Division of the British Standards Institution.

The first main activity carried out by the certification body is to assess the top-level quality system documentation. This is usually carried out 'on site' so that any queries can be resolved on the spot in the interests of customer satisfaction. When the quality manual has been 'passed', then the date of the assessment can be set by mutual agreement. By passing the manual the certification body is effectively saying that 'provided you run your business the way you say you do in your quality manual, then you will pass the assessment'.

The second main activity is the assessment itself. The assessors will be looking for differences between what is stated in the top-level quality manual and what happens in practice. When such a difference is discovered the assessor will raise a 'non-conformity' report, which will reference a particular section of the standard.

Non-conformity reports are assigned a level of seriousness. If the non-conformance is considered to represent a major failure in the quality system, then the assessment will be failed. An example of a 'major' non-conformance would be if the assessors discovered that internal quality assessments were not being carried out, there was no complaint procedure, or processes had not been adequately defined against customer requirements.

If the non-conformance is not considered to be so serious, then a 'minor' non-conformance is raised. But beware! If several minor non-conformances are raised against the same section of the standard, then these can be combined into a major non-conformance and the assessment will be failed. There is no set number dictating when a minor non-conformance becomes a major one; this is down to the discretion of the lead assessor.

The assessors also have the option to raise 'observations', which are not considered to be non-conformances but are warning signs that if a situation is not corrected a non-conformance could well occur. It is recognized that the non-conformance approach has to have a level of discipline so that the standards are maintained. However, unlike the 'old days', when non-conformances were handed out as a punishment, now they provide a valuable form of feedback to support an organization in its improvement activities.

At the end of the assessment, the assessors give a recommendation regarding whether the organization should be certified or not. This recommendation is subject to the receipt of a corrective action plan detailing how the non-conformances raised will be cleared. It is not up to the assessors to award the certificate, and the governing body must ratify their recommendation.

One of the problems encountered when a third-party assessor encounters a 'total quality' organization is that there can be conflict over the timeliness of corrective action. A total quality organization will seek to discover and remove the root cause of a problem, and this may take considerably longer than a 'quick fix' required to clear an assessment point. Wherever possible, root cause elimination should be encouraged by the assessment team, even if the assessment points remain outstanding longer as a consequence. This is especially important in view of the corrective and preventative action requirements of the standard.

Phase 3 – Maintenance

The receipt of the certificate is not the end of the process. The certification body will generally conduct surveillance visits twice a year to ensure that conformance to the standard is still being maintained. Although in theory these visits could be unannounced, the certification body works in partnership with the certified organization to ensure that maximum value is obtained from the surveillance activities. For example, at least one member of the original assessment team usually conducts the first visit to ensure continuity.

At the first visit the team will confirm that the non-conformances raised in the original assessment had been effectively cleared. Over the course of a two-year cycle, the surveillance visits will address every section of the standard on a systematic basis.

8.6 Company evaluation against the standard – the internal quality assessment process

Internal quality assessments have become an applied management tool to check compliance of an organization to various standards, including ISO9001. The requirements of ISO9001 call for the organization regularly to assess its quality system using an independent internal resource. In this way, the systems can be monitored and improved.

In practice, the process of the internal assessments does not vary a great deal from the process for an external assessment, although the degree of learning will be different. A third party suffers in that it does not know an organization as well as it knows itself. Also, the maturity of the quality culture of the certification body may not be as advanced as that of the host company. On the positive side, the external assessors have much wider industry knowledge and have a habit of asking 'simple, obvious' questions that a large organization may overlook. The benefits from both processes are of great value.

The internal quality assessment process is discussed in two parts. The first part describes how a typical internal assessment is conducted, while the second part moves on to a discussion of how an internal quality assessment programme can be used to promote continuous improvement.

A typical internal quality assessment process

The internal assessment programme typically assesses the entire quality system over a one-year assessment cycle. The procedure has the four main stages:

1. Plan the assessment
2. Conduct the assessment
3. Report the assessment findings
4. Close off the assessment points.

Plan the assessment

First, the senior assessor should define the scope and purpose of the assessment – for example, is it to check compliance or effectiveness, or to verify corrective action? Next, the assessment team is selected. Only assessors who have been trained to conduct assessments and are independent of the area to be assessed should be used. The assessment team members should collectively have

Table 8.6: Qualities of the lead assessor and assessor team members

- Experience of the type of quality system standard against which the assessment is to be conducted (for example, manufacturing, computer software or service standards)
- Experience of the type of service or product and its associated regulatory requirements (for example, healthcare, food, insurance, nuclear devices)
- Need for professional qualifications or technical expertise in a particular discipline
- Skill in managing a team
- Ability to make effective use of the skills of the various members of the assessment team
- Personal skills to deal with assessors
- Any required language fluency
- Absence of real or perceived conflict of interest
- Any other relevant factors

the skills to conduct the assessment, which includes having any specialist knowledge required for the area. Table 8.6 gives guidance regarding the qualification criteria of assessment team members.

It is not suggested that every assessment team member should have these qualities, but there should be representation across the team. These skills also hold for the role of assessors, which will be discussed in Part 3 of this book.

Once the assessment team has been established, members of the team review the relevant standard and top-level quality documentation. From this review, a checklist of areas to examine is compiled; this helps with the planning of the assessment and serves as a record of events. A detailed schedule giving the role of each assessor, the areas they are to visit and areas to be examined can then be developed. The process for constructing the checklist is not unlike the process described for site visits in the total quality frameworks, which will be discussed in Part 3 of this book.

Conduct the assessment

An assessor typically starts with an opening meeting. Here, the purpose and scope of the assessment may be reinforced and assessment plan confirmed.

It is usual for the senior or lead assessor to start by assessing the senior management, whilst the other assessors tackle the production or service areas. During the course of the assessment the assessors will confer to see how well the 'top-down' picture compares with the 'bottom-up' one.

During the assessment, staff are interviewed and asked questions to determine whether procedures are understood and are being carried out as stated in the documented quality system. The general process is to 'observe, verify and record'. Information gained during the interview is confirmed by watching the process as it is being done, and by reviewing records that have previously been generated. Any significant observations should be recorded.

Report the assessment findings

At a closing meeting, a verbal summary of the findings (both positive and negative) is presented to the management team. Any non-conformances that have been observed and reported will be 'signed-off' by an area representative who witnessed the event. This is to confirm that the observation took place.

After the closing meeting a formal report containing all the non-conformances is issued so that the particular area can prepare its corrective action plan.

Close off the assessment points

After the corrective action has been taken, a follow-up review by one of the assessment team should be conducted to ensure that the corrective action has been effective.

Quality assessments as a continuous improvement tool

Returning to Figure 8.6, we can see how a quality management system maps against the Deming Plan–Do–Check–Act improvement cycle. Taking the quality assessment specifically, we can see that it plays a vital role in the 'check' stage. It is a way of ensuring that the disciplines laid down in the quality manual have been fully implemented. Closer inspection reveals that there is more to it than just this.

People at all levels throughout an organization either make or are involved in the making of decisions. The output of the decision-making process is only as good as the input. Viewed in a positive light, assessments are fact-finding activities that examine objective evidence in an unbiased manner so as to provide reliable input for decisions. A central purpose of an assessment should be to obtain correct information that will be used as essential input to assist in the decision-making process. This will allow quality problems and costs to be prevented or rectified.

It is worth at this stage recounting the words of A. P. Sloan, who, when recalling his days at the head of General Motors, wrote:

> *... and I do not mean audits in the usual financial sense but one that contemplates a continuous review and appraisal of what is going on throughout the enterprise ... This audit function ... is of the highest value to the enterprise and its shareholders. I cannot conceive of any board of directors being better informed and thus able to act intelligently on all the changing facts and circumstances than is the board of General Motors.* (Sloan, 1996)

We can therefore define an assessment as an unbiased fact-finding exercise that substantially improves the quality of decisions by helping to avoid the risks associated with them. Assessments provide objective management information that improves decision-making.

Turning specifically to quality assessments, the information collected can fall into one of four categories:

1. Interpretation of the ISO9001 standard
2. Scope of the approach taken
3. Implementation of the quality practices
4. Improvement opportunities.

We will now discuss each of these in turn. It should be noted that there are two main dimensions, approach and deployment, and we will be returning to these dimensions when we discuss the evaluation processes for the business frameworks.

Interpretation of the ISO9001 standard

The interpretation of ISO9001 for a particular industry can often be subjective, despite the fact that guidelines are available to assist in this process. Sometimes assessors will form a view on what is wrong and what is right based on their experience. Whatever the case, observations raised allow a debate to take place on what is best for the organization. By challenging the basic assumptions made during the original interpretation, there is an opportunity to improve the approach that has been taken.

Scope of the approach taken

Sometimes the approach that has been taken is good, but it does not have a wide enough scope. There will therefore be an improvement benefit if the approach is applied to other areas.

For example, consider the case where all employees in an organization have been given total quality management awareness training. The approach taken by the company for new employees is that they too will be subjected to total quality management awareness training. However, an assessment reveals that there is no provision to train any temporary staff that are employed and, what is more, temporary staff are used in the reception area where the first point of contact with customers is made. Clearly it will be an improvement if the scope of the approach is widened to include temporary staff.

Implementation of the quality practices

Since an assessment systematically analyses objective evidence and presents facts rather than value judgements, it corrects pre-conceived ideas about the status of a company's management systems, procedures, methods and training requirements. This also involves the correction of particular notions about whether or not various parts of the company are working in a manner that is consistent with the policies and objectives delegated by the board of directors.

It is common for senior and middle management to assume that authorized procedures are being followed at all times, whereas in fact any similarity between authorized procedures and actual practice can be purely coincidental. The senior management team obtains its information through the channels that run upward through the organization's hierarchy. As the information is passed from level to level, it is inevitably distorted and filtered before it ever reaches senior management. This can be disastrous in extreme cases, and costly at other times. However, an assessment report bypasses a number of management levels and reaches senior management in its original form. This gives an undistorted picture of company operations and the effectiveness of the various departments and managers within the organization.

All too often quality assessments are not seen as opportunities for improvement but as policing activities – especially when the findings circumnavigate the usual management levels. This is unfortunate. If an assessment reveals that a procedure is not being carried out in line with the defined instructions, the reason for this must be understood. There may be any one of many reasons, including the following:

- The procedure may be wrong
- The operator may be untrained in the operation
- The operator may not be aware of the latest procedure
- The operator may simply want to do things his or her own way.

Whatever the reason, the assessment will form a basis for improvement action provided the results are used in a positive way.

Improvement opportunities

Improvement opportunities have already been discussed in the preceding three sections. The improvement opportunities discussed here are mainly those generated by the report process and by the observations made by the assessment team, outside the scope of an assessment to the ISO standard.

Taking the report process first, since the assessment report will reach senior management directly, it will promote communication between the lowest and the highest levels within an organization. It enables employees at all levels to suggest improved methods of operation. The people performing the operations are more closely involved with the product or service, and are normally in the best position to see the truth about the practical implementation of the quality system and suggested improvements.

This is one area where the assessment process scores over the evaluation processes used in the award processes described in the previous chapters. With the evaluation processes, the communication between the parties is not always dynamic and does not take place in real time.

The second aspect is the commonsense observations made during the course of the assessment, or those ideas generated by the assessor challenging the way in which the work is being performed.

For example, during an assessment of a service company that had two locations, an assessor questioned how the paperwork was protected during the transfer of work between the two locations. By walking through the process, it was discovered that although there was an established procedure for protecting the paperwork during transport, there was no way of ensuring that the paperwork that was sent actually arrived! This point was so obvious it had been overlooked and an improvement action was immediately implemented, preventing what could have been a complete disaster.

8.7 The ISO9004:2000 performance improvement standard

So far we have concentrated on the ISO9001:2000 standard and looked at its contents and the way that organizations are assessed against its requirements. The ISO9004:2000 'Guidelines for performance improvement' is based on the same eight management principles and process-based quality management system model,

4 Quality management system	5 Management responsibility	6 Resource management	7 Product realization	8 Measurement, analysis and improvement
4.1 Managing system and processes	5.1 General guidance	6.1 General guidance	7.1 General guidance	8.1 General guidance
4.2 Documentation	5.2 Needs and expectations of interested parties	6.2 People	7.2 Process related to interested parties	8.2 Monitoring and measurement
4.3 Use of quality management principles	5.3 Quality policy	6.3 Infrastructure	7.3 Design and development	8.3 Control of non-conformity
	5.4 Planning	6.4 Work environment	7.4 Purchasing	8.4 Analysis of data
	5.5 Responsibility, authority and communication	6.5 Information	7.5 Production and service provision	8.5 Improvement
	5.6 Management review	6.6 Suppliers and partnerships	7.6 Control of monitoring and measuring devices	
		6.7 Natural resources		
		6.8 Financial resources		

Key	
No significant change	
Minor change	
Major change or new addition	

Figure 8.10 Comparison of ISO9001:2000 and ISO9004:2000 (Source: ISO (2000b, 2000c))

but goes beyond the basic requirements of ISO9001:2000 to include the satisfaction of interested parties and the performance of the organization. Unlike ISO9001:2000, it is not possible to achieve certification against the standard, but organizations following this standard would meet the needs of ISO9001:2000.

The ISO9004:2000 standard is similar in structure to the ISO9001:2000 standard. A comparison highlighting the differences is given in Figure 8.10.

Figure 8.8 demonstrates the degree of change between the two standards. Of the 23 sections in the 9001 standard, 10 have undergone some minor revision and 6 have been added or subjected to major change. One of the other significant changes is that ISO9004:2000 contains advice on self-assessment as well as audits.

Considering the major changes, subsection 4.3 adds a specific reference to the eight management principles that were given in Table 8.2 and form the basis of the ISO9000 series of standards. Under the Resources section, other resources that are found in the business excellence frameworks, such as information resources and financial resources, have been added. This brings the ISO9004:2000 closer to these models.

The change in subsection 7.2 from 'Customer-related processes' to 'Process related to interested parties' indicates a widening scope in this area. Example processes that have been listed include market research, including sector and end-user data, competitor analysis, and benchmarking.

The difference between ISO9001:2000 and ISO9004:2000 has been expressed as a general widening of scope in the standard as it approaches a business excellence framework, as shown in Figure 8.11. With the introduction of ISO9004:2000, there is now a much better transition path between ISO9001 and business excellence. An excellent comparison between ISO9001, Baldrige

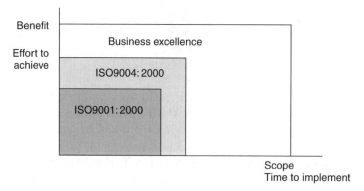

Figure 8.11 ISO9000 and business excellence

and the EFQM Excellence Model® is given in the BSI Publication *Beyond Registration*.

8.8 Summary

In this chapter we have examined the ISO9000:2000 series of quality assurance standards, with a particular focus on ISO9001:2000. We have looked at this standard from a business improvement point of view and not simply from the normal certification standpoint, and have examined the ISO9004:2000 performance improvement standard. When doing this, the ISO9000 series of standards can be seen as an important element of a 'business excellence' framework.

We have looked briefly at the certification and assessment processes. The certification process may be compared with the award processes discussed in the previous chapters, and the assessment process with the evaluation method. When applied effectively, the assessment process is one of the most powerful evaluation techniques, both for use in an 'award' situation and a self-assessment situation.

References

ECforBC (2000). *The Model in Practice*. London: British Quality Foundation.

ISO (2000a). *ISO9000:2000. Quality Management Systems – Fundamentals and Vocabulary*. London: British Standards Institution.

ISO (2000b). *ISO9001:2000. Quality Management Systems – Requirements*. London: British Standards Institution.

ISO (2000c). *ISO9004:2000. Quality Management Systems – Guidelines for Performance Improvements*. London: British Standards Institution.

ISO (2002d). *The ISO Survey of ISO9000 and ISO 14000 Certificates, International Standards Against*. London: British Standards Institution.

Naveh, E., Marcus, A. *et al.* (1999). *ISO9000 Survey '99*. New York: McGraw-Hill.

Sloan, A. P. (1996). *My Years with General Motors*. Doubleday.

Tanner, S. J., Pertwee, C. and Bailey, M. (2003). *Beyond Registration*. London: British Standards Institution.

Part Three

Self-Assessment

The key steps in self-assessment

9.1 Introduction

In the previous chapters we have evaluated the major excellence frameworks used in self-assessment, and taken an overview of the award processes.

Organizations can position themselves against a selected framework in a variety of ways. However, each of these ways has certain common processes. This chapter is concerned with the detail of these common processes, which include the steps shown in Figure 9.1.

We will examine each of these processes in turn. Each of the processes is a key step in the self-assessment process, irrespective of the excellence framework chosen. The different approaches to self-assessment are considered in Chapter 11. In the following discussions, we will generally assume that an award process is being followed.

9.2 Choosing the framework

The Baldrige, EFQM, Deming, Australian, Canadian and Singapore frameworks were compared in Chapter 2 and explored in more detail in Chapters 4–7. The award frameworks share a similar purpose, core values and concepts and criteria. The similarities between the various models far outweigh the differences. Some of the frameworks are based on a synthesis of best practice excellence concepts found in other award models. For example, the Singapore

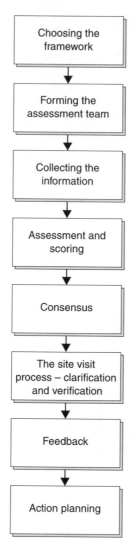

Figure 9.1 Self-assessment steps

Excellence Framework is based on the Baldrige, EFQM and Australian models.

All the frameworks, with the exception of the Deming framework, have moved from quality frameworks to business or organizational excellence frameworks. The information given in EFQM booklets such as *The EFQM Excellence Model*® covers many areas that are detailed in the Baldrige 'Criteria for Performance Excellence' guidelines. The Baldrige criteria guidelines are generally more detailed, offer more guidance, and sometimes take a more rigorous approach.

It should be noted that in all the award frameworks the categories are to an extent purely based on expert opinion, and have not been subjected to the rigorous empirical tests that are frequently used in the management sciences. Over the years, some Baldrige items have been moved between different categories as part of the process of clarifying and improving the model. The management sciences are littered with 'social-scientific' and largely unsuccessful attempts to produce unified frameworks of excellence or TQM, so expert opinion may not be a bad substitute provided it produces a pragmatic solution! The criteria or categories are weighted according to their relative importance, and this is also arbitrary, although it does represent the consensus of some important 'experts'. In the case of the European model, the views of approximately 1000 business leaders were sought in establishing the criteria weightings.

The Baldrige criteria guidelines have been available since 1988, and the EFQM guidelines became available in 1991. Both have undergone significant development over the years. It is highly likely, therefore, that organizations that have used self-assessment for several years will have systems based on either the Baldrige or the European model, or will have developed their own model. US-based or -owned companies are most likely to use the Baldrige framework, although many of their European-based operations have adopted the European model. Similarly, European-based or -owned companies are most likely to use the EFQM Excellence Model. A valuable aspect of self-assessment is the ability to make year-on-year objective comparisons. Clearly it would be difficult to make meaningful comparisons if the excellence model used were frequently changed. Both the Baldrige and the EFQM models offer some stability in this area.

Perhaps organizations should develop their own hybrid models, taking the 'best from the best'? In the past, some organizations (such as Rank Xerox and IBM) with greater experience of self-assessment have developed their own hybrid frameworks. These are generally based on the Baldrige criteria, but include specific areas of interest to the company. However, whilst these hybrids can be tailored to specific organizational requirements, there are definite advantages in adopting one of the main excellence frameworks, such as the EFQM Excellence Model® or Baldrige model, rather than developing in-company hybrid versions. Simple adoption of the 'standard' framework facilitates benchmarking and networking with other organizations. It also allows the organization to benefit from the annual review and refinement of a recognized framework. If tailoring is required, this can be done at the detailed sub-criterion level whilst still retaining the advantages of adopting a more universal model. If used properly, there should be some customization at the 'areas to address' level anyway. The frameworks, and the EFQM Excellence Model® in particular, are not intended to be prescriptive at the detailed level.

In summary, there is no 'best' framework; only an appropriate framework. The choice of framework will depend upon many factors, including the geographic location of the organization, and its experience with self-assessment.

9.3 Forming the assessment team

A key step in the process is forming the assessment team. The excellence criteria address a wide range of areas, including human resource management/organizational behaviour (leadership and people management and people satisfaction results), business analysis (all the results' criteria) and process management. No single person is likely to have an in-depth knowledge of all these areas, and hence it is essential that the assessment team members be drawn from a broad cross-section of functional areas. They will certainly not be a group of 'quality' specialists. The team should also have credibility to ensure buy-in to the self-assessment process and the dissemination of the self-assessment results. The senior assessor or examiner plays a critical team leader role in the self-assessment process.

The role of the senior assessor/examiner is to:

- Facilitate the development of a high-performing team to achieve the specified objectives
- Help the team in specific stages of the assessment process, e.g. consensus, site visit etc.
- Share his or her own learning and experiences to facilitate a successful outcome
- Provide technical insights into the content and use of the chosen excellence framework
- Mentor and appraise the team.

The senior assessor should be capable of taking a holistic view across all functional areas, and of leading and motivating the assessment team. A good rapport with senior management is essential, as is a knowledge and passionate belief in quality and excellence and its strategic importance. In recent years the EFQM has introduced a feedback process during training to enable senior assessors to become more effective leaders.

The senior assessor/examiner has specific requirements from the team. These include:

- To be committed to the team and its objectives
- To deliver timely input in accordance with agreed timescales
- To deliver clear and concise input based on fact
- To ensure availability to carry out agreed tasks in the assessment process, and to attend key meetings
- To work in a constructive manner
- To keep an open mind and be prepared to change views where necessary
- To 'own' the findings of the team.

It is essential that assessors receive prior training to ensure that they have:

- A good understanding of the excellence model to be used
- A good understanding of the key steps in self-assessment
- A clear understanding of the whole assessment process
- An ability to assess any submission consistently
- An ability to form a judgement on all aspects of an organization's performance, including financial performance
- A clear understanding of the role of self-assessment in driving continuous improvement
- The skills necessary to collect and analyse relevant data
- The skills in writing and giving effective feedback
- The ability to work well in a team.

A key objective of this training is to enable assessors to carry out assessments in a more systematic and consistent manner. The usual practice is to form teams of approximately six assessors and train them using the same materials and calibrated case studies used for the Award assessors. This approach ensures that organizations achieve greater consistency in their assessment process. In some instances this in-depth approach may be too time consuming, and a more general 'awareness'-type training process may be more appropriate. However, this may result in less objectivity and reduced learning.

If the organization has no experience of performing broad operational reviews or assessments, then outside expertise will be useful and provide the internal team with a 'hands-on' learning experience as well as saving time and effort. There are a growing number of people who have received EFQM assessor training, Baldrige examiner training or the national equivalent training and have sufficient experience to play a positive role in this way. Even if the organization has its own team of experienced assessors, an outside expert can be a valuable addition to the team. This person will not be biased by the corporate experience or culture that can blind an organization to different ways of operating.

The assessment team members need to have an eye for detail, see the context of evidence presented, have a good knowledge of the excellence model, and be committed to the assessment process. Individuals are quite different when it comes to handling large amounts of information. Some people have a natural ability for processing large amounts of information, whilst others almost appear to rely on a sixth-sense and are very good at seeing the bigger picture. The study of individual preferences is well established in the social sciences, and may help in producing a better-balanced team.

For example, the Myers–Briggs Type Indicator (MBTI) enables people to develop a better understanding of their own motivations, strengths and potential areas for growth, as well as facilitating a better understanding of other people. In particular, the MBTI attempts to describe how people take in information and how they organize the information and come to a conclusion. This is central to the assessment process. The use of an instrument such as the MBTI may help to form and develop more effective assessor teams. Simply taking a group of trained assessors does not automatically lead to an effective team. The team dynamics can be very complex.

9.4 Collecting the information

Self-assessment is an organizational health check based on a comprehensive internal assessment of organizational activities and their performance, and stakeholder perception. It involves assessing what an organization does and what it achieves. Many organizations are awash with data, which unfortunately is not always used effectively. Similarly, organizations usually have procedures explaining what they do in their main operational areas. A critical part of self-assessment involves making what is done and achieved match with what the criteria are asking for. The questions posed at criterion and sub-criterion level are designed to provide insights into organizational capability and performance, and it is therefore very important that organizations thoroughly understand the criteria before embarking upon the information-gathering phase.

The information requirements will be largely determined by the self-assessment approach taken. For this discussion we will assume that an award-type process is being used, although in Chapter 10 we will consider other approaches to self-assessment.

In the award-type process, there is a requirement to produce a position statement, not exceeding 75 pages, that explains what the organization does and what it achieves. This submission is the basis for a fact-based assessment (see Chapter 12 for more information on preparing a submission document).

All the main excellence frameworks give clear examples of the information requirements in the sub-criteria and 'areas to address' listings, or category, item and notes listings. An effective way of collecting information is to break down each item, item question, sub-criterion or area to be addressed into a set of questions or statements. For example, against each enabler sub-criterion or sub-item, the following questions could be posed:

- What do you currently do in this area?
- How do you do it?
- What results are you trying to achieve?
- How widely are these practices used?
- For new approaches, were they deployed in a systematic way?
- How is your approach reviewed and what improvements are undertaken following review?
- How is your approach integrated into normal business operations?

There are small differences in the scoring systems used in the various excellence models, but in essence to achieve a 75 per cent score in an item or enabler criterion an organization has to demonstrate:

- Clear evidence of an effective systematic approach with a clear rationale; a well-defined and developed process that focuses on organizational and stakeholder needs
- Clear evidence of good integration with the organizational needs, strategy and plans, and with other relevant approaches
- No significant gaps in deployment – structured and systematic deployment to approximately 75 per cent of potential in all relevant areas and activities
- Clear evidence of regular fact-based assessment of the effectiveness of the approach and deployment, and clear evidence of refinement and improvement as a result of organizational learning.

Similarly, against each of the results items or criteria explanation should be sought regarding:

- The measures used to monitor performance
- The extent to which the measures cover the range of the organization's activities
- The relative importance of the measures presented

- The organization's actual performance and performance against target
- Comparisons of performance with external organizations, such as competitors and 'best in class' organizations.

The advantage of this approach is that it should encourage the maximum amount of information to be collected in a structured way.

Results data should be presented as trend data wherever possible, and comparisons with own targets and external benchmarks are important. Again there are small differences between the various models, but in essence to achieve a 75 per cent score in a results item criterion an organization has to:

- Demonstrate that current performance is good to excellent in key areas – most results have strong positive trends or sustained excellent performance over at least three years
- Show favourable comparisons with its own targets in most areas
- Show favourable comparisons with external organizations in many areas
- Demonstrate that most of the results are caused by the approach taken
- Demonstrate that the scope of the results address key stakeholder requirements, most relevant areas and activities.

A good graphical presentation of results is shown in Figure 9.2.

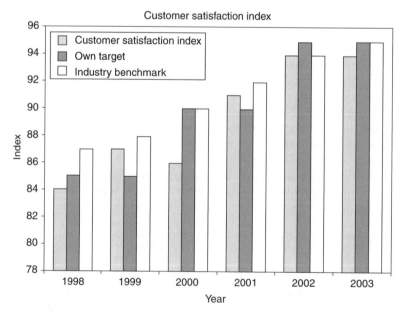

Figure 9.2 Year-on-year comparison of customer satisfaction index

It is important to explain how targets are derived. Targets based on the trend line of year-on-year improvement are not sufficient in themselves. The absolute level should be justified, and this can only be done through benchmarking. Adverse results and trends should always be accompanied by an appropriate explanation, and 'sleeping' targets in particular should be questioned.

In collating the best possible 'picture' of the organization, data collection options include:

- Use of documented procedures, for example in the Quality/Business Management System
- Referral to internal documentation, such as management reports, scorecards, etc.
- Surveys
- In-depth interviews using structured or semi-structured interview pro formas
- Discussion group or focus group sessions
- Use of existing results, reformatting where necessary to suit the specific sub-criteria
- Site visits to verify or clarify a specific approach, deployment or result.

A good submission has certain desirable features:

- It should address the criteria in a factual and concise way. In the European Quality Award process, applicants are limited to 75 pages. The Baldrige Award has a limit of 50 pages, two columns per page, for the criteria responses.
- Evidence must fit the criterion. It is important to ensure that criteria responses focus on information that is directly relevant to the needs of the criteria.
- Cross-references should be used wherever appropriate. The criteria are not mutually exclusive, and there may be many instances where responses to different sub-criteria or items are mutually reinforcing. In such cases it is preferable to cross-reference rather than repeat information presented elsewhere.
- A clear distinction must be maintained between enablers and results or the 'hows' and the 'whats'. Each criterion or item question is prefaced with the word 'how'. Responses should provide as complete a picture as possible to enable meaningful assessment. A common failing is to present enabler information in a results criterion.
- Results should be presented in a user-friendly way, and graphical representation used extensively.

The end result of this data collection phase is the production of a submission document describing what the organization does and what it achieves. This document is the 'primary evidence' used in the assessment process.

9.5 Assessment and scoring

The first task of the assessment team is to carry out an individual assessment and score the submission. Assessors review the entire submission document, identify the strengths, areas for improvement, and site visit or clarification issues. This information is recorded in a scorebook. Individual scoring is carried out by applying the scoring guidelines described in the appropriate excellence framework to the summary information captured in the scorebook. An extract from a scorebook used in an internal self-assessment is shown in Table 9.1.

Table 9.1: Extract from a scorebook

People strengths

- The principles of the HR policy and strategy are clearly defined and reviewed annually for strategic fit with operational plans.
- The staff perception survey is well established and is providing evidence of positive improvement and perception.
- HR performance improved by moving responsibilities to line managers, and they came 14th out of 39 in the internal customer satisfaction survey.
- A personnel committee advises the Board on all matters affecting staff relationships.
- Induction training is available for all new recruits within three months of joining the company, and is currently being reviewed to reflect changes in organization structure and new corporate visions and values.
- Matrix reporting structures are used to provide flexibility to respond to workload variations, and to encourage sharing of skills and workload.
- The competency-based career development model has resulted in major improvements in staff satisfaction with career development. Pioneering this approach enables them to act as a role model.

People areas for improvement

- Induction training is not mandated or controlled.
- The approach to managing the resource level during periods of major change (downsizing) has not been covered in any detail. This is considered to be a critical area, given the level of rationalization that has gone on.
- The use to which employee satisfaction information is put has not been fully described. Throughout the submission the main uses appear to be to identify problem areas and confirm the effectiveness of corrective action. The information is put to limited use in determining policy and strategy.
- HR is not yet an example of excellence, achieving only an average position in the internal customer satisfaction survey.
- There is limited evidence to indicate the involvement of staff during the development of the HR policy.
- There is limited evidence of benchmarking and measurement.

People site-visit issues

- Check 'flexible menu' of terms and conditions.
- Check staff satisfaction on identification of training and development requirements.
- What is the interrelationship between HR and the personnel committee?
- Who developed the HR policy? Who reviews it?
- Look at the HR plan. How is this aligned to policy and strategy?
- Check involvement of staff in HR policy and plans development.
- Check how equal opportunities policy is implemented.

Assessors will already have had some experience at scoring as part of their assessor training. However, there will still be considerable assessor-to-assessor variation in the assessments – it is not unusual to see a three-to-one scoring variation between assessors. Reasons for this scoring variation may include:

- Individual assessors' own business or organizational background
- Individuals' ability to process large amounts of information
- Differing interpretations of the item and sub-item or criterion and sub-criteria
- The assessors' approach to 'processing' the submission
- Differing perceptions of excellence
- The critical approach taken to evidence presented
- Differing cultural background.

Assessment and scoring is not an exact science, but the rigorous use of the scoring guidelines and training can help to minimize this variation. The scoring guidelines are used constantly throughout the assessment process, and represent a sort of continuous calibration process. An assessor's approach to processing the information can have a significant effect on the score. A good approach is quickly to read through the whole submission once, and then to work on the sub-criteria details. Sometimes it is like being a detective, and evidence can turn up in the most unlikely places. The sub-criteria are not mutually exclusive, and a good assessor constantly checks between criteria to validate information. For example, an enabler assessment may use information presented in an appropriate results criterion to validate the assessment.

The scoring systems used in the awards may also be used in internal assessments. These scoring systems have been considered in previous chapters, and are printed in most of the excellence model publications. Alternatively, organizations may wish to tailor the scoring to their specific needs or use a simplified scoring system.

Scoring is a frequently debated subject. The EFQM has had several task forces looking at this over the last few years, and the Baldrige scoring system has also evolved over the years. For the EFQM approach, each part of the enabler criterion or item is scored on the basis of three factors, approach, deployment, and assessment and review:

- The degree of excellence of the approach
- The degree of deployment of the approach
- The use made of learning to improve performance.

The excellence of the approach is assessed by considering how the organization addresses each enabler sub-criterion. The score given takes into account:

- The appropriateness of the approach – it should have a clear rationale, a well-defined process, and focus on stakeholder needs
- The degree to which the approach has been integrated into normal operations and supports other approaches
- The degree to which the approach supports strategy and plans.

The degree of deployment, on the other hand, is concerned with the extent to which the approach has been implemented, taking into account its full potential. The score takes into account the appropriateness and effective application of the approach:

- Vertically through all relevant levels of the organization
- Horizontally through all relevant areas and activities
- In all relevant processes

- To all relevant products and services
- In its method of deployment.

The use made of learning to improve performance considers the innovation and learning aspects. The score takes into account:

- The use of measurement of both the approach and its deployment
- The learning activities that identify and share good practice and improvement activities, including learning from other organizations
- How measurement and learning is used to improve performance.

Results are also assessed on a two-dimensional scale, namely:

1. The degree of excellence of the results, which takes account of
   - The existence of positive trends and/or sustained excellent performance
   - Comparisons with own targets
   - Indications that negative trends are understood and addressed
   - Comparisons made with external organizations, including 'best in class' organizations
   - The organization's ability to sustain its performance
   - The extent to which the results have been caused by the approaches.
2. The scope of the results, which takes into account
   - The extent to which the results cover all relevant areas of the organization
   - The extent to which a full range of results, relevant to the criteria, are presented
   - The extent to which the relevance of the results presented is understood.

This multidimensional approach has many advantages. It is important to separate approach/deployment/assessment and review from results/scope. However, combining the scores to give a single figure for an enabler or a result can pose problems. Simple arithmetic averaging is used, with the proviso that the resulting figure should look 'right' when weighed against the evidence. However, this latter qualification can contribute to additional scoring variations.

When considering a two-factor scoring system, such as that used with Baldrige, the obvious anomalies occur with a poor approach widely deployed or a good approach that has only been partly deployed. For example, a poor approach (say 20 per cent) deployed across the whole organization (say 100 per cent) would average out at 60 per cent. Clearly this is not a sensible score. Subjectivity now enters into the process, by deciding how far this overall score should be moved down. Does 50 per cent, 40 per cent, 30 per cent etc. feel 'right'? A zero score on either approach or deployment is ruled to give a zero overall score. Part of the

Approach

% scores	0	25	50	75	100
0	0	0	0	0	0
25	0	25	25	25	25
50	0	25	50	60	75
75	0	25	60	75	85
100	0	25	75	85	100

Deployment

Figure 9.3 The approach–deployment grid

problem lies in the process of calculating an arithmetical average. A geometric average (the square root of the product of the two scores) gives a better scoring system, and removes some of the anomalies of the present system. For example, with a 25 per cent approach deployed to 75 per cent of the potential, the two different averaging techniques give:

Arithmetic mean   50 per cent

Geometric mean   43 per cent

The geometric mean takes more account of the poor approach.

An approach–deployment scoring matrix using a geometric mean score is shown in Figure 9.3. The figures in the body of the matrix are the geometric means of the appropriate approach and deployment scores, suitably rounded to a sensible figure.

A matrix approach can be utilized in various ways to aid scoring objectivity. All the excellence frameworks assess the enabler approaches along three key dimensions:

1. Soundness and effectiveness of the approach
2. Integration in normal operations in support of policy and strategy
3. Assessment, learning and improvement.

It is generally accepted that overperformance in any one of the above dimensions can compensate for underperformance in any of the others. However, in practice it is difficult to carry out the necessary mental juggling when looking at the conventional scoring charts. The matrix shown in Figure 9.4 can help.

A further refinement of matrix scoring approaches is shown in Figures 9.5 and 9.6. These scoring systems are based on an approach

Dimension \ Score, %	0	25	50	75	100
Sound and effective approach	No evidence of a sound and effective approach	Some evidence of an effective and sound approach	Evidence of an effective systematic approach	Clear evidence of an effective systematic approach	Comprehensive evidence of an effective systematic approach
Integration into normal operations	No clear approach to ensuring integration	Approach is not fully aligned with policy and strategy and is only partially integrated	Approach is aligned with policy and strategy and partially integrated	Approach is well integrated and aligned with policy and strategy	Approach is fully integrated and aligned with policy and strategy
Assessment, learning and improvement	No system for assessment, learning and improvement in place	Early signs of systematic assessment and improvement is evident	Regular systematic fact-based assessment of key processes takes place	Clear evidence of learning and improvement based on regular assessment	Extensive evidence of organizational learning and improvement
Role-model status				Award Standard	World Class

Figure 9.4 The approach scoring matrix

Deployment		0	40	65	85	100
Degree to which approach is implemented in a structured way	100%	0	40	65	85	100
	75%	0	35	60	75	85
	50%	0	30	50	60	65
	25%	0	25	30	35	40
	0%	0	0	0	0	0
		0%	25%	50%	75%	100%
Assessment, review and learning		No evidence or anecdotal	Occasional assessment learning and improvement evident	Evidence of systematic assessment learning and review	Clear evidence of systematic assessment learning and review	Extensive evidence of organizational learning
Integration		No evidence or anecdotal	Some areas of integration into normal operations	Evidence of integration into normal operations	Clear evidence of integration into normal operations	Comprehensive evidence of integration into normal operations
Sound effective approach		No evidence or anecdotal	Some evidence of a systematic effective approach	Reasonable evidence of an effective systematic approach	Clear evidence of an effective systematic approach	Comprehensive evidence of an effective systematic approach
Element		Degree of excellence				
		Approach				

Figure 9.5 Enabler scorecard

Scope

Scope		0%	25%	50%	75%	100%
Degree to which results address relevant areas	All 100%	0	40	65	85	100
	Most 75%	0	35	60	75	85
	Many 50%	0	30	50	60	65
	Some 25%	0	25	30	35	40
	No 0	0	0	0	0	0

Element	0%	25%	50%	75%	100%	Overall percentage score
Results caused by approach	No results or anecdotal information	Some cause and effect links	Many cause and effect links	Most results caused by approach	All results caused by approach	
Comparison with external benchmarks	No results or anecdotal information	Some comparisons	Favourable in some areas	Favourable in many areas	Excellent in most areas – 'best in class' in many areas	
Comparison with own targets	No results or anecdotal information	Appropriate comparisons in some areas	Favourable and appropriate comparisons in some areas	Favourable and appropriate comparisons in many areas	Excellent and appropriate comparisons in most areas	
Performance levels and trends	No results or anecdotal information	Positive trends and/or satisfactory performance on some results	Positive trends and/or sustained good performance on many results over at least 3 years	Strongly positive trends and/or sustained excellent performance on most results over at least 3 years	Strongly positive trends and/or sustained excellent performance in all areas over at least 5 years	
			Degree of excellence			
			Results			

Figure 9.6 Results scorecard

originally used in Saga Petroleum, Norway, in conjunction with some of the members of the EFQM.

The figures in the body of the matrix represent the expert view of a large number of assessors trained for the European Quality Award process. The use of the matrix is illustrated in Figure 9.5. The approach has been assessed according to the following dimensions:

Sound and effective approach	Good evidence
Integration	Some integration
Assessment, learning and improvement	Subject to occasional review

This gives an 'average' approach of approximately 30 per cent.

The deployment is scored as 50 per cent, giving an overall score of 30 per cent. This is significantly less than the arithmetical mean of 40 per cent. The scoring process is certain to be developed as organizations gain greater experience of self-assessment.

Whatever the scoring system used, it is clear that if an organization does not have an effective and sound approach that is well integrated into the organization, or does not regularly assess its approach and learn and improve from the assessment, or does not fully deploy its approach, then there are significant opportunities for improvement against the enabler criterion and the assessment must result in a low score. Similarly, if an organization's results do not show improvement trends, or there are no benchmarks, or results are presented for non-value-adding processes, then there are opportunities for improvement against the results criterion.

Figure 9.7 gives a schematic representation of all the inputs to the process of reaching a score against the sub-criteria.

The '50 per cent' approach is frequently taken as a starting point in the scoring process. This involves comparing the organization's

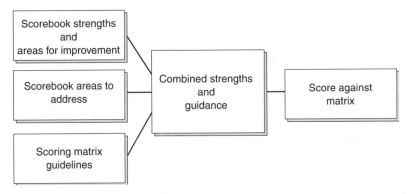

Figure 9.7 Inputs to the scoring process

evidence against the 50 per cent rating on the scoring charts, and moving up and down the scales based on the evidence presented.

A useful guideline when scoring is the number of strengths and of areas for improvement recorded on the score sheet. If there are several strengths and few areas for improvement, then the chances are that the score will be above 50 per cent. Conversely, if the number of areas for improvement outweighs the strengths, then the score will be considerably lower. Care needs to be taken, however, as sometimes a strength or an area for improvement far outweighs a number of other items – for example, having no approach in a critical area far outweighs some attempt to address more minor aspects of business excellence.

9.6 Consensus

Following the individual assessment and scoring, members of the assessment team come together to share their views on the submission and to reach consensus on the strengths, areas for improvement, site-visit issues and scores. Given the wide assessor-to-assessor variation that can typically be expected, a good consensus process is essential to the self-assessment process. This is not just an averaging process aimed at generating an agreed score. Consensus is a learning opportunity for each assessor, and provides the opportunity for the team to take an overview of the total information available from each individual assessment, reassess the evidence, and reach consensus. For the purpose of an award process, consensus is defined as:

- Agreement in the team of the strengths, areas for improvement and site-visit issues for each sub-criterion
- A score on this view of the sub-criterion that the whole team can support
- An agreed view of the key strengths, key areas for improvement and key areas requiring further clarification.

An overview of the consensus process is shown in Figure 9.8.

The senior assessor plays a key role in the process, and is responsible for organizing and running the consensus meeting. Planning and preparation are critical to the success of a consensus meeting. The process can be streamlined if individual assessors record their individual assessments in electronic versions of the scorebook, as this allows the senior assessor to combine the individual assessments and make available an overall list of the strengths and areas for improvement of all the team members prior to the consensus meeting.

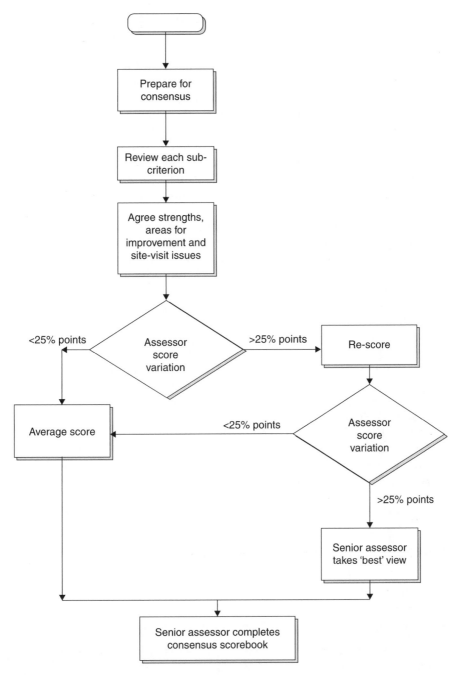

Figure 9.8 The consensus process

The team review this pre-consensus view at the consensus meeting. The first step in reaching consensus is to form a shorter list of the key strengths and areas for improvement of each sub-criterion by eliminating any duplications and grouping key points together wherever possible. The members of the team then carefully re-read the appropriate criteria and the scoring chart and independently re-score to reach a consensus view. Low-scoring team members will raise their score if they see that they have missed some vital evidence, and high scorers will lower their score if they can accept that they have over-rated a particular sub-criterion. It is most important to check against the relevant scoring chart continually. This is an ongoing calibration check.

Time is always a major constraint, both in internal company assessments and in award processes. There is a temptation simply to average the scores and accept the comments, but this approach is only taken by inexperienced teams who lose sight of the fact that reaching consensus is a process with the primary objective of providing valuable feedback; the score is a secondary concern. For this reason, the feedback is debated before the scores are considered.

Few organizations can afford the luxury of assessors debating the scoring variation when they are within 20–25 percentage points. Some practical compromise to the strict meaning of consensus has to be made, and a set of basic rules is necessary to speed the consensus process. The rules used in EQA assessments are shown in Table 9.2.

If there is insufficient convergence of views after re-scoring, the senior assessor has to take the 'best view' and record the reasons for the failure to reach consensus. Typically, forming a best view is not difficult; it simply represents a majority view. Failure to reach consensus can frequently be due to an individual assessor having a particularly strong view coupled with unwillingness to

Table 9.2: Rules for reaching a consensus score

Assessor score variation	Rule
Range less than 25% points	Team leader averages all the assessor scores
Range greater than 25% points	Assessor team discusses, re-assesses and re-scores
	Senior assessor can take a 'best' team view if required, and record any differences of opinion

move. However, there is a danger of group-think taking over the consensus process. It is possible for the assessor team to converge on an incorrect score and ignore the odd lone voice, and the senior assessor must handle the group dynamics with some care. Self-assessment is a fact-based exercise, and individual assessors should be encouraged to make their case on the available facts and not their opinions.

The consensus view and score are recorded in a consensus scorebook, which is used to generate the feedback report. It is therefore essential to write comments in a manner that may be quickly transcribed into the feedback report. There is always a danger that in the 'heat' of the assessment process, assessors will write brief one-liners that provide few insights for the feedback report!

The consensus process adds objectivity and robustness to the whole assessment process. No single assessor would be able to obtain the best overall view of an organization in the usual timescale allowed; however, an assessor team working effectively can get very close to the best overall view and provide an objective assessment of the organization. It is vital to remember that consensus is not just about scoring but is also the part of the assessment process that offers one of the greatest learning opportunities through the sharing of knowledge.

9.7 The site-visit process – clarification and verification

It is almost impossible to capture the true position of an organization in a 75-page submission document. During the assessment process, many areas requiring clarification will be identified. It is also necessary to confirm the validity of the submission. These tasks can be carried out during site visits to the organization.

There may also be a significant time lapse between the preparation of the submission and its subsequent assessment. In the interim new information may arise, and most award bodies lay down rules as to what may be accepted as additional supporting evidence. The EFQM's policy on this is that:

- New initiatives started after the submission may not be taken into account by the assessors
- Existing ongoing initiatives not mentioned in the submission document may be considered if they are brought to light during the site visit, and assessors may make an appropriate adjustment to the score
- Applicants may present the latest data points or trends for any results presented in the submission document.

In internal self-assessments (i.e. not as part of an award application), a site-visit process should be integrated into the data collection phase to ensure greater objectivity. However, there will still be a need for further clarification and verification following the individual and consensus assessments.

Planning is the key to a successful site visit. A planning meeting should be held approximately two weeks prior to the site visit in order to decide:

- Which site or business units should be visited
- Who will be involved – the whole team, part of the team?
- What information is needed to clarify or verify specific issues
- How the questions will be framed
- Who will ask the questions.

The outcome of the consensus process is a list of issues requiring clarification covering the whole excellence model. It is important to match assessors' experience and skills to the task. For example, a person with operations management experience may be best suited to seeking clarification on process management issues and health and safety issues, while an assessor from a marketing background may be best placed to seek clarification on customer satisfaction issues.

The senior assessor is responsible for the conduct of the site visit. The site visit should commence with a short introductory meeting with the management team heading the business or organization being assessed. The introductory meeting covers:

- Introduction of the assessors involved in the site visit
- An introduction by the senior management team
- A brief overview of the self-assessment process to date
- The objectives of the visit
- The site-visit agenda.

Requests for information to clarify specific issues can be supplemented by interviews with individuals and teams. The latter acts as a deployment verification. If several sites are to be visited it is useful to prepare a checklist to test the 'feel' of the organization. A simple check on the following can build confidence in the validity of the submissions:

- How the team is greeted
- Whether the employees appear knowledgeable and helpful
- The standard of housekeeping
- The openness of managers.

A short meeting at the end of the site visit is important. This enables appropriate thanks to be made to the organization.

The keys to an effective and efficient site visit are:

- Careful and detailed planning by the assessment team prior to the site visit
- A clear site-visit agenda detailing information requirements and responsibilities
- A clear focus on those factors that have a significant effect on the overall score
- Good team working
- Flexibility – it may be necessary to adjust the plan part way through the visit
- Firm control of the process – the agenda should not be surrendered to the senior management team
- Thorough documentation of the site-visit findings
- Summarizing the findings immediately following the site visit.

If the submission has been well prepared, the site visit should only result in relatively small adjustments to the score. The resources put into the process should reflect the weighting of the model. For example, in the EFQM Excellence Model®, customer satisfaction with a weighting of 20 per cent merits closer attention because of its impact than does the impact on society with a lower weighting of 6 per cent. It is not admissible to present whole new areas of information to be assessed at this stage of the process. Site visits are primarily concerned with verifying the fact-based assessment findings.

9.8 Feedback

The feedback report is the major output from the assessment process. The report is a final analysis of the organization, and represents the accumulated knowledge acquired by the assessor team from the members' individual assessments of the submission, the team consensus meeting and the site visits. The report is a concise presentation of the key strengths and areas for improvement, and provides a benchmark comparison of the organization's progress towards organizational or performance excellence through the scoring profile achieved. An example of a scoring profile is shown in Figure 9.9. This information can alternatively be presented as a radar diagram (see Figure 9.10), which gives an overall picture at a glance.

The feedback report should be tactful and constructive, and be based on the facts presented for assessment – not opinions. The wording of the report should be non-prescriptive and avoid recommending specific solutions. It is unwise to tell a management team how to run its own organization!

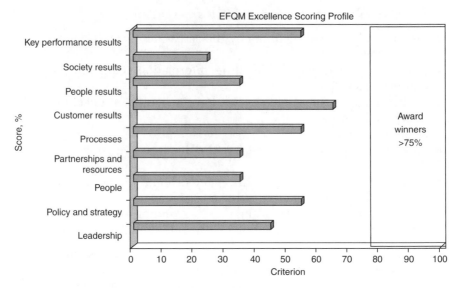

Figure 9.9 Eastern Division scoring profile

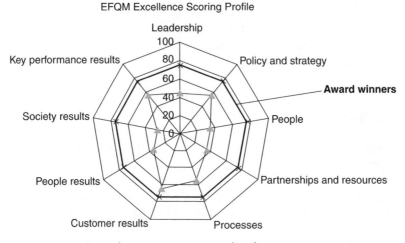

Figure 9.10 Southern Region score radar diagram

The detailed content of the feedback report should include:

- An overview of the assessment process
- An executive summary giving a concise general impression of the submission – this includes the main themes and some comments on the submission document
- A review of each criterion, giving the main themes for each
- A list of the key strengths and areas for improvement for each sub-criterion

- The overall score (note that this is only given in score bands 0–50, 51–100 etc. in some award processes)
- The scoring profile, i.e. the score for each criterion – in the award process, these results are given in score bands for each criterion (0–5 per cent, 5–10 per cent etc.).

An extract from a feedback report for an organization, simulating an award-type process, is shown in Appendix 9.1.

The senior assessor is responsible for preparing the feedback report. Two common processes used to generate the report are:

1. The senior assessor writes the complete report and circulates a draft to the assessor team for comments and improvements; this feedback is then incorporated into the final report.
2. The senior assessor allocates specific criteria to team members, who then draft their part of the feedback report. The senior assessor then collates the document and circulates the complete feedback report to the team for final comment.

The feedback report is an opportunity to present a balanced view of the organization, dwelling on both positive aspects and improvement opportunities, and positions the organization relative to the most successful exponents of excellence.

9.9 Action planning

The feedback report is a rich source of improvement opportunities. Both the Baldrige and EFQM Excellence Models have over 30 sub-criteria or items, and the potential to be overwhelmed by improvement opportunities is clearly real. A rigorous prioritization technique is essential. This should take account of the relative weightings of the criterion and, even more importantly, the relative leverage to the organization. Techniques such as meta-planning and affinity digraphs help to structure the many areas for improvement into clusters with key themes.

Another way of making the process more manageable is to encourage individual members of the senior management team to take ownership of specific criteria. They are then responsible for taking the outputs from the assessment in their allocated criteria, developing a set of action plans and cascading improvement activities down through the organization.

There is always the danger that the feedback report will simply generate a higher level of firefighting. A more strategic view should be taken. Wherever possible, the timings of the assessments should be phased to align with the business planning cycle. Ideally, the assessment should be one of the inputs to the business planning process and totally integrated with it.

9.10 Summary

In this chapter we have looked in detail at the key processes in the self-assessment cycle. These include choosing an appropriate framework, forming the assessment team, collecting the data to be assessed, feedback, and action planning. These processes are important irrespective of the excellence framework used. Understanding them and practising them are important steps in developing a self-assessment capability. As a result of this development, organizations may wish to tailor specific sub-processes to their needs and design improved processes. A good example of this is the matrix scoring method.

Self-assessment is a team-based activity. Individual scoring variation can be large, and the team-based consensus process gives the overall process considerable robustness and provides a major learning opportunity through the sharing of knowledge.

Self-assessments usually generate many improvement opportunities, and it is important to prioritize this information and use it to drive business improvement. Organizations are increasingly turning to excellence-based self-assessments for business planning and monitoring purposes.

In the next chapter we will look at some of the main approaches to self-assessment. These will use some of the processes discussed in this chapter, and explore in greater detail the data collection and assessment processes.

Appendix 9.1 The feedback report

Section 1: Overview of the assessment process

Evaluation of XYZ's 200X EQA Report

Introduction
One of the benefits of applying for the European Quality Award or the Regional Award is the feedback all applicants receive on the application they presented.

It has been a privilege to be given access to your company through your 200X EQA Report. Your application was assigned to an experienced team, who worked hard to assess your application as fairly and objectively as they were able. The purpose of the feedback is to give an indication of the score given to your application, along with the main strengths and areas for improvement – as perceived by the team of assessors.

The feedback report is aimed primarily at improvement. We hope you will find the comments made constructive and in the spirit of continuous improvement, which is at the heart of Business Excellence. The fact that, based on your 200X EQA Report, your company would be unlikely to win the European Quality Award should not be taken as criticism, but more as the opportunity to make a good business better.

We have deliberately avoided making suggestions on possible approaches to securing improvement; this is outside the scope of our feedback. The assessors do not provide advice in this area as part of the assessment process.

The feedback report is divided into three sections. The first section is a brief overview of the process followed for assessing your submission. This is to help you understand the work on your application leading up to the feedback report. The second section begins with general comments on the application as a whole, followed by detailed comments on strengths and areas for improvement in respect of the Award criteria. This section is based on the observations of the team who assessed your application, and is written in the team's words. The third section is a Table that shows, for each of the criteria, the score achieved by your application within bands of 10 percentage points, and the overall score achieved within bands of 100 points on the scale 0–1000.

Overview of the assessment process

Assessors
The first stage was to assign a team of five assessors to your submission. The assessors were experienced line managers and quality managers; some academics were also involved. All the assessors had been suitably trained, the main objective of this training being to ensure consistency, so far as possible, in the scoring of applications for the Award.

Assessor teams were put together bearing the following points in mind:

- no conflict of interest between the assessor and the applicant company
- a blend of skills and experiences.

One of the team was nominated Senior Assessor and asked to lead and manage the assessment of the submission. This person was the most experienced EFQM/EQA assessor, and is currently in his fifth year as an assessor for the European Quality Award.

The assessment process
Copies of your submission were sent to each member of the assessor team to assess independently. Each of the criteria were assessed from the points of view of strengths and areas for

improvement, and a score was assigned based on charts 1 and 2 of the Application Brochure.

The next stage was for the Senior Assessor to arrive at a consensus view that fairly reflected the opinions of the whole team. This was achieved at a consensus meeting, where the findings of the whole team were presented and debated.

The preparation of a consensus scorebook recording the consensus findings marks the completion of the first stage of the assessment process.

In the actual award process, the consensus report is considered by a team of Jurors, who select the applicants to receive a site visit. The purpose of the site visit is to verify the submission and clarify any issues.

The preparation of the feedback report is the responsibility of the Senior Assessor. The words used are those of the assessor team.

This feedback report was generated from the consensus report.

Section 2: Comments of assessor team

General comments on the submission

The team compliments XYZ on a well prepared, professionally produced report, which has obviously involved a high commitment of time and resources.

Leadership by all levels of management is exemplified by the long-term commitment to Business Excellence that has been demonstrated by managers since 1995. Many mentions are made of senior management involvement in training, indicating a highly visible involvement in leading Business Excellence. Similarly, managers appear to be actively involved in the various Quality Forums, and the Quality Council. However, the management involvement in the recognition process is not clear, and this is reflected in a significant level of people's dissatisfaction with recognition.

XYZ's adoption of the EFQM Excellence Model® as the basis for its promotion of Business Excellence provides a clear working framework and a sound process for the approach to Policy and Strategy. There is good evidence of a systematic review of Policy and Strategy using a wide range of inputs, although exactly how policy and strategy and priorities are defined is unclear. The Business Planning Process itself is not transparently clear.

Management of people is well defined, although very little evidence is presented to assess the level or involvement of individuals or teams in continuous improvement. It is also not clear how improved communication is received or actioned.

The approach to resource management is systematic and is well integrated into the business planning process. All capital expenditure proposals are required to evaluate the positive impact upon customers, users and processes.

There is evidence of a systematic approach to identifying critical processes and process management. Audits undertaken within the planning process are used to review processes and identify the need for improvements. However, the actual process of identifying the critical processes is not clear, and there appears to be some ambiguity over what constitutes a business process.

Statistics presented for 'Customer Results' indicate that XYZ has consistently outperformed its main competitors for at least five years, although many of the graphs presented are so badly scaled that it is impossible to comment on trends or absolute levels. The EFQM system is heavily dependent on trend data (chart 2).

Trends in many areas of 'People Results' are improving, and the 'Committed People Index' has maintained a significant lead over the benchmark quoted. However, there appears to be a selective presentation of the survey results, and many important areas have been omitted, e.g., satisfaction with pay, employment conditions, etc.

Evidence of a systematic approach to the collection of societal perception data is not provided, but it is apparent that the company is proactive in some initiatives to protect the environment and plays a significant role in the local community. With regards to Key Performance Results, XYZ has shown a positive trend in the last few years for many key indicators, such as sales, profit and capital employed. However, many indicators have been fairly static since 1991/92, e.g. market share, and sales have persistently fallen short of target over the period 1990/91 to 1993/94. The presentation of indexed data prevented the assessors from commenting on the excellence of the results.

Overall, XYZ, with a sum between 401 and 500, is assessed to be a company with a top-led Excellence process, making good progress in most areas of the model. The team feels that the approach is well planned, but many aspects of the review process are unclear. As a general comment, learning does not appear to be an activity that receives much support. The results data have not been particularly well presented, and this has had a significant negative impact on the overall assessment. The relationships between the indicator results and outcomes have not been well articulated.

We compliment XYZ on its process, and wish the company success should it proceed to a wider-based application for the European Quality Award in future years.

All the comments contained in this report have been made to recognize success in Business Excellence, and we hope that they will provide a focus for further improvement.

Section 3: Summary of scores of assessor team

Percentile ranges

Criterion	0–10	11–20	21–30	31–40	41–50	51–60	61–70	71–80	81–90	91–100
1. Leadership						*				
2. Policy and strategy							*			
3. People						*				
4. Partnerships and resources						*				
5. Processes						*				
6. Customer results				*						
7. People results					*					
8. Society results			*							
9. Key performance results						*				

Points

	0–100	101–200	201–300	301–400	401–500	501–600	601–700	701–800	801–900	901–1000
Total points awarded					*					

Approaches to self-assessment

10.1 Introduction

In the previous chapters we have examined the main self-assessment frameworks based on the widely recognized quality awards and the key processes in self-assessment. There are many ways of carrying out the actual self-assessment in an organization. Many approaches share common key processes, such as individual assessment, consensus, etc. However, each approach differs substantially in how the data is collected to produce the position document that provides the basis of the information to be assessed. Data collection methods range from discussion or focus group approaches to the full award-type process.

The main approaches used are:

- Questionnaire and survey approaches
- The matrix approach
- The workshop approach
- The pro-forma approach
- Award-type processes
- e-approaches
- Hybrid approaches.

The approaches make use of many of the key self-assessment processes described in Chapter 9, and follow a common overall process outlined in Figure 10.1.

The design criteria phase involves developing clear objectives for the self-assessment and identifying any resource limitations. It is important that the approach used for self-assessment matches

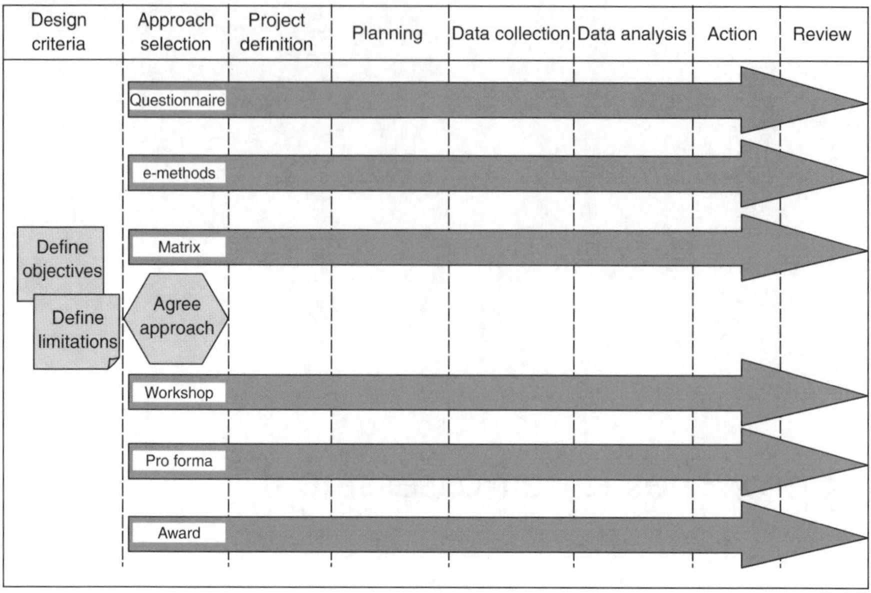

Design criteria	Approach selection	Project definition	Planning	Data collection	Data analysis	Action	Review

Questionnaire

e-methods

Matrix

Define objectives

Define limitations

Agree approach

Workshop

Pro forma

Award

Figure 10.1 The excellence blueprint

the organization's needs, and these needs, as well as the self-assessment approach, may change over time. The limitations may involve budget, people's time and availability, timescales etc. These considerations determine the selection of the most appropriate approach. More information on how the approach to self-assessment changes over time is given in Chapter 11.

In this chapter we will examine each of these approaches with a view to making informed choices about their appropriateness in any given situation. Each approach has its own specific advantage, disadvantage and resource implication. In addition, we will describe how the excellence frameworks can be used to assess processes.

10.2   Questionnaire and survey approaches

The questionnaire approach uses a set of questions or statements derived from the adopted excellence framework. The questionnaires collapse the criteria into a series of summary statements that require respondents to assess the current status or performance of their organization on a relatively simple scale. At the simplest level, yes–no responses are recorded. More sophisticated questionnaires employ Likert-type interval scales. Some questionnaires

Table 10.1: Excellence questionnaire using a Likert-type scale

Leadership – role modelling a culture of excellence

Circle the number against each statement that best represents your view	*Strongly agree*	*Disagree*	*Agree*	*Strongly agree*
Managers have communicated a set of values that support excellence	1	2	3	4
Managers have developed and communicated improvement objectives	1	2	3	4
Managers encourage, fund and support improvement	1	2	3	4
Managers are personally and actively involved in improvement activities	1	2	3	4

require respondents to give a score of between 0 and 100 per cent for each of the questions posed, with 100 per cent representing a fully deployed approach that is subject to regular review and refinement, and 0 per cent indicating that it simply doesn't happen. Table 10.1 shows part of a questionnaire using a Likert-type scale. A four-point scale has been used to overcome respondents' tendency to choose a middle option. The scores in the body of the matrix can be used to generate an overall assessment score, which can be normalized to fit in with the total scores from other assessment approaches. Typical questionnaires can contain up to 100 questions addressing all the criteria. As questionnaire fatigue is a well-known ailment, excessively lengthy questionnaires should be avoided!

The questionnaire approach is the least resource-hungry approach, and can be completed very quickly. It provides an excellent method for collecting information on people's perceptions within the organization. The questionnaire can be used in a variety of ways, and is frequently used as a data-gathering tool in the more sophisticated approaches to be discussed in later sections.

The assessment process follows a simple six-step process, which is outlined in Figure 10.2.

Planning	Briefing	Data collection	Data analysis	Action	Review

Produce project plan · Brief target survey group · Complete questionnaires · Analyse questionnaires · Identify priority actions / Implement improvements · Review

Figure 10.2 The excellence questionnaire blueprint

1. *Step 1 – Planning.* Project definition involves being clear on the objectives and deliverables of the self-assessment. This clarity of purpose can then be translated into a project plan that details the main activities, timescales and resource requirements.
2. *Step 2 – Briefing.* There needs to be prior communication with the target survey group prior to sending out the questionnaire. This communication should make clear the purpose of the survey, and provide some background information on the excellence framework.
3. *Step 3 – Data collection.* Data collection involves all those activities that ensure that the questionnaires reach the required target group and are returned within the required timescale.
4. *Step 4 – Data analysis.* The analysis phase involves the consolidation of all questionnaires and the extraction of useful information using tables, graphs and other diagrams.
5. *Step 5 – Action.* Surveys usually generate a wealth of information, and there is a need to identify priority actions and implement improvements. Focus is the key at this stage.
6. *Step 6 – Review.* This stage involves reviewing the response to the survey, the survey instrument itself, the key survey findings, and improvement activities.

Questionnaires can be used in surveys to test the 'state' of excellence in an organization. Demographic questions, such as work location, department, position etc., are usually included in survey instruments. A major attraction of surveys is the coverage that can be achieved. Hundreds of employees can be surveyed relatively quickly and at a low cost. Employees typically need about 30 minutes to complete the questionnaire. The data can easily be analysed on a spreadsheet, which will also allow further analysis by key demographic variables such as job position.

The sampling method is dictated by the objectives of the study. If the objective is to get an overall view in a large organization, it may be appropriate to take a diagonal slice of the organization containing several hundred employees. Other studies may be concerned with looking at the perception gaps between senior and middle management. In this case, samples would be drawn from these two levels. There is generally little practical purpose in worrying about statistical purity. We are not in the realms of political opinion polls! However it is always wise to strive for a good representative sample.

The results of part of a survey of a small business unit employing approximately 200 people are shown in Figure 10.3.

The purpose of this survey was to investigate perception gaps between managers and staff. There was a response rate of 69.5 per cent, with 35 managers and 104 staff returning the questionnaire. Figure 10.3 shows management and staff responses to four questions in sub-criteria 1d of the EFQM Excellence Model®. Clearly, enabling people to take part in improvement and recognizing individuals and teams present major opportunities for improvement in this organization.

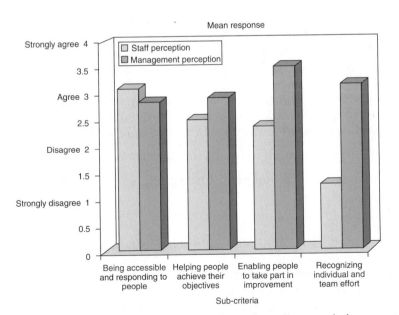

Figure 10.3 Leaders reinforce a culture of excellence with the organization's people

Response rates to questionnaires can be highly variable. Reliance on internal mailing for the distribution and collection of questionnaires can sometimes result in disappointingly low response rates. In many instances it may be more appropriate to administer the questionnaire in small group sessions; this allows for a more thorough explanation of the purpose of the questionnaire, and enables points from respondents to be clarified quickly.

Questionnaires are clearly prescriptive in nature, and do not offer the individual learning opportunities provided by the other methods of self-assessment discussed later in this chapter. The usefulness of the output is in part limited by the design of the questionnaire. Despite these shortcomings, surveys can be useful in identifying performance gaps and generating a quality profile. However, they cannot generally be used to monitor progress on a regular basis, as people become conditioned to the questionnaire.

In summary, the benefits of a questionnaire or survey approach are that:

- It provides a quick way of getting the organization's profile against the chosen excellence framework
- It is a simple introduction to self-assessment
- Questionnaires can be tailored to specific organizational needs
- It has a low resource requirement
- Training requirements are minimized – basic awareness training in the excellence framework will suffice
- It can achieve high levels of involvement within the organization – responses can be stratified by function/department, level etc.
- Results and learning opportunities can be quickly found and cascaded down into the organization, and actions taken
- It can be used as an input to more sophisticated approaches.

However, this simple approach has some limitations:

- The assessment outputs represent perception and require validation
- The approach does not highlight specific strengths or areas for improvement
- The objectivity and accuracy of the approach depend upon the quality of the questions
- The element of prescription in the questions limits learning
- Ownership of issues is not encouraged
- When used as a survey instrument, response rates may be low, giving rise to concerns over the validity of the approach.

10.3 The matrix approach

Organization or business improvement matrices are not a new concept – various maturity grids have been in common usage for some time. However, the development of an achievement matrix built on the assessment excellence framework and tailored specifically to the organization's needs is a relatively new development, and can provide a very effective approach to self-assessment. The matrix can help in developing understanding of the assessment criteria in a very practical and organization-specific way, and allow teams to assess their progress quickly and simply. The matrix can be used at any level in the organization.

One of the first excellence matrices originated with British Gas plc, and this matrix is shown in Table 10.2. Note that British Gas plc has subsequently been spun off into several separate companies – Transco, Centrica, and BG. Some of these newer companies continued to use the matrix, and the approach has also been adopted by several other organizations.

The matrix consists of the nine categories of the EFQM Excellence Model® framework. Under each heading, ten steps are listed in a logical sequence from first beginnings (Step 1) to a good European standard of operation (Step 10). Within each of the nine categories, the steps reflect progress in terms of:

- The approach adopted
- The levels of deployment of the approach
- The results achieved.

The matrix can be used to give a snapshot of the current position of the organizational or business unit, and enables improvement opportunities to be identified.

A six-step assessment process using the matrix is illustrated in Figure 10.4.

The key stages of this process are:

1. *Step 1 – Planning.* Project definition involves being clear on the objectives and deliverables of the self-assessment. This clarity of purpose can then be translated into a project plan that details the main activities, timescales and resource requirements. The assessment team should be identified at this stage in the process. Typically the team will include the unit manager and his or her direct reports, but it may be a diagonal slice through the unit. The approach is particularly suited to small teams. The self-assessment is facilitated by a fully trained assessor, whose prime role is to help the team deliver the assessment exercise objectives.
2. *Step 2 – Briefing.* The purpose of this stage of the process is to ensure that the team is clear about the objectives and deliverables

Table 10.2: The excellence matrix

		Enablers			
Step	Leadership	Policy and strategy	People management	Resources	Processes
10	All managers are proactive in sustaining continuous improvement	Mission and business policy statements cover the whole of the business, and everyone understands them	All actions are directed towards realizing the full potential of all employees	The organization's resources are deployed effectively to meet policy and strategy objectives	Key value-added processes are understood, formally managed and continuously improved
9	Managers are able to demonstrate their external involvement in the promotion of total quality as a business philosophy based on their own experience	A process is in place to analyse competitor business strategy and modify unit plans as a result, in order to develop and sustain a competitive advantage	Employees are empowered to run their business processes	A process is in place to identify additional resources that can be used to strengthen competitive advantage	The existence of a formal quality management system can be demonstrated
8	Managers have a consistent approach towards continuous improvement across the unit	The policy and strategy processes are benchmarked	The human resource plan for the unit supports the company's policy and strategy for continuous improvement	A system is in place to review and modify the allocation of resources based on changing business needs	Process performance is demonstrably linked to customer requirements

7	The management team is proactive in valuing, recognizing and rewarding all employees for continuous improvement	A process is in place to modify policy and strategy as a result of business and operational information	A process is in place to encourage creativity and innovation amongst all employees	A process is in place for identifying, assessing and evaluating new technologies and their impact on the business	A mechanism is in place for developing and using appropriate measures which evaluate key processes
6	Managers are visibly involved in the development and support of improvement teams and act as champions	A process is in place to assess the continuing relevance of plans as a result of business and operational information	Improvement teams have been established and supported	Systems are in place to track, monitor and review targeted areas to reduce all other waste including time and rework	The process results are reviewed and fed back into the improvement cycle
5	A process is in place to ensure managers are working with customers and suppliers, and that the effectiveness of this process can be assessed	The unit has policy statements and strategy that cover the nine EFQM business improvement matrix headings	Training and development needs are regularly reviewed for all employees and teams. Skill gaps relevant to personal aspirations and business needs are identified	Systems are in place to track, monitor and review targeted areas to reduce material waste	An improvement mechanism for key value-added processes has been implemented

(continued)

Table 10.2: Continued

			Enablers		
Step	Leadership	Policy and strategy	People management	Resources	Processes
4	A process is in place to ensure managers are visibly involved as role models in business improvement within the unit. The effectiveness of the process is reviewed	A process exists, and is reviewed, which promotes a clear understanding of the company's and unit's mission, CSF and policy statements, so that everyone knows and understands these	An effective appraisal system is in place for all employees	A process is in place to manage the dissemination of relevant information to customers, suppliers and employees	An improvement mechanism has been identified and targets for improvement have been set
3	A process is in place to ensure mutual understanding of business issues through two-way communication both vertically and horizontally throughout the unit	A process is in place to collect relevant external information to enable a review of CSFs and business plans	A process is in place for two-way communication of business information within the unit	Partnerships with suppliers are being developed to jointly improve quality, delivery and performance	The effectiveness of existing key value-added processes is assessed
2	A process is in place to create and	A process is in place to collect relevant	A public commitment has been given to	A process is in place to identify suppliers	Key value-added processes are

continually increase an open awareness of business issues throughout the unit	internal information to enable a review of CSFs and business plans	develop all employees to achieve business goals	for key resources	identified, flowcharted and/or documented. Ownership is established
1	The management team has a process in place to develop members' own awareness of the concepts of total quality	The unit management team has developed a mission statement and critical success factors (CSFs)	A process is in place to canvas and track employee opinions	A process is in place to identify what resources are available and how they are being deployed	The main processes within the business unit are identified

(continued)

Table 10.2: Continued

Step	Customer satisfaction	People satisfaction	Impact on society	Business results
		Results		
10	There is a positive trend in customer satisfaction. Targets are being met. There are some benchmarking targets across the industry	Regular comparison with external companies shows employee satisfaction is comparable with other companies and has improving trends	Views of local society are proactively canvassed. Results are fed back into the company's policies	There are consistent trends of improvement in 50% of key results areas. Some results are clearly linked to approach
9	75% of customer satisfaction targets are being met	Results indicate that employees feel integrated into the work environment	Benchmarking has started for 25% of impact on society targets	All targets are being met and showing continuous improvement in 25% of trends
8	50% of customer satisfaction targets are being met	Results indicate that people feel valued for their contribution at work	50% of impact on society targets are being met	75% of targets have been achieved. Able to demonstrate relevance of key results areas to business
7	All employees understand targets relating to customer satisfaction	Results indicate that people can express their feelings confidently and openly	Results are linked to environmental and social policy. Policy is reviewed	Performance against others in the industry is compared and targets are reset

6	The drivers of customer satisfaction have been identified and are used to modify targets	Targets are set in key improvement areas and are published	There is an increased public awareness of policies	Improving and adverse trends have been identified, understood and linked to enablers
5	Compare customer satisfaction levels within the company. Results have a positive trend and some are meeting targets	Trends are established. Positive and negative trends are understood. Parameters measured are relevant to employees	There are consistently improving trends in relevant results areas	50% of internal targets have been met
4	The relevance of targets to customer satisfaction can be demonstrated	The effectiveness of two-way internal communications is measured	Local perceptions and needs are researched and targets are set for improvement	Trends are compared against the unit's goals and financial objectives
3	Targets are set for improvement	Data is used to plot trends for employee satisfaction	Employees' awareness of relevant results areas is measured	Relevant results are communicated to all employees and key results are published regularly
2	Data is used to plot trends of customer complaints	Key measures of employee satisfaction have been identified	Trends are established and a process is in place to track progress	A system exists for measuring and monitoring key results areas
1	Customer complaints are logged, and reacted to on an *ad hoc* basis	Employee grievances are reacted to on an *ad hoc* basis	Result areas have been identified	The unit's key financial and non-financial objectives have been identified

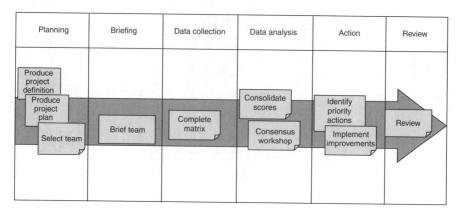

Figure 10.4 The excellence matrix blueprint

of the exercise, and that members understand the assessment process. The team members come together for a briefing on the matrix and its use. Each team member is issued with a copy of the matrix and supporting documents, which explain how the self-assessment will be conducted.

3. *Step 3 – Data collection.* Each team member returns to his or her unit and rates the unit on the matrix using hard supporting evidence rather than opinion or perception. Some matrices use a RAG (red–amber–green) colour-coding scheme for the rating exercise.

4. *Step 4 – Data analysis.* Individual assessments are returned to the facilitator for collation of the overall picture. Approximately one week after the briefing session, the team meets to discuss members' individual matrix assessments and generate a consensus assessment based on the overall picture compiled by the facilitator. This team view provides a more objective view of the unit, based on shared knowledge.

5. *Step 5 – Action.* The information from the consensus forms the basis for further discussions, and improvement action plans are subsequently generated.

6. *Step 6 – Review.* The review stage involves assessing the outcomes of the process against the original objectives and taking on board any learning points that will improve the process in the future. It is beneficial to repeat the process on a regular basis, say every six or twelve months, as part of an ongoing review of progress.

This practical matrix approach has many attractive features but, like all approaches, it requires reviewing from time to time. For example, many of the statements at Step 10 in the matrix shown are rather less demanding than might be expected from world-class organizations. However, the matrix is capable of being developed to capture world-class enabler-type activities and results. The British Gas Matrix has proved to be a very popular self-assessment tool, and many organizations have adopted this approach.

The key benefits of this approach are that:

- The matrix is simple to use
- The resource requirements in the assessment process are relatively low and the training requirements are minimal
- The matrix can be tailored to the specific requirements of the organization
- The matrix facilitates the understanding of the excellence criteria and self-assessment process
- The matrix facilitates objectivity and an efficient assessment process
- The matrix is good for facilitating discussion in the team and for team building
- The output is suitable for action planning.

The main limitations are that:

- Lists of key strengths and areas for improvement may not result from the assessment process
- The output is dependent on the matrix design
- There are medium to high development resource implications if an organization decides to design its own matrix
- The matrix can lead to a prescriptive approach
- A one-to-one correspondence between the matrix elements and excellence model criteria may not be evident, which makes comparisons and benchmarking against award winners more difficult.

10.4 The workshop approach

Workshop or discussion group self-assessment is one of the simplest forms of self-assessment, and avoids the need to produce a lengthy submission document to be assessed. Groups such as management teams, departmental teams, improvement teams etc. use the chosen excellence framework to guide their discussions about the strengths and improvement opportunities of their organization, unit or department in the categories of the excellence framework. An assessor who has been trained to award standards will usually facilitate the teams.

The workshop approach is particularly useful for management teams; a typical process is shown in Figure 10.5.

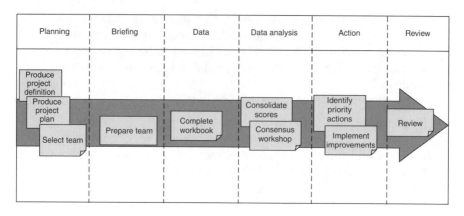

Figure 10.5 The workshop excellence blueprint

The key steps in the process are:

1. *Step 1 – Planning*. This step broadly follows the process outlined in Section 10.3), with the proviso that the team is drawn
   from the management team of the unit being assessed. One of
   the real advantages of this approach is that it requires the
   active involvement of the management team in the end-to-end
   assessment process. Of course, that can also be its downfall if
   there is a lack of buy-in at the start of the process! Another
   clear advantage of the approach is that managers should have
   the necessary good overall knowledge of the organization,
   department or unit undergoing self-assessment to ensure an
   objective assessment.
2. *Step 2 – Briefing*. In the process illustrated, the team is brought
   together in a one-day facilitator-led awareness workshop to
   develop members' understanding of the self-assessment
   process. The workshop also enables the team to practise self-
   assessment in a limited way by choosing an area and assessing
   its strengths and improvement opportunities. This is always a
   useful learning opportunity, and helps build confidence in the
   process. At the end of the workshop, each team member agrees
   to sponsor a criterion and is charged with the responsibility of
   collecting information about this criterion. Workbooks, based
   on the excellence framework, are usually issued to ensure that
   the data collection process is carried out in a systematic way.
   The workbook requires the key strengths, areas for improvement and clarification issues to be identified. An example of a
   workbook structured along the EFQM RADAR® scoring guidelines is shown in Table 10.3.
3. *Step 3 – Data collection*. Usually the sponsor will set up a
   small team of 'experts' from his or her operational unit to

facilitate the collection of this information. It is important to maintain a good momentum with this process, and a period of approximately four weeks should be sufficient to collect all the necessary information. The data collection phase usually provides major insights and early learning opportunities for the management team. This may be the first time that they have run an excellence 'ruler' over their organization. This stage of the process is over when a fully completed workbook is returned to the facilitator.

4. *Step 4 – Data analysis.* Individual workbooks are returned to the facilitator for collation of the overall picture. This overall picture is circulated to the management team prior to members attending an assessment workshop. Ideally this workshop should be a two-day event, but it can be compressed into one long day. The workshop also covers steps 5 and 6 in the process, i.e. action and review. The trained assessor helps the team form a consensus view of the organization's strengths and improvement opportunities based on the available information facilitates the workshop. The workshop is structured along the following lines:

   - The facilitator briefs the team on the objectives and deliverables for the workshop
   - Each criterion sponsor presents the information gathered against his or her criterion, i.e. strengths, areas for improvement and clarification issues
   - The information is validated with the rest of the team, any agreed amendments are recorded, and an agreed list of strengths and areas for improvement is finalized
   - The revised evidence is scored on an individual basis
   - The facilitator gains consensus on the score.

5. *Step 5 – Action.* A key output from the assessment is the development of an action plan to address the identified improvement opportunities. In most self-assessments there will be many improvement opportunities, and it is essential to develop priorities. The final stage of the process involves each senior manager cascading the results of the assessment throughout the organization and initiating improvement activities. These activities should not be delegated, and it is important for senior managers to be seen to be actively involved in the improvement process.

6. *Step 6 – Review.* The review stage involves assessing the outcomes of the process against the original objectives and taking on board any learning points that will improve the process in the future. The management team will want to consider the benefits of repeating the exercise on a regular basis.

Table 10.3: Assessment workbook based on the EFQM Excellence Model®

Criterion 1 – Leadership

Excellent leaders develop and facilitate the achievement of the mission and vision. They develop the organizational values and systems required for sustainable success, and implement these via their actions and behaviours. During periods of change they retain a constancy of purpose. Where required, such leaders are able to change the direction of the organization and inspire others to follow.

Criterion part 1a – *Leaders develop the mission, vision, values and ethics and are role models of a culture of excellence.*

RADAR® element	Attributes	Evidence
Approach Sound and integrated (provide example)	*Sound:* ● Approach has a clear rationale ● There are well-defined and developed processes ● Approach focuses on stakeholder needs *Integrated:* ● Approach supports policy and strategy ● Approach is linked to other approaches as appropriate	

Deployment Level of implementation and systematic	*Implemented:* ● Approach is implemented *Systematic:* ● Approach is deployed in a structured way
Assessment Linkage to which results	*Measurement:* ● Regular measurement of the effectiveness of the approach deployment is carried out *Linkage to results:* ● Demonstrate linkage to results
Review Examples of improvement and use of learning	*Learning:* ● Learning activities are used to identify and share best practice and improvement opportunities *Improvement:* ● Output from measurement and learning is analysed and used to identify, prioritize, plan and implement improvements

A simpler but more subjective process than that described above involves the management team coming together for a two-day workshop to brainstorm strengths and improvement opportunities against each criterion. The output from each brainstorm is evaluated, a consensus is reached, and the outputs are captured in a documented form. 'Criterion champions' who are responsible for cascading group discussions down into the organization and initiating improvement activities can then take these outputs forward.

The main advantages of workshop or discussion group approaches are that:

- The approach is faster than award-type processes and is relatively inexpensive – there are no major training requirements
- The approach encourages ownership of the self-assessment process and its outcomes, and is less threatening than second- or third-party assessment
- The self-assessment exercise provides a team-building opportunity
- Scoring is generally of secondary importance to the group discussions that highlight improvement opportunities and help develop a common view
- An agreed list of key strengths and areas for improvement is produced, which forms the basis for action
- Management team assessments encourage ownership of the outcomes, effective prioritization and action planning.

The main limitations are that:

- The accuracy of the assessment is limited to the knowledge and insight of the group, and thus it is important that the group contains a range of knowledge and experience that allow the criteria to be addressed in a meaningful manner
- Biased scoring can result owing to the team's lack of experience of the scoring process or members' unwillingness to face up to the sometimes stark facts!
- Evidence of the extent of deployment is sometimes difficult to assess in this process
- The outcome can be highly dependent on the skills and persuasive power of the facilitator; this is certainly true for more 'difficult' management teams!

The workshop approach can be used to monitor the organization on an ongoing basis – say annually – but some conditioning of the discussion groups is to be expected. As groups become more knowledgeable and experienced in self-assessment, they may take a 'harder' view on scoring. However, this will mainly influence the earlier time period comparisons.

10.5 The pro-forma approach

Data collection is clearly one of the major resource-hungry elements in the assessment process, and the use of pro forma can significantly reduce the amount of work involved in undertaking and documenting the self-assessment. A set of one page pro forma can be developed for each criterion part. An example of a completed pro forma is shown in Figure 10.6.

The criterion and sub-criterion details are printed at the top of the form, and the 'body' of the pro forma enables strengths, areas for improvement and supporting evidence to be captured.

The pro forma can be completed on an individual or a team basis. The evidence captured on the pro forma can then be assessed in the usual way, using individual and consensus assessments.

Criterion 2 – Policy and Strategy

Sub-criterion 2d. How policy and strategy are communicated and deployed through a framework of key processes

Areas to address could include how the organization:	Key strengths
• Communicates and cascades policy and strategy • Deploys the policy and strategy through a framework of key processes • Aligns, prioritizes and communicates plans, objectives and targets • Evaluates people's awareness of policy and strategy	• *Senior management briefing roadshows are used to communicate policy and strategy* • *Local managers use the 'team briefing' process at unit level* • *Unit, team and individual scorecards translate policy and strategy into operational plans* • *The annual staff satisfaction survey tests people's awareness and understanding of policy and strategy* **Key areas for improvement** • *Individual scorecards are not always clearly aligned to policy and strategy* • *Results from the staff satisfaction survey indicate a awareness of policy and strategy in some areas*

Notes & evidence

• *Roadshow timetable published annually*
• *Scorecards published at unit level – individual scorecards used as part of annual appraisal process*
• *Staff satisfaction data available for 1999, 2000, 2001, 2002 and 2003*

Score	Approach	Deployment	Assessment and review	**Overall** %
	65	50	50	55

Figure 10.6 The excellence pro forma

A well-designed set of pro forma can be particularly useful for larger organizations, and facilitates comparisons between business units or departments and the sharing of best practice. This enables organization-wide improvement plans to be developed.

A typical assessment process is shown in Figure 10.7.

The key steps in the process illustrated are:

1. *Step 1 – Project definition.* The process illustrated is a more exhaustive process than the approaches we have already considered. It is therefore important to develop a proposal for the exercise that 'sells' the concept of self-assessment and the associated benefits to the management team. The proposal should clearly explain the approach, timescales and costs. The proposal document translates into a project management plan once the go-ahead has been agreed.

2. *Step 2 – Planning.* The planning stage is concerned with team selection, customizing the materials, mobilizing the team, training, and planning the data collection phase. The team typically consists of a cross-section of managers and other stakeholders in the self-assessment process who are involved in the total assessment process. A trained assessor facilitates the team. It is also important to mobilize some internal administrative support. Some customization of materials may be required to capture the culture and working practices of the organization being assessed.

   Team mobilization occurs at an initial one-day briefing workshop, which covers a session on the excellence framework, the assessment process and how to use the pro forma.

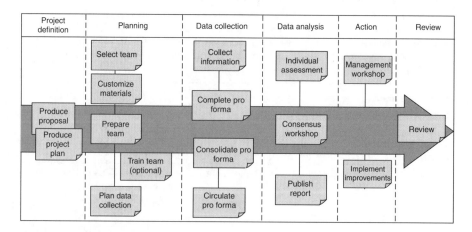

Figure 10.7 The excellence pro-forma blueprint

Outline data collection plans are also developed in the workshop. Use is frequently made of criterion sponsors or champions in this process. Sponsors or champions are responsible for collecting information against the criterion they 'own' or 'sponsor'.

In some variants of this process, the team involved in the assessment is trained to award standard. This generally results in a more objective assessment, but on the down side, there are clearly significant resource implications.

3. *Step 3 – Data collection*. This phase commences with the criterion sponsors or champions forming a small team to gather the available information against their criterion. It can sometimes be difficult to pull together information that meets the demanding requirements of the excellence model. Data collection surgeries, in which the facilitator reviews the information for its relevance and quality and makes constructive suggestions, can help overcome this common roadblock. Completed pro forma are returned to the facilitator for consolidation, and the complete 'picture' is then circulated to the team. The data collection phase usually takes four to six weeks.

4. *Step 4 – Data analysis*. In this phase, individual team members carry out an assessment based on the complete set of pro forma. It is usual to allow one week for this. The facilitator then consolidates individual assessments. A consensus workshop is held to gain consensus on the overall 'picture' assembled in the pro forma and on the score. The workshop is also used to develop the key findings from the self-assessment, which provide the basis of subsequent improvement activity. This feedback report is published prior to the next phase.

5. *Step 5 – Action*. Approximately two weeks after publication of the feedback report, the team members come together in an action-planning workshop to prioritize opportunities for improvement, identify quick wins, and ensure that the resulting improvement activity is aligned with strategic objectives.

6. *Step 6 – Review*. The final phase of the process involves reviewing the self-assessment approach, checking that the original objectives have been met and identifying the key learning points that can be used in the next cycle of self-assessment.

The main advantages of the pro-forma approach are that:

- It encourages the collection of fact-based evidence in a much more time-efficient manner than award simulation processes
- It can result in objective scores that are comparable with those generated by the award simulation process

- The assessment generates a list of key strengths and areas for improvement, which are the basis for action planning
- It can potentially involve a range of people at various stages in the process.

The main limitations are that:

- The pro forma can be completed on a superficial basis and jeopardize the outcome of the assessment; strong and effective facilitation is required
- The pro forma can give a summary and incomplete 'picture' of the organization.

10.6 Award-type processes

An award-type process involves the preparation of a document describing what the organization has achieved and is achieving, and how the results are actually achieved. The self-assessment process is similar to that for an award application, except that the actual assessment is carried out by trained assessors from within the company or by external assessors. Two teams are generally required for this approach: the first is involved in gathering the information and writing the report, and the second is involved in assessing the report, identifying strengths and improvement opportunities, and preparing the feedback. The length of the submission document can vary greatly. The European Quality Award allows a submission document of up to 75 pages, whereas the limit for the Baldrige Award is 50 pages. This may seem rather excessive, but experience in this field shows that it is sometimes difficult to limit an enthusiastic team to an arbitrary 75 pages. However, some organizations adopt a very focused approach and require the submission document to be in the form of a relatively short management report. Submission documents can vary from approximately 20 pages to over 100 pages. A case study showing how an organization approached the production of its submission document for an internal assessment can be found in Chapter 12.

In this section, we outline the award approach to facilitate a comparison with the other approaches described.

The actual process of generating the submission document and carrying out the assessment varies widely from organization to organization. One particular approach that has been found effective is outlined in Figure 10.8.

The key steps in this process are:

1. *Step 1 – Project definition.* This involves much the same steps as were described in section 11.5 for the pro-forma process.

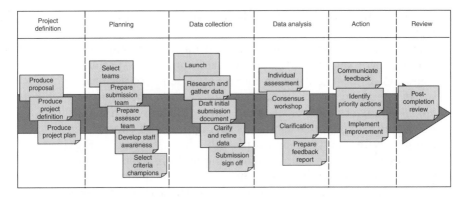

Figure 10.8 The award simulation blueprint

A sound proposal and project plans are even more crucial, given the resource requirements for this approach.

2. *Step 2 – Planning.* The award simulation process usually involves two key teams: the submission team and the assessor team. Some individuals may be involved in both teams but, given the scale of the task, it is impractical to involve all members of the submission team in the assessment process.

The first step involves forming the team that has the responsibility for preparing the submission. The criteria address a wide range of areas, including human resource management/organizational behaviour (leadership and people management and results), business analysis (all the results' criteria), and process management. No single person is likely to have an in-depth knowledge in all these areas, and hence it is essential that the submission team members are drawn from a broad cross-section of the organization and have the necessary insights and access to the information required. It is preferable that the submission team is led by a senior manager who has been trained to award standard, and it is also advantageous if the team includes other members who have been trained to this level.

The assessor team should also be mobilized at an early stage in the process. The team should have credibility to ensure buy-in to the self-assessment process and the dissemination of the self-assessment results. The team leader, typically a senior manager, should be capable of taking a holistic view across all areas of the unit being assessed, and of leading and motivating the team. All the team members should be trained to award standards.

Many staff in the organization being assessed are likely to be involved in the self-assessment, either at the information-gathering phase or the subsequent improvement activity phase. It is vital to brief staff about the self-assessment and how it will impact on them.

The whole assessment process is usually facilitated by a Quality or Excellence Group, which contains experienced assessors. If the organization has no experience of performing broad operational reviews or assessments, then outside expertise will be useful and provide the internal team with a 'hands-on' learning experience as well as saving time and effort. There are a growing number of people who have received EFQM assessor or Baldrige examiner training and are keen to play a positive role in this way via their self-assessment networks. Even if the organization has its own team of experienced assessors, an outside expert can be a valuable addition. This person will not be biased by the corporate culture, and may facilitate a more questioning approach that ultimately leads to greater learning.

During the planning phase, individual members of the submission team are asked to champion or sponsor specific criteria or examination areas. Criteria champions are responsible for collecting all the necessary information for a successful assessment.

3. *Step 3 – Data collection.* At the launch phase, the Quality or Excellence Group initially issues a 'Model Booklet' to the submission team, describing the self-assessment model to be used and outlining the process. The objective at this stage of the process is to develop a good awareness of the chosen model and the role of self-assessment. This is followed up approximately two weeks later with a half-day preparation workshop for the submission team. The purpose of this workshop is to develop a greater understanding of the self-assessment model and process. In particular, the workshop concentrates on developing the skills necessary to gather and analyse data. The team is given the opportunity to practise the submission preparation part of self-assessment against selected sub-criteria or examination areas. For example, the team may look at the people management area and address the following questions:

- What do we do in this area?
- How do we do it?
- How widely is it deployed?
- How well is it integrated into our normal business operations?
- How is its effectiveness measured and assessed, and what improvements are undertaken based on the key learning from the assessment?

This should result in a concise factual statement of the team's view of its approach and its deployment in this area. The team is then in a position to assess strengths and improvement opportunities. There is generally a great deal of learning that goes on during the information-gathering process. In many cases teams quickly realize that there are significant gaps in their approach. The actual assessment process will confirm these gaps as well as highlighting other opportunities.

The Quality Group plays an important facilitation role at this stage of the process in ensuring that the submission addresses the specific criterion. Some common problems encountered are that:

- Evidence is presented in the wrong sections
- Sources of information are not adequately cross-referenced
- Anecdotal evidence tends to be presented, and there is an inadequate explanation of specific approaches or their deployment
- Results are not presented in a way that allows easy analysis – the use of graphs should always be encouraged.

A period of four to six weeks is usually allowed for research and gathering data. During this stage of the process the criteria champions will draft an initial response and copy this to the Quality Group. Some further clarification and refinement of the information may be necessary prior to a one-day submission workshop. During this workshop, criteria champions share their draft submission with the other team members by presenting their key findings. Further work on clarifying and refining the submission takes place before an agreed submission document is signed off for assessment.

4. *Step 4 – Data analysis.* At this stage of the process, a separate team of trained assessors or examiners carries out the assessment in a similar way to the actual award process. It is usual to allow a further four to six weeks for this assessment from the receipt of the initial submission to preparation of a feedback report.

5. *Step 5 – Action.* The second major learning point (the first being preparing the submission) comes at a half-day feedback workshop. The senior assessor makes a presentation to the management team, outlining the business unit's strengths and improvement opportunities and assessment score. It is generally wise to feed back the score last or get it over with fairly quickly; there is a tendency to get 'hooked up' on the score, and this is not the main learning point. There is also a danger that some organizations may have a league table mentality. This simply destroys the whole process, and is a serious barrier to continuous improvement.

Each member of the management team receives a comprehensive feedback report. This is used to prioritize action plans addressing the major improvement opportunities.

6. *Step 6 – Review*. The whole process is finally completed by a post-completion review, which aims to review the main lessons learnt from the overall process. This review involves representatives from the team involved in preparing the submission, the assessor team, and the Excellence/Quality Group.

The main advantages of the award simulation approach are that:

- It provides comprehensive insights into the capability and performance of the organization
- It produces details on strengths and areas for improvement
- It produces self-assessment results that are directly comparable to actual award assessments
- It provides excellent learning opportunities for the submission and assessor teams
- It provides a powerful communication and reference document
- It provides a wealth of 'quality' output for action planning.

The main limitations of the award simulation approach are that:

- It has high resource requirements and a lengthy cycle time
- It may not be as objective as it should be – the results can be influenced by creative writing!
- It may be used at an inappropriate stage of the organization's journey to excellence, and distract the organization from more pragmatic improvement activities.

10.7 e-approaches

Questionnaire, matrix and pro-forma approaches clearly lend themselves to e-data capture methods via PC-based checklists, questionnaires and pro forma. The self-assessment approach is broadly similar to the approaches described above, but the 'tools' to facilitate the self-assessment are clearly different.

Appendix 10.1 provides a full description of one such e-self-assessment tool, BQFsnapshot. BQFsnapshot is one of a range of self-assessment products that can be obtained from the British Quality Foundation. This e-approach provides a powerful but simple to use software tool for assessing an organization of any size or sector against the eight fundamental concepts of business excellence.

10.8 Hybrid approaches

It is possible to combine several of the approaches previously described for the purpose of obtaining a more objective and accurate assessment – for example, a survey may be used as a deployment check in an award-type process. Similarly, checklists can be used in the discussion group methods. The combinations are limitless. A typical hybrid process could follow the process outlined below:

1. Top team facilitator-led discussion group workshop. This develops the understanding of criteria and generates an executive team snapshot of strengths and areas for improvement.
2. Top team interviews. Assessment team carry out interviews with the top team to generate a clear picture of approaches taken within each of the criterion parts.
3. Structured interviews. Assessment teams carry out a series of structured interviews in a diagonal slice of the organization to check consistency of the approach and the deployment.
4. Surveys of the workforce are carried out to supplement the information found in (3) above.
5. The organization's existing data, e.g. quality systems, performance data etc. are collated to complete the process of obtaining an objective position statement of where the organization is.

Ultimately there is no right way of carrying out a self-assessment, but there is an approach that is appropriate to the needs of your organization. In the final analysis, the assessment process should identify fact-based improvement opportunities that spur the organization on to higher performance levels, irrespective of the data collection method.

10.9 Process assessments

Excellence frameworks can provide valuable insights into the 'excellence' of processes, particularly the enabling environment in which processes operate. This is illustrated in Figure 10.9, which shows the results of a process assessment against a hybrid EFQM/Baldrige excellence framework. Problems with this process, an accounting process in a large global oil company, included:

- High rates of error and re-work
- High customer dissatisfaction
- High people dissatisfaction.

The excellence assessment of the enabling environment of the process provided insights into the many causes of these

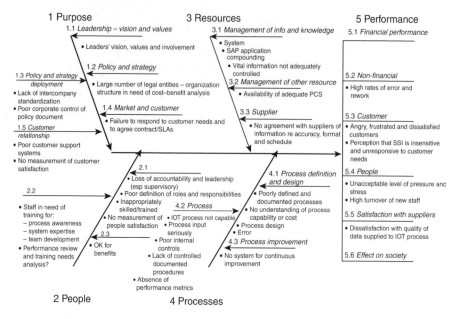

Figure 10.9   The excellence process enabler diagram

problems, and Figure 10.9 represents a sort of excellence cause and effect diagram.

10.10   Comparison of approaches

The approaches described in the previous sections are listed in Table 10.4, together with the main advantages and limitations of each approach.

There is no 'best' approach for an organization. It is important to weigh up the advantages and limitations, and adopt an approach suitable for a particular organization.

The two critical criteria to evaluate are the quality of learning, and resource requirement. Generally, greater personal and organizational learning will require more resources, although diminishing returns can set in – for example, a good pro-forma approach can deliver nearly just as much learning as an award process with significantly less resource consumption. Excellence maturity, i.e. where the organization is on the route to excellence, will also dictate the most appropriate approach. An organization embarking on self-assessment may wish to evaluate the use of questionnaire and matrix approaches before advancing to more resource-consuming approaches such as pro-forma and award-type approaches. These ideas are illustrated in Figure 10.10, and a more detailed discussion is given in Chapter 11.

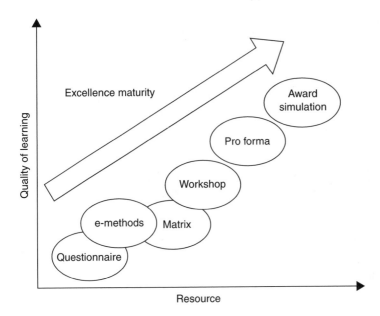

Figure 10.10 Excellence maturity and learning

10.11 Summary

In this chapter we have looked at the main approaches to self-assessment. Many of the approaches contain some of the common elements discussed in previous chapters. Each approach has its own specific advantage, disadvantage and resource implication. We have essentially been discussing 'smart' ways of collecting the assessment data. This may be facilitated by the use of e-based approaches involving screen-based pro-forma and scoring systems, but the fundamental purpose of self-assessment should always be kept in mind and the technology should not mask the purpose.

The award-type process, as used in the European Quality Award and Malcolm Baldrige National Quality Award, probably produces one of the most objective statements of an organization's current position, and provides a major learning opportunity for the team compiling the data and the assessor team. The considerable resources required to produce the detailed position statement, or submission document, can be managed by the adoption of hybrid approaches and the use of criterion champions to collect data on individual criteria. However, other approaches can also provide valuable organizational insights with less resource demands.

Table 10.4: Self-assessment approaches – key advantages and limitations

Approach	Advantages	Limitations
Questionnaire and survey	• Provides a quick way of getting the organization's profile against the chosen excellence framework	• Assessment outputs represent perception and require validation
	• A simple introduction to self-assessment	• Approach does not highlight specific strengths or areas for improvement
	• Questionnaires can be tailored to specific organizational needs	• Objectivity and accuracy of the approach depend upon the quality of the questions
	• Low resource requirement	• Element of prescription in the questions limits learning
	• Training requirements minimized – basic awareness training in the excellence framework will suffice	• Ownership of issues is not encouraged
	• Can achieve high levels of involvement within the organization – responses can be stratified by function/department, level etc.	• When used as a survey instrument response rates may be low, giving rise to concerns over the validity of the result
	• Results and learning opportunities can be quickly found and cascaded down into the organization, and actions taken	
	• Can be used as an input to more sophisticated approaches	

Matrix	• Simple to use	• Lists of key strengths and areas for improvement may not result from the assessment process
	• Resource requirements in the assessment process are relatively low and the training requirements are minimal	• Output is dependent on the matrix design
	• Can be tailored to the specific requirements of the organization	• Medium to high development resource implications if an organization decides to design its own matrix
	• Facilitates the understanding of the excellence criteria and self-assessment process	• Can lead to a prescriptive approach
	• Facilitates objectivity and an efficient assessment process	• One-to-one correspondence between the matrix elements and excellence model criteria may not be evident, making comparisons and benchmarking against award winners more difficult
	• Good for facilitating discussion in the team and for team building	
	• Output is suitable for action planning	
Workshop	• Approach is faster than award-type processes and is relatively inexpensive – there are no major training requirements	• Accuracy of the assessment is limited to the knowledge and insight of the group; thus it is important that the group contains a range of knowledge and
	• Encourages ownership of the self-assessment process and its outcomes	

(continued)

Table 10.4: *Continued*

Approach	Advantages	Limitations
	and is less threatening than second- or third-party assessments	experience to allow the criteria to be addressed in a meaningful manner
	• Self-assessment exercise provides a team-building opportunity	• Biased scoring can result due to the team's lack or experience of the scoring process or unwillingness to face up to the sometimes stark facts!
	• Scoring is generally of secondary importance to the group discussions, which highlight improvement opportunities and help develop a common view	• Sometimes difficult to assess evidence of the extent of deployment
	• Agreed list of key strengths and areas for improvement is produced, which forms the basis for action	• Outcome can be highly dependent on the skills and persuasive power of the facilitator. This is certainly true for more 'difficult' management teams!
	• Management team assessments encourage ownership of the outcomes, effective prioritization and action planning	
Pro forma	• Encourages the collection of fact-based evidence in a much more time-efficient manner than award simulation processes	• Can be completed on a superficial basis and jeopardize the outcome of the assessment. Strong and effective facilitation is required

Award simulation

- Can result in objective scores that are comparable with those generated by the award simulation process
- Generates a list of key strengths and areas for improvement, which are the basis for action planning
- Can potentially involve a range of people at various stages in the process
- Provides comprehensive insights into the capability and performance of the organization
- Produces details on strengths and areas for improvement
- Produces self-assessment results that are directly comparable to actual award assessments
- Provides excellent learning opportunities for the submission and assessor teams
- Provides a powerful communication and reference document
- Provides a wealth of 'quality' output for action planning

- Can give a summary and incomplete picture of the organization
- High resource requirements and lengthy cycle time
- May not be as objective as it should be – the results can be influenced by creative writing!
- May be used at an inappropriate stage of the organization's journey to excellence and distract the organization from more pragmatic improvement activities

Self-assessment is essentially concerned with organizational learning. There is no 'right' approach only an approach that suits your organization. There is a considerable opportunity to integrate the various types of audits and assessments (quality, safety, environmental, financial etc.) into a powerful total system that maximizes the organizational learning in a more efficient way.

Appendix 10.1 BQF SNAPSHOT – a software tool for self-assessment

Introduction

BQF SNAPSHOT is a powerful but simple to use software tool for assessing an organization of any size or sector against the eight fundamental concepts of business excellence. The following provides an overview of the potentials of the software. An example of BQF SNAPSHOT in action gives a description of its use, with illustrations taken from 'real life' practice.

BQF SNAPSHOT helps the senior management of an organization team to develop a practical improvement plan to enhance performance. BQF SNAPSHOT is designed as a framework for self-evaluation using a questionnaire approach against the eight fundamental concepts of excellence.

BQF SNAPSHOT is designed to support both those undertaking their first venture into the world of self-evaluation and experienced users of the excellence model. Alongside many others, features include:

- Workbook documents, which can be downloaded and used in groups to support independent scoring prior to debate to agree the consensus position
- A framework to record the position for 64 issues that are related to the concepts of excellence
- A feature to show the summary position against the concepts of excellence
- Cross-referencing to the excellence model to give an indicative points score out of 1000 and a percentage for each of the 32 sub-criteria
- A feature to compare files to show progress over time, to identify the gap between current performance and target or to compare different organizations
- Space to record strengths and opportunities for improvement, action planning support and illustrative guidance on excellence model practice.

BQF SNAPSHOT is divided into eight parts that deal with each of the eight fundamental concepts of excellence. These concepts are indicative of an organization's ability to achieve and sustain outstanding results for all their stakeholders. They are:

1. *Results orientation*. The needs of stakeholders are met and balanced. Stakeholders may include employees, customers, suppliers, shareholders and society.

2. *People development and involvement.* There is a culture of trust and empowerment that allows all employees to develop and contribute to their full potential.
3. *Customer focus.* There is a clear understanding of the needs of both current and potential customers, and a passion for meeting needs and exceeding expectations.
4. *Continuous learning, improvement and innovation.* Knowledge is shared to maximize performance, with learning, innovation and improvement encouraged.
5. *Leadership and constancy of purpose.* Leaders have a clear sense of direction and purpose, which they communicate effectively throughout the organization.
6. *Partnership development.* There are mutually beneficial relationships with all partners.
7. *Management by process and facts.* All activities are managed in a systematic and effective way, taking into account all stakeholders' perceptions.
8. *Public responsibility.* The organization fosters a positive and mutually beneficial relationship with society and the community.

The potentials of BQF SNAPSHOT

Truly excellent organizations are measured by their ability to achieve and sustain outstanding results for all their stakeholders, such as customers, employees, shareholders and the community. This requires a management approach based on the eight fundamental concepts.

For an organization to be truly outstanding, it requires a management approach based on these concepts. BQF SNAPSHOT will not only measure an organization's profile against these concepts; it will also help to develop a practical business plan of key issues to consider for improvement.

Self-assessment is a recognized and powerful way of driving improvement within an organization. It enables an organization to compare itself against the most demanding measures. There are many pathways to excellence, and not all organizations are ready to embark on a long and sometimes difficult journey. BQF SNAPSHOT, however, gives assistance for going in the right direction by providing a profile of the organization as it stands now. This helps to prioritize what are the most important factors for improvement, and to stimulate interest and commitment in taking an organization forward on the first steps of the journey to excellence.

Preparing for evaluation

When undertaking self-evaluation, available information from as many sources as possible should be considered. These can include:

1. Performance data regarding your organization
2. External reports
3. Feedback from stakeholders, including
   - Customers – e.g. letters, complaints, surveys etc.
   - Staff – e.g. surveys, discussions etc.
   - Community – e.g. statutory authorities and representatives of society etc.
   - Views and experience of senior managers.

The usual scoring process starts with members of a group scoring each issue, individually, on an initial basis using the hard-copy scoring sheets. The resulting outcomes and initial scores can then be discussed and debated in a group to establish a consensus score. It may be helpful to have an 'expert' advisor facilitating the process to establish the consensus score. Once a consensus has been reached, scores can be recorded in the software.

The recommended scoring approach is to address the issues as grouped around the fundamental concepts of the model. Scoring the issues in the eight sections in the BQF SNAPSHOT software will focus on understanding the concepts of excellence. The software provides profiles and scores for both criteria and sub-criteria sections of the excellence model.

It is suggested to score an organization rigorously by using the following principles:

- It is important to remember that each section has both enabler and result issues, with different scoring scales
- For each issue, set the score on the slider bar and select the button so that the score reflects an accurate, or conservative, position
- Listen and take on board the views of everyone who has experience regarding the issue
- Aim to establish a realistic, conservative, consensus score for each issue.

BQF SNAPSHOT provides several options once the scoring of the organization has been completed. One possibility is to use the 'group' feature to bring together the scores of individuals or departments; another possibility is to analyse the strengths and opportunities for improvement and flag the issues for improvement.

Furthermore, an action plan can be prepared to improve the issues that were identified.

Analysis

The analysis function of BQF SNAPSHOT has a wide variety of elements. Scores can be viewed grouped in different themes related to management practice. The relationship between unsatisfactory performance and weak management practice can be identified and reflected on (the results linkages). The organization's position for each sub-criterion of the model can be analysed. Moreover, issues where improvement will drive improvement in other issues can be uncovered – 'the drivers for improvement'. In addition, important issues that need improvement can be highlighted.

There are several recommended steps when identifying issues for improvement:

- 'Flag' the results issues that require improvement first, and possibly state your target for the scale of improvement on the 'action points' screen
- Look for the enablers where improvement will drive improvement in the results that need to be improved
- Keep the number of enablers issues 'flagged' for improvement to a manageable number (ten to fifteen)
- Separately list the key issues holding back development of the organization and make sure that the improvements 'flagged' address these key issues
- Use a group file to flag issues for a whole organization where separate scored files have been created.

After the issues to improve for either an individual or a group have been identified, a file detailing improvement action plan needs to be prepared (see 'Action planning' section below).

File comparison

With BQF SNAPSHOT, any number of files can be compared. There is a wide variety of features available, including a comparison of files for the same organization which have been scored at different times. This illustrates change over time. Additionally, files for different departments or business units can be compared and an average position established. This creates an overall position and identifies specific, or common, problems. The performance of the organization can be compared in relation to targets. This gap analysis may highlight priorities for improvement. Using the benchmarking feature, an external comparison with the practice and performance of other organizations can be made.

Action planning

With this function of BQF SNAPSHOT, a detailed improvement action plan can be produced for any issue identified. An action plan can be displayed in a number of formats. The action plan can be printed or transferred to other BQF SNAPSHOT files, and can also be exported to other applications.

For a successful completion of the action plan, it is important to gain commitment from everyone involved in the process. This can be achieved by communicating the plan to all who are drawn into the continuous improvement initiative. It is also important to monitor progress and provide support where necessary. During the course of the programme necessary changes will need to be addressed as these are exposed. BQF SNAPSHOT helps to achieve these planned improvements in practice and performance.

An example of a BQF SNAPSHOT application

In this section we look at BQF SNAPSHOT in action, using a case example. The example takes one area – leadership – and follows through some of BQF SNAPSHOT's features, showing its application. One of many advantages of the software is that it provides an easy to use but very effective way of assessing an organization. It allows quick completion of a complex self-assessment, and the many features provide a comprehensive overview of the organization on the way to excellence. Figure 10A provides an example of a scoring against the leadership criteria.

Model criteria – leadership

How leaders develop and facilitate the achievement of the mission and vision, develop values required for long-term success and implement these via appropriate actions and behaviours, and are personally involved in ensuring that the organization's management system is developed and implemented.

1a.	Leaders develop the mission, vision and values, and are role models of a culture of excellence	**34**
1b.	Leaders are personally involved in ensuring the organization's management system is developed, implemented and continuously improved	**35**
1c.	Leaders are involved with customers, partners and representatives of society	**24**
1d.	Leaders motivate, support and recognize the organization's people	**31**

Figure 10A Leadership criteria

In addition to the scoring per criterion, a breakdown of the percentage contribution of each of the areas to address per criterion is also possible. An example for (1b) is shown in Figure 10B.

A further useful feature of BQF SNAPSHOT is that the concepts of excellence can be displayed 'sorted by strengths' (Figure 10C) and 'sorted by weaknesses' (Figure 10D). This provides a quick health check of an organization and instantly shows where it stands regarding the concepts of excellence.

There are plenty more exciting features available at the touch of a button. For example, notes on strength, opportunities and evidence can be printed (Figure 10E), which provide a convenient reference for future planning.

A similarly useful output of BQF SNAPSHOT is the summary score of the EFQM Excellence Model® (see Figure 10F). This gives an instantaneous outline of the performance against each criterion. In addition, an easy to understand calculation of how the scores have been computed is also provided. This may be useful for explaining the process to people who are unfamiliar with the EFQM Excellence Model®.

A very useful function of the BQF SNAPSHOT software is the examples of illustrative practice. These not only give the reader interesting clues about what companies do in all areas of the Excellence Model, but also provide an interesting learning opportunity. An example is given in Table 11.1.

The last feature of BQF SNAPSHOT we would like to draw upon is benchmarking links. Using this option, organizations from all sectors are able to compare themselves against others.

In summary, BQF SNAPSHOT is an easy to use tool that helps make the complex process of self-assessment efficient and effective. It assists in gaining agreement and commitment amongst those undertaking self-assessment. Together, this ensures a successful implementation process of the excellence model.

Acknowledgements

The authors acknowledge the contribution of Dr Joachim Bauer, who largely wrote this appendix.

We are also pleased to acknowledge the assistance of the British Quality Foundation, who gave us permission to include this section and allowed us to use some of their materials. In particular, we acknowledge the kind help of Mr John Smith of the BQF.

% Score – 1b – Leader Organization

Development Issues

Governance   58%

Leaders have established a framework to manage the organization as expected by all stakeholders

Policy co-ordination   55%

A structured policy reference framework exists to communicate key aspects and standards of management practice

Process management   38%

The organization has established effective process management, involving co-ordination with partners/suppliers, and continuous review and improvement

Knowledge management   35%

Knowledge is researched, developed and shared to benefit customers and the organization

Performance measurement   28%

The organization has effective performance measurement systems

Process definition   28%

The key processes and systems required by the organization are established

Improvement culture   23%

Leaders constantly promote a culture of continuous improvement at all levels, using innovation, technology, learning, involvement and partnership

Management by fact   15%

Leaders ensure that decision-making in the organization is based on relevant, reliable, factual information

Average score for this sub-criterion: 35%

Figure 10B Contribution of sub-criteria – Leader Organization

Average scores for each section

Customer focus	32%
People development	30%
Leadership	30%
Public responsibility	24%
Results orientation	23%
Management by fact	23%
Continuous improvement	21%
Partnership development	20%

Figure 10C Concepts of Excellence – sorted by strengths

Average scores for each section

Partnership development	20%
Continuous improvement	21%
Management by fact	23%
Results orientation	23%
Public responsibility	24%
Leadership	30%
People development	30%
Customer focus	32%

Figure 10D Concepts of Excellence – sorted by weaknesses

Issue Notes on Present Strengths (1) Improvement Opportunities (2) and Supporting Evidence (3)

1a Leader vision

Results focus
1) IT and operations areas quite well advanced

1b Leader Organization

Performance measurement
1) A framework exists in some departments
2) Effectiveness questionable
   Are they the right measures?
   Not necessarily related to customer requirements
   Standardization potential
   Not measures that support improvement
   Communication mechanisms weak
   Integrity of data questionable

1c Leader involvement

Customer consultation
1) Exists
2) Not good at defining customer requirements in relation to each business unit
   Communications

Figure 10E Assessment details

EFQM Excellence Model Summary Score

1. Enablers criteria

Sub-criterion	**1a** 34%	**2a** 33%	**3a** 27%	**4a** 25%	**5a** 27%
Sub-criterion	**1b** 35%	**2b** 20%	**3b** 37%	**4b** 20%	**5b** 25%
Sub-criterion	**1c** 24%	**2c** 35%	**3c** 37%	**4c** 31%	**5c** 35%
Sub-criterion	**1d** 31%	**2d** 34%	**3d** 30%	**4d** 23%	**5d** 33%
		2e 35%	**3e** 38%	**4e** 18%	**5e** 36%
Sum	124%/4	156%/5	168%/5	117%/5	156%/5
Criterion Score	31%	31%	34%	23%	31%

2. Results criteria

Sub-criterion	**6a** 20%	**7a** 17%	**8a** 14%	**9a** 21%
	$\times 0.75$ 15%	$\times 0.75$ 13%	$\times 0.25$ 4%	$\times 0.50$ 11%
Sub-criterion	**6b** 19%	**7b** 14%	**8b** 25%	**9b** 21%
	$\times 0.25$ 5%	$\times 0.25$ 4%	$\times 0.75$ 19%	$\times 0.50$ 10%
Criterion Score	20%	16%	22%	21%

3. Calculation of total points

Criterion	Score	Factor	Points
1 Leadership	31%	$\times 1.0$	31
2 Policy and strategy	31%	$\times 0.8$	25
3 People	34%	$\times 0.9$	30
4 Partnerships and resources	23%	$\times 0.9$	21
5 Processes	31%	$\times 1.4$	44
6 Customer results	20%	$\times 2.0$	40
7 People results	16%	$\times 0.9$	15
8 Society results	22%	$\times 0.6$	13
9 Key performance results	21%	$\times 1.5$	32
Total points			**251**

Figure 10F Excellence Model – scoring summary

Building an excellence platform

11.1 Introduction

This chapter builds on the previous two chapters, where we looked at the key steps to self-assessment and described various approaches to self-assessment. This chapter puts the previous two chapters into context, and shows that over time there is more to self-assessment than simply choosing an approach and implementing it. Although there is a degree of repetition in this chapter and the last two chapters, we feel that it is important to give the reader an overall picture of self-assessment in action. It also provides greater insight for the more experienced practitioner.

To be of value to an organization, self-assessment in its wider context is a change management approach. As such, there is a need to provide support mechanisms and to recognize that there will be barriers to implementation and cost implications. It is also important to acknowledge that as an organization matures its challenges will change, as will the approach it needs to take.

This chapter introduces the 'self-assessment roadmap', which maps out the progress of self-assessment over time, the support mechanisms required, and the barriers an organization is likely to face. Becoming a world-class organization takes time and often the process cannot be accelerated, as there is a need to embed excellent activities as well as an excellence culture. The self-assessment roadmap features three main phases. The first is concerned with getting started, and the second with using the results of the self-assessment to drive the organization forward to a position where it is delivering excellent results. In the third phase the results are world-class as the business systems are subjected to continual refinement so that the advantages gained are sustained.

11.2 Introduction to the self-assessment roadmap

We envision the building of world-class capability to be similar to building a house. First of all the foundations have to be laid, secondly, the house has to be built and, finally, the house is occupied and the benefits of ownership are enjoyed. However, it has to be remembered that the property must be maintained and improved if it is to retain its value.

The self-assessment roadmap, which is based on many years' practical experience, is shown in Table 11.1. The roadmap is divided into three phases: entry, user and world-class. Each phase will be described in greater detail below, and here we simply explain the format of the roadmap and some of its principles.

The three phases have been given these names to capture the emphasis of the phase. There is also a relationship between the performance of the organization in terms of the self-assessment score and the time since implementation. Figure 11.1 shows this relationship, which it will be appreciated is a generalization – one organization might be scoring over 600 points on its first self-assessment (although this would be unusual) and another might still be scoring less than 300 points after five years due to lack of progress. The main thing to note is that most organizations see an

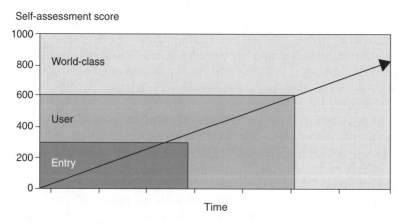

Figure 11.1 Looking at the score over time

Table 11.1: The self-assessment roadmap

Aspects	Phase 1 – Entry *Laying the foundations*	Phase 2 – User *Building the house*	Phase 3 – World-class *Reaping and maintaining the benefits*
Features of phase			
Typical score	Up to 350 points	350 to 600 points	600 points and above
Time from start	First 2–3 years	2–5 years	Over 5 years' experience
Issues to address	Getting buy-in Getting started Temptation to tie self-assessment result with personal performance Performance measurement systems (other than financial) often poor	Novelty of approach being lost Competition on scoring Areas are not actually as good as they think they are Danger of change of leadership, as not fully embedded	Complacency and loss of focus if external recognition achieved Operational pressures Finding areas to improve Limited scope of business excellence model chosen
Leadership			
Role and responsibilities	To be the first to experience Demonstrate commitment to process To provide vision and direction Establish support systems	Demonstrate commitment to process To provide vision and direction To provide support To improve leadership as part of improvement To share progress with other areas	Demonstrate commitment to process To provide vision and direction To provide support To improve leadership as part of improvement To be role models

(continued)

Table 11.1: *Continued*

Aspects	Phase 1 – Entry Laying the foundations	Phase 2 – User Building the house	Phase 3 – World-class Reaping and maintaining the benefits
Self-assessment approach			
Rigour	Very simple approach High level Limited data collection	Greater accuracy Richer feedback Need for confirmation of real progress Examination of results/ enabler linkages	Holistic, but accurate feedback at high level Measure of integration of approaches within business Diagnostic in nature Approaches may vary dependent on level
Effort (£ and resource)	Minimal but may incur third-party costs for support	More time and effort for each assessment More assessments leading to greater investment	Lower than previous phase due to greater integration with 'business as usual'
Level of cross-sharing/ learning	Focused on unit undergoing assessment Results often 'confidential'	Some promotion an adoption of good practice More sharing of results	Free exchange of best practice
Organizational elements			
Level of deployment/ involvement	Restricted to higher levels Limited involvement of others in self-assessment	Deployment to lower levels More people involved in the assessments	Self-assessment deployed throughout organization

Alignment with strategic objectives	Weak Unrelated improvement planning at lower levels	Improvements aligned with business plans	Fully integrated with 'business as usual' Achieving excellence leads to organizational advantage
Support mechanisms			
Communication/promotion	Either widespread with multi-channels or low key Use of intranet to exchange information	Widespread broadcasting reinforcing benefits of activity Regular updates on progress Consider rebranding	Integrated with normal business communications
Education/experience	Awareness training for leaders Training limited to facilitators and focused on process not concepts Few real experts	Training provided to key personnel on both concepts and process Business excellence included in induction programme More experts, some with external experience	Network of experts established, many in line positions High percentage of staff received training, with many delivering training
Support systems	Establishment of facilitator support structure Establishment of a reward and recognition system	Introduction of good practice database Continued dependence on support systems	Less emphasis
Integration with other systems	Established systems form the foundations of the first assessments Gaps in existing systems identified	Enterprise level system often defined Close integration with HR and performance measurement systems	Full integration

(continued)

Table 11.1: Continued

Aspects	Phase 1 – Entry *Laying the foundations*	Phase 2 – User *Building the house*	Phase 3 – World-class *Reaping and maintaining the benefits*
		First use of self-assessment to inform and deploy strategy	
Benefits/ deliverables	'Strategic' level improvements Mainly cultural at lower levels	Fundamental building blocksof excellence put into place High level of improvement activity Some quantifiable demonstration of benefit Organization more receptive to change More customer-focused attitude	Improvements contributing to achievement of business objectives Continued improvement in performance Desired culture continuously reinforced

increase in scoring over time, and that the focus of the activity changes at various stages.

Looking at the three phases, in the entry phase the organization has started to implement self-assessment as a vehicle for improving its performance over the longer term. The objective is one of awareness of self-assessment; data collection is limited and data are often mainly qualitative in nature, which means that they are based on people's perceptions and not solid facts. Because most of the effort goes into completing the self-assessment, there is limited improvement activity after the self-assessment. Simple methods are used for self-assessment, and the score will typically be less than 350 points out of 1000. Most of the benefits are cultural, as the organization recognizes the benefits of working more efficiently in a way that focuses on the customer and not the organization. The entry phase generally lasts for around two years, within which time the organization completes at least two self-assessments.

The second phase, the user phase, is entered when the benefits of self-assessment have been recognized and understood, and people are prepared to invest time and effort to use the information from the self-assessment to drive improvement activities through to completion. Data will be more readily available, and decisions will be based on facts and not opinions as a result of using a more rigorous approach to self-assessment. During this phase the fundamental building blocks of business excellence are put into place as the score increases, recognizing improved approaches and real benefits – such as reduced costs, higher people and customer satisfaction, and better alignment of activities.

The real benefits from business excellence are reaped when the organization reaches the world-class phase. This is when the understanding of business excellence is fully developed and is embedded into the 'learning organization'; when the approaches are continuously reviewed and refined, fuelled by insights from external organizations. Performance will be 'best in class' in several areas, and the typical self-assessment score will be 600–850 points out of 1000 – in reality there is of course always some opportunity for improvement, and hence a perfect score of 1000 is unrealistic.

The self-assessment roadmap in Table 11.1 has several aspects, which are explained in Table 11.2. These aspects represent the features and main streams of activity that support self-assessment. In the next sections each of these aspects (with the exception of the features) will be described in more detail, together with an explanation as to how the approach changes over time.

Table 11.2: Aspects of the self-assessment roadmap

Aspect	Description
Features of phase	The score obtained during self-assessment will increase as the business excellence platform is built within the organization, and an indication of the scores that should be expected is given in the roadmap. It should be noted that the scores refer to those using an accurate self-assessment methodology, such as an award-style assessment. In the earlier phases, because simpler self-assessment methods are being used there will be a tendency to over-score – 50–150 points is not unusual in the entry phase
	The roadmap also indicates the typical times that an organization spends in a particular phase
Issues to address	These are the main challenges of the phase, which include the barriers to overcome and the problems that might be encountered
Leadership	Leaders have a key role to play in the success of building an excellence platform. They also have particular responsibilities that remain fairly constant over time

Self-assessment approach	The approach to self-assessment will change as the needs of the organization change. In the early days a simple, quick-to-use approach is most appropriate, but in time there will be a need for a more rigorous approach that delivers richer improvement data. The costs will also change over time, as will the level of sharing
Organizational elements	With time, self-assessment will involve more areas and more people as the benefits from the approach are delivered. There will also be greater alignment between the strategic objectives and the improvement activity
Support mechanisms	A number of support systems will need to be put into place to ensure that the self-assessments are successful. These may include communication, education, and activities such as a facilitator network and a reward and recognition scheme. The integration of such activities with other organizational activities must also be considered
Benefits/deliverables	The benefits delivered vary from being strategic to operational, and through all phases there will be a positive impact on the culture of the organization as the business excellence philosophy is embedded

11.3   Aspects of the self-assessment roadmap

Issues to address

As with every initiative, there are always barriers to getting started. Some will be due to a lack of awareness, but others will be due to previous experiences. This is especially the case with self-assessment where there has previously been a total quality management programme that is considered to have been a failure.

Increasing awareness, especially at the senior levels where people have a lot of things competing for their attention and time, can be difficult. It is for this reason that the roadmap has a leadership aspect, a communication/promotions aspect, and an education aspect, as a lot of effort has to go into communication in the early days. This is at a time when there are no support structures in place, the philosophy is not embedded into the organization, and success rests with a band of disciples.

Previous experience can also act as a positive or negative influencing force. If the organization has had a total quality programme that has been labelled a failure, there is often a resistance to self-assessment. There are some close links with total quality management and business excellence, but it is important to communicate the differences. Some of these are listed in Table 11.3. Where there has been a highly successful total quality management programme, business excellence and self-assessment are the natural progression to extend the scope and benefit from the activities.

Often the desire to commence self-assessment is halted because leaders hear about another bandwagon they can jump onto. A particular example is the current high level of interest in Six Sigma, balanced scorecards, and the revised ISO9000 series of standards. These deliver benefits to an organization but, as we saw in Chapter 1, they are within the scope of a business excellence approach and are not a replacement for it.

It is important that the need for the initiative is linked with the success of the organization so that these barriers may be overcome. Sometimes this can be difficult in the early days, when there may be a lack of clarity regarding the direction the organization is taking. This is often compounded by poor performance measurement systems, when the only reliable, historical measures are financial measures. It cannot be overemphasized that business excellence is a philosophy that will have a resultant impact on the culture of the organization. Culture changes are not achieved overnight.

One issue that can become more significant as the organization moves from the entry phase to the user phase relates to personal performance measurement. There is a temptation to tie

Table 11.3: Comparing self-assessment and total quality management

Similarities	Differences
• Need for leader commitment and continuity	• Leaders are directly involved in business excellence
• High dependence on people's involvement	• TQM is internally focused, whereas business excellence includes a range of stakeholders
• Embeds a quality philosophy	• Business excellence is less prescriptive – there is no 'magic'
• Process improvement at the centre of the approach	• Business excellence covers all the organization's approaches
• Focus on the customer	• Business excellence requires mature performance measurement systems and external comparisons
• Delivers both 'hard' and 'soft' benefits	• Business excellence has a direct link to the organization's strategy, supporting the achievement of the strategic objectives
• Benefits delivered over time – it is not an overnight process	• Self-assessment allows a direct comparison with other companies
• Communication, education and other support systems, such as reward and recognition, vital to success	
• External support often required to support programme, especially in the early years	

self-assessment results to personal performance, and this is a dangerous seed to sow. Scoring is a 'necessary evil'. In the early days the organization will be focused on the score and on the need to be seen conducting a self-assessment, especially if to do so is a directive from top management. The benefit of the approach is often off people's radar screen.

Although many areas will demonstrate commitment, there will be others that will see the need to conduct a self-assessment as an unnecessary distraction from normal business activities. As time progresses and the understanding of self-assessment and its benefits materialize there will be more commitment to the approach, but this will take several self-assessment cycles. Repeated self-assessments will drive up the self-assessment score to the point where some areas will think they are 'world-class' when in fact they are only on the first rung of the ladder. As awareness of business excellence and what 'world-class' really means improves, and as the approach to self-assessment becomes more rigorous and accurate, some senior managers are going to have to recognize that they are not as good as they thought. This leads to a barrier in getting the organization from the entry to the user phase, and from the user phase to the world-class phase. If scores have been tied to personal performance or, even worse, bonuses, this will be a still higher barrier. Even when there is no tie to personal performance, competition between different business areas will lead to the barrier.

Apart from scoring, an organization faces other issues when it is in the user phase. After two to three years the novelty of the approach may start to wear off, and so there may be a need to relaunch the programme to keep it fresh and in people's minds. This will be at a time when the real benefits are only just starting to come through and there is the temptation to jump onto another bandwagon. There is also a danger of the whole programme being blown off course by a change of leadership if sustainable self-assessment approaches are not fully embedded within the first two to three years. New leaders often have new ideas, and politics often dictate that credit should not be given to a previous job incumbent.

It should also be remembered that the business excellence models do not stand still and there is a need to keep in line with the current thinking. When considerable effort has been put into training and support materials, the last thing you want is to find that there has to be a major update. However, keeping in line not only allows continued comparisons with other organizations; it also provides refreshment and new thinking. This need to keep in line follows through into the world-class phase, where there is a danger of complacency creeping in. Many organizations get knocked backwards by internal organizational change in response to threats or opportunities in the external environment. When this happens the organization's systems need to be brought into line, and this can take considerable effort. It is easy to slip back to the user phase.

Things can also go wrong and the benefits start to get lost if the organization achieves some form of external recognition, such as winning a Quality Award. Human nature dictates that people work hard towards a goal, but once it has been achieved the organization loses focus. This concern is particularly damaging if the organization is successful in marketing itself to the external assessors, and it is really only in the user phase when it achieves the recognition. There is a danger that it could go backwards even faster under these conditions.

Criticism from other areas of the business may also undermine the value from business excellence. This can be a problem with jealousy or 'not invented here', and is particularly apparent when external recognition is involved. We know several organizations that have achieved some form of external recognition only to come under attack from other parts of the organization, as they 'know what they are really like'.

In the unlikely event that everything is stable and the organization is not fighting to keep up the standard of performance, a problem can be resistance to taking improvement action. Organizations can get so welded to their approaches that there is resistance to change. It is well recognized that an organization's core competencies can lead to its destruction, and there have been many calls for an organization to 're-invent' itself every few years. It also has to be recognized that whatever business excellence model has been chosen to build the platform of excellence, this too will be limited in its scope. Some of the longer-standing 'role model' business excellence organizations have started to outgrow their models, and are now looking for other vehicles to take their organizations forward.

Leadership

The requirements placed on the leaders remain relatively constant throughout. They have the responsibility to lead and support the process, and take the overall lead. It is recommended that the senior leaders be the first team to conduct a self-assessment, to get the process rolling. As noted by John Sharpe, who is the ex-President of one of the major Unilever Business Groups:

The shared understanding and commitment gained by the top team from doing the self assessment themselves is an essential ingredient for real understanding of the process and its benefits.

The commitment gained from 'doing it oneself' greatly increases the chance of long term success.

Apart from being the first to experience the process, in the early stages there will be a need to resource the support structure and fund the development of the approach. This is especially the case where there is limited in-house expertise and thus a need to engage consultants to provide the support. This is the quickest way to get going, but the responsibility should never be abdicated to the third party.

The leaders should establish the direction at the outset, and make the link to the strategy and the benefits to the business. For example, it has been known for the CEO to set the goal of 'becoming world-class within five years' to provide a stimulus. This can have a negative long-term effect if it causes the focus to be exclusively on the score achieved as discussed above, but there is no doubt that such a statement gets people's attention.

As self-assessment becomes more visible within the organization leaders have to be on their guard, as their actions will give an indication as to how important they feel business excellence is to the organization. In one instance, in a worldwide organization, the senior management teams in one of the countries completed their self-assessment in a two-hour Board meeting as an agenda item. It is accepted that this part of the organization was firmly rooted in the entry phase, but just think of the message it sent to people when management teams in other areas were taking a full day to complete their self-assessments.

Leaders also have to understand the concept that their own leadership style will be under scrutiny as part of self-assessment. This makes many leaders uncomfortable and even resistant to the process, especially if it is also feared that there will be an attack on the effectiveness and efficiency of their functional area as well, suggesting that they are poor leaders. The truly great leaders embrace these concepts, and work to improve their effectiveness as individuals.

Once the user phase is entered, leaders will devote more time to sharing their experiences and progress with others. This will start to involve more external organizations when the world-class phase is reached. In some ways the user phase is the most precarious, as after two to three years there is more chance of a change to a senior leadership team. This incurs the risk of a change in direction or of dilution, as new team members have to be brought into the process. The risk reduces when the world-class phase is achieved, as at this point the whole philosophy is embedded into the organization and success is less dependent on a single individual.

Self-assessment approach

The self-assessment process is capable of being applied more rigorously as experience of self-assessment increases over the years. This will give more accurate and detailed feedback, but such rigor will be distracting in the entry phase, where the improvement opportunities are often large scale and obvious – such as the need to install or improve performance measurement systems. A more rigorous self-assessment methodology will be looking for the enabler–results linkages as part of the evaluation and improvement planning activity. The self-assessment can also be used as a critical working document for recording evidence, and will be used in future self-assessment activities. By way of example, Table 11.4 illustrates the way that the approach to self-assessment may vary over time. This table also shows the linkage between the roadmap and the approaches given in Chapter 10.

There is also the consideration that more rigorous assessment takes more time and involves more people, which may present a barrier in the earlier days when the full benefits of self-assessment are not understood. The level of involvement of staff in the self-assessment process can vary from just the assessment team and facilitator to the entire organization. To consider the options, four scenarios have been prepared demonstrating various levels of involvement (see Table 11.5). The approach chosen will vary

Table 11.4: Example self-assessment approaches through the phases

	Entry phase	*User phase*	*World-class phase*
Features	Highly prescriptive	Some tailoring	Customized
	Focus on 'whats'	Focus on 'hows'	Focus on linkages across the model
	Scoring based on counting	Scoring based on extended scoring matrix	Scoring based on extended scoring matrix
	Limited results data	Current results data	Extended time results data
Typical approach to self-assessment	Simple questionnaire	Pro forma	Award style

Table 11.5: Examining levels of involvement

Scenario	Level of involvement	Advantages	Disadvantages
Self-assessment team plus facilitator	Low	Exercise contained in top team Clarity of data during consensus meeting	Limited views taken into account Limited buy-in to improvement plans May be difficult to accept a realistic score Staff may feel isolated if not involved
Self-assessment team plus direct reports to top team	Low to medium	Greater buy-in from managers for improvement action More accurate and balanced views during consensus Easier to debrief management after the assessment	Managers and the team may need training to participate Staff may feel isolated if not involved Management could defend their own corner, leading to conflict and devaluing the process
Self-assessment team plus cross-functional teams	Medium	Greater buy-in, especially if the team members involve a range of people in their areas More extensive data collected with a wider	Staff not selected to participate may feel isolated Increased resource requirements

| All staff | High | range of views
Accuracy of the data improves

Wide deployment of self-assessment
Acceptance of improvement action throughout the organization
Improved communication

Wide range of views collected
Can use internal marketing techniques to increase participation | Training could be a major factor
Increased resources with possible short-term effect on the organization
Time to conduct assessment increases |

from organization to organization, and will depend on which phase the organization is in. As an organization moves from the entry to the user phase, the level of staff involvement is likely to increase.

In general, the higher the level of involvement, the greater the accuracy and benefit to the organization will be. The downside is that the assessment will take longer, require more resources and be more difficult to co-ordinate, as shown in Figure 11.2. The advantages and disadvantages of the various levels of involvement are shown in Table 11.5.

As discussed in Chapter 9, one of the key activities of self-assessment is the consensus stage, and the level of involvement and time invested in this activity will have a marked effect on the output from the self-assessment. Consensus is where the team meets to agree the results of the assessment, and it involves considering the evidence, compiling the feedback and agree the scores. As a general rule, the more time spent preparing for and conducting the consensus, then the greater the benefit. This relationship is shown in Figure 11.3.

Three basic scenarios have been developed to illustrate the different approaches that may be taken. The first, 'show and go', represents the scenario where preparation for consensus is kept to an absolute minimum and everyone shows up for the meeting with limited or no sharing of information. The second scenario, 'share and go', is where the evidence is circulated before the meeting so that some preparation may take place. Finally we have 'pre-consensus', where the evidence is shared and feedback collected prior to the meeting. Under this scenario everyone is up to speed and there is partial agreement, so the focus will be on producing the feedback that will be used for improvement planning. These three scenarios are summarized in Table 11.6.

A final feature of the self-assessment approach that varies over the phases is the level of sharing of information at the end of the process. In the entry phase, it is not uncommon for scores to be kept confidential as business areas are concerned that they will be regarded as deficient. There is also likely to be a low level of sharing of good practice from the strengths identified, as there may be few actual strengths and a 'not invented here' culture. As the level of experience increases and the culture changes to support sharing, there will be a marked change. It is not unusual to find that, in the user phase, promoting good practice will be clearly evident, as business areas are keen to show their strengths. When the world-class phase is reached there will be more pride in learning from others, so the focus will be implementing on others' ideas.

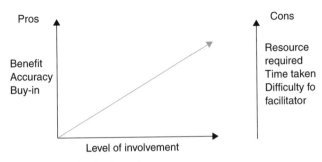

Figure 11.2 Trading level of involvement

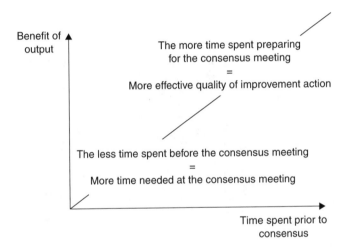

Figure 11.3 Time spent on consensus

Organizational elements

The previous section considered the level of involvement during the self-assessment, but there is another level of involvement that relates to how far the self-assessment approach is deployed throughout the organization. Unless the organization is relatively small, it is likely that there will be a number of divisions, departments and even teams. Under these circumstances, just how far self-assessment will be extended is a key consideration. The answer to this question will vary from organization to organization, but it is likely that in the first year or so the self-assessment will be restricted to the top level of management. It is usually a

Table 11.6: Three scenarios for preparing for consensus

Scenario	Description	Advantages	Disadvantages
Show and go	Team arrives at the consensus meeting with their data. As each area is discussed the data are shared and the team's conclusions reached	Very little time is taken to prepare for consensus Each team member has responsibility for a specific checklist area Most likely approach during the entry phase	Absorption and collation of data has to be achieved in real time Lengthens consensus meeting Accuracy of data is likely to suffer
Share and go	The team members circulate their data prior to consensus so that other team members can read all the information and data. This allows team members time to prepare for consensus, and limits the number of surprises on the day	Allows participants to be better prepared for consensus Areas of inaccuracy or conflict can be discussed in advance Linkage between enablers and results easier to identify	More effort required to prepare for consensus May encourage participants to prepare defences to protect their areas Preparation will be devalued if some team members fail to prepare for the meeting

| Pre-consensus | Each team member circulates evidence and data for their area of responsibility. Team members then feed back to each other so summaries can be prepared prior to consensus | Most likely approach for business units in the 'user' phase
Linkages between enablers and results easier to identify
Consensus concentrates on areas of improvement, not accuracy of the data
Higher likelihood that team members will prepare for consensus
Quality of improvement action taken should be more effective
Considered to be 'best practice' by external assessors | Preparation for consensus requires more resources
Cycle time for the assessment will be lengthened
Assessment process more difficult to co-ordinate
Change of team membership during the assessment process more difficult to manage
Greater demand on support from facilitator |

mistake to insist that all units conduct a self-assessment from day one, for both practical and cultural reasons. From a practical perspective, the logistics are quite significant and it is likely that the approach required at team level will vary from the approach at organizational level. For example, the results set for a team would be different from the results set for an organization.

The cultural perspective is as, if not more, important. In the early days of the entry phase, it is unlikely that everyone will support the self-assessment activity. It is important that the senior leaders are the first ones to buy-in and support the process, so that when the benefits are challenged at lower levels there is unwavering commitment from the leaders.

A second organizational consideration is the alignment of the improvement actions with the strategic objectives. In the early days there will be some large-scale improvements, but the majority of lower-level improvements will be 'TQM'-type improvements, where a major cultural benefit will result from people's involvement. In the later phases the self-assessments will be more in line with 'business as usual', and as a consequence more closely aligned with the needs of the organization.

It is highly recommended that improvement planning be conducted some time after completion of the self-assessment. This is to allow time for the team to reflect on the main conclusions, stand back, review and look at best practice. This is captured in the 'rule of three':

> At the end of the assessment the top team should take a step back from all the detail and ask itself the question 'What are the three things that would have the most significant effect on improving business performance in the next year?'.
>
> By defining three main themes and broad action plans, management is more able to build the improvement goals into the ongoing planning process and achieve more in the end.

There are two suggested approaches to improvement planning, which are outlined below. The organization must determine the approach best suited, and it is likely that the improvement plan approach will be used in the early days, with a move to an integrated approach over time.

The 'separate improvement plan' approach

For organizations new to self-assessment, it is appropriate for the improvement action planning to be contained in an improvement action plan. This section focuses on giving guidance regarding the completion of such a plan.

The self-assessment will lead to the calculation of the overall score and will capture the main strengths and areas for improvement. The team should agree both the key strengths and key areas for improvement once consensus is complete, and the whole assessment can be reviewed.

Once the key areas for improvement have been established, a plan should be generated outlining the action to be taken to address the area of concern. Areas of improvement normally fall into one of the five categories listed in Table 11.7. Each area to be addressed should be coded and treated accordingly.

For each key area of improvement, it is recommended that the following be considered:

- The setting of SMART objectives reflecting the improvement that is sought
- A list of actionable steps that will lead to the improvement in performance
- Each action step to have a person assigned to it as the person responsible for the achievement of the action
- A date by which each action will be achieved.

The list of actions should be compiled into an improvement plan. This action plan should be monitored on a regular basis, and ideally this should be part of the normal management processes.

The 'integrated with business planning' approach

In some ways this is a much more straightforward approach than the one described above. It will, however, take a little longer, as it involves the screening of the improvement opportunities once they have been coded.

Each potential area for improvement is screened against the following tests. In taking the suggested improvement action, will it:

- Deliver a measurable benefit to the business?
- Support the achievement of one or more strategic objectives?
- Close a significant gap in performance, when the area's performance is compared with best in class?

If the answer to the questions is yes, then an appropriate activity should be added to the organization's business plan for stewarding as part of the business planning process. By taking this action the improvement activity will not only clearly support the business, but also the improvement activity will be fully integrated into normal business planning and the management control processes.

Table 11.7: Types of improvement from self-assessment

	Description	Suggested action
Submission report issues	These are issues where there is no under-lying problem and the issue is a result of lack of clarity in the evidence. Such issues may be due to the unfamiliarity of the assessment team with the business area	Improve evidence on next self-assessment
Deployment issues	These are issues where the approach is sound, but it has not been fully deployed. This is an issue of conformance. The deployment could be related to a lack of results data	Ensure that the approach is deployed to the relevant areas. It should be noted, however, that such lack of deployment might be intentional, as when deploying an approach in a systematic manner
Process improvements	Here, the approach has been deemed to lack effectiveness and/or efficiency. This may be caused by a lack of review and refinement	Establish a process improvement activity
Strategic issues/gaps	An area has not been addressed – for example, lack of an approach such as no employee survey. These issues are more likely to occur during the entry phase	Establish an improvement project to address the issue. These will be larger-scale, longer-term improvements
Philosophy issues	More holistic than approach issues, these will be themes that are identified from the assessment. Examples are limited review and refinement across several approaches, or a general lack of trends, targets and comparisons in the results areas	This may be addressed through time as the number of review or measurement cycles increases. Alternatively there may be a need to establish an improvement project, which will embrace many processes

Support mechanisms

A number of support mechanisms are listed on the roadmap, and each is discussed here in turn.

Communication

A variety of different media may be used for communications. These include:

- e-mail
- Local intranet facility
- Local magazines
- Organization cascade meetings
- Board and management team meetings and minutes.

All these channels may be used to communicate the objectives, the process, the timetable and the results of the self-assessments. However, 'branding' is also important to get some identity, and organizations often have their own logo or theme to support the approach.

There will be several communication events throughout the self-assessment cycle. These include the launch of the self-assessment for a particular year, regular updates on progress and the communication of the learning, and reinforcement of the benefits at the end of the cycle. The launch tends to be the most major event, and this may be supported by a number of things, for example:

- A communication package, giving the materials and support documentation for the facilitators
- A letter from the most senior leader
- An organization-wide cascade to brief all staff
- A set of slides and briefing notes that facilitators can use to brief their teams
- A leaflet explaining the particular business excellence model
- Posters advertising the self-assessment round.

Education

The level of education required will vary for the different roles in the process. It is normal to give the senior leaders a brief executive overview of business excellence and self-assessment, but most of their education will come from their involvement in the programme. There is a similar need to provide support for the managers and teams that conduct the self-assessments. The facilitators, who in turn will have been educated by the core team responsible for the self-assessment activity, normally provide this support.

It is not uncommon to find that in every self-assessment cycle an annual training workshop will be held for the new facilitators, and a refresher day for the previous facilitators. The refresher training for the previous facilitators also allows them to be briefed first-hand on any changes to the self-assessment process, such as when moving between the different phases of the self-assessment roadmap. Facilitator training will cover the objectives of improving their knowledge of business excellence, as well as the specific details of the self-assessment approach that will be used. Figure 11.4 illustrates a typical one-day programme for facilitators.

The core team members are likely to have had experience in conducting self-assessments as part of an external award programme, or at least to have been trained as external assessors. As experience with self-assessment increases and the organization moves through the various phases, it is useful if selected facilitators are given the opportunity to experience an external process. This ensures that first-class expert support is available at the point where the self-assessments are being conducted.

Support systems

Most of the activities in this section of the roadmap provide support in some way, but three areas are of particular note as they are implemented specifically to support the self-assessment activities. These are the facilitator support network, the reward and recognition scheme, and a database for the sharing of good practice – which is needed as the organization moves from the entry to the user phase to support the increased learning that will be evident.

In this section we will focus on the facilitator network. It is common to have a central support team managing the overall process, with facilitators providing support in local areas. To ensure that the business excellence philosophy gets embedded into the organization, a facilitator should serve a two-year term and certainly no more than three years. Ideally the facilitators will be part time, but in larger areas of the organization full-time facilitators are not uncommon.

In pursuit of business excellence, organizations are increasingly recognizing the need to gain the full involvement of their employees in the improvement process. The role of the facilitator is key to achieving this. The facilitator's task is to help to create an environment in which employees at all levels can contribute to the continuous improvement of working practices at the point of operation.

A One-Day Seminar

Objectives:

By the end of the seminars, delegates will be able to:

- Explain the principles behind the Excellence Model
- Describe the process for conducting a self-assessment
- Discuss the benefits that organizations who are practising self-assessment have achieved
- Refer to an action plan for conducting self-assessment within their own part of the organization.

Pre-seminar work:

Before attending the seminars, delegates will be given a case study to read.

Outline programme:

Approximate timing	Session	Content
09:00	Introduction	• Introduction of delegates • Purpose of seminar • Schedule for the seminar • Seminar administration
09:15	Key stakeholders exercise	• Understanding the stakeholders in an organization
09:30	Key business excellence concepts	• Review key business excellence concepts to ensure a common level of understanding
10:00	Designing a framework exercise	• Delegates will be asked to design their own business excellence framework
10:30	Basic principles behind the European Business Excellence Model	• Historical background • A simple model • Building the model • Enablers and results
11:00	Coffee	
11:30	Providing feedback against the model exercise	• Analysing the 'Strengths'and 'Areas for Improvement'in selected enabler areas of the case study
12:30	Scoring an organization against the model	• Principles behind the scoring matrix • Introduction to the scoringmatrix
13:00	Lunch	
14:00	Scoring the case study exercise	• Scoring enablers • Scoring results
15:00	Benefits from self-assessment	• Results from independent research • Benefits experienced by some case study companies
15:30	Tea	
16:00	Key steps in self-assessment	• A simple self-assessment process • Data collection methods • Assessment methods
16:30	A way forward in your organization	• What are the lessons from this Seminar? • What should you do next in your organization?
17:30	Seminar close	

Figure 11.4 Outline one-day seminar for facilitators

It is necessary to consider key features of the exact role facilitators are expected to fulfil. In addition to meeting the needs of the programme, the role definition should consider the following four points:

1. *The core skills required.* These are common to all facilitator roles, and as a minimum comprise:

   - The teamwork process
   - Structuring a meeting
   - Observing a group
   - Giving feedback
   - Active listening
   - Intervention in a group
   - Tools and techniques for process improvement
   - Dealing with resistance.

   These are the skills that need to be practised and deployed by facilitators in their role of oiling the wheels of the team process. Appropriate feedback and intervention, effective meetings with good communication, and use of relevant data – properly analysed and presented – all contribute to the smooth running of the team and good decision-making. In this way, much potential conflict can be avoided.

2. *The facilitator as supporter.* In addition to exercising the core skills, a facilitator needs to understand the interpersonal and group issues in a team that may be getting in the way of task achievement. This includes understanding potential sources of conflict that can arise, particularly when the team comes under pressure to produce results. Techniques such as the Myers–Briggs Type Indicator (MBTI) provide a means of increasing facilitators' awareness of their own preferred ways of working and those of others. The insight gained from this into the profile and dynamics of the whole team enables them to recognize the value of the differences between individual team members and to build constructively on them.

3. *The facilitator as leader.* A facilitator is often required to take the role as leader of a group. This requires particular skills in addition to those listed above, such as understanding leadership styles, dealing with resistance, and approaching problem solving in a clear and systematic way. Facilitators should explore their own leadership style and how to apply it in the context of a problem-solving methodology. Such a methodology should be designed to help the leader gain maximum participation from everyone in the team as it moves from task definition to task completion.

4. *The facilitator as teacher.* The responsibility for encouraging improvement teams to learn and use the systematic tools of quality improvement recognizes a wider role of the facilitator as internal consultant. This role demands not only competence in the use of the techniques by the facilitator, but also the ability to communicate and teach them to others. To improve their own understanding and communication skills, facilitators could prepare and deliver short lectures on the key aspects of the tools and techniques of quality improvement. Receiving feedback from colleagues would help facilitators to improve their performance.

Not all of these roles will be exercised, depending on the organization concerned and its particular aspirations. In the case of organizations engaged in organization-wide business improvement initiatives, all of the roles tend to assume prominence at different times.

One of the best ways of gaining support is to establish relationships with people who can help. Two types of relationship, each with different objectives, are suggested for facilitators: mentors and buddies.

Quite often, new facilitators feel undefended when trying to influence powerful senior management teams. For this reason it is suggested that each facilitator establishes a mentor who can give support and guidance at difficult times. Ideally, this mentor should be a member of the senior management team.

Not all facilitators will feel the need to have a mentor. It is a concept worth considering if they are new to the facilitation role, feel exposed when addressing the senior management team, or simply want to receive constructive feedback to improve performance.

Every facilitator should have a 'buddy'. A buddy is a person from whom the facilitator can seek help and advice, and with whom he or she can exchange ideas. Ideally the buddy will be local, and it is useful if he or she has different areas of expertise. During the self-assessment process the buddy is the facilitator's first line of support.

It is often useful to establish a list of frequently asked questions to help facilitators. A sample list of questions is given in Table 11.8.

Integration with other systems

Established systems form the foundation of the first assessments on the way to building an excellence platform. Gaps in existing systems will be identified during the entry phase, and many of these will relate to performance measurement systems.

Table 11.8: Sample frequently asked questions

Question	Response
How do I get hold of external comparison data?	Some data have been included in the support documentation drawn from internal sources. If you want to collect your own data, you will find useful data in publicly available information. You might like to try the following public information to begin your search:
	Company reports
	Business reports
	Quality newspapers
	Trade magazines
	Conference presentations.
	Trade contacts can be a useful source of information, but care must be taken when using these sources. The European Code of Conduct provides useful guidance on best practice in this area.
How does our questionnaire score compare against the scores given to companies as part of the European Award process?	As a rule of thumb, if you reduce your questionnaire score by about 100–200 points you will be close to the score you would achieve in an external assessment.
	The actual scores required to win an award are not published, but we know from people who work as external assessors that the range of scores is approximately as follows:

To reach the final site-visit stage of the award process, an organization needs to score above 450 points

To win a prize, the score is going to be in the region of 600–700 points

To win the award itself a score or over 700 points is required and 750 is a likely benchmark.

What do I do if I cannot get the team to agree at the consensus meeting?

You may be surprised to learn that this often occurs during external assessments, as at the end of the day the final score comes down to an assessor's perception and this perception is coloured by the assessor's background and experience. So if your team cannot reach agreement on a consensus point, there is no need to worry.

The best process to follow is to review the information against the scoring guidelines, starting with a 50% score and moving the score either up or down, depending on the wording. If the team is still in disagreement, then get the self-assessment team leader to make the final decision. The reason for the disagreement should be recorded, and you should get the team to agree that if more information should become available to prove the point one way or the other, the team should revisit its decision.

It must be remembered that the score is not the important issue when conducting the self-assessment. Capturing the evidence and data and planning the improvement actions that are going to improve business performance far outweigh the need for absolute accuracy in the score.

What do I do if not all the self-assessment team can make the consensus meeting?

The best course of action is to rearrange the consensus meeting on a date suitable for all participants.

(continued)

Table 11.8: *Continued*

Question	Response
	Going ahead with the meeting without team members is not desirable, as this could affect the ability to take the improvement actions identified as a result of the assessment.
What do I do if we get to the consensus meeting and not all the evidence and data are available?	It is better to postpone the meeting until they are available Making decisions on incomplete information is not desirable. It is important that any actions that are taken make the best use of available resources. If decisions are made without the full information it is possible that the actions may not be the best actions, or the actions may not be effective.
What do I do if the team leader dominated the process?	You are likely to know that this will happen before the self-assessment process commences. This is also likely to be a problem that has far-reaching effects outside of the self-assessment process. The best advice is to invest time in preparation. Draft a plan that you feel will be acceptable to all stakeholders. You should also review the 'people issues' section so that you can prepare to tackle the interpersonal conflicts that might occur.
What should I do if I do not agree with the process that the team is following?	You should not lose sight of the fact that the self-assessment process is the team's process and not yours. You should use your people skills and expertise to influence the team as much as possible. It is also worth remembering that there is the possibility that the team will come up with an improved process!

What should I do if I do not agree with the team's strengths, areas for improvement and score?

It is the team's decision as to how it assesses the business. If you feel that the team is misguided, based on your experience, ensure that the team focuses on the facts and not on emotions.

For example, if only limited evidence is available, then by referring to the scoring guidelines it will be clear that a score of 100 per cent is not appropriate. Similarly, if people think they know what happens but do not have the hard evidence or data, they should be challenged until they accept that they are giving an emotional response and not one based on fact.

Some of the measures on the Business Unit's scorecard are milestones and not performance measures. Should I include these measures in the assessment?

Ideally an organization should use performance measures that can be tracked over a period of time and be compared to other areas of the operation or externally.

A performance measure such as '*deliver the Disneyland Paris project on time*' is a milestone and not a performance measure as such, although milestones may be extremely important for the business. If these types of measure exist on the scorecard, the best approach is to convert them to process-based measures. For example, the milestone measure above could be re-worded as '*key projects delivered on time*'.

By the time that the user phase is reached, an enterprise level system will have been defined. An enterprise level system consists of a list or picture of the highest-level process in the organization, supported by the detail of which sub-processes support the high-level processes. There will also be close integration with HR systems, and performance measurement systems will be in place for all types of performance measures. It is likely that the organization will see the first use of self-assessment information to inform and deploy the strategy. At this point the excellence platform will have been built, and it is during the world-class phase that it is continually reviewed and refined with a view to obtaining outstanding and sustainable levels of performance.

Benefits/deliverables

In the entry phase, many of the improvements will be large scale and strategic in nature. This is for a number of reasons. First, as self-assessment activity commences it is likely to be confined to the highest levels of the organization. In addition, in the early days the improvements will focus on the gaps that the self-assessment identified. There will be effects on the culture, and for the majority of people this is where most benefit will be realized in the early days, as a new results-focused, learning culture starts to emerge. It is interesting that organizations that have experienced total quality management, even if it has been perceived as a success, find getting started with self-assessment much easier, as the culture is more receptive and closer to what an excellence culture is like.

By the time the user phase has been reached, the fundamental building blocks of excellence will have been put into place and there will be a high level of improvement activity. Some quantifiable demonstration of the benefit from the improvement activity will be available, and the organization will be much more receptive to change. A customer-focused attitude will prevail.

In the world-class phase, improvements will be contributing to the achievement of business objectives and there will be a continued improvement in performance whilst the desired culture is continuously reinforced.

11.4   Using the roadmap

In this section we include a simple plan for the self-assessment activity to help make it a success. This is based on the process shown in Figure 11.5 and summarized in Table 11.9. The planning pro forma is given in Figure 11.6.

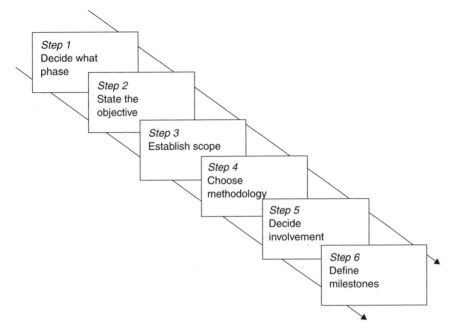

Figure 11.5 Simple planning approach

Step 1: Deciding the phase

We have already described the three phases of the journey to world class (entry, user and world-class) and the different approaches to self-assessment that are likely to be followed in each phase. It is important to determine the approach phase for the organization to ensure that the most suitable means of self-assessment is used. As organizations move from one phase to another, the data collection and analysis will become more sophisticated. The plan needs to take account of this to ensure that maximum payback is achieved.

The following criteria should be used to determine which phase the area to be assessed is in. An area that has moved into the user phase will be able to answer yes to each question:

- Has the area undertaken self-assessment before?
- Was last year's score more than 350?
- Is there evidence that self-assessment is a recognized and widely used business improvement tool in the area?
- Are data on the performance of the business area readily available?
- Are there signs of improving performance trends?
- Is the area ready to take positive improvement plans forward?

Table 11.9: The six steps summarized

Step 1: Deciding the phase	The self-assessment phase that the organization is in – 'entry', 'user' or 'world-class'. Many of the planning definitions and decisions will hinge on determining the phase. The guidelines contain the criteria that should be used to determine the phase
Step 2: Stating the objectives	Each area's own objectives in undertaking self-assessment – what do you want to do, and what do you want to get out of it?
Step 3: Establishing the scope	The decisions as to which area(s) will be covered and the level of staff involvement
Step 4: Choosing the methodology	The way that the data are collected and improvements planned will vary from area to area
Step 5: Deciding who will be involved	Who will be involved at each stage?
Step 6: Defining milestones and activities	Detail on activities, timing and involvement for each of the six steps

When the world-class phase is reached, a different set of questions will be answered in the affirmative:

● Was last year's score above 450 points, meaning that it would have received a site visit in an external award process?
● Are the improvement activities small in scope?
● Are data available for all key results for at least three years, with targets and some external comparisons?
● Have there been several review cycles?

Step 2: Stating the objectives

Time should be taken to state clearly and concisely the overall business purpose of the self-assessment. A means of achieving this is repeatedly to ask the question 'why?', to get at the reason rather than the activity. For example, in a domestic situation

Step 1	**Phase:**	**Entry**	or	**User**	or	**World-class**

Step 2	**Objective(s)**
	Identify 'why' this self-assessment is being undertaken – what will be achieved and when. For each, use **S**pecific **M**easurable **A**chievable **R**elevant **T**imed criteria.

Step 3	**Scope**
	Which area will be covered? (Tick all areas included)

	Board	Division	Factory	Department	Function
	Level of staff involvement:	**Low**	or	**Medium**	or	**High**

Step 4	**Methodology for data collection:**
	Preparation for consensus: **Show and go,** **Share and go** or **Pre-consensus**
	Improvement planning: Separate improvement plan or **Integrated with business plan**

Step 5	**Who is involved at each stage?**
	Identify the names, main duties and responsibilities of all involved staff
	The launch:
	Completion of the self-assessment plan:
	Data collection:
	Performing the assessment:
	Developing the improvement plan:
	Post-completion review and learning from it:

Figure 11.6 Self-assessment planning pro forma

(*continued on next page*)

Step 6

Milestones

For each, identify

- Who is responsible for achieving the milestone
- When the milestone is to be achieved by
- The activities necessary to achieve the milestone, who else will be involved and their responsibilities

Ref.	Milestone	Responsibility of	To be achieved by	Activities and who
1	The launch brief has been held			
2	The self-assessment plan has been signed off			
3	The data (as defined in the plan) have been collected			
4	Consensus has been reached			
5	The improvement plan is complete			
6	A post-completion review has been held and learning points agreed			

Figure 11.6 *Continued*

someone might intend to vacuum the carpet. Is the objective to impress an imminent visitor, to minimize health risks, or to test the effectiveness of the vacuum cleaner?

The objective(s) needs to be clear so that everyone has the same clear view of what the assessment is to achieve, and all are on the same wavelength.

The objective(s) must be 'SMART':

Specific, so that everyone is clear on what is to be achieved
Measurable, so that attainment will be known
Achievable, so that tasks are realistic
Relevant, so that it has a firm business basis
Time-based, so that it is a finite activity and can be controlled.

The objectives for an area in the 'entry' phase are likely to include:

- Awareness of the self-assessment process and the benefits to all people in the area
- Identification of business measures that need to be put in place in order to move into the 'user phase', whereby self-assessment becomes a recognized and widely used business improvement tool.

The objectives for an area in the 'user' phase are likely to include:

- Reviewing the success of past business improvement action
- Looking for enabler–results linkages in the collected data as part of the evaluation and improvement planning
- Prioritizing the opportunities for improvement to those giving most benefit
- Monitoring the progress of the improvement plans and reviewing the achievements made
- 'Tightening up' on the evidence available to justify strengths in order to put the area on a strong footing for the deeper analysis required for the world-class phase.

The objectives for an area in the 'world-class' phase are likely to include:

- Establishing exactly how well the organization performs against external organizations
- Further improving and protecting current performance levels
- Reinforcing and retaining the positive excellence culture
- Extending the learning from external organizations
- Identifying strengths and weaknesses as input for the strategic planning process
- Confirming that the strategy is delivering the levels of performance required.

Step 3: Establishing the scope

The scope of the self-assessment consists of two factors:

1. *Which area will be covered?* The scope section should be completed to show exactly which areas will be covered by the self-assessment. If there is more than one area, more than one box should be ticked. Possible options are:

   - Board
   - Division
   - Factory
   - Department
   - Function.

2. *What level of staff involvement will there be at each stage?* As the number of staff involved with the self-assessment increases, so will the payback. This is because there will be a wider deployment of self-assessment, the improvement actions will be more generally accepted and owned throughout the business unit, and communication will be improved. The investment is in the additional resources and time that will be needed.

As each organization moves through the phases on the journey to world class, there will be a need and an appetite for increased staff involvement. This is a necessary requirement in order that business excellence becomes fully embedded, that review and refinement become natural, and that the organization's standing against its competitors and other world-class companies is generally understood.

An organization may elect to restrict involvement to the top team, or it may involve all staff, or it may choose any combination in between. Each organization will need to consider carefully the level of staff involvement, as this will have an impact on the approach that will be taken and the detailed planning. The increasing involvement of staff can be considered on an annual basis, or planned in advance.

The level of staff that will be involved at the various stages should be considered. After consideration, the level of involvement should be stated in terms of 'low', 'medium' or 'high'. Table 11.10 below gives guidance on the various levels of involvement.

Step 4: Choosing the methodology

There are three main variables: the way that the data are collected, the degree of preparation for the consensus meeting, and the way that improvement action is planned.

Table 11.10: Levels of involvement

Level of involvement	Explanation and example
Low	Involvement in the self-assessment limited to less than 25% of the population of the organization – for example, confining the self-assessment to the senior management team
Medium	Between 25 and 75% of workers are involved in the self-assessment. This is the widest range, and it will depend on the total number of people in the organization. Such levels of involvement could be achieved if teams were used to collect the data
High	Involvement of more than 75% and approaching all staff in the organization. This could be achieved if all staff contributed to the data collection stage of the process

1. *Data collection.* An area in the entry phase will be limited to data collection by a simple checklist, whilst an area in the user or world-class phase will need to include collecting data on the performance of the organization, the analysis of improvement trends, prioritization of improvement opportunities, and the development of improvement plans. Here, it should be stated how the data will be collected, analysed and turned into a form suitable for improvement planning.
   Responsibility for data collection can also be taken in different ways, from 'criterion champions' to 'experts'. The critical issue is to plan for broad viewpoints on all criteria to limit the risk of isolated views, which could distort the assessment.
2. *Preparation for consensus.* There are three approaches for preparing for consensus: 'show and go', 'share and go' and 'pre-consensus'.
3. *Improvement planning.* An area in the user phase or world-class phase will be more likely to integrate improvement planning with the business planning activity. On the other

hand, entry-phase business units will find that the generation of a separate improvement plan may be the best approach.

Step 5: Deciding who will be involved

There are several stages in the self-assessment. These are:

- The launch
- Completion of the self-assessment plan
- Data collection
- Performing the assessment
- Developing the improvement plan
- Post-completion review and learning from it.

The names, main duties and responsibilities of all staff involved at each stage should be stated. In addition to those with responsibility for collecting the data, people with expertise on specific subjects (such as specialist processes, finance, technology or accommodation) should be identified, along with those who will take responsibility for involving the levels of staff identified in the scope section.

The self-assessment team has the responsibility of collecting sufficient data to identify strengths and areas for improvement, in approach and deployment, excellence and scope of the results. These will need to be assessed in a consistent fashion. There are a number of approaches that can be taken in choosing the self-assessment team and assigning roles within it.

There should be a mix of relevant skills present in the team make-up. In addition to data collectors, there is a need for expertise on the business excellence model to gain consensus and facilitation skills to draw out strengths and areas for improvement.

The responsibility for collecting the data for each of the criterion needs to be assigned and documented in the plan. Consideration should be given to what action is necessary to ensure full cooperation of all those who need to be involved.

Step 6: Defining milestones and activities

The table contained on the second page of the pro forma should be completed, and the following identified for each of the six milestones:

- The person who has the overall responsibility for ensuring that the milestone is reached successfully. This will include making decisions and re-planning if 'the unexpected' happens.
- When the milestone will be reached.

- Details of activities necessary to complete the milestone, who will undertake the activity, who else needs to be involved, and who will be impacted.

The milestones are:

1. *The launch brief has been held.*
2. *The self-assessment plan has been signed off.*
3. *The data (as defined) have been collected.* Exactly which data are to be collected, and in what form, must be defined here. This will certainly vary between areas at entry phase and those at the user phase. At the entry phase, the data will probably be limited to evidence of approach and deployment of the approach. Results data are likely to be limited. At the user and world-class phases, data will need to be collected showing the performance of the organization. Data may include trends, performance against own targets, and performance against competition, and may also include evidence of review and refinement activity.
   There can be different approaches. For example, are the assessors to collect data and bring it to the consensus meeting, or is it to be provided to the lead assessor, who will collate and perform some initial analysis before the consensus meeting?
4. *Consensus has been reached.* The means to achieve consensus will need to be planned in advance of the data collection. At the user phase there will be a greater importance on reaching consensus, since the improvement planning will depend on a more rigorous approach to a consensus of strengths and areas for improvement. The means of documenting this as evidence will need to be addressed.
5. *The implementation plan is complete.* At the user phase, the precise content of the implementation plan will need to be decided. As each area moves through this phase, the level of activity with this plan will increase. In addition to action plans and accountabilities, the plan will show targets and other comparative measures. The plan may well refer to benchmarking projects, internal or external.
6. *A post-completion review has been held and learning points agreed.* In addition to identifying what went well and what could have gone better, the team needs to identify how learning can be taken forward into next year's process.

11.5 Summary

This chapter has introduced the self-assessment roadmap, which was developed based on many years of practical experience helping organizations in their quest to building an excellence platform so that they can become world-class, with outstanding performance that is sustained over many years.

The roadmap has three phases: the entry phase, the user phase and the world-class phase. The approach to self-assessment, the support required and the benefits achieved vary across the phases. In the entry phase the self-assessment approach is very simple and the improvements large scale as the gaps in the excellence platform are identified. The benefits are mainly cultural. The entry phase is probably the most challenging phase, as self-assessment and the concepts have to be introduced at a time where there may be resistance and the benefits are not easy to measure.

The user phase sees the delivery of more measurable benefits, but there is a need to remain focused on the longer-term goal of becoming world-class. The self-assessment approach gets more rigorous, and self-assessment is extended to more areas of the organization. The support systems still play a critical role as approaches are designed, deployed and improved. By the time that the organization is ready to enter the world-class phase, the building blocks of excellence have been built and the review and refinement cycles continuously improve the organization's performance. There is less dependence on the support systems as the business excellence philosophy becomes fully embedded into the organization.

This chapter has referred to several areas that were first discussed in Chapters 9 and 10, such as the different approaches to self-assessment. This chapter has built on this earlier discussion and, using the business excellence roadmap, has shown how to get self-assessment activities up and running.

Writing an award submission document

12.1 Introduction

Of the many approaches to self-assessment seen in Chapter 11, the award submission is the most time- and resource-consuming approach, but it does give the most detailed feedback when assessed by an experienced team. The purpose of conducting an award-style assessment could be to gain recognition through an award process. If this is the case, then this chapter will help in compiling the submission document and preparing for the site visit, if appropriate. If the desire of the organization is to perform an award-style self-assessment for internal purposes, whether or not a team external to the organization conducts the assessment, this chapter will also be of interest. Even if another self-assessment approach is being used, many of the approaches described in the chapter will be of use in putting evidence together.

The material was developed as part of a long-term programme to meet the aspirations of a division of a leading multinational FMCG organization that had set itself the target of becoming 'world-class' as measured by assessment against the EFQM Excellence Model®. As this stretching target was approached, there was a need for a more rigorous approach to self-assessment so that detailed feedback could be considered and actions taken as part of business planning activities.

The chapter starts with a review of the background to the case study. This is followed by a description of the project plan, and an insight into the tools that were used to aid the compilation of the submission document. It should be noted that this case study is based on a large multinational organization, and so some of the tools described may not be appropriate for other organizations. In addition, with many organizations moving away from paper to IT based information systems the use of paper templates may seem archaic. The main objectives of these templates are to demonstrate the principles being discussed and to stimulate the best use of the process in a particular organization by providing a list of requirements. By the end of the chapter the process of writing a submission will be clearer, and readers will be well placed to plan their own projects.

12.2 Background to the case study

The organization this chapter is based on achieved many benefits from the approach described. It is worth noting that the process was used for three annual cycles, but at no time was an application for a quality award submitted. What we describe below are the key elements from the third cycle, as this was the most advanced approach. The project had very clear aims.

1. To build on the progress made in previous years by preparing a submission document based on the learning and subsequent improvements made, for use as the reference document for the self-assessment
2. To engage the organization in the site-visit experience to maximize ownership and learning from the self-assessment
3. To use the outcomes from the self-assessment to drive improvement in the business, at the same time measuring the progress that has been made towards 'world-class'.

Although the self-assessment included an independent external assessment, we only include the preparations for the site visit in this chapter.

The context of the programme was defined at the start of the project. It had been declared that a key aim of the Board was to lead the organization to becoming world-class as measured by the EFQM Excellence Model®. Progress towards this goal had been marked, with the self-assessment score at the time of the third cycle being in the 600–650 point range. The organization had already seen improved performance, which could be attributed to the business excellence approach. The concept of business excellence had been well accepted, and the philosophy was becoming embedded throughout the organization. The external assessors in previous self-assessment had been impressed by the commitment and passion they found for excellence at all levels of the organization.

Although several main areas for improvement had been identified, plans were already in place to improve performance further. Feedback from staff to the assessment had also been extremely positive. The site visit was found to add value, and many enthusiastic suggestions were made regarding how the submission document could be improved in future assessment cycles.

Being realistic, a number of limitations were identified at the outset of each assessment cycle. These included the facts that the organization was large and diverse, that there were different levels of deployment of the principles of excellence at the numerous sub-units, and that the data collection phase had to ensure that the information collected was as representative as possible. There was also enormous pressure on Board Members' time but it was necessary to obtain their involvement in the project to gain their ownership. This was a limitation for all staff involved in the project.

The level of investment required to deliver the project was also recognized right at the start. Internal resources were used to co-ordinate activities, manage the communication process and contribute to the submission document. The internal team also co-ordinated the design and printing of the submission report, which was a major task in its own right. A number of Board-level criterion sponsors led criterion teams, which consisted of business excellence facilitators (approximately 50 facilitators were involved in total). These teams were responsible for providing the evidence for the submission document for their criteria, and for reviewing and refining the submission document. A number of associated experts were also identified as being in a position to contribute expertise to the submission document.

External project support was required for the preparation of the submission document over an 8-month period, and there was the need to finance a six-person external assessment team to conduct the self-assessment. Other costs included designing and printing the submission document, and an allowance was made for travel and accommodation. The cost of the design of the submission document was significant, given the problems faced with the need to present representative data in the results section. This point is elaborated further later.

Despite the level of investment, the expected benefits from the work were extremely clear. These included:

1. Further confirmation of the progress the organization had made towards becoming a business excellence organization.
2. Confirmation of the progress being made on improvement activities, and the provision of a comprehensive platform on which to base further improvement activities over the next twelve to eighteen months.

3. The capturing of the knowledge and approaches used throughout the organization, making the submission document a valuable resource in its own right.
4. Publication of the submission document and report in a suitable format to enhance communication about business excellence and the progress made to date, both within the division and to other parts of the organization. This was particularly valuable for new-joiners.
5. Enhancing the organization's chances of a successful outcome if a competitive award application was ever submitted.

Although an application for an award was never submitted there is no doubt that, had this happened, some level of recognition would have been achieved.

We now move on to describe the work in more detail.

12.3 Outline plan for an award submission self-assessment

It is not the purpose of this book to discuss project management approaches, but it should be recognized that the approach we are about to describe is a project-based approach. As such, the main elements of the project plan have been given so that they may be taken and used in a particular organization's project planning approaches.

The project approach followed a goal-directed methodology (Andersen *et al.*, 1998). It was recognized that the importance of the success of the project required that it be delivered in a robust and professional way. Therefore, all project activity was being undertaken against a framework of proven project disciplines aligned to the normal project lifecycle. Tracking was achieved using a project timetable, and resource requirements were captured. Reporting took place by reviewing progress with the project team on a monthly basis, and a post-completion review was conducted at the end of the project to capture learning.

Figure 12.1 provides a milestone plan for the project, Figure 12.2 a generic schedule, and Figure 12.3 a generic resource requirements summary. The actual timings and resources will, of course, depend of the organization. These figures do, however, provide a baseline on which to build plans.

The approach has four results streams: project co-ordination, results evidence, enabler evidence, and submission report. Table 12.1 provides an overview of the purpose and contents of each of the resource themes.

More detail on each of these results streams will be given in the next section. The purpose of this section is to provide an

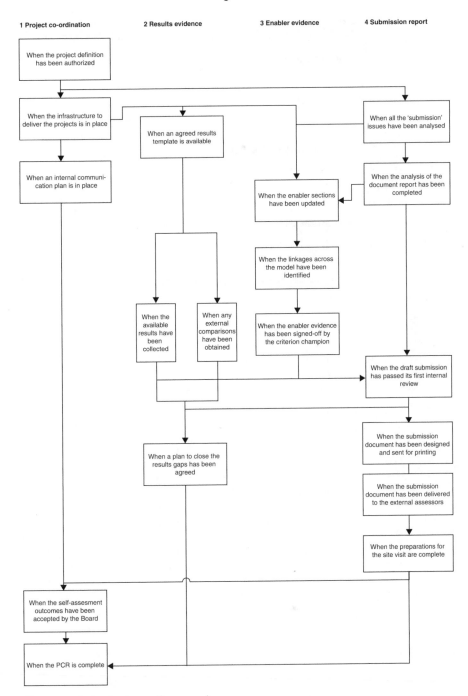

Figure 12.1 Project milestone plan

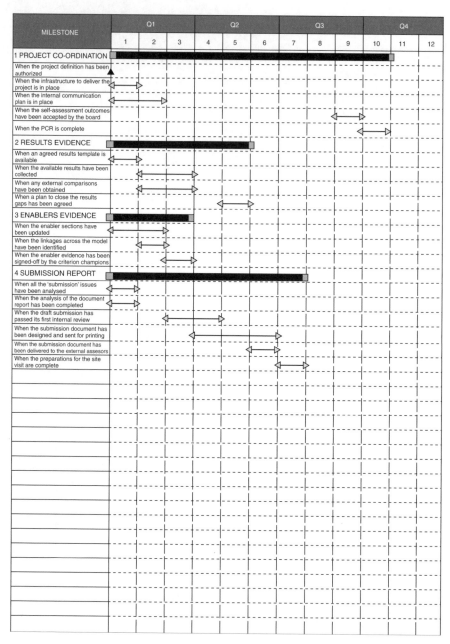

Figure 12.2 Outline schedule

Man-days summary by months

Activity track	Resource	Quarter 1			Quarter 2			Quarter 3			Quarter 4			Total
		M1	M2	M3	M4	M5	M6	M7	M8	M9	M10	M11	M12	
Project co-ordination	Project team	3	1	1	1	1	1	1	1	3	3	1	1	18
	External support	2								1	2			5
Results evidence	Project team	2	4	4		2								12
	Criterion teams and experts	2	4	4		1								11
	External support	2	4	4		1								11
Enabler evidence	Project team	2	2	2										6
	Criterion teams and experts		5	3										8
	External support	2	2	2										6
Submission report	Project team	2		5	5	10	8	7						37
	Criterion teams and experts			1	1	1		1						4
	External support	2		5	5	5	1	2						20
	External assessment team							15	30					45

Man-days summary by resource

		M1	M2	M3	M4	M5	M6	M7	M8	M9	M10	M11	M12	
	Project team	9	7	12	6	13	9	8	1	4	3	1	1	74
	Criterion teams and experts	2	9	8	1	2		1		1				23
	External support	8	6	11	5	6	1	2			2			42
	External assessment team							15	30					45

Figure 12.3 Resource requirements summary

Table 12.1: Overview of results streams

Results theme	Purpose	Contents
Project co-ordination	To manage the project from initiation to completion	• Gaining agreement to project plan • Establishing the infrastructure to deliver the project • Managing the major stakeholders (the Board and Staff). A significant effort goes into communication • Ensuring the learning from the project is captured
Results evidence	Collecting the results data for the submission	• Establishing what data must be collected and collecting it • Establishing ownership of the data • Identifying external comparisons • Planning to fill any data deficiencies
Enabler evidence	Documenting the enabling approaches	• Identifying the approaches and their level of deployment • Collecting evidence of assessment and review • Resolving differences in approaches in different areas • Identifying the drivers of results
Submission report	Producing the submission report and managing the assessment	• Analysing the feedback from the previous assessment • Collating the submission report and managing the reviews of content • Co-ordinating the design and printing of the submission report • Preparing for and managing the site visit

overview and to show the linkages between the various activities. Figure 12.2, which contains the schedule, provides guidance on the timings for each of the milestones. The information in this schedule has been used to derive the resource matrix, which is given in Figure 12.3. This matrix identifies five types of resources. Table 12.2 defines these resources, and outlines their main responsibilities.

12.4 Description of individual results streams

The previous section described the overall project, and in particular the interfacing and dependence of the various milestones within each results stream. In this section we will describe the key aspects to each results stream in turn, providing an overview of the tools that were developed.

Project co-ordination

The project co-ordination results stream sought to maintain control over the project, and in particular to manage the key stakeholders. A project definition was produced and agreed by the Board before any work commenced. The contents of the project definition contained many of the items covered in the section above, and these included:

- Project identification
- Project aims, scope and objectives
- Business context
- Limitations
- Benefits
- Investment in internal resources, external resources and costs
- Milestone plan and outline schedule.

Once authorized, the project kicked off on all the other results streams. For the project co-ordination results stream, this involved getting all the resources in place. The primary activities were to agree which Board member would look after each criterion of the model, and to inform the facilitators and the subject experts of the roles that they would play.

Formulating and implementing the communication plan was a critical activity. The communication, which continued throughout the project, had two main objectives. First, there was a need to inform the various parties of their responsibilities and provide reports on progress throughout the project so that momentum was continuous. The second objective was one of 'internal marketing' to reinforce the purpose and value of the project to both internal

Table 12.2: **Project resources**

Resource	Description	Main responsibilities
Project team	The main internal team who manage project. These will normally be internal people although the external support will work as part of the project team	• Managing the progress of the project • Managing the interfaces between the various stakeholders (Board, facilitators, experts, external support, assessment team) • Formulating and implementing the communication plan • Contributing to and writing the submission document • Managing the design and printing of the submission document • Managing the site visit • Communicating the feedback report, which includes presenting findings to the Board
Criterion teams	These are the representatives of the business areas who provide a link between the areas and the project team. Led by a main Board Member, the criterion teams normally consist of local facilitators	• Providing data and evidence to the project team • Signing-off parts of the submission document • Managing the site visit in their areas of the organization
Experts	These are specialists who provide an expert insight, but are not directly involved in the project. The experts are normally functional specialists	• Provide their opinion on their areas of expertise, for example, on approaches and measures • A Valuable source of leads for benchmarking activities
External support	External resource and expertise used to support the project on a temporary basis. External consultants fall into this category	• Provide support for the project team and are often full members • Are treated separately for the purposes of budgeting, as their time has to be paid for

Table 12.2: *Continued*

Resource	Description	Main responsibilities
External assessment team	Conduct the assessment	• Assess the submission document • Plan and conduct the site visit • Provide the feedback report

and external stakeholders. It must be remembered that one of the benefits of self-assessment is the effect it has on the culture, and this internal marketing activity supported the culture change.

When the results from the self-assessment were available, they were presented to the Board to get their agreement to the findings. Once this penultimate milestone had been achieved the project team conducted a post-completion review. The post-completion review covered all aspects of the project, including the perception of the value of the project from the Board members, facilitators and staff who were involved in the site-visit process. Costs and timings against the base-line plan were also compared.

Results evidence

One of the major issues facing the organization at the start of the work was 'What results should we put in the submission document?'. There is no simple answer to this question, for several reasons. First, with such a diverse organization the financial measures were only the really consistent measures throughout the organization. Where non-financial measures existed, they varied from area to area. Secondly, the measures that did exist had not been derived from the EFQM Excellence Model®, and so there was bound to be a mismatch between the requirements of an excellence approach and the measures that were in place.

Part of this mismatch was caused by the lack of measures that should rightly be in place if the organization was a 'world-class' organization. However, there was another problem that needed attention, and this had more to do with the way that assessments are conducted. Collating the results data was difficult owing to the fact that the organization was a large multinational that operated in many countries and with many products. To manage the business, management teams would collect and act upon data relevant to their area of responsibility – for example, the market share of Brand X would be monitored in Country Y. If an attempt were made to report the market share of Brand X across the organization, data not required to manage the business would be being sought solely for the purpose of the self-assessment. Aggregating the data adds no value to the organization. As a consequence, it was necessary to collect all the original data that came from a variety of sources and present a representative sample in the submission document. We shall return to this problem when discussing the design of the submission document below.

To solve the problem 'results templates' were constructed, defining the measures that were required for the submission document. These templates, and there was one for each results criterion, were constructed from several inputs:

- In-use measures that could be identified from the various business areas
- Results that were defined on the simple questionnaire-based self-assessment tool
- Requirements of the EFQM Excellence Model®
- Output from a benchmarking exercise that studied the results used by award applicants that had published their submission documents.

Figure 12.4 provides an extract from the people measures results template. In the example a number of potential measures have been listed, with a rationale for each measure. The shading of the measure confirms that the measure is in use somewhere, and 'SC' indicates that the measure may be found on a scorecard. 'SR' notes that the measure was included in a previous submission document. Where measures existed, the source of the measurement data and owner were also recorded.

The first step described is essentially an analytical activity to determine the measures that should be monitored so that the results may be included in the submission. The list of potential measures was quite long, and there was a need to reduce the list and to define at what level the measure should be used. For example, a measure relevant to product development would be expected in the product development function, and not in sales. The subject experts played a key role in reducing the measures to an agreed set of measures, which were then presented to the criterion champions for sign-off. Another template was produced to present the agreed measures, and an example of this is shown in Figure 12.5.

This second template varied from the previous template in more ways than just containing the agreed measures. On the left-hand side the leading or indicator measures were listed, with their corresponding main outcome measures on the right-hand side. So in the example, results such as Recordable accident

Proposed measure	Rationale	SC	SR	Databases	Data owner
Number of changes to skills and competence dictionary	Demonstrates the continual review of required skills and competencies				
% Cost of training by job type	Measure considered relevant by four award winners				
% Cost of training by work level	Demonstrates training is available to all, measure considered relevant by one award winner.				
Absenteeism	Measure considered relevant by all award winners		✓		Human relations
List cover	Shows identification of potential high flyers, measure considered relevant by one award winner	✓	✓		Human relations
TPM involvement	Supports involvement and improvement culture, measure considered relevant by four award winners		✓	Factory records	Manufacturing excellence
Survey response rate	Supports involvement and improvement culture, measure considered relevant by four award winners	✓	✓	Bi-annual survey	Human relations
Employee suggestion received	Supports Involvement and improvement culture, measure considered relevant by four award winners		✓		Local facilitators
Employee suggestion implemented	Supports involvement and improvement culture, measure considered relevant by four award winners				
Number of awards given for improvement	Supports involvement and improvement culture, measure considered relevant by four award winners				
Number of team-based rewards	Supports involvement and improvement culture, measure considered relevant by four award winners		✓		Local facilitators
Number of networks (formal and informal)	Measures of communication opportunities				
Number of magazines published					

Figure 12.4 Extract from people performance indicators results template

Left section — Indicator/driver measure

Category	Indicator/driver measure	C	B	L	P
Satisfaction	Recordable accident frequency rate	×		×	×
	Site safety performance	×		×	×
	Lost time accidents	×		×	×
	Ave time in job	×	×	×	
	Employee turnover – regretted losses	×		×	×
	Absenteeism	×		×	×
	Grievances	×		×	×
	Participation in cultural, recreational and social activities	×		×	
Services	Number of clicks on HPCE Home/News pages	×			
	Results of benchmarking of terms and conditions			×	
Other	Number of improvement projects as result of survey	×	×	×	×

Segmentation level: C / B / L / P

Right section — Outcome measure

Category	Outcome measure	C	B	L	P
Satisfaction	**Employee survey**				
	Overall satisfaction	×	×	×	×
	Pay and benefits	×	×	×	×
	Organization's environmental policy and impact	×	×	×	×
	Working environment (physical)	×	×	×	×
	Working environment (cultural)	×	×	×	×
	Health and safety conditions	×	×	×	×
	Job security	×	×	×	×
	Peer relationships	×	×	×	×
	Management of change	×	×	×	×
	Organization's role in community and society	×	×	×	×
Other	Company image	×	×	×	×
	Quality	×	×	×	×
	Access to information	×	×	×	×
	Customer focus	×	×	×	×
	Likelihood to leave	×	×	×	×
	Staff awareness of improvements as result of survey	×	×	×	×

Segmentation level: C / B / L / P

Key on segmentation: C = Corporate, B = Brand/Product, L = Local company, P = Process

Figure 12.5 Extract from people results template

frequency rate, Employee turnover – regretted losses, and Absenteeism are all considered to be the indicating results of people satisfaction. Making the link between these types of results is an important feature of the EFQM Excellence Model®, and the relationship was discussed in Chapter 5. The templates also include the 'Segmentation level' to indicate where the result is applicable using the key given in Table 12.3.

Once the measures have been defined, the next task is to collect the data. A data collection template such as that shown in Figure 12.6 facilitates the process. On the template the measures to be collected in particular business areas are listed, with the target (T) and result (R) for each year. These are taken from the completed results template that was given in Figure 12.5. In the column marked 'INTBP' any internal benchmarks (BM) may be noted, and in the 'EXTBP' external comparisons may be noted. The 'ID' refers to an identification number, so that the source of the comparison may be noted. The collection of the results data

Table 12.3: Segmentation levels

Code	Segmentation level	Description
C	Corporate	Results for the corporation, such as overall turnover, profit and share dividends
B	Brand	Results associated with brand performance, such as market share, product range and customer satisfaction
L	Local company	Results for the operating companies that market, sell and manage logistics within the various countries that the organization operates. Example results are turnover, customer satisfaction and people satisfaction
P	Process	Results associated with the operating processes. These include product development, supply chain, and human resources. Example results for each type of process are sales from innovation, direct operating cost and training effectiveness

People results performance indicators

Business area:

Performance measures	History										INTBP		EXTBP	
	Year -4		Year -3		Year -2		Year -1		Year		BM	ID No	BM	ID No
	T	R	T	R	T	R	T	R	T	R				

Key: T = Target, R = Result, BM = Benchmark, ID = Identification number, INTBP = Internal best practice, EXTBP = External best practice

Figure 12.6 Data collection template

and the comparisons are considered to be two activities in the milestone plan, as it is best to collect external comparisons on a centrally co-ordinated basis and the results templates are designed to be used at a business unit level. The columns are included on the template so that the project team may collate any known internal or external comparisons during the course of the project.

It is extremely unlikely that all the data required will be available. A final milestone in this result stream is therefore to produce a plan to close any gaps between the data required and the data available. This plan is best produced once the internal review of the submission document is complete, as this review may throw up some additional areas that need to be covered. As the plan will be a living plan, additions may be made at any stage – for example, once the external feedback is received, or when the Board has discussed the results.

Enabler evidence

The collection of the enabler evidence is an iterative process, and as this case study reflects the third cycle most of the enabler information would already have been collected. At this point it is worth reflecting on how the original enabler information was collected. To do this, a set of 'enabler worksheets' were produced to capture the enabler information for each enabler criterion. An example worksheet is given in Figure 12.7. On these worksheets the requirements of the EFQM Excellence Model® were broken into sub-criteria, and each sub-criterion was broken down into the guidance, p.115. For each area to address, evidence was collected for each aspect of the RADAR® scoring system, namely:

- Approach: sound and integrated together with example
- Deployment: level of implementation and systematic
- Assessment: linkage to which results
- Review: examples of improvement and use of learning.

The approach was designed because it forced coverage of all the aspects of the EFQM Excellence Model®, and did not require people to have a detailed knowledge of the EFQM Excellence Model®. The process used to collect the evidence is shown in Figure 12.8.

The first versions of the workbooks were used as the basis for interviews with the criterion leaders, who were at Board level, and it was important to get their ownership of the information. Because of their position, the criterion leaders provided the 'corporate view'. The worksheets were therefore issued to the facilitators to obtain their feedback. This had two purposes. First, it

Relevant element to consider:	RADAR® Aspect	Evidence
Developing human resource policies, strategies and plans	Approach Sound and integrated together with example	
	Deployment Level of implementation and systematic	
	Assessment Linkage to which results	
	Review Examples of improvement and use of learning	

Figure 12.7 Blank enabler worksheet

confirmed that what was thought to happen at the top of the organization actually happened on the ground. Secondly, the facilitators were able to provide extra evidence through examples, which strengthened the 'deployment' aspect of the submission as 'real life' situations could be described. With many of the examples being graphics, some of these were selected for inclusion in the submission document. Whilst this consultation process took place, additional feedback was sought from the subject experts.

Once all the feedback had been analysed it was discussed with the criterion leaders so that they were aware of and agreed with any changes. This led to refinements being made to the workbooks, which then provided the database of evidence from which the submission was finally written.

The enabler workbooks were kept current, and were updated as a result of feedback from the internal reviews and external assessment. It would have been an easier task simply to update the submission document for subsequent external assessments, but as the submission document with its limited length of 75 pages only

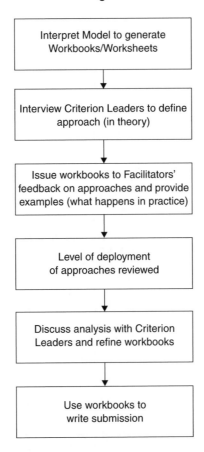

Figure 12.8 Approach to collect enabler evidence

provides a summary of the activities, it was decided always to work from the enabler evidence when putting the submissions together. There was also another piece of analysis work that needed to be completed before the submission document could be written, and this could not have been achieved working from the submission document. This was the analysis of the linkages across the model, and the need to demonstrate continuous progress. The concept of the 'driver tables' was designed to meet these needs.

The main purpose of the driver tables was to establish the link between the enablers and results. An extract from a driver table for people is shown in Figure 12.9. The main enablers were listed in the table, and the year that they were introduced was noted. In the next column, the sub-criteria supported by the enabler are listed. As an example, 'Annual communication events' were

Enabler	<99	99	00	01	02	03	Sub-criteria	Key?	Motivation	Satisfaction	Achievements	Involvement	Services to people
Local company mission statements developed	4						1a		4				
Local company county recognition schemes implemented	4						3e		4				
Annual communication events	4						1a, 1d, 2e, 3a, 3b, 3e	4	4				
Communication feedback sessions held		4					1a 1d, 2e, 3a, 3b, 3e		4				
First Annual Objectives Booklet issued to all staff, which included the European Values		4					1d		4				
First bi-annual people survey		4					1a, 1d, 2a, 2c, 3a, 3d		4				
Local people surveys based on the corporate methodology first used to achieve more regular feedback			4				3a, 3d		4				
Regular country visits by Board members introduced		4					1d, 3d		4				
'Year of programmes first introduced with 'Year of the Consumer', supported by the President's Award			4				1d, 3e	4	4				
Communication officer appointed			4				3d		4				
Variable pay targets and bonuses for managers	4						1d, 3e	4	4				
Balanced scorecards linking business to individual objectives developed				4			2c, 2e, 3a, 3b		4				

Figure 12.9 Extract from a people driver table

introduced in 1996, and support the 1a, 1d, 2e, 3a, 3b, 3e sub-criteria of the EFQM Excellence Model®. Whether or not the enabler was considered key is also noted, together with the area of the results where the effect of the enabler is expected to materialize.

The last task in this work stream was to get the final sign-off of the criterion leaders to both the enabler evidence in the worksheets, and the driver table contents. The project could then move onto the important stage of writing the submission.

Submission report

In the situation where there had been a previous submission, the first task of this results stream was to refer to the analysis the previous feedback report. On receipt of the feedback report, each comment was considered and coded using the categories listed in Table 12.4.

For the submission report results stream, all the items placed in the third category were extracted and taken into account when writing the new submission document. The external assessors were also asked to provide their comments on the submission document, and these were taken into account.

The submission was written from the results data that had been collected, and from the enabler evidence. As a starting point to balance the level of information, the EFQM Excellence Model® was analysed to derive a table of target page lengths for each of the sub-criteria. The breakdown for the 2003 version of the model is given in Table 12.5. It should be remembered that this breakdown was quite arbitrary, and does not allow for the overview section. However, it formed the basis of the starting point. It is also worth noting that as the final document was typeset, the text reduced in page-length terms from a word-processed document to a final printed version. A 10 per cent reduction in page length is not unusual, and this should be allowed for when writing the submission if it is to be typeset.

The solution chosen involved selecting consistent examples and engaging a designer to produce graphics that communicated the key points being made. For example, as 'market share' across all the countries where a particular product was sold was a meaningless result, results were presented by country, keeping the product in the brand consistent. This target per country had to be added together with the competitors' position. A related graphic kept the product and country constant, and charted the performance over time against target.

An organization will want to produce the submission document in line with its corporate identity, and there are many examples of submission documents that have been published in the

Table 12.4: Submission report classifications

Category	Action taken
Improvement opportunity	Improvement used as an input into either short-term or longer-term improvement planning. A short-term issue would be an item such as the need to improve deployment, and a long-term action where there was no existing approach. 'Short-term' was defined as meaning that action would be taken within the year, and 'long-term' as where some action would be taken but it was not expected to address the issue within a one-year timeframe
No action decisions	No action. The limitations of the assessment process were considered to have been the root of the comment. This could have been caused by a number of reasons, such as the action not being aligned to the long-term strategy of the organization, a personal preference of a member of the external assessment team or where there was conflicting feedback
Submission report issues	These were items where it was felt that greater clarity in the submission document could have prevented the comment and so no improvement action was necessary. However, there was an opportunity to improve the future submission document, perhaps by including or clarifying a graphic

public domain. A review of such documents was conducted, and it was decided that the preferred format was to use a two-column approach, broken up into criteria by dividers, with each criterion being broken down into sub-criteria and 'guidance points'. The decision to present the evidence in this way was taken so as to maximize the consistency during the assessment process. It is

Table 12.5: Breakdown of 2003 EFQM Excellence Model® by sub-criterion

1	*Leadership – 100 points*	*7.5 pages*
1a	Leaders develop the mission, vision, values and ethics and are role models of a culture of excellence	1.5
1b	Leaders are involved in ensuring that the organization's management system is developed, implemented and continuously improved	1.5
1c	Leaders interact with customers, partners and representatives of society	1.5
1d	Leaders reinforce a culture of excellence with the organization's people	1.5
1e	Leaders identify and champion organizational change	1.5
2	*Policy and strategy – 80 points*	*6 pages*
2a	Policy and strategy are based on the present and future needs and expectations of stakeholders	1.5
2b	Policy and strategy are based on information from performance measurement, research, learning and external related activities	1.5
2c	Policy and strategy are developed, reviewed and updated	1.5
2d	Policy and strategy are communicated and deployed through a framework of key processes	1.5
3	*People – 90 points*	*6.75 pages*
3a	People resources are planned, managed and improved	1.3
3b	People's knowledge and competencies are identified, developed and sustained	1.3
3c	People are involved and empowered	1.3
3d	People and the organization have a dialogue	1.3
3e	People are rewarded, recognized and cared for	1.3

(continued)

Table 12.5: *Continued*

4	*Partnerships and resources – 90 points*	*6.75 pages*
4a	External partnerships are managed	1.3
4b	Finances are managed	1.3
4c	Buildings, equipment and materials are managed	1.3
4d	Technology is managed	1.3
4e	Information and knowledge are managed	1.3
5	*Processes – 140 points*	*10.5 pages*
5a	Processes are systematically designed and managed	2.1
5b	Processes are improved, as needed, using innovation in order to fully satisfy and generate increasing value for customers and other stakeholders	2.1
5c	Products and processes are designed and developed based on customer needs and expectations	2.1
5d	Products and services are produced, delivered and serviced	2.1
5e	Customer relationships are managed and enhanced	2.1
6	*Customer results – 200 points*	*15 pages*
6a	Perception measures (75%)	11.25
6b	Performance indicators (25%)	3.75
7	*People results – 90 points*	*6.75 pages*
7a	Perception measures (75%)	5
7b	Performance indicators (25%)	1.75
8	*Society results – 60 points*	*4.5 pages*
8a	Perception measures (25%)	1.2
8b	Performance indicators (75%)	3.3

Table 12.5: *Continued*

9	*Key performance results – 150 points*	*11.25 pages*
9a	Key performance outcomes	5.6
9b	Key performance indicators	5.6
	Enablers total	37.5
	Results total	37.5
	Grand total	75

known that most assessors compare submissions against the model criteria, and such an approach avoids areas of the model being missed by accident.

There is one downside to this approach, which is worthy of mention. The approach makes the assessment simpler for the assessors, but it does devalue the document for internal purposes due to the high level of repetition that can occur when approaches are repeatedly referenced throughout the document. When deciding on the format, it is important to keep the main audiences' needs in mind.

The issue of the aggregation and segmentation of results data was raised earlier, and now is a good time to return to the subject. On the aggregation issue, it has already been noted that there is a temptation to develop some 'corporate-level' results purely for the submission report. The problem with this is that at site visit there will be no evidence that the results being defined are 'key outcomes', and people interviewed will not recognize the data. The solution was to make it absolutely clear in the submission document exactly what corporate level results were pertinent.

Segmentation of the results data presented another issue. One of the major problems faced was 'How do we present representative results data for all our areas of operation and keep the submission within the 75-page limit?'. The magnitude of the problem is brought home when considering the number of factors that impacted the results for the case study organization. These factors included:

- Decision on actual measure used
- Year of result to give trends
- Brand and products within brand, all of which are different
- Country
- Competitors, which varied from country to country depending on their market position
- Targets given the brand, product and country.

Because of these complexities, a significant amount of effort went into working with the designer to produce the graphics for the submission document. It may be that another organization's submission report is not as complicated, but it is worth noting that what appears to be a simple task can take many weeks to complete. With experience, it became clear that the results data had to be progressively worked on throughout the project to get the graphics right. It was not a task that could be left right until the end.

Once the submission report had been drafted, it was subjected to several internal reviews. The first review involved the project team and criterion leaders reviewing the document to check for accuracy and inconsistencies. The second review involved an independent team of trained assessors, and their task was to provide a review with a particular focus on the interrelationships across the submission. When writing submissions by criterion it is easy to get trapped into a 'silo' mentality, so there is a need to check for consistency across the various sections. Once this review had approved the document, it was sent to the printers for typesetting and printing. If organizations do not wish to have their submission document typeset, the alternative would be to send it direct to the external team so that team members may conduct their assessment, which will typically take up to fourteen days.

The last activity in this results stream was to prepare the organization for the site visit. The external assessment team provided a list of the places members wanted to visit, people they wanted to interview, the criteria they would be examining, and any focus groups they wanted to hold. These arrangements were made between the senior assessor and the project team leader, and this resulted in a timetable for the visit.

There were four main roles within the site-visit process, excluding the assessment team itself, and these roles are defined in Table 12.6. Remember that this approach was designed for a large complex organization, and a simpler approach may be more suited to another.

The project team provided central co-ordination before, during and after the site visit. Where the assessment team split into small teams (usually pairs), it was useful for lead facilitators to be identified to work with each pair of assessors. This not only ensured that any problems during the site visit were quickly resolved, it also allowed valuable feedback to be collected during the site visit. The latter was best managed using a pro forma to collect feedback. Such a pro forma is given in Figure 12.10, together with its instructions in Figure 12.11.

Table 12.6: Site-visit roles

Role	Responsibilities
Project team	• Manages the logistics of the site visit • Acts as a central contact point • Is the place to go if there are any problems or questions that cannot be answered locally • Is the focal point for receiving documents
The lead facilitators	• Manage the site-visit team during the week • Ideally be present at all their team's interviews • Identify the key themes that are coming out of the site visit • Be the ears of the organization, to bring the feedback report to life • Observe the site-visit process with a view to improving the way the site-visit team is managed next time • Attend a debriefing session soon after the site visit to capture learning
The local facilitators	• Circulate relevant parts of the submission report to interviewees to help them prepare • Ensure that the site is ready for the visit – for example, brief site personnel on what will happen during the site visit, and check that the mission and values have been displayed (visible clues) • Act as a co-ordination point when the team is on their site • Direct the team to the right person to answer members' questions if a question is raised that cannot be answered accurately by an interviewee on the schedule • Answer points of clarification • Provide data requested, whether this is during the site visit or after the visit if it is not available (to be sent to the project team)
Interviewees/focus group members	• Answer the site-visit team's questions as accurately as possible • Say when they do not know • Provide documents and information if not available at the interview

Site:	Lead facilitator:
Assessor:	Interviewee/focus group:
Key themes from the interview:	
Site-visit comment:	

Figure 12.10 Site-visit feedback form

Instructions for use

The 'Site-visit feedback forms' are to be used by all lead facilitators to record the key learning points from each of the interviews or focus groups held during the site visit. The forms will provide us with two useful areas of feedback:

- Information on those areas within the submission document that needed further clarification and that were of interest to the assessors.

- Information on the way in which the site visit was conducted.

This information will be used to better prepare us for the site visit next year.

The form

1. Complete the names of the site, the assessor, and the interviewee. If the form is being used to record a focus group session, then indicate this in the correct box. You do not have to name all of the attendees.

2. Key points from the interview – make a note of any areas of the submission the assessor wants to validate or verify.

3. Use this section also to make a note of the key themes being explored by the assessor.

4. Site-visit comment – use this box to make any notes on how the assessors conduct the interview, any additional information the assessors request.

Figure 12.11 Site-visit feedback form instructions

It is always valuable to issue a briefing note to all stakeholders prior to the visit. This should remind people of the aims, objectives and benefits of the project, introduce the assessment team, explain what will happen during the visit, and give guidance on how to prepare and provide the schedule with local details. Publishing a list of 'Dos and Don'ts' for the facilitators and interviewees just prior to the site visit will also be helpful. Sample lists are provided in Figures 12.12 and 12.13 respectively.

12.5 Summary

In this chapter we have looked at a process for compiling a submission document. This process has been successfully used

Do
Before

- Read the submission document
- Make sure you are aware of any local initiatives that were mentioned in the submission
- Make sure all the interviewees are prepared and are not anxious
- Make sure everyone on site knows the schedule
- Ensure the mission and values are readily noticeable about the site
- Make corporate business excellence literature available in the meeting room
- Make sure all materials are up to date, for example, have the latest goals documentation
- Make sure the facilities are prepared – flip charts, paper etc.
- Ensure the site is clean and tidy
- Make sure there is protection in case it rains, if the assessors are visiting multiple buildings on site

Safety and site welcome

- Advise the assessors of emergency procedures in case of fire etc.
- Provide them with a list of telephone numbers in case they get separated from the lead facilitator
- Ensure you follow local security measures
- Be pleasant and helpful
- Be on time for the assessors
- Offer the assessors refreshment
- Provide the assessors with a quiet room where they can talk privately and make calls to the other site-visit teams
- Check the schedule with the assessors on arrival to make changes if necessary

During

- Keep to the schedule but remain flexible
- Talk about the strengths of the organization
- Give the assessors some time on their own – usually over lunch
- Check at regular intervals that the assessors have everything they need
- Check at regular intervals to see if there are any changes required to the schedule
- Make sure the assessors are not having language problems
- Find someone to answer the assessors' questions if the interviewee can not

After

- Check at the end of the day that the assessors are happy they have achieved everything they needed to
- Do what you have said you will do, e.g. provide additional support materials

Don't

- Make up an answer
- Try to hide anything
- Make assumptions about what the assessor means – ask if you are not sure

Figure 12.12 Facilitator 'dos and don'ts'

Do

- Read the submission document
- Make sure you are aware of any local initiatives that were mentioned in the submission
- Have a selection of key documents readily available making sure you have the latest versions
- Make a list of potential questions and prepare potential answers
- Be aware of the results that are being achieved due to our approaches
- Have examples where the approaches have been reviewed and improved
- Be in a position where you can explain the rationale behind the targets that have been set and refer to external comparisons
- Make it clear that business excellence is not a new concept – we have been improving for several years
- Try and answer the questions accurately
- Tell the assessor if you don't know the answer to the question
- Talk about the strengths of the organization
- Be pleasant and welcoming
- Ensure your working area is clean and tidy

Don't

- Make up an answer
- Try to hide anything
- Make assumptions about what the assessor means – ask if you are not clear
- Stretch the interview to use up time. If it finishes early this may be because the assessors have to see additional people
- Give your prepared answers without checking that you are answering the assessors' question
- Elaborate unnecessarily
- Leave things lying around that you do not want the assessor to see
- Argue with the assessor
- Worry about the interview

Figure 12.13 Interviewee 'dos and don'ts'

several times. The approach is both systematic and structured, and it is important to remember that in its current form it will probably have to be adapted for individual organizations. For example, a target organization may be not as complex as the case study organization, and may choose to use a technology-based rather than a paper-based approach to collect the information. In both cases, the pro forma provided may be taken as a checklist of potential requirements.

It will now be clear that writing a submission document is not an easy process, and takes both time and effort. The increased quality of the feedback far outweighs the cost, provided the organization has several years' experience with self-assessment and a degree of maturity in their approaches. The submission document itself has other benefits, such as providing a way to capture current information and approaches, and as a vehicle for summarizing the way the organization works for newcomers.

It should also be remembered that the awards assessment approach is worth considering even if there is no intention of entering a submission into an award process. It is also likely that some of the methods described in this chapter will be of value, even if a simpler form of self-assessment is being used.

Reference

Andersen, E. S., Grude, K. V. *et al.* (1998). *Goal Directed Project Management.* London: Kogan Page.

Further reading

The following articles and books provide further useful information on:

- Total quality management in general
- Specific frameworks in detail (ISO9000, Deming, Baldrige etc.)
- The practice of self-assessment
- The experiences and performance of role model companies.

Chapter 1

Deming, W. E. (2000). *The New Economics*. Cambridge, Mass.: Institute of Technology.

ECforBE (2002). *The Model in Practice*. London: British Quality Foundation.

Garvin, D. A. (1988). *Managing Quality: The Strategic Competitive Edge*. New York: The Free Press.

Oakland, J. S. (2003). *Total Organizational Excellence*. Oxford: Butterworth-Heinemann.

Oakland, J. S. (2003). *TQM: Text with Cases*. Oxford: Butterworth-Heinemann.

Chapter 2

Curkovic, S., Vickery, S. *et al.* (2000). Quality-related action programmes: their impact on quality performance and firm performance. *Decision Sciences*, **31(4)**.

Douglas, T. J. and Judge, W. Q. (2001). Total quality management implementation and competitive advantage: the role of structural control and exploration. *Academy of Management*, **44(1)**.

ECforBE (1997). *Evaluating the Operation of the European Quality Model for Self-assessment*. Leeds: European Centre for Business Excellence.

ECforBE (1999). *The x-Factor: Winning Performance through Business Excellence*. Leeds: European Centre for Business Excellence.

ECforBE (2000). *The Model in Practice*. London: British Quality Foundation.

ECforBE (2002). *The Model in Practice*. London: British Quality Foundation.

EFQM (1999). *The EFQM Excellence Model*. Brussels: European Foundation for Quality Management.

Fisher, C., Dauterive, J. *et al.* (2001). Economic impact of quality awards: does offering an award bring returns to the state? *Total Quality Management*, **12(7 & 8)**.

GAO (1991). *GAO Management Practices: US Companies Improve Performance through Quality Efforts*. Washington, D.C.: General Accounting Office.

Helton, R. (1995). The Baldie play. *Quality Progress*, **February**.

Hendricks, K. B. and Singhal, V. R. (1999). Don't count TQM out. *Quality Progress*, **April**.

Hillman, A. J. and Keim, G. D. (2001). Shareholder value, stakeholder management, and social issues: what's the bottom line? *Strategic Management Journal*, **22**.

NIST (2002). *Baldrige Winners beat the S&P 500 for the Eighth Year*. Gaithesburg: NIST.

Oakland, J. S. (1999). Winning performance through business excellence. *Credit Control*, **20(7)**.

Pannirselvam, G. P. and Ferguson, L. A. (2001). A study of the relationships between Baldrige categories. *International Journal of Quality and Reliability Management*, **18(1)**.

Powell, T. C. (1995). TQM as competitive advantage. A review and empirical study. *Strategic Management Journal*, **16**.

PriceWaterhouseCoopers (2000). *Report on the Evaluation of the Public Sector Excellence Programme – Main Report*. London: PriceWaterhouseCoopers.

Przasnyski, Z. H. and Tai, L. S. (2002). Stock performance of Malcolm Baldrige National Award winning companies. *Total Quality Management*, **13(4)**.

Terziovski, M. and Samson, D. (1999). The link between total quality management practice and organisational performance. *International Journal of Quality and Reliability Management*, **16(3)**.

Williams, R. and Boudewijn, J. (1994). Quality leadership in Taiwan. *European Foundation for Quality Management.*

Wisner, J. D. and Eakins, S. G. (1994). A performance based assessment of the US Baldrige Quality Award winners. *International Journal of Quality and Reliability Management,* **11(2)**.

Chapter 3

Mahoney, F. X. and Thor, C. G. (1994). *The TQM Trilogy.* New York: Amacon.

Vokurka, R. J. and Stading, G. L. (2000). A comparative analysis of national and regional quality awards. *Quality Progress,* **August**.

Chapter 4

Case, K. E. and Bigelow, J. S. (1992). Inside the Baldrige Award guidelines. *Quality Progress,* **November**.

Crosby, P. B. and Reimann, C. (1991). Criticism and support for the Baldrige Award. *Quality Progress,* **May**.

Garvin, D. A. (1991). How the Baldrige award really works. *Harvard Business Review,* **November/December**.

George, S. (1992). *The Baldrige Quality System.* NJ: John Wiley.

Hart, W. L. and Bogan, C. E. (1992). *The Baldrige.* New York: McGraw Hill.

Neves, J. and Nakhai, B. (1994). The Evolution of the Baldrige Award. *Quality Progress,* **June**.

NIST (2002). *Malcolm Baldrige National Quality Award Criteria.* US Department of Commerce, National Institute of Science and Technology (www.quality.nist.gov).

Chapter 5

ECforBE (2000). *The Model in Practice.* London: British Quality Foundation.

ECforBE (2002). *The Model in Practice.* London: British Quality Foundation.

EFQM (1999). *The EFQM Excellence Model.* Brussels: European Foundation for Quality Management.

EFQM (2003). *The Fundamental Concepts.* Brussels: European Foundation for Quality Management.

Chapter 6

Ishikawa, K. (1987). The quality control audit. *Quality Progress,* **January**.

JUSE (1990). *The Deming Prize Guide for Overseas Companies.* Tokyo: Union of Japanese Scientists and Engineers.

Yoshizawa, T. (1995). QC diagnosis and management review through quality strategy deployment. *Proceedings of the 1st World Congress of TQM, Sheffield, UK.* London: Chapman and Hall.

Chapter 8

Dale, B. G. and Oakland, J. S. (1991). *Quality Improvement Through Standards.* Cheltenham: Stanley Thornes.

ISO9000 (2000). *Quality Management Systems – Fundamentals and Vocabulary.* London: British Standards Institution

ISO9001 (2000). *Quality Management Systems – Requirements.* London: British Standards Institution.

ISO9004 (2000). *Quality Management Systems – Guidelines for Performance Improvements.* London: British Standards Institution.

ISO (2002). *The ISO Survey of ISO 9000 and ISO 14000 Certificates, International Standards Against.* London: British Standards Institution.

Sayle, A. J. (1988). ISO 9000 – progression or regression? *Quality Assurance News,* **14(2)**.

Chapter 9

Conti, T. (1991). Company quality assessments. *The TQM Magazine,* **June** and **August**.

Conti, T. (1992). A critical review of the correct approach to quality awards. *Proceedings of the EOQ 36th Annual Conference.* Bedford: IFS Publications.

Myers, D. H. and Heller, J. (1995). The dual role of AT&T's self-assessment process. *Quality Progress,* **January**.

Chapter 10

Fiero, J. and Holmes, G. (1993). Using Baldrige assessments at the departmental level. *Journal for Quality and Participation,* **16(3)**.

Finn, M. and Porter, L. J. (1994). TQM self-assessment in the UK. *The TQM Magazine,* **6(4)**.

Hakes, C. (1994). *The Self-assessment Handbook*. London: Chapman and Hall.

Harmon, M. (1992). Internal award programs: Benchmarking the Baldrige to improve corporate quality. *Quality Digest*, **12(5)**.

Hayes, F. W. (1994). The Baldrige process. *Executive Excellence*, **June**.

Chapter 11

Conti, T. (2002). A roadmap through the fogs of quality and organizational assessment. *7th World Conference for Total Quality Management*. Verona: Sinergie-Cueim.

Oakland, J. S. (1999). *Total Organizational Excellence*. Oxford: Butterworth-Heinemann.

Oakland, J. S. (2003). *TQM: Text with Cases*. Oxford: Butterworth-Heinemann.

Chapter 12

EFQM (1999). *Submission Writers' Handbook*. Brussels: European Foundation for Quality Management.

Index

Page numbers in *italic* refer to information in figures or tables.